Building Multimodal Generative AI and Agentic Applications

Shaping concept to code for the future of multimodal and advanced agentic GenAI applications

Indrajit Kar

bpb

www.bpbonline.com

First Edition 2026

Copyright © BPB Publications, India

ISBN: 978-93-65898-385

To View Complete
BPB Publications Catalogue
Scan the QR Code:

Dedicated to

My parents, my wife, my kids, and the mother

About the Author

Indrajit Kar is a distinguished AI thought leader, author of 5 AI/ML books, innovator, and author with over 22 years of experience driving transformative AI-led products and platforms across industries. Throughout his career, he has led numerous high-impact teams responsible for developing end-to-end solutions in AI, ML, GenAI, and data science - guiding projects from conceptualization and design to deployment and scaling.

In his current role as head of AI, Indrajit spearheads large-scale initiatives that deliver measurable business impact across a diverse portfolio of global clients. His work is rooted in deep technical expertise across GenAI, **large language model** (**LLM**) architectures, MLOps, natural language processing, and computer vision. He has played a key role in integrating LLMs and autonomous AI agents into real-world applications spanning sectors such as e-commerce, healthcare, life sciences, telecommunications, and manufacturing.

Indrajit is also a strategic advisor and collaborator to C-level executives, helping enterprises unlock business value through advanced AI product and platform transformations. His leadership consistently bridges the gap between cutting-edge research and enterprise-scale implementation, accelerating AI adoption across organizations.

A recognized voice in the AI community, Indrajit has authored two books, including one dedicated to GenAI and its industry applications. He has also contributed extensively to AI research, with 27+ published papers, 21 patents filed, and multiple accolades, including eight Best Paper Awards from reputed conferences and institutions. His work often explores the intersections of innovation, scalability, and responsible AI.

With a legacy of leading R&D programs and having managed AI services and productization efforts for Fortune 500 companies, Indrajit continues to shape the future of intelligent systems. His passion for innovation, combined with a vision for ethical and scalable AI, drives his mission to empower businesses and communities through transformative technology.

About the Reviewers

❖ **Dhanveer Singh** is a technology leader at Capital One USA with over 19 years of experience in software engineering, cloud architecture, and large-scale system modernization across financial services, insurance, and retail. He specializes in AWS, microservices, containerization, DevOps, big data, and AI/ML, delivering secure, high-performing platforms that process billions of transactions and serve millions worldwide.

An advocate of cloud-native architectures and automation, Dhanveer has led transformative initiatives in cloud cost optimization, resilience engineering, and cybersecurity automation, driving measurable efficiency and advancing enterprise digital transformation. He has also filed multiple patents in areas of data integration, transformation, data security, and cloud automation, underscoring his focus on innovation.

Beyond his technical leadership, he contributes as a reviewer and TPC member for international journals and conferences, serves as a judge for global IT and cybersecurity awards, and mentors through STEM and CodeDay programs.

Dhanveer is a Fellow of IETE and IAENG, and an active IEEE and ACM member.

❖ **Harvendra Singh** is a distinguished technology leader specializing in cloud engineering, architecture, automation, and AI-powered solutions. He designs and implements scalable, secure systems utilizing Azure, .NET, C#, Python, GCP, Kubernetes, Databricks, and other cutting-edge technologies. With expertise in cloud-native applications, microservices, event-driven architectures, and distributed systems, Harvendra drives innovation in cloud and AI ecosystems, delivering high-impact solutions that drive business value and sustainable growth.

❖ **Manish Jain** is the vice president and head of AI architecture at Firstsource Solutions, where he leads enterprise-wide AI transformation for Fortune 100 organizations. With more than 20 years of technology leadership, including over a decade driving advanced AI innovation, he has earned recognition as an architect of transformative solutions that deliver quantifiable business impact. In addition to corporate responsibilities, his acts as a technical consultant for Deeplearning.ai and mentors at Analytics Vidhya. He also serves as a manuscript reviewer for prominent AI publishers such as Manning and Packt, positioning him at the crossroads of research and practical enterprise applications. Manish is unique blend of deep technical expertise and proven executive leadership enables him to guide organizations through the strategic and operational aspects of AI transformation. His commitment to advancing the AI community is evident in his advisory and mentoring roles, as well as his involvement in peer-reviewed publishing.

These experiences make a compelling authority on the imperatives of AI transformation and the practical challenges of scaling AI across complex enterprise environments, consistently linking innovation with measurable outcomes.

Acknowledgement

I extend my deepest appreciation to my family, parents, wife, in-laws, and children, whose steadfast encouragement and belief in me have been the cornerstone of this journey. Heartfelt thanks to BPB Publications for their patience and trust, allowing the book's multi-part publication to thoroughly cover the dynamic field of AI. I am also grateful to my companies for fostering growth and providing opportunities to develop GenAI and agentic applications, which informed the insights shared here. To everyone who supported me, seen and unseen, your guidance and encouragement have profoundly shaped this journey, for which I am eternally thankful.

Preface

We are living in the age of intelligent collaboration, where AI is no longer just a tool, but a partner capable of retrieving knowledge, generating ideas, reasoning through problems, and interacting across modalities like text, images, and voice. The emergence of multimodal and agentic applications marks a turning point in how we build, deploy, and rely on AI.

This book, *Building Multimodal Generative AI and Agentic Applications*, is a practical guide for those who want to move beyond theory and actually build the future of AI systems. Across 18 chapters, you will move step-by-step from fundamentals to advanced implementations, starting with retrieval, generation, and orchestration; progressing into multimodal workflows that combine text, images, and voice; and then advancing toward real-world applications like text-to-SQL systems, OCR, fraud detection, and AI operations.

Every chapter is designed to be hands-on and approachable. You will find conceptual explanations, system design principles, code walkthroughs, and to do exercises that push you to experiment and learn by doing.

The goal of this book is not only to explain how these systems work, but also to empower you to build your own scalable, multimodal, and agentic AI applications, applications that are reliable, safe, and impactful.

Whether you are an engineer, researcher, or leader in technology, I hope that this book equips you with the knowledge, confidence, and inspiration to shape the next-generation of AI.

Chapter 1: Introducing New Age Generative AI - This chapter introduces the key building blocks of modern AI systems. It begins with an overview of generative AI and then explores retrieval systems, generation systems, and the strengths of each. It covers how **retrieval-augumented generation** (**RAG**) generation combines the two, and how orchestration helps different AI components work together. The chapter also explains tokens, vector databases, and reranking methods, along with the differences between bi-encoders and cross-encoders. Finally, it discusses essential topics like guardrails for safe AI use, the role of agents, and the importance of Model Context Protocols.

Chapter 2: Deep Dive into Multimodal Systems - This chapter focuses on vision-language models and their role in multimodal AI. It explains what vision-language models are, compares different implementation approaches, and explores how they differ from broader multimodal GenAI systems. The chapter also looks at vision-language models in more depth and introduces ways to classify multimodal systems based on their outputs.

Chapter 3: Implementing Unimodal Local GenAI System - This chapter explores the practical side of building GenAI systems. It begins with the role of GPUs in today's AI landscape and how to make use of a local GPU. The chapter then introduces Ollama, including how to generate a PDF document with it. Moving forward, it explains how RAG works, along with the key challenges involved in implementing RAG effectively.

Chapter 4: Implementing Unimodal API-based GenAI Systems - This chapter provides a hands-on introduction to working with OpenAI's APIs and models. It explains how to move from using OpenAI for basic tasks to building more advanced agentic AI solutions. You will learn how to perform multi-document queries, implement a modular retrieval-augmented generation system using OpenAI and Faiss, and explore a set of to do steps for extending these capabilities further.

Chapter 5: Implementing Agentic GenAI Systems with Human-in-the-loop - This chapter focuses on designing and advancing agentic generative AI systems. It starts with principles of architecting such systems and then walks through an end-to-end **human-in-the-loop (HITL)** RAG workflow. From there, it explores how HITL setups can evolve into multi-agent HITL RAG systems. The chapter concludes by clarifying the differences between agentic AI and AI agents, highlighting their distinct roles and applications..

Chapter 6: Two and Multi-stage GenAI Systems - This chapter provides a deep understanding of the concepts of interactions within dense retrieval systems and their importance in RAG. It explains the role of interaction models in two-stage RAG systems and compares different reranking strategies, including late interaction, full interaction, and multi-vector models. The chapter then introduces two-stage and multi-stage RAG architectures, discusses grading mechanisms for evaluating retrieved results, and demonstrates how to implement a multi-stage RAG workflow with routing for more accurate and efficient responses.

Chapter 7: Building a Bidirectional Multimodal Retrieval System -This chapter introduces multimodal systems and how they can be classified based on their outputs. It then explains the working of a multimodal retrieval system and provides a code implementation with step-by-step explanation. The chapter closes with a to do section, giving readers practical exercises to apply and deepen their understanding.

Chapter 8: Building a Multimodal RAG System - This chapter focuses on practical approaches to generation and evaluation using LLMs. It begins with the implementation of generation techniques, followed by an introduction to the concept of LLM-as-a-judge and its application in building recommender systems. The chapter also covers how to incorporate grading mechanisms with OpenAI to improve evaluation. It concludes with a to do section, giving readers exercises to apply these ideas in practice.

Chapter 9: Building GenAI Systems with Reranking - This chapter explores the concept of reranking and its critical role in improving retrieval and RAG systems. It explains how reranking is applied in both text-based and multimodal contexts, with a focus on using cross-encoders in multimodal RAG. The chapter also introduces the cross-encoder architecture in multimodal settings and the idea of multi-index embedding within RAG systems. Alongside these concepts, it provides a code implementation with detailed explanation and concludes with a to do section to help readers practice and solidify their understanding.

Chapter 10: Retrieval Optimization for Multimodal GenAI - This chapter examines how to make retrieval systems more efficient and effective. It begins by outlining common drawbacks of retrieval systems, then introduces various optimization techniques to address these limitations. The chapter also explores retrieval optimization in detail, showing how these methods can be applied to improve performance. It then shifts focus to multimodal RAG systems, explaining how adaptive index refresh can enhance their accuracy and responsiveness. Finally, it provides a to do section with exercises for readers to apply these ideas in practice.

Chapter 11: Building Multimodal GenAI Systems with Voice as Input - This chapter explores how RAG extends beyond just image and text. It introduces the core concepts of expanding RAG to other modalities and shows how speech interfaces can be integrated into the RAG architecture. The chapter also provides a step-by-step code implementation of a voice-enabled RAG system, demonstrating how to bring these ideas into practice.

Chapter 12: Advanced Multimodal GenAI Systems - This chapter highlights the importance of reasoning in GenAI systems. It explains the different types of reasoning used in GenAI and why they matter for building more reliable and intelligent models. The chapter also introduces key benchmarks that are used to evaluate reasoning capabilities in AI systems.

Chapter 13: Advanced Multimodal GenAI Systems Implementation - This chapter focuses on how reasoning can be enhanced in GenAI through effective prompting techniques. It then explores specialized architectures that bring reasoning into play at different stages—first during reranking, where results are refined, and then at the recommendation stage, where reasoning helps deliver more accurate and context-aware suggestions.

Chapter 14: Building Text-to-SQL Systems - This chapter delves into the complexities of text-to-SQL and why it is considered a challenging problem. It begins by explaining the basic concepts and then explores real-world applications where text-to-SQL can make a significant impact. The chapter discusses the key challenges involved, followed by practical guidance on designing an effective text-to-SQL system. It also covers entity extraction using large language models, highlighting how this integrates with text-to-SQL to improve performance. Finally, the chapter emphasizes how such systems can enhance data accessibility and literacy, while also introducing performance metrics and best practices to ensure reliability.

Chapter 15: Agentic Text-to-SQL Systems and Architecture Decision-Making - This chapter presents the design and implementation of an agentic text-to-SQL system tailored for real-time retail intelligence. It explains the system's architecture in detail, along with code walkthroughs for better understanding. A step-by-step pipeline is provided to show how the system processes queries, leading to meaningful outputs. The chapter concludes by demonstrating the actual results generated by the text-to-SQL system and how they address the original problem statement.

Chapter 16: GenAI for Extracting Text from Images - This chapter introduces three different approaches to applying GenAI for optical character recognition. It explains how OCR works on images, as well as how it can be extended to multimodal documents that combine text, images, and other elements. The chapter concludes with a to do section, giving readers practical exercises to apply and reinforce what they have learned.

Chapter 17: Integrating Traditional AI/ML into GenAI Workflow - This chapter explores how traditional machine learning models can be integrated into GenAI workflows through a detailed case study. It presents a practical use case of hybrid ensemble learning for telecom fraud detection, showing how models like XGBoost can be wrapped and enhanced within an LLM-powered system. The chapter also provides a comparative overview of different ways ML models can be combined with GenAI to create hybrid solutions. It concludes with a to do section, offering readers hands-on activities to deepen their understanding.

Chapter 18: LLM Operations and GenAI Evaluation Techniques - This chapter highlights the importance of operations in building and running production-grade GenAI applications. It compares evaluation methods for LLMs and RAG systems, introduces the concept of RagOps, and emphasizes the need for continuous monitoring and observability platforms. The chapter also explores how graph-enhanced RAG can improve recommendation systems and provides a comparison of different Ops practices in modern software development. Finally, it offers practical guidance on setting up MLflow for managing experiments and deployments.

Code Bundle and Coloured Images

Please follow the link to download the
Code Bundle and the *Coloured Images* of the book:

https://rebrand.ly/78f896

The code bundle for the book is also hosted on GitHub at
https://github.com/bpbpublications/Building-Multimodal-Generative-AI-and-Agentic-Applications.
In case there's an update to the code, it will be updated on the existing GitHub repository.

We have code bundles from our rich catalogue of books and videos available at
https://github.com/bpbpublications. Check them out!

Errata

We take immense pride in our work at BPB Publications and follow best practices to ensure the accuracy of our content to provide an indulging reading experience to our subscribers. Our readers are our mirrors, and we use their inputs to reflect and improve upon human errors, if any, that may have occurred during the publishing processes involved. To let us maintain the quality and help us reach out to any readers who might be having difficulties due to any unforeseen errors, please write to us at: errata@bpbonline.com

Your support, suggestions and feedback are highly appreciated by the BPB Publications' Family.

At www.bpbonline.com, you can also read a collection of free technical articles, sign up for a range of free newsletters, and receive exclusive discounts and offers on BPB books and eBooks. You can check our social media handles below:

Instagram   *Facebook*   *Linkedin*   *YouTube*

Get in touch with us at: business@bpbonline.com for more details.

Piracy

If you come across any illegal copies of our works in any form on the internet, we would be grateful if you would provide us with the location address or website name. Please contact us at business@bpbonline.com with a link to the material.

If you are interested in becoming an author

If there is a topic that you have expertise in, and you are interested in either writing or contributing to a book, please visit www.bpbonline.com. We have worked with thousands of developers and tech professionals, just like you, to help them share their insights with the global tech community. You can make a general application, apply for a specific hot topic that we are recruiting an author for, or submit your own idea.

Reviews

Please leave a review. Once you have read and used this book, why not leave a review on the site that you purchased it from? Potential readers can then see and use your unbiased opinion to make purchase decisions. We at BPB can understand what you think about our products, and our authors can see your feedback on their book. Thank you!

For more information about BPB, please visit www.bpbonline.com.

Join our Discord space

Join our Discord workspace for latest updates, offers, tech happenings around the world, new releases, and sessions with the authors:

https://discord.bpbonline.com

Table of Contents

CHAPTER 1
Introducing New Age Generative AI

Introduction

This chapter sets the stage for mastering new age **generative AI** (**GenAI**) systems by introducing essential concepts and foundational technologies. We begin by exploring the difference between retrieval systems and generation systems, followed by an in-depth look at vector databases, search algorithms, embedding techniques, indexing, and reranking, all critical for building intelligent, efficient AI solutions. Key reliability mechanisms, such as reflection and guardrails, are discussed to ensure outputs remain robust and aligned with user intent.

We then dive into advanced prompting methods like **chain of thought** (**CoT**) to guide AI models through structured reasoning processes. Moving into agentic AI, the chapter covers agents, tools, reasoning, planning, and action execution, expanding into the design of multi-agent systems capable of complex, collaborative tasks. A comparative overview of **large language models** (**LLMs**), **large vision models** (**LVMs**), and emerging **large action models** (**LAMs**) is provided, along with practical insights into local model deployment and **graphics processing unit** (**GPU**) infrastructure planning.

Further, we introduce speech technologies, including **automated speech recognition** (**ASR**) and generation, and explain the critical role of memory management in agent-based architectures. Finally, we present industry standards like **Model Context Protocol** (**MCP**) and differentiate the evolving responsibilities of a GenAI developer vs. a GenAI engineer, preparing readers for advanced system design.

Structure

This chapter covers the following topics:

- Overview of generative AI
- Retrieval system
- Generation systems
- Understanding where generation systems excel
- Retrieval-augmented generation
- Orchestration in AI systems
- Tokens in AI systems
- Vector database
- Reranking
- Bi-encoders vs. cross-encoders
- Guardrails
- Agents
- Model Context Protocols

Objectives

This chapter aims to equip readers with a comprehensive understanding of the key building blocks essential for designing and deploying modern GenAI systems. By exploring concepts such as retrieval and generation systems, vector databases, embedding techniques, advanced prompting strategies, agentic architectures, and multi-agent collaboration, readers will gain a strong foundation for building intelligent, scalable AI solutions. Additionally, the chapter introduces critical topics like local model deployment, GPU infrastructure, speech processing, memory management in agents, and industry standards like MCPs. These foundational elements are crucial for advancing toward multimodal, reliable, and production-ready AI applications.

Overview of generative AI

The evolution of generative models represents one of the most significant paradigm shifts in AI. In the pre-**generative pre-trained transformers (GPTs)** era, GenAI was shaped by powerful techniques such as Boltzmann machines, **variational autoencoders (VAEs)**, **generative adversarial networks (GANs)**, and autoencoders. These models achieved groundbreaking results by generating unstructured data like images, audio, and even text. For instance, GANs revolutionized realistic image synthesis, while VAEs enabled probabilistic generative modeling of complex data spaces, including speech and document generation.

While impressive, these earlier systems generally focused on single-domain generation with limited ability to reason, plan, or generalize across tasks. They lacked the rich contextual understanding, dynamic reasoning, and task-driven flexibility that define modern AI experiences.

The true *paradigm shift* occurred not directly with GPT models, but with the introduction of the transformer architecture itself in 2017 (in the seminal paper *Attention Is All You Need* by *Vaswani et al.*). The transformer introduced the concepts of self-attention, parallel processing, and positional encoding, enabling models to scale massively in both size and capability, far beyond the limits of traditional **recurrent neural networks (RNNs)**, **long short-term memories (LSTMs)**, or **convolutional neural networks (CNNs)** based generative models.

Building on the transformer foundation, GPTs ushered in the era of *open-ended generation* models capable of not just recreating data but performing tasks like conversation, reasoning, summarization, code generation, and multimodal synthesis. The modern GenAI systems now exhibit semantic awareness, dynamic problem-solving, and multimodal understanding across text, images, and speech.

Several key advancements define this new age, which are as follows:

- Massive pre-training on diverse, heterogeneous datasets.
- Scaling laws showing predictable improvements with more parameters, data, and compute.
- CoT prompting techniques for guided reasoning.
- Agentic AI architectures where models not only generate but also reason, plan, and act.
- Multi-agent systems collaborating toward complex goals.
- Multimodal generation across text, vision, and audio modalities.
- Private and local deployments driven by improvements in GPU infrastructure and efficient models.

Note: The scope of this book is focused exclusively on new-age GenAI systems. If you seek to explore the foundations of older generative models, including Boltzmann machines, autoencoders, VAEs, and GANs, you can refer to another book authored by me and my co-author, titled "Learn Python Generative AI: Journey from Autoencoders to Transformers to Large Language Models" (published by BPB Publications). It provides a detailed walkthrough of the classical generative modelling journey leading to today's cutting-edge systems.

In this book, we move beyond classical generation, focusing on designing, building, and deploying reasoning, planning, and action-oriented GenAI—the systems that are now transforming industries, enterprises, and everyday experiences. Understanding this transition is key: *what started as data mimicry has evolved into intelligent, multimodal agents capable of augmenting and automating human thought itself.*

While generative models have evolved to create rich, human-like outputs, not all AI solutions rely solely on generation. In fact, many of the most powerful AI systems today combine retrieval with generation to ground their outputs in real-world information, improve reliability, and reduce hallucinations.

Before exploring generation strategies, it is essential to first understand retrieval systems, the backbone of how AI finds, filters, and brings relevant knowledge into the conversation. Retrieval forms a critical pillar of modern AI infrastructure, supporting tasks ranging from search engines and recommendation systems to advanced **retrieval-augmented generation (RAG)** pipelines.

In the next section, we will explore what retrieval systems are, how they differ from pure generative models, and why they are indispensable for building accurate, scalable, and production-grade AI applications.

Retrieval system

GenAI systems today are celebrated for their creativity and reasoning abilities, but behind many of these intelligent behaviors lies a strong foundation built on retrieval mechanisms. Retrieval is often the hidden engine that allows AI to ground its outputs in real-world knowledge, find relevant facts, and maintain coherence across conversations or tasks. To truly appreciate how retrieval has become such a critical pillar of modern AI, it is important to first understand how it evolved, from simple keyword matching to sophisticated, learning-driven, and memory-augmented techniques.

Prior to understanding modern retrieval systems, it is helpful to trace their evolution briefly, which is discussed in the following table:

Year	Milestone	Description
1970s-2000s	**Term frequency–inverse document frequency (TF-IDF), Best Matching 25 (BM25).**	Early keyword-based retrieval methods focused on matching exact terms.
2020	**Dense passage retrieval (DPR)**	Introduced dense embeddings to semantically match questions and documents.
2021	Hybrid retrieval	Combined sparse (BM25) and dense (DPR) methods to improve robustness.
2020–2022	RAG	Tight integration of retrieval with generation models to enhance grounding.
2023+	In-context learning retrieval, memory-augmented retrieval.	Dynamic, reasoning-driven retrieval embedded inside LLM workflows.

Table 1.1: Historic timelines of retrieval systems

With the preceding background, given in *Table 1.1*, in mind, it becomes clear that retrieval is no longer a simple lookup process; it has evolved into a dynamic, intelligent layer that actively augments the reasoning capabilities of AI systems. In the following sections, we will explore how retrieval systems work, the key components that make them powerful, and how they integrate seamlessly with generative models to build reliable, context-aware AI applications.

The foundation of modern retrieval systems can be traced back to early innovations like DPR, introduced by *Facebook AI Research* (now *Meta AI*) around 2020. DPR was a major breakthrough compared to traditional sparse retrieval methods (such as TF-IDF and BM25) because it introduced dense vector representations for both queries and documents. This allowed semantic retrieval, finding information based on meaning rather than relying purely on keyword overlap.

Dense retrieval marked a major turning point: models could now encode the meaning of a query and a document into a shared embedding space where similarity could be computed efficiently. Instead of matching exact words, dense retrieval matched concepts and ideas. However, early dense retrievers still had limitations: they sometimes retrieved irrelevant passages due to coarse semantic matching, and scaling them to millions or billions of documents required solving difficult engineering challenges around efficiency and latency.

Sparse retrieval

Sparse retrieval methods like TF-IDF and BM25 rely on matching exact keywords and term frequency statistics. While older, they remain highly effective in cases where precision is critical and queries are closely tied to specific terminology, such as in legal document search, scientific literature, and enterprise document retrieval, where exact matches matter more than general semantic similarity. Sparse retrieval also scales very efficiently with traditional inverted index techniques and remains a strong baseline in many real-world search systems.

Dense retrieval

Dense retrieval methods, introduced with models like DPR and **Approximate Nearest Neighbor Negative Contrastive Learning for Dense Text Retrieval** (ANCE), marked a major shift from sparse term-matching techniques (e.g., BM25) toward semantic vector-based retrieval. Dense retrievers excel when dealing with open-domain search, ambiguous queries, or when synonyms and paraphrases are common, for example, in customer support bots, multilingual retrieval, or semantic **frequently asked questions** (**FAQs**) matching. Dense retrieval allows systems to understand the intent behind a question, even when the exact words differ between the query and the document. The following figure shows the basic flow of semantic retrieval using a vector database:

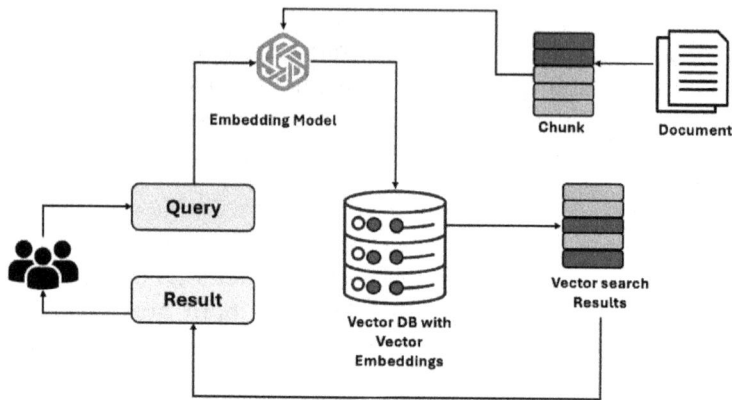

Figure 1.1: Basic flow of semantic retrieval using a vector database

Note: To maintain clarity and simplicity, this figure illustrates document chunking and embedding as part of the overall RAG process. In practice, these steps—chunking and embedding of documents- are performed offline during the indexing phase and not during real-time query execution. This simplification applies across all figures and workflows presented in the chapters of this book.

The following figure illustrates the offline phase of a RAG pipeline, where raw documents are first processed using language chunking tools (e.g., Llama-based parsers or LangChain utilities) to divide them into manageable segments. These chunks are then passed through an embedding model, such as OpenAI's embedding API, to generate dense vector representations. The resulting embeddings are stored in a vector database, forming the searchable index that powers downstream retrieval during real-time query execution. This preprocessing step is critical to enabling fast, scalable, and semantically rich document retrieval in multimodal or LLM-based applications.

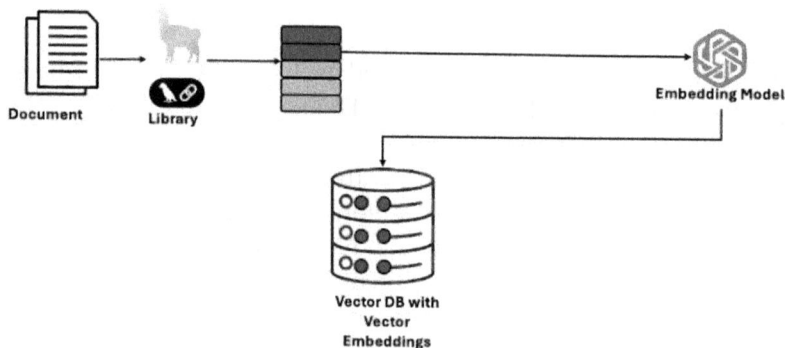

Figure 1.2: Offline document indexing and embedding workflow

Reflecting on the evolution, today's retrieval systems have dramatically advanced beyond the early DPR architecture:

- **Hybrid retrieval**: Modern systems increasingly combine sparse and dense retrieval (e.g., BM25 + dense embeddings) to balance recall and precision, especially valuable in long-tail queries or domain-specific knowledge bases.

- **Multi-vector representations**: Advanced methods like *ColBERT* (late interaction models) encode multiple vectors per document rather than a single one, improving retrieval accuracy without sacrificing too much speed.

- **Retriever-generator fusion (RAG systems)**: Retrieval is no longer a standalone step; it is now tightly integrated into the generation pipeline. Models like RAG retrieve documents dynamically during inference and condition the generated output, improving factual accuracy and reducing hallucinations.

- **Memory-augmented retrieval**: Agentic AI systems use episodic memory, blending external document retrieval with internally learned knowledge to continuously adapt and improve over time.

- **Learning-to-retrieve (LTR) and in-context retrieval**: Some newer architectures like *Retro* and *RePlug* move beyond static indexes, enabling the model itself to learn retrieval strategies during inference, deciding *what* to retrieve based on the reasoning context dynamically.

Additionally, vector database technology has matured rapidly. Tools like **Facebook AI Similarity Search (Faiss)**, Milvus, Qdrant, Azure AI Search, and Pinecone offer scalable, high-speed vector search, supporting billions of embeddings with **approximate nearest neighbor (ANN)** algorithms, metadata filtering, and hybrid retrieval capabilities—all critical for powering modern enterprise-grade RAG systems.

It is crucial to recognize that retrieval today is no longer just about fetching documents. It has become an intelligent augmentation mechanism, involving filtering, reranking, reasoning, and dynamic knowledge grounding. Retrieval is evolving from a backend lookup service into a frontline reasoning component of next-generation AI.

Thus, understanding retrieval deeply, not simply as a search technique but as an intelligent augmentation strategy, is essential for building reliable, scalable, and goal-driven new-age GenAI applications.

Retrieval systems are typically evaluated based on metrics like recall@k, precision@k, and **Mean Reciprocal Rank (MRR)**, which measure how effectively the system retrieves relevant documents among the top results. We will cover retrieval evaluation in greater detail later, but for now, it is important to remember that retrieval quality is judged by both accuracy and ranking efficiency.

Generation system

As we have seen, retrieval systems focus on finding the most relevant existing information. However, many real-world tasks demand more than just retrieval—they require creation, reasoning, and original synthesis. This is where generation systems come into play.

In this section, we will explore what generation systems are, how they operate, and the core techniques that power them. We will discuss different types of generation tasks, such as text, image, and audio creation, and understand key mechanisms like autoregressive modeling, diffusion models, and sampling strategies. Additionally, we will cover important concepts like temperature control, prompt design, and the balance between creativity and factuality.

We will also examine the typical challenges faced by generation systems, such as hallucination, coherence issues, and safety risks, and highlight where these systems truly excel, especially in tasks that demand open-ended creativity or complex problem-solving. Finally, we will briefly introduce how retrieval and generation are increasingly being combined in modern AI architectures to build more grounded and intelligent systems.

Let us begin by understanding the fundamental nature of generation systems and how they differ from purely retrieval-based approaches.

Generation systems are AI models designed to produce new content, rather than simply retrieve it. They can generate text, images, audio, code, and even multimodal outputs by learning complex patterns from training data. Unlike retrieval, which surfaces information that already exists, generation enables models to compose new sentences, invent new images, and solve new problems dynamically at inference time.

Modern generation systems are typically large-scale neural networks or LLMs trained with billions of parameters on massive datasets across multiple domains. The following figure shows the types of LLMs and generation models:

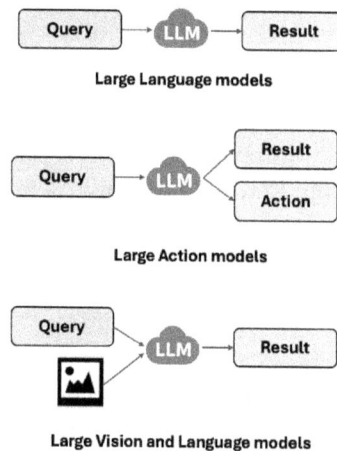

Figure 1.3: Types of LLMs and generation models

Types of generation systems

GenAI systems span multiple modalities, each designed to create content such as text, images, or audio based on user input, showcasing the versatility and power of modern **machine learning (ML)** models. Let us look at the types of generation systems:

- **Text generation**: Models like GPT, Llama, and Claude specialize in generating coherent paragraphs, answering questions, summarizing articles, translating languages, or even writing poetry and code. They are autoregressive, meaning they predict the next token based on previous tokens—enabling them to build long, meaningful sequences word by word.

- **Image generation**: Models like DALL·E, Stable Diffusion, and Imagen generate images from text prompts (text-to-image generation). These systems rely on techniques like diffusion models or GANs to iteratively create realistic images from random noise, conditioned on user instructions.

- **Audio generation**: In audio generation, models like Whisper (for ASR) and VALL-E (for speech synthesis) produce human-like speech or even create music. These models learn representations of sound waves and either recognize speech (ASR) or generate audio based on text inputs.

Core techniques behind the generation are as follows:

- **Language models**: Language models are trained to predict the next word (token) given a previous sequence, and so they are called **autoregressive models**, as explained in *Figure 1.3*. Large models like GPT-3/4/o3, Llama, or Claude learn contextual relationships and world knowledge through self-supervised learning, enabling diverse generation tasks such as answering questions, summarizing documents, and creative writing.

- **Vision models**: Models like DALL·E and Stable Diffusion apply transformer-like architectures to image patches or latent representations, allowing text-to-image generation. They capture the structure, style, and content of visual elements in latent spaces.

- **Diffusion models**: Diffusion models start with random noise and iteratively denoise it to create a realistic sample. Popular for generating high-fidelity images (e.g., Stable Diffusion, Imagen), they have also been adapted for audio and even 3D model generation. Diffusion models are being actively adapted for language tasks, though they are still less mature and less dominant than transformer-based models (like GPT). The field of language diffusion models is rapidly evolving, and several research efforts have shown that diffusion-based generative models can be competitive with or complementary to autoregressive language models.

Autoregressive generation

In autoregressive models (like GPT), each output token is generated one at a time, conditioned on previously generated tokens. This sequential token-by-token generation allows models to produce highly coherent outputs, but can also lead to error accumulation if not managed carefully. The following figure explains how LLM generates in an autoregressive manner (one token at a time):

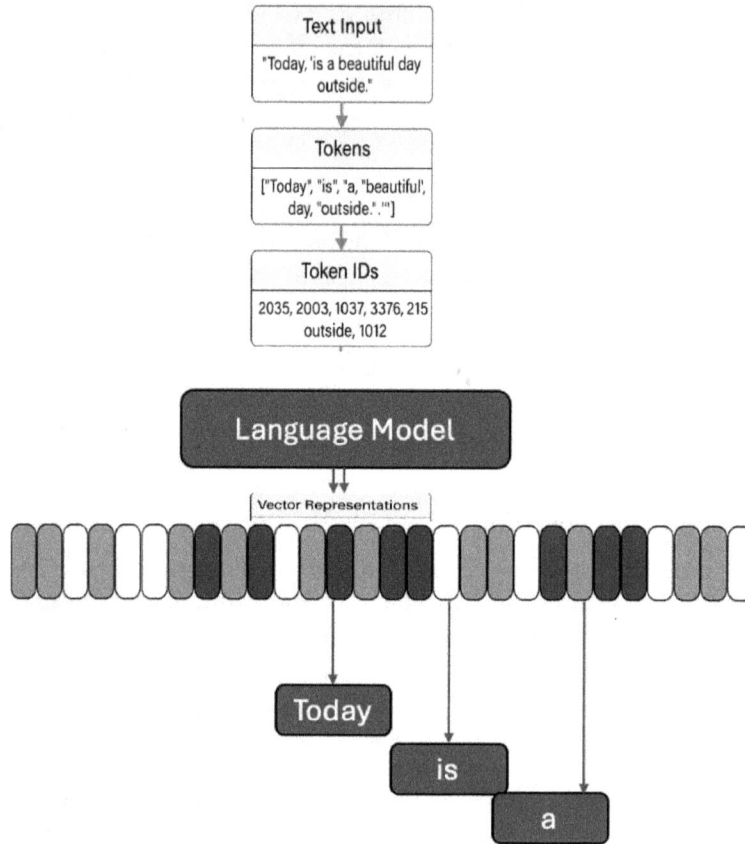

Figure 1.4: *LLM generation in an autoregressive manner (one token at a time)*

The following are the temperature and sampling strategies:

- **Temperature**: Controls the randomness of the generation. Lower temperature | more deterministic and factual outputs. Higher temperature | more creative and diverse outputs.

- **Top-k sampling**: Limits the next token choice to the top-k most probable tokens.

- **Top-p (nucleus) sampling**: Selects from the smallest set of tokens whose cumulative probability exceeds top-p.

Tuning these parameters allows fine control over creativity vs. precision in AI generation.

Prompting strategies

Prompts are critical for steering the behavior of generation systems. Advanced prompting techniques like CoT enable multi-step reasoning by encouraging models to explain their thought process before answering. We will explain these in more detail in the next section.

Understanding where generation systems excel

Generation systems are particularly powerful in the following:

- Open-ended creativity tasks (storytelling, image creation, poetry, coding).
- Complex reasoning and problem-solving beyond retrieval capabilities.
- Personalization and dynamic response generation (chatbots, educational tutors).
- Bridging gaps where no pre-existing data exactly fits the query.

Combining retrieval and generation

While generation systems are incredibly powerful at creating new content, they sometimes struggle with factual accuracy, up-to-date knowledge, and grounding their outputs in real-world information. To overcome these challenges, modern AI architectures increasingly combine the strengths of retrieval and generation, giving rise to a powerful paradigm known as RAG.

In the next section, we will explore how RAG systems work, why they are critical for building reliable AI applications, and how they seamlessly integrate retrieval and generation into a unified, intelligent workflow.

Retrieval-augmented generation

RAG is an advanced AI architecture that combines retrieval and generation into a unified workflow. Instead of relying solely on a model's internal knowledge (which may be outdated or incomplete), a RAG system first retrieves relevant external information and then generates an answer conditioned on that retrieved content.

RAG emerged to address key challenges faced by pure generation models, which are as follows:

- **IIallucination**: It sometimes generates fabricated, plausible-sounding but incorrect outputs.
- **Stale knowledge**: Pre-trained models have a static knowledge base (cutoff dates).
- **Groundedness**: Users often demand outputs linked to verifiable, real-world information.

RAG bridges these gaps, making outputs more accurate, grounded, and up-to-date.

RAG working

A RAG system typically involves two major steps, which are as follows:

1. **Retrieval step**: Given a user query, the system first retrieves the top-k most relevant documents or chunks from an external knowledge base (e.g., a vector database).

2. **Generation step**: The retrieved documents are passed as **context** to a language model (LLM), which generates the final answer conditioned on the retrieved information.

Thus, the model is not generated from memory alone; it is reading first, then reasoning.

Architecture of a basic RAG pipeline

The following list outlines how a basic RAG pipeline looks like:

- **Query understanding**: The input query is processed, optionally rephrased or expanded, to optimize retrieval.

- **Retrieval**: A dense or hybrid retriever fetches the most relevant documents from a vector database or search engine.

- **Context preparation**: Retrieved documents are selected, truncated, chunked, and formatted to fit within the LLM's input context window.

- **Generation**: The LLM is prompted with both the original query and the retrieved documents to generate a grounded, contextually rich response.

- **Output delivery**: The model's final response is returned to the user.

Types of RAG architectures

There are many different types of RAG architectures evolving today, depending on how retrieval and generation are orchestrated. However, to keep the scope focused, the following are the two most common and practical ones:

- **Single-stage RAG**:
    - A simple pipeline: retrieve | generate.
    - Used when retrieval quality is high and latency needs to be minimal.

  The following figure shows a single-stage RAG architecture:

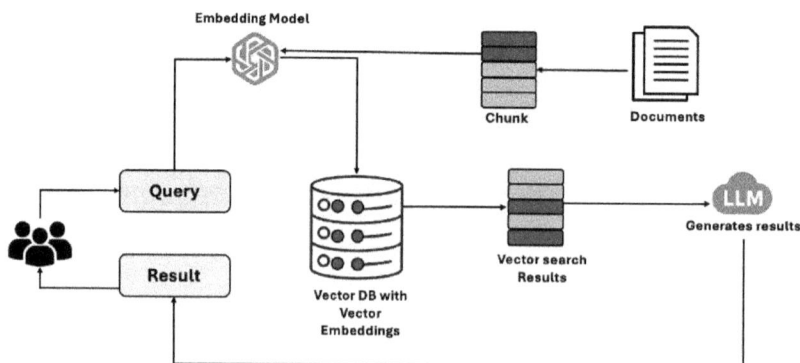

Figure 1.5: Single-stage RAG architecture

- **Two-stage RAG**:
  - o Retrieval | reranking | generation.
  - o After initial retrieval, a second model (e.g., cross-encoder) reranks documents to improve the quality before passing them to the generator.
  - o Reduces hallucination by focusing the generation only on the most relevant documents.

The following figure shows a two-stage RAG architecture:

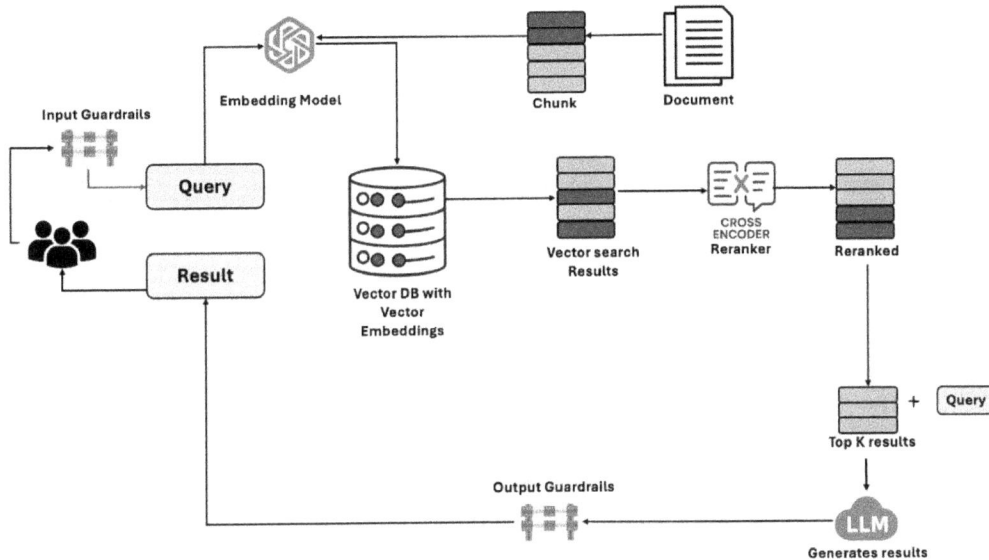

Figure 1.6: Two-stage RAG architecture

Iterative RAG

The following are the two iterative RAG:

- Retrieval and generation happen across multiple turns.
- The model can retrieve additional documents dynamically if the first batch is insufficient, refining the answer step-by-step.

Vector databases and RAG

Vector databases are critical infrastructure for efficient RAG systems.

- **Purpose**: They store document embeddings and enable fast semantic search based on vector similarity.
- **Examples**: Faiss (Meta), Qdrant, Milvus, Pinecone, Weaviate.

ANN algorithms are used for scalability, finding *close enough* vectors quickly rather than exact matches, enabling real-time retrieval over millions or billions of documents.

Vector stores also allow metadata filtering (e.g., date, author) and sharding for distributed retrieval, essential for scaling enterprise RAG systems.

Prompt engineering for RAG

How the retrieved content is formatted and fed into the LLM significantly affects output quality.

Key techniques include the following:

- **Chunking**: Breaking large documents into smaller pieces to fit multiple passages into the prompt.

- **Windowing**: Sliding a fixed-size window over documents to capture local context around keywords.

- **Context management**: Selecting the most relevant chunks without exceeding the model's token limit.

Well-constructed prompts ensure the LLM focuses on the most important information during generation.

Advanced RAG techniques

As RAG systems evolve, advanced techniques are being developed to enhance retrieval quality, improve response accuracy, and enable more context-aware generation. The following are some of the advanced RAG techniques:

- **RAG with reranking**:
  - Use a reranker (like a cross-encoder) to evaluate and reorder the retrieved documents based on fine-grained relevance scoring before generation.
  - Improves precision without significantly increasing retrieval time if optimized properly.

- **Memory-augmented RAG**:
  - Retrieval is not only from static knowledge bases but also from episodic memories-storing past conversation snippets or learned experiences.
  - Enables dynamic, personalized, and context-aware responses in multi-turn dialogue systems.

- **Multimodal RAG**:
  - Extend RAG to retrieve both text and images (or videos, audio).

    o **Example**: In a medical assistant role, retrieve x-rays and patient notes together, feeding both into a multimodal model like GPT-4V or Flamingo.

Applications of RAG

RAG systems have rapidly gained adoption across industries. Let us understand its applications:

- **Enterprise chatbots**: Customer service bots grounded in company knowledge bases.
- **Document QA systems**: Answering queries from large corpora like research papers, legal documents, or technical manuals.
- **Knowledge management**: Organizing and dynamically accessing enterprise knowledge in real-time.
- **Personalized AI assistants**: Tailoring responses based on user-specific documents, emails, notes, etc.

In every case, RAG ensures the AI system produces reliable, verifiable, and grounded outputs.

Orchestration in AI systems

As AI systems become increasingly complex, especially with the rise of RAG and agentic AI systems, the need for intelligent orchestration has become critical. Orchestration refers to how different components, such as retrieval engines, language models, memory modules, and external tools, are managed, sequenced, and coordinated dynamically to achieve a specific goal.

Unlike traditional single-call LLM applications, RAG systems and agentic systems involve multi-step reasoning and dynamic decision-making, requiring sophisticated orchestration frameworks.

Orchestration in RAG systems

In RAG systems, orchestration involves the following:

- **Query understanding**: Preprocessing user queries before retrieval.
- **Document retrieval**: Interfacing with vector databases (e.g., Faiss, Qdrant, Pinecone) to fetch top-k relevant documents.
- **Context preparation**: Chunking, selecting, and formatting retrieved documents to fit within the LLM's context window.
- **Prompt construction**: Dynamically inserting retrieved knowledge into well-structured prompts.
- **Response generation**: Using the LLM to generate outputs grounded in the provided documents.
- **Post-processing (optional)**: Filtering, reranking, or verifying model outputs.

Frameworks like LangChain, LlamaIndex, and Haystack specialize in orchestrating these steps automatically, making it easier to build scalable and production-ready RAG pipelines.

The following figure explains how LangChain is orchestrating the entire RAG process:

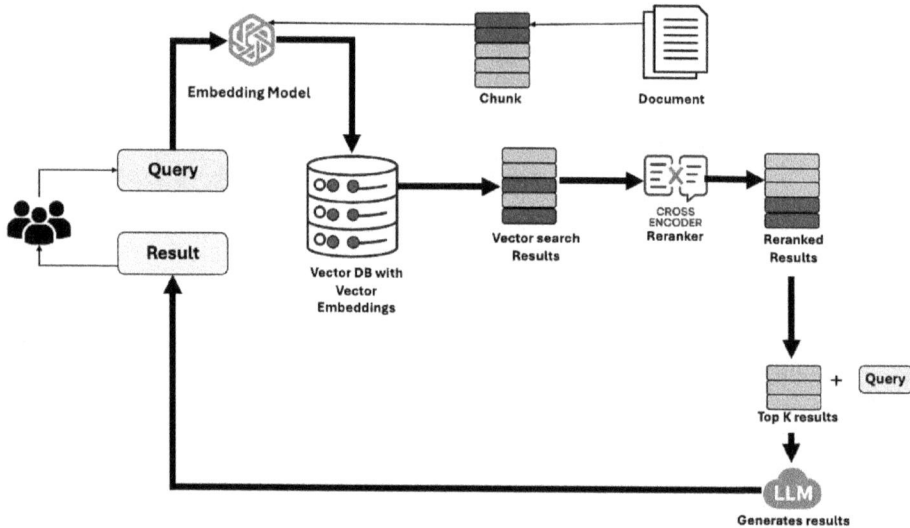

Figure 1.7: The fat lines are orchestrated by LangChain or similar orchestrators

Good RAG orchestration ensures the following:

- Minimal latency
- High retrieval quality
- Tight coupling between retrieval and generation
- Robust handling of token limits and memory

Orchestration in agentic systems

In agentic systems, orchestration becomes even more dynamic.

An agent is an AI entity capable of the following:

- Reasoning about a task.
- Choosing actions (e.g., tool usage, API calls, retrievals).
- Executing actions step-by-step.
- Reflecting and adjusting its plan dynamically based on intermediate results.

Agentic orchestration involves the following:

- **Tool selection**: Deciding which external tools or functions to call based on the current goal.

- **Multi-step planning**: Sequencing actions logically toward solving complex problems.
- **Memory management**: Retaining past actions, intermediate results, and conversation history to guide future steps.
- **Error handling**: Retrying or recovering gracefully if an action fails.
- **Goal management**: Continuously checking whether the final task objective has been met.

Frameworks like LangChain Agents, LamaIndex, Haystack, etc., provide orchestration primitives for agentic systems, allowing AI models to behave like autonomous, multi-step decision-makers.

Good agentic orchestration ensures the following:

- Task decomposition into manageable actions.
- Dynamic adaptation to unforeseen outcomes.
- Human-like reasoning chains that span multiple tool interactions.

While orchestration focuses on managing the overall flow of complex AI systems, another foundational concept operates at a much lower level - how information itself is represented and processed inside models. Before any retrieval, generation, or reasoning can happen, input text must be broken down into a form that models can understand—a process known as **tokenization**.

To fully appreciate the capabilities and limitations of AI systems, it is essential to understand what tokens are, how tokenization works, and why it plays a critical role in shaping performance, cost, and design choices.

Let us now understand tokenization.

Tokens in AI systems

In modern AI systems, particularly LLMs, the concept of **tokens** is fundamental to how inputs and outputs are processed. A token is not necessarily a word; it can be a word, a part of a word (subword), or even punctuation and special characters, depending on the model's tokenizer.

Tokenization is the process of breaking down text into discrete units that the model can understand and process. Models like GPT-3, GPT-4, and Llama do not operate directly on raw text; they operate on sequences of tokens.

There are different types of tokenization strategies, like the following:

- **Word-level tokenization**: In early models, one token often corresponded to one full word (e.g., *dog*, *running*). This approach is simple but inefficient for handling rare or compound words.

- **Subword-level tokenization [Byte-Pair Encoding (BPE)]:** Used by most modern LLMs (including GPT, BERT). Common word parts are merged (e.g., *run + ning | running*) to reduce the vocabulary size while still handling rare words efficiently.

- **Character-level tokenization:** Each character (including spaces and punctuation) is treated as a token. It increases sequence length dramatically and is less common in large models due to computational cost.

- **Byte-level tokenization:** Some models tokenize based on raw bytes (e.g., GPT-2 uses byte-level BPE), allowing flexible multilingual processing without complex pre-tokenization.

The number of tokens determines:

- The cost (for APIs like OpenAI's GPT-4 pricing is per 1,000 tokens).

- The context window size (how much information the model can *see* at once).

- Model behavior and the truncation happen if input exceeds maximum token limits (e.g., GPT-4 turbo supports 128K tokens max).

Thus, understanding tokens, what they represent, and how they are counted is critical for optimizing performance, controlling generation length, managing costs, and designing effective prompt engineering strategies.

For example, the input *Today is a beautiful day outside.* might be split into subwords like (*To, day, is, a, be, aut, iful, day, out, side*) depending on the tokenizer.

Once split into tokens, each token is then mapped to a unique token ID using a vocabulary table (pre-built during model training). Each token ID corresponds to an integer that the model understands internally. For instance:

- *To* | 98

- *day* | 1452

- *beautiful* (split into subwords) | 2932 and 1709

Thus, the entire input sequence is transformed into a vector of token IDs—a list of numbers that the model can operate on.

At this point, the token IDs are passed through an embedding layer. This embedding layer converts each token ID into a high-dimensional vector (e.g., 768-dimensional) that captures semantic relationships between tokens. Tokens that are semantically related (e.g., *dog* and *puppy*) will have embeddings that are close in vector space.

From there, the token embeddings move through the model's architecture, the attention layers, transformer blocks, and eventually lead to output generation or reasoning.

In summary, tokenization bridges the gap between human language and machine understanding. It translates messy, variable-length human text into standardized numerical forms that deep learning models can efficiently process. Without tokenization, modern language models would not be able to handle the complexity and diversity of human communication. The following figure shows the tokenization process flow in modern language models:

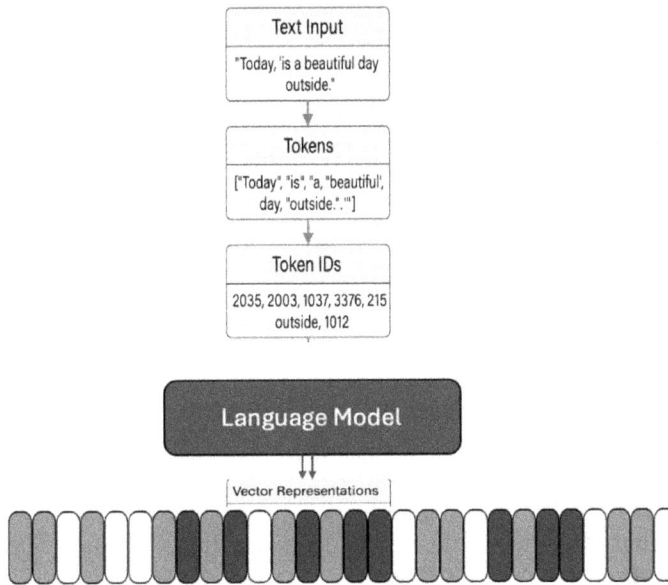

Figure 1.8: Tokenization process flow

Vector database

While tokenization enables language models to process and understand text inputs at a granular level, handling large-scale retrieval tasks requires a different kind of representation. Instead of working directly with tokens, retrieval systems operate on dense vector embeddings—mathematical representations that capture the semantic meaning of text, images, or other data types. To store, search, and retrieve these embeddings efficiently, vector databases have become an essential component of modern AI architectures.

Let us now explore the role of vector databases and how they power scalable, high-performance retrieval systems.

Before we explore vector databases further, it is important to first understand where they fit among other types of databases.

Let us look at the types of databases, which are as follows:

- **Relational databases**: Organize data into structured tables of rows and columns; best for structured data with SQL querying. (e.g., MySQL, PostgreSQL)

- **Key-value stores**: Store simple key-value pairs; optimized for fast lookups. (e.g., Redis, DynamoDB).

- **Document databases**: Manage semi-structured data in flexible formats like **JavaScript Object Notation (JSON)**. (e.g., MongoDB, CouchDB).

- **Graph databases**: Store relationships between entities using nodes and edges. (e.g., Neo4j, ArangoDB).

- **Wide-column databases**: Organize data into column families for efficient large-scale reads/writes. (e.g., Cassandra, HBase).

- **In-memory databases**: Store data in **random access memory (RAM)** for ultra-fast access. (e.g., Redis, Memcached).

- **Time-series databases**: Specialized for sequential, time-stamped data. (e.g., InfluxDB, TimescaleDB).

- **Text search databases**: Optimized for full-text indexing and search. (e.g., Elasticsearch, Solr).

- **Spatial databases**: Store geographic/spatial data. (e.g., PostGIS).

- **Blob stores**: Manage large binary files like images and videos. [e.g., Amazon **Simple Storage Service (S3)**].

- **Ledger databases**: Immutable record-keeping [e.g., Hyperledger Fabric, **Amazon Quantum Ledger Database (QLDB)**].

- **Hierarchical databases**: Tree-like parent-child structured data. [e.g., IBM **Information Management System (IMS)**.

- **Vector databases**: Store high-dimensional embeddings for semantic search and similarity operations. (e.g., Faiss, Chroma, Pinecone).

Among these, vector databases have become essential for AI, retrieval, and agentic reasoning systems.

Understanding vector databases

Vector databases are designed to store and retrieve dense vector embeddings, numerical representations of unstructured data such as text, images, or audio. Unlike relational or document databases, vector databases perform similarity searches based on distance metrics like cosine similarity or Euclidean distance rather than exact matching.

They enable AI models to retrieve semantically similar items efficiently, a critical operation for RAG and memory-augmented agentic systems.

Indexing algorithms in vector databases

Efficient vector search is fundamental to AI-driven applications, but performing brute-force searches over millions of high-dimensional vectors is computationally intensive. To address this challenge, vector databases use specialized indexing algorithms that improve search speed while balancing accuracy and memory efficiency.

The following are some commonly used indexing techniques:

- **Flat (brute-force search)**: Every query is compared against all stored vectors.
  - Offers the highest accuracy.
  - Slow and not scalable for large datasets.
- **Inverted File Indexing (IVF)**: Vectors are grouped into clusters, and searches are restricted to the most relevant clusters.
  - Significantly faster than brute-force.
  - Maintains good accuracy with improved efficiency.
- **Hierarchical navigable small world (HNSW)**: A graph-based structure that enables fast and accurate ANN searches.
  - Well-suited for real-time search.
  - Balances high recall with low-latency.
- **Product quantization (PQ)**: Compresses vectors into compact representations for scalable search.
  - Suitable for very large datasets.
  - Efficient in both storage and retrieval with reasonable accuracy.

Each of these indexing methods offers a different balance between speed, accuracy, and memory usage. The best choice depends on the specific needs of the application, including dataset size, performance requirements, and infrastructure constraints.

Search algorithms in vector databases

Vector databases are designed to store and retrieve high-dimensional vector embeddings efficiently, key to powering modern AI applications like semantic search, recommendation systems, and image similarity. Once data is encoded into vector embeddings and indexed, search algorithms are used to retrieve the nearest neighbors to a given query vector.

The two main approaches are as follows:

- **Exact search**: This method compares the query vector against every vector in the database to find the most similar ones. It offers high recall and accuracy but is computationally expensive and slow, making it suitable only for small datasets or offline analysis.
- **ANN search**: Instead of exhaustive comparison, ANN algorithms search for a smaller subset of the database to find results that are *good enough*. This trade-off between speed

and precision is essential for scaling millions or billions of vectors, enabling real-time search and inference.

Common ANN techniques include the following:

- **HNSW**: A graph-based method known for fast and accurate retrieval.
- **IVF + PQ**: It combines clustering and compression for memory efficiency.
- **ScaNN**: A high-performance ANN algorithm developed by *Google*, optimized for large-scale production environments.

Most production-grade vector databases (like Faiss, Milvus, or Pinecone) rely on ANN search to deliver low-latency, high-throughput performance without sacrificing too much on relevance or recall.

Embeddings and embedding models

At the core of vector databases lies the concept of embeddings. Embedding is a dense numerical vector that captures the semantic meaning of an input (text, image, audio) in a way that similar inputs are closer together in the vector space.

For example, two sentences about *dogs* will have embeddings close together even if they use different wording.

Embedding models are neural networks trained to map inputs into these vector spaces. Some popular types of embedding models are as follows:

- **Text embeddings**:
  - OpenAI's text-embedding-ada-002
  - **Sentence-BERT (SBERT)**
  - Hugging Face MiniLM
- **Image embeddings**:
  - CLIP (OpenAI)
  - DINOv2 (Meta)
- **Multimodal embeddings**:
  - CLIP (joint vision-language)
  - Flamingo (DeepMind)

Embedding models are crucial because the quality of retrieval depends heavily on the quality of embeddings.

Importance of vector databases for RAG and agentic systems

In RAG pipelines, embeddings of queries are matched against stored document embeddings inside a vector database to retrieve the most relevant knowledge for grounding responses.

In agentic systems, an agent might need to:

- Retrieve past experiences
- Fetch external knowledge
- Search through the tool outputs

All dynamically at runtime, based on vector-based similarity, not just keyword matching.

Thus, vector databases enable semantic memory and scalable, intelligent retrieval, two cornerstones of the new age of GenAI. The following figure represents the workflow of a similar search pipeline using embeddings, where input data is transformed into vectors to retrieve semantically similar results:

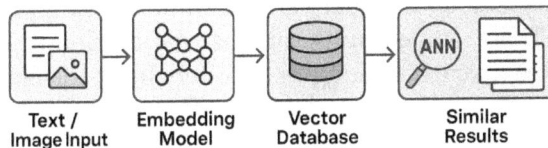

Figure 1.9: Basic flow of semantic retrieval using a vector database

While vector databases enable fast and efficient retrieval of semantically similar documents, the top results returned by similarity search are not always perfectly aligned with the user's true intent. Retrieval-based purely on vector similarity can sometimes surface documents that are only loosely relevant, leading to less accurate or less grounded final outputs.

To address this challenge, an important refinement step called **reranking** is often introduced. Reranking allows AI systems to reorder and prioritize retrieved documents based on deeper relevance scoring, improving the quality of the inputs ultimately passed to the language model for generation.

Let us now understand reranking, why it is needed, how it works, and the different approaches used in modern AI pipelines.

Reranking

The concept of reranking is not new to AI. It has deep roots in recommendation systems and search engines.

In traditional recommendation pipelines (e.g., recommending products, movies, articles), the system typically retrieves a broad set of candidates, say, the top 100 or top 1000 items, based on rough matching like user history or content similarity. However, these initial candidates are often imperfect, as retrieval systems prioritize recall, getting as many potentially good items as possible, even at the cost of precision.

Thus, a reranking step is introduced, details as follows:

- A more sophisticated model (often a deeper neural network) re-evaluates the initial set and reorders them based on more accurate relevance scores.

- The goal is to maximize precision at the top and ensure the first few items shown to the user are the most relevant and impactful.

This two-stage approach, retrieval and reranking, is now fundamental not just in recommendation systems but also in modern RAG pipelines and search engines.

Bi-encoders vs. cross-encoders

Bi-encoders and cross-encoders are two popular architectures used for tasks like semantic search and ranking in **natural language processing (NLP)**.

Bi-encoders independently encode the query and document into separate vector embeddings using the same model. These embeddings can then be efficiently compared using cosine similarity or other distance metrics, making bi-encoders ideal for large-scale retrieval where speed and scalability are critical.

Cross-encoders, on the other hand, jointly encode the query and document by feeding them together into a transformer model. This allows the model to consider cross-attention between tokens, resulting in more accurate relevance scoring. However, this approach is computationally expensive and slower, limiting its use in real-time or large-scale systems.

In the context of retrieval and reranking, a common pattern is to use bi-encoders for fast candidate retrieval, followed by cross-encoders for reranking the top results to improve precision, balancing efficiency and accuracy effectively:

- **Bi-encoders**:
    - Encode the query and documents separately into dense vectors.
    - Similarity is computed after encoding, usually via dot product or cosine similarity.
    - Extremely fast and scalable, and ideal for first-pass retrieval from large corpora.
    - **Examples**: DPR, Sentence Transformers.

- **Cross-encoders:**
    - Concatenate the query and document together and encode them jointly.
    - The model sees both pieces together and can model fine-grained interactions.
    - Much slower than bi-encoders because every query-document pair needs to be recomputed.

- o However, much more accurate at judging true relevance.
- o **Examples**: BERT for passage ranking, MiniLM for reranking.

Cross-encoders for reranking

In RAG pipelines or AI search systems, the typical workflow is as follows:

- Use a bi-encoder retriever to fetch top-k candidates quickly.
- Apply a cross-encoder reranker on these k candidates (e.g., top 100) to rescore and reorder them.
- Select the top-n reranked documents (e.g., top 5 or top 10) to feed into the generation model.

Due to the cross-encoder model's deep interactions between the query and candidate documents, it significantly improves the quality of retrieved information, leading to better-grounded, more accurate, and more contextually relevant outputs during generation.

Thus, reranking, especially using cross-encoders, is a vital tool in building high-precision, production-grade AI retrieval systems today, as shown in the following figure:

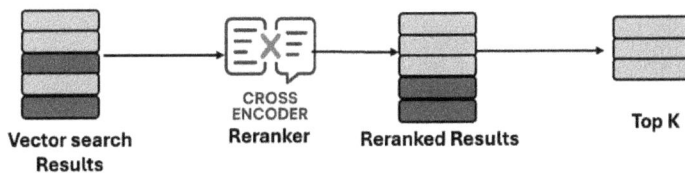

Vector search Results · CROSS ENCODER Reranker · Reranked Results · Top K

Figure 1.10: *Reranking architecture for improving document relevance*

While reranking improves the quality and relevance of retrieved information, it does not inherently guarantee that the AI's final output will always be safe, unbiased, or aligned with application requirements. Even with high-precision retrieval, generation models can still hallucinate, introduce sensitive content, or produce outputs that deviate from user expectations. To address these risks, modern AI systems implement guardrails, structured controls, and validation mechanisms designed to monitor, filter, and shape model behavior. In the next section, we will explore the concept of guardrails, why they are essential, and how they are applied across retrieval and generation pipelines.

Guardrails

As AI systems become increasingly capable, the need for guardrails, structured controls that guide and constrain model behavior, has become critical. Guardrails ensure that models act safely, ethically, and in alignment with application or organizational goals, even when handling complex, open-ended inputs.

While reranking helps in surfacing more relevant and factual information, it does not inherently prevent hallucinations, bias propagation, policy violations, or user manipulation. LLMs are powerful but non-deterministic; even with clean inputs, they can produce unsafe, offensive, or misleading outputs if left unchecked. Guardrails help maintain trust, safety, and compliance. They are all crucial factors when deploying AI systems in real-world environments, especially in the enterprise, healthcare, finance, and education sectors. The following figure illustrates the architecture of a RAG system enhanced with guardrails, reranking, and LLM-based response generation:

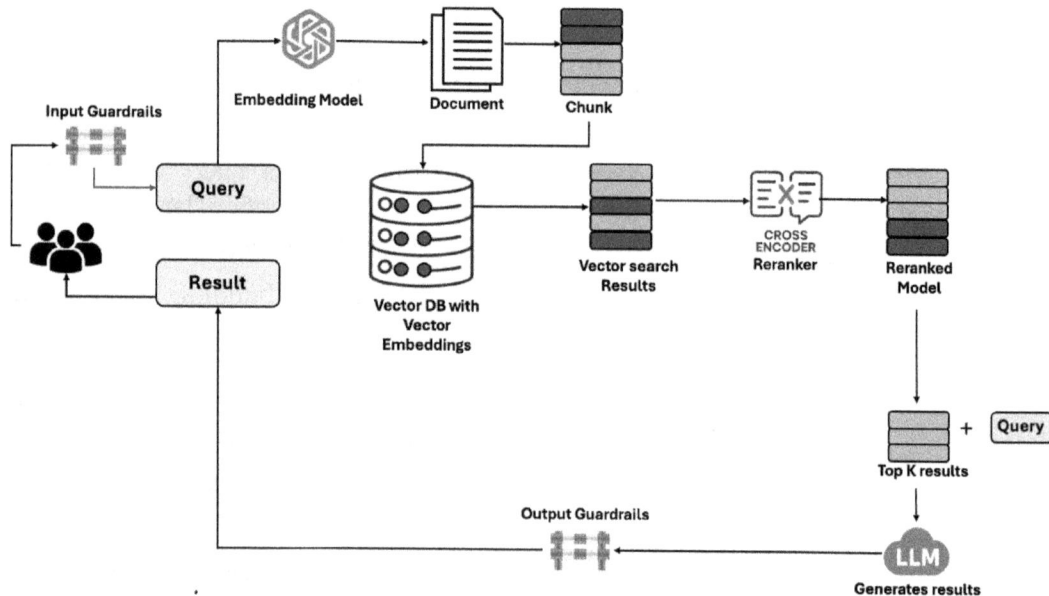

Figure 1.11: End to end figure of guardrail enabled GenAI system

Types of guardrails

Guardrails typically operate at two major stages, which are described in the following list:

- **Input guardrails**: They filter, rephrase, or block problematic user queries before they reach the model. Examples include:

    o Detecting and blocking malicious prompts (e.g., asking the model to generate harmful content).

    o Rewriting vague, ambiguous, or risky queries into safer forms.

    o Adding disclaimers or constraints to the prompt to set clear expectations for model behavior.

- **Output guardrails**: Output guardrails analyze, validate, and modify model-generated outputs before they are delivered to the user. Examples include:

o Removing toxic, biased, or unsafe content.

o Ensuring outputs comply with organizational policies (e.g., no sharing of personal data).

o Fact-checking answers against trusted knowledge bases before displaying them.

o Enforcing tone, style, or content formatting requirements (e.g., professional, neutral).

Methods of applying guardrails

Guardrails are implemented through a combination of techniques:

- **Prompt engineering**: Structuring prompts carefully to guide safer behavior.
- **Moderation APIs**: Running outputs through toxicity and safety detectors (e.g., OpenAI Moderation API).
- **Policy engines**: Defining explicit allowlists and blocklists for topics, keywords, or behaviors.
- **Post-generation filtering**: Analyzing and editing or discarding unsafe responses before sending them to users.
- **Rule-based enforcement**: Using pre-set rules to catch specific violations.
- **Retrieval-augmented guardrails**: Using RAG to cross-validate facts or check consistency before output.

Without guardrails

Without guardrails, AI systems are vulnerable to the following:

- **Jailbreaking**: Users craft tricky prompts to force the model to bypass restrictions and generate forbidden outputs.
- **Hallucination**: The model invents plausible but false information without validation.
- **Bias amplification**: The model unintentionally reinforces stereotypes or unfair content.
- **Security risks**: Revealing sensitive information, leaking system details, or enabling harmful actions.

These risks can cause reputational damage, compliance violations, user harm, and even legal consequences for organizations.

Industry examples of guardrail solutions

The following leading AI platforms have recognized the need for robust guardrails and built specialized frameworks:

- **NVIDIA NeMo guardrails**:
  - Open-source toolkit focused on trustworthy conversational AI.
  - Supports input filtering, output moderation, conversation flow control, and grounded generation.
  - Allows developers to define *rails* declaratively using YAML files to enforce behavior across bots and assistants.

- **Azure AI Prompt Shields**:
  - Microsoft's enterprise-grade solution is integrated with the Azure OpenAI Service.
  - Detects and blocks prompt injection attacks, offensive content, and jailbreak attempts.
  - Provides both proactive input screening and reactive output moderation, making it highly effective for regulated industries.

- **OpenAI Moderation API**: One of the most widely used tools for automatic content safety checks is the OpenAI Moderation API. This API analyzes both user inputs and model outputs to detect sensitive content across categories such as:
  - Hate
  - Harassment
  - Sexual content
  - Violence
  - Self-harm
  - Misleading information

The Moderation API returns detailed scores indicating the likelihood of a violation, allowing developers to:

- Automatically block unsafe queries or completions.
- Flag outputs for human review.
- Customize workflows based on severity thresholds.

By integrating the Moderation API into production pipelines, developers ensure that models behave consistently with safety and compliance standards, without requiring constant manual monitoring.

These tools show that guardrails are no longer optional and are foundational to building responsible, production-ready AI applications.

While retrieval, reranking, and guardrails significantly enhance the reliability and safety of AI systems, true intelligent behavior requires models to go beyond single-turn responses. Modern AI applications increasingly involve agents. They are systems capable of autonomous reasoning, decision-making, planning, and tool use. Although we will explore agents in greater depth in *Chapter 5, Implementing Agentic GenAI Systems with Human-AI Interaction*, it is important to introduce the core concepts: how agents leverage tools, perform reasoning, develop plans, execute actions, maintain memory across tasks, and collaborate in multi-agent systems to solve complex goals. Understanding these foundational ideas will prepare us for building more dynamic, adaptable AI solutions in the chapters ahead.

Agents

A GenAI agent is an intelligent software system that uses generative models, such as LLMs or diffusion models, to understand, reason, and create content in response to user input or environmental stimuli. It can perform tasks like answering questions, generating text or images, summarizing content, or even collaborating in problem-solving. GenAI agents often integrate with tools or APIs and can operate autonomously or within a larger multi-agent system. They observe inputs, make decisions based on learned patterns, and take actions aligned with their goals, mimicking human-like cognition in creative and functional contexts. Refer to the following list to build a deeper understanding of agents:

- Tools are external functions, APIs, or utilities that an agent can call upon to extend its capabilities beyond pure text generation. Instead of trying to answer all questions from its own knowledge, an agent can access search engines, databases, calculators, knowledge graphs, or custom APIs to gather real-time information or perform specific operations. Tools make agents more powerful, enabling them to interact with the external world, retrieve up-to-date facts, query private data, or execute tasks that a model alone could not accomplish reliably.

- Reasoning refers to the agent's ability to think through problems step-by-step, rather than immediately generating an output. Through reasoning, an agent evaluates the current situation, decides what it knows, identifies what it needs to find out, and chooses a sequence of actions that move it closer to solving the task. Reasoning allows agents to break down complex goals into manageable subproblems, handle uncertainty, and adapt their behavior dynamically based on new information or unexpected results.

- Planning builds upon reasoning and involves the structured organization of future steps to achieve a given objective. A well-designed agent does not simply react one step at a time but is capable of constructing a flexible, goal-directed plan—a deliberate sequence of tool calls, decisions, and actions that lead to a successful outcome. Advanced agents enhance their planning through techniques like self-reflection, evaluating their intermediate steps and adjusting strategies if needed, and CoT prompting, which encourages systematic, multi-step reasoning before execution. This enables agents not only to set intermediate goals and prioritize tasks but also to improvise dynamically when faced with unexpected results or incomplete information. Effective planning allows agents to navigate complex, multi-stage processes efficiently rather than acting impulsively or getting trapped by early errors. The ability to plan, reflect, reason through chains of logic, and adapt in real-time is critical for solving real-world tasks that require sustained, coherent progress across multiple actions and decision points.

- Action represents the execution phase where an agent implements a specific step in its plan, such as calling an external tool, making an API request, saving information to memory, or returning an answer to the user. Actions are the *doing* part of agentic systems, where reasoning and planning turn into observable operations. Importantly, actions can be dynamic based on the results of previous actions; the agent may revise its plan, reason again, and take different subsequent steps. This continuous loop of thinking and acting distinguishes agents from static models.

- Memory and multi-agent collaboration are advanced concepts that further enhance an agent's capabilities. Memory allows agents to retain information across different steps, sessions, or even tasks, providing continuity, personalization, and long-term learning. Instead of starting from scratch every time, an agent with memory can recall past interactions, intermediate results, and evolving user preferences. Multi-agent collaboration expands this even further: multiple specialized agents can work together, sharing tasks, delegating responsibilities, and communicating with each other to solve complex goals more efficiently than a single agent could. Systems with memory and collaboration capabilities begin to resemble coordinated, modular ecosystems of intelligent agents working towards shared objectives. The following figure illustrates how an agent interacts with its environment and takes action:

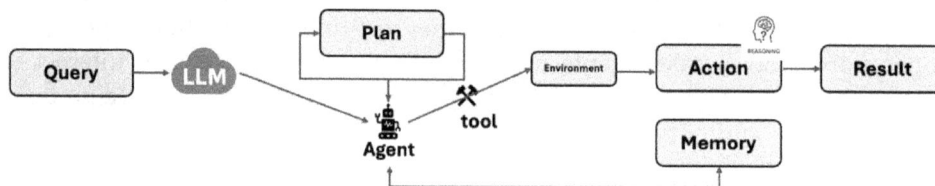

Figure 1.12: *Agents flow, how an agent interacts with environment and takes action*

Agentic RAG vs. non-agentic RAG

In a non-agentic RAG system, the process is linear and static: a user query is embedded, a retriever fetches top-k documents, and the language model-generates an answer using the retrieved context. Each step follows a fixed pipeline without dynamic decision-making. Non-agentic RAG excels in simple question answer tasks where the initial retrieval is usually sufficient, but it struggles when retrieval results are noisy, ambiguous, or insufficient for complex reasoning.

In contrast, an agentic RAG system introduces dynamic control, reasoning, and adaptability. An agent first assesses the query, retrieves initial documents, and reasons about whether the information is sufficient. If not, the agent can reformulate the query, perform multiple retrievals, choose different tools (like search APIs or databases), reflect on intermediate results, and dynamically plan multiple steps to arrive at a better-grounded answer. Agentic RAG systems can iteratively retrieve, rerank, reason, and synthesize across multiple knowledge sources, adapting in real-time to solve complex, multi-hop, or ambiguous queries.

Thus, while non-agentic RAG is simple and fast for straightforward tasks, agentic RAG is critical for building truly intelligent, reliable systems that can handle uncertainty, incomplete data, or evolving information needs. *Figure 1.13* illustrates a multi-agent system featuring an orchestration agent and two additional agents capable of performing joint tasks as well as individual tasks:

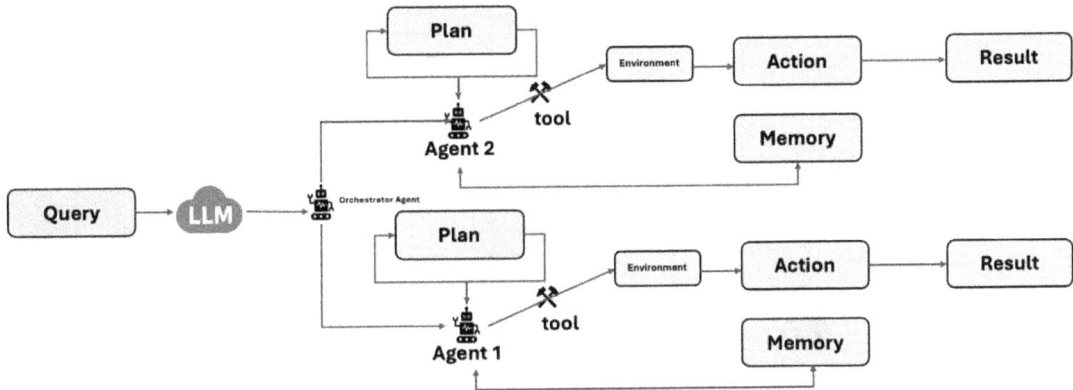

Figure 1.13: Multi-agent systems with an orchestration agent

Model Context Protocols

Agentic systems empower AI models to reason, plan, and execute tasks autonomously by dynamically using tools, APIs, and external knowledge sources. However, without a standardized way to discover and interact with these tools, scaling becomes chaotic and fragile. This is where the MCP is essential. MCP provides a universal, language-agnostic interface for agents to seamlessly access tools, data, and prompts, ensuring secure, modular, and dynamic integration.

MCP is an open standard designed to simplify and standardize how AI models interact with external tools, data sources, and APIs. Introduced by *Anthropic*, MCP acts as a universal communication layer, much like a USB-C for AI, enabling AI assistants and agents to seamlessly retrieve structured information, invoke actions, or apply domain-specific prompts without custom integrations for every backend system.

At its core, MCP establishes a client-server architecture where servers expose three primitives: tools (functions that perform actions), resources (data like documents or APIs), and prompts (guidance for AI behavior). MCP uses lightweight, language-agnostic protocols like JSON-RPC over transports such as studio or HTTP/SSE, making it easy to integrate across diverse environments.

By adopting MCP, developers can build scalable AI systems where new tools and data sources can be dynamically discovered and utilized without retraining models or hardcoding APIs. MCP also ensures modularity, security, and future-proofing, critical for sectors like healthcare, finance, and enterprise automation. As AI ecosystems grow increasingly complex, MCP provides a foundation for building interoperable, secure, and agile AI systems that can reason and act across multiple domains through a unified interface.

Together, agentic systems and MCP enable AI to operate more intelligently and reliably, adapting to real-world complexities without hardcoded dependencies, unlocking powerful applications across industries like healthcare, finance, and education. *Figure 1.14* shows how MCP establishes a client-server architecture and interacts with external tools, data sources, and APIs:

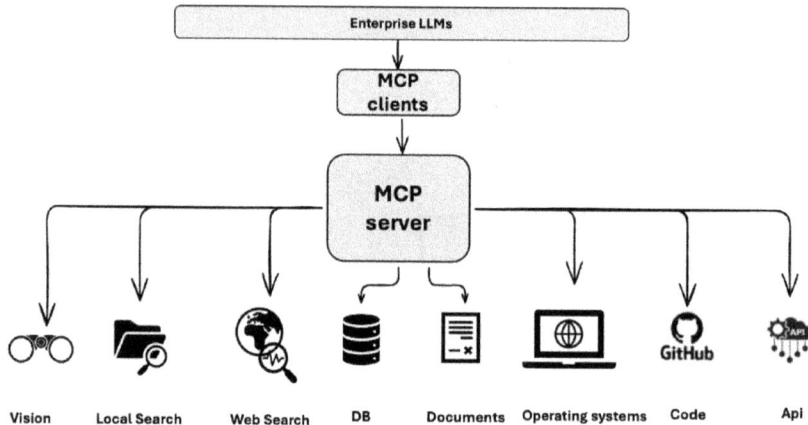

Figure 1.14: *MCP establishes a client-server architecture and interacts with external tools, data sources, and APIs*

Conclusion

In this chapter, we laid the foundation for understanding how modern GenAI systems are designed and orchestrated. We began by differentiating between retrieval systems and generation systems, exploring how each plays a critical role in building intelligent AI solutions. We discussed the evolution from traditional keyword-based retrieval to dense vector search powered by embeddings, and how vector databases enable scalable, real-time semantic retrieval. Moving beyond basic retrieval, we introduced reranking techniques, particularly the use of cross-encoders, to refine and prioritize retrieved documents for greater relevance and precision. We then emphasized the importance of guardrails to ensure AI outputs are safe, ethical, and aligned with real-world usage standards. Finally, we introduced the emerging world of agentic AI systems, covering key concepts such as tool use, reasoning, planning, action, memory, and multi-agent collaboration.

In the next chapter, we explore the expanding frontier of multimodal systems, where AI applications are no longer limited to a single mode of input or output. The focus then shifts to multimodal GenAI architectures, where text, images, and structured data interact within unified frameworks. Readers will learn how AI systems transform text into images, interpret images into descriptions, combine inputs for new outputs, and even translate natural language into **Structured Query Language (SQL)**. This sets the foundation for building rich, contextually aware AI experiences.

CHAPTER 2

Deep Dive into Multimodal Systems

Introduction

The first chapter introduced the foundations of modern **generative AI (GenAI)**, covering retrieval systems, generation models, **retrieval-augmented generation (RAG)**, orchestration, tokenization, vector databases, reranking, guardrails, agent systems, and **Model Context Protocols (MCPs)**. These core components established the groundwork for building intelligent, text-driven generative systems.

Building on this foundation, this chapter explores the evolution of AI into multimodal domains, where text, images, and other data types are processed together. We begin by explaining cross-encoders and bi-encoders within the context of **vision-language models (VLMs)**, followed by a discussion on multimodal vector embeddings and the design of multimodal vector databases.

The chapter further clarifies how VLMs differ from broader multimodal GenAI systems. Practical applications, including text-to-image generation, image-to-text captioning, text and image-to-image synthesis, and text-driven specification and image generation, are covered. Additionally, we explore how text-to-SQL query generation expands the potential of multimodal AI systems.

Through this chapter, we move from understanding the basic mechanisms of generative models to developing systems capable of sophisticated, cross-modal reasoning, positioning us for advanced applications in real-world environments.

Structure

In this chapter, we will learn about the following topics:

- Understanding vision-language model
- Implementation comparisons
- Multimodal generative AI systems vs. VLMs
- Vision-language models
- Output-based classification of multimodal systems

Objectives

This chapter aims to equip readers with a comprehensive understanding of the key building blocks essential for designing and deploying modern GenAI systems. By mastering concepts such as retrieval and generation systems, vector databases, embedding techniques, advanced prompting strategies, agentic architectures, and multi-agent collaboration, readers will gain a strong foundation for building intelligent, scalable AI solutions. Additionally, the chapter introduces critical topics like local model deployment, **graphics processing unit (GPU)** infrastructure, speech processing, memory management in agents, and industry standards like MCPs. These foundational elements are crucial for advancing toward multimodal, reliable, and production-ready AI applications.

Understanding vision-language models

VLMs form the foundation of multimodal AI systems that bridge the gap between visual and textual understanding. Unlike traditional GenAI, which primarily processes text or images in isolation, VLMs are designed to jointly interpret, align, and generate across both modalities. As organizations increasingly look to create systems that *see* and *talk*, VLMs have become critical for applications such as **visual question answering (VQA)**, captioning, cross-modal retrieval, and even text-driven image generation.

Building on the foundations laid in the previous chapter, where we discussed core generative and retrieval concepts, this section delves into the architecture, types, and capabilities of VLMs, highlighting how they extend the principles of tokenization, vector embeddings, retrieval, and generation across multiple data forms.

Categories of vision-language models

VLMs are powerful AI systems that integrate visual and textual understanding, enabling machines to process, interpret, and generate information across both modalities. As the field evolves, VLMs are increasingly specialized in serving diverse applications, from retrieving the right image for a search query to generating detailed image descriptions or even reasoning over documents. To better understand their capabilities and design, VLMs can be broadly categorized based on their core objectives: retrieval, captioning, and QA, generative synthesis, multimodal reasoning, and instruction-tuning. Each category reflects a unique architectural focus and supports real-world applications across industries like e-commerce, accessibility, education, and design. VLMs can be broadly classified based on their primary tasks and architectural design goals, which are as follows:

- **Retrieval-focused VLMs**: These models are trained to align images and text into a shared embedding space, allowing efficient cross-modal retrieval. A key objective is to find the most relevant image given by a text query (or vice versa):

    o **CLIP (OpenAI)**: Trained on 400 million image-text pairs; it learns to embed images and their associated text descriptions closely in the latent space.

    o **ALIGN (Google)**: Scales the retrieval paradigm to billions of noisy image-text pairs from the web.

    o **DeCLIP**: Improves over **Contrastive Language–Image Pretraining** (**CLIP**) by considering harder negatives and better contrastive losses.

    o **Applications**: Image search engines, content moderation, e-commerce product discovery.

- **VQA and captioning VLMs**: These models are designed to answer questions about images or generate captions that describe images:

    o **Learning Cross-Modality Encoder Representations from Transformers (LXMERT) (Facebook)**: LXMERT merges separate visual and language representations via a cross-modal transformer.

    o **UNiversal Image-TExt Representation Learning (UNITER) (Microsoft)**: UNITER trains a unified representation for both vision and text, achieving strong VQA results.

    o **VisualBERT**: It incorporates visual region features early into **Bidirectional Encoder Representations from Transformers** (**BERT**) text transformer, improving captioning and VQA.

    o **Applications**: Accessibility tools (e.g., image descriptions for the visually impaired), visual assistants, and content tagging.

- **Generative VLMs**: These models generate new images or detailed text from inputs across modalities:

    o **DALL·E 2 (OpenAI)**: Generates photorealistic images from text prompts.

    o **Imagen (Google)**: State-of-the-art text-to-image generation model, focusing on ultra-high-quality images.

    o **Parti (Google)**: Autoregressive model generating images by modeling sequences of visual tokens.

- o **Applications**: Creative design, game development, marketing visuals, virtual worlds.

- **Multimodal reasoning VLMs**: These models go beyond retrieval or generation, performing logical reasoning across modalities, such as inferring relationships between images and text, or solving complex visual-text tasks:

  - o **Flamingo (DeepMind)**: Few-shot visual reasoning with flexible conditioning on images and text.

  - o **Kosmos-1 (Microsoft)**: Extends multimodal reasoning to documents, images, **Optical Character Recognition (OCR)** text, and even visual math problems.

  - o **Applications**: Multimodal chatbots, document understanding, and education technologies.

- **Instruction-tuned VLMs**: The following recent models are aligned using human-like instructions, improving their ability to generalize across new tasks without explicit retraining:

  - o **BLIP (Salesforce)**: Bootstrap learning from captioning and retrieval; can both generate captions and retrieve images.

  - o **BLIP-2 (Salesforce)**: Connects a vision encoder with a frozen language model (e.g., OPT, Flan-T5) for zero-shot VQA and generation.

  - o **MiniGPT-4**: Lightweight, open-source approach to build a MiniGPT-4-like multimodal model.

  - o **Applications**: Zero-shot captioning, task-oriented multimodal systems, robotic perception.

Core architectural components of vision-language models

Despite task differences, most VLMs share common design principles, like the following:

- **Cross-encoders vs. bi-encoders**:

  - o Cross-encoders jointly process both image and text during inference, allowing richer interaction but slower retrieval. It takes both the image and text input together and processes them through a *single, joint transformer model*. The image is usually represented as a sequence of visual tokens (e.g., from a **Vision Transformer (ViT)** or a **convolutional neural network (CNN)** with spatial flattening), and the text is tokenized as usual.

    These two sequences are then concatenated and passed into a transformer that performs self-attention across the entire joint sequence, meaning:

- Text tokens attend to image tokens.

- Image tokens attend to text tokens.

- Tokens attend to each other within their modality as well.

This full cross-attention allows rich, fine-grained interactions between vision and language representations at every layer. For example, a word like *dog* can attend to specific image patches showing the dog, and vice versa.

Figure 2.1 depicts a cross-encoder-based VLM architecture designed for tasks requiring deep joint understanding of images and their corresponding textual descriptions, such as matching product photos with detailed specifications. Unlike dual encoders that generate separate embeddings for images and text, this approach does not rely on embeddings but instead computes a direct relevance score by processing the input as a combined pair. Through merged attention or cross-attention mechanisms, the model captures fine-grained interactions across modalities. This setup is ideal for scenarios where alignment precision is critical, such as e-commerce product verification, VQA, and multimodal document understanding.

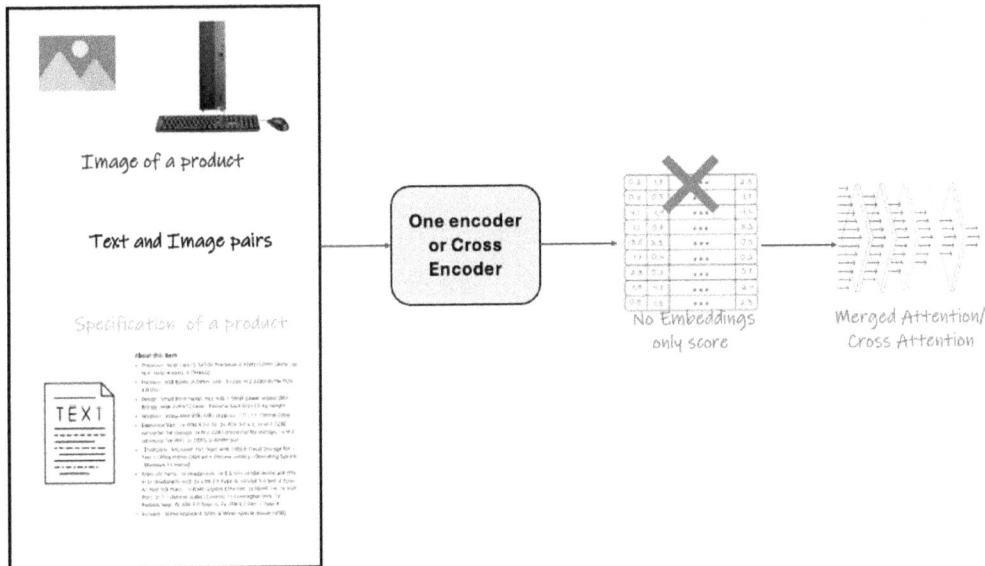

Figure 2.1: *Cross-encoders jointly process both image and text*

o Bi-encoders encode image and text separately and compare their embeddings later, enabling faster, scalable retrieval (as used in CLIP).

The image and text are encoded separately into their own embeddings using two independent encoders, typically: a vision encoder (e.g., a ViT or CNN) processes the image and produces an image embedding vector. A text encoder (e.g., a transformer-based language model like BERT) processes the text and produces a text embedding vector.

Importantly, the image and text do not interact during encoding.

There is no cross-attention between image and text features during inference.

Once both embeddings are generated independently, they are compared after encoding, often by computing a similarity score such as:

- Cosine similarity
- Dot product
- Euclidean distance

The following figure depicts how closer the two embeddings are in the vector space, the more relevant they are considered to each other:

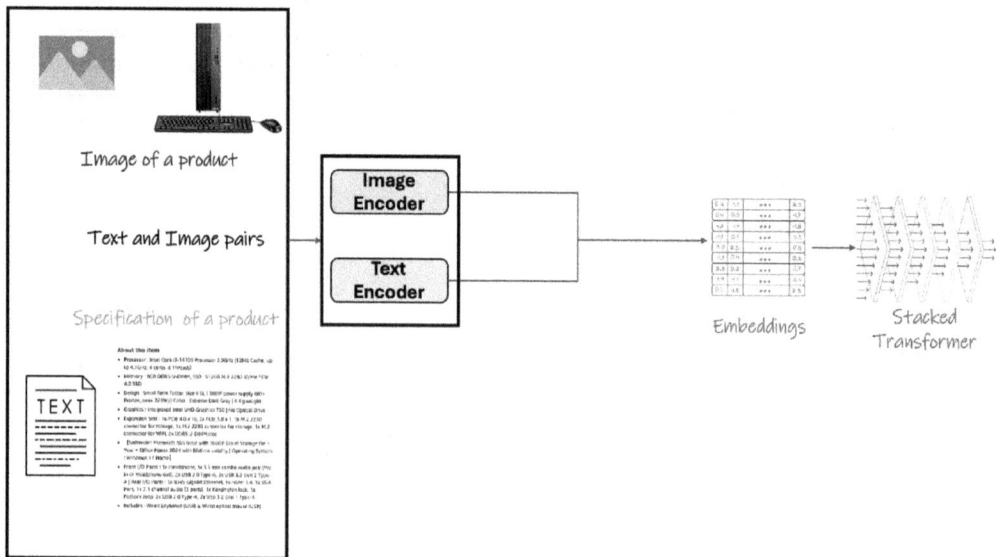

Figure 2.2: *Bi-encoders encode image and text separately*

- **Fusion mechanisms**: Some models (like LXMERT, VisualBERT) use early or late fusion to combine visual and textual information during model training.

  Fusion mechanisms in VLMs refer to how information from different modalities, typically visual features from images and textual features from language, is combined to form a joint representation. Effective fusion is crucial for enabling models to reason across both vision and text inputs.

There are several types of fusion strategies. Early fusion combines image and text embeddings at the input stage, allowing the model to jointly learn cross-modal interactions from the beginning. Late fusion processes each modality separately and merges their output at a later stage, typically before final decision-making. Intermediate fusion (or cross-modal fusion) combines features after partial processing, allowing for more sophisticated interactions between modalities during the model's forward pass. Fusion mechanisms are often implemented using cross-attention layers, where features from one modality (e.g., image regions) attend to features from the other modality (e.g., text tokens). This is similar to how transformers use attention to relate different parts of a sequence, but here the attention operates across modalities. Cross-attention enables models to selectively focus on relevant parts of an image when processing text and vice versa.

Thus, while fusion mechanisms refer broadly to the combining of modalities, cross-attention is a specific technique often used within fusion strategies.

VLMs represent a critical evolution in AI, merging the strengths of computer vision and **natural language processing** (**NLP**) into unified, powerful architectures. From retrieval and captioning to multimodal reasoning and instruction-tuning, VLMs are paving the way for the next-generation of intelligent systems capable of interacting with the world through multiple senses. As we proceed deeper into multimodal GenAI systems in the next sections, the capabilities and limitations of VLMs provide a vital reference point, highlighting the opportunities and challenges of building truly versatile, human-like AI.

Challenges in vision-language models

Despite their growing success across tasks such as VQA, image captioning, and cross-modal retrieval, VLMs face several critical challenges that limit their broader applicability and real-world deployment. These challenges stem from both architectural limitations and practical constraints in data, performance, and generalization:

- **Data requirements and quality**: VLMs require vast amounts of aligned image-text data to learn meaningful cross-modal representations. High-quality datasets like COCO, Visual Genome, or LAION provide a starting point, but they are often biased toward Western, internet-centric content. This restricts generalization to domain-specific or non-English environments. Moreover, creating curated, well-aligned image-text pairs at scale is expensive, and noisy captions can degrade model learning.

- **Modality imbalance**: In many cases, the textual modality dominates model learning due to its semantic richness, leading to underutilization of the visual signal. This imbalance reduces the effectiveness of vision-text fusion and results in suboptimal performance on tasks requiring fine-grained visual understanding, such as object grounding or scene description.

- **Limited multimodal reasoning**: While VLMs can align text and image features, their ability to perform logical reasoning across modalities remains weak. They struggle with tasks requiring temporal understanding, numerical reasoning, or multi-step inference, especially when information must be drawn jointly from visual elements and textual context.

- **Generalization across domains**: Most VLMs are trained on web-scale and generic datasets and fail to generalize to specialized domains, such as medical imaging, scientific literature, or industrial settings. Fine-tuning helps, but it often requires large labeled datasets in the target domain, which may not be readily available.

- **Efficiency and latency**: VLMs are computationally expensive to train and deploy. Architectures that use cross-attention between vision and text tokens (e.g., UNITER, LXMERT) scale poorly at inference time. This limits their feasibility in low-latency or resource-constrained environments, such as mobile devices or edge computing.

- **Lack of tool integration**: Unlike modular GenAI systems, most VLMs are not designed to interface with external tools, like databases, APIs, or vector stores. This limits their utility in dynamic environments where contextual grounding or external memory access is required.

Overcoming these challenges requires innovations in data curation, model architecture, training efficiency, and integration with retrieval or orchestration systems, many of which are addressed in broader multimodal GenAI frameworks.

Multimodal GenAI system

Training VLMs is an extremely resource-intensive process. These models require millions or even billions of aligned image-text pairs to learn meaningful multimodal representations. Curating such massive datasets involves substantial effort, including data collection, cleaning, filtering for quality, and sometimes human labeling to ensure proper alignment. Beyond data, computational costs are also very high. VLMs typically use large architectures, such as ViT for images and transformer-based encoders for text. Training them from scratch demands extensive GPU or TPU clusters running for weeks or even months. For example, models like CLIP (OpenAI) and ALIGN (Google) were trained on datasets that regular organizations cannot easily replicate due to hardware, storage, and energy costs. Moreover, achieving good generalization requires diverse and broad datasets, covering a wide range of visual and textual concepts, further increasing data acquisition challenges. Fine-tuning a pretrained VLM is more feasible for most organizations, but even that can be expensive if large-scale domain adaptation is needed.

Therefore, while developing a VLM from scratch offers full control and potential innovation, it is often prohibitively expensive. Many practical systems today rely on fine-tuning or adapting open-source pretrained VLMs instead of training entirely new models. An alternative to training large VLMs from scratch is building multimodal RAG systems. In multimodal RAG, as shown in *Figure 2.3*, separate retrievers fetch relevant text, image, or mixed-modal data from external sources, and a generator synthesizes a response based on the retrieved information. This approach bypasses the need for massive pretraining by leveraging existing multimodal embeddings and vector databases. It allows flexible integration of text, images, or both as context for downstream tasks like QA, captioning, or summarization, making it a more efficient and scalable method for deploying multimodal AI systems without the heavy costs of end-to-end training.

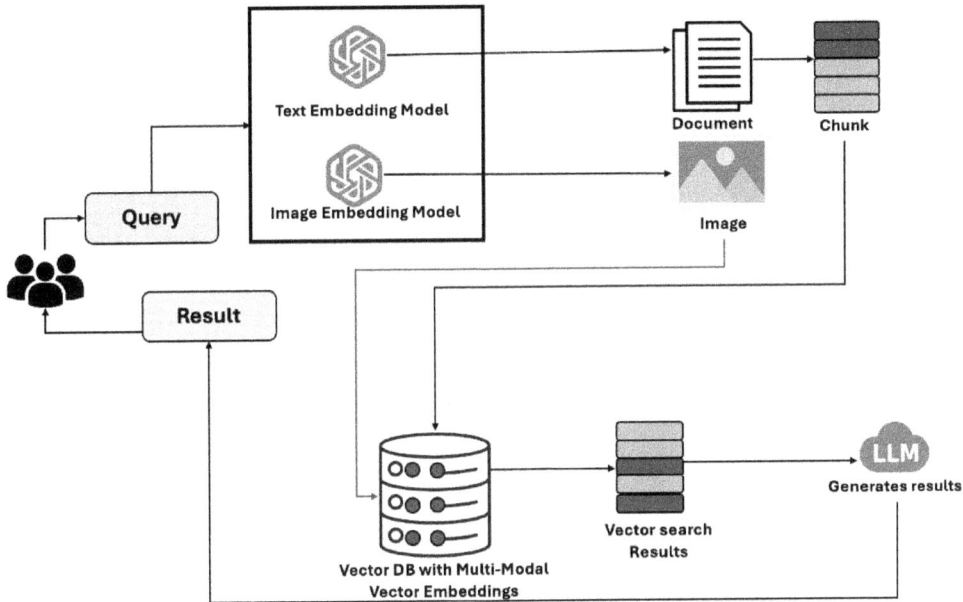

Figure 2.3: *Multimodal RAG system, using two embedding models, one for text and one for image*

Let us understand the multimodal RAG system, an efficient way to build multimodal AI capabilities without training large VLMs from scratch. This system intelligently retrieves and generates answers by leveraging both text and image data. The following is a detailed step-by-step explanation of the process:

- **User query submission**: A user initiates the process by submitting a query.

  The query can be:

  o Text-only (e.g., find smartphones with a good camera),

  o Image-only (e.g., uploading a smartphone photo),

  o A combination of text and image (e.g., a photo with the text prompt, *show similar models*).

  The system must handle different modalities and interpret them appropriately.

- **Embedding generation**: The query, whether text, image, or both, is processed through specialized embedding models, like the following:

  o **Text embedding model**: Converts the text input into a dense vector that captures its semantic meaning.

  o **Image embedding model**: Converts the image into a similar high-dimensional vector space representation.

By encoding both modalities into a shared embedding space, the system ensures that similar concepts from text and images can be compared meaningfully.

- **Preprocessing of knowledge base**: In preparation for retrieval:
    - Documents are broken into smaller, meaningful parts called chunks (e.g., paragraphs, sections).
    - Images are also prepared and associated with their corresponding textual metadata if available.
    - Both text chunks and images are embedded using the different embedding models used for the query. However, please take note that the same embedding models can also be used in specific contexts, and we will talk about this in the following chapters.
    - The resulting embeddings are stored inside a multimodal vector database.

This step ensures that all knowledge assets—text and images—are searchable through vector similarity.

- **Vector database search**: Once the query is embedded:
    - The system performs a vector search against the multimodal vector database.
    - It finds the most semantically similar documents, paragraphs, or images to the user's query.
    - The retrieval happens in embedding space, which allows for flexible matching beyond exact keyword or pixel similarity.

This search step ensures that the most relevant knowledge pieces, irrespective of modality, are fetched.

- **Retrieved results consolidation**:
    - The vector search results include text chunks, images, or both.
    - These results from the retrieved context will assist the final response generation.
    - Retrieved content provides factual grounding for the generative model, improving its accuracy and relevance.

- **Response generation by LLM**:
    - The retrieved multimodal content is then fed into a LLM.
    - The LLM synthesizes the final answer or output using the retrieved knowledge as context.
    - It may combine text explanations, describe images, or generate creative outputs depending on the query.

This design ensures that the model does not hallucinate answers but grounds them in actual retrieved knowledge.

- **Returning the result**:
    o The final result is returned to the user.
    o The output could include text-based answers, references to images, or multimodal summaries based on the retrieved information.

Thus, users receive high-quality responses generated efficiently through retrieval and augmentation.

This multimodal RAG architecture efficiently merges text and image retrieval with generative capabilities. It bypasses the need for massive VLM pretraining, reduces computational costs, and enables scalable deployment of multimodal systems. By separating retrieval and generation, organizations can build powerful AI solutions with existing embedding models and LLMs, making it an attractive option for real-world multimodal AI applications.

Multimodal vector embedding

Now you know that in the era of GenAI, the ability to work across multiple modalities, text, images, audio, video, and structured data, is no longer a luxury but a necessity. Multimodal RAG systems are at the forefront of this evolution, enabling more context-rich, informative, and human-like responses by augmenting LLMs with relevant information retrieved from diverse data sources. However, the effectiveness of such systems is heavily dependent on their underlying vector representations, specifically, the ability to generate multimodal vector embeddings that unify information across formats in a comparable, semantically rich space.

Multimodal vector embeddings are essential because they form the backbone of similarity search in a RAG pipeline. A standard text-only RAG system may suffice for applications limited to documents, webpages, or textual knowledge bases. However, real-world information is often multimodal. For example, user manuals contain both text and diagrams; product specifications include tabular data and annotated images; customer support interactions may involve voice transcripts and screenshots. A system that cannot simultaneously understand and retrieve relevant information from these heterogeneous formats will miss critical signals, leading to suboptimal generation quality.

To enable cross-modal retrieval, each piece of content, whether it is an image, paragraph, or audio clip, must be embedded into a vector space. However, unlike unimodal systems, where all embeddings are derived from the same encoder and live in a uniform latent space, multimodal systems require a more sophisticated design. As explained in *Figure 2.2*, separate encoders (e.g., CLIP for images, Sentence Transformers for text, and Whisper for audio) are often used to generate modality-specific embeddings. These embeddings must then either be mapped into a shared latent space or linked via indexing strategies that allow for efficient similarity computation across modalities.

For example, consider a user asking, *show me laptops with ports like this*, while uploading an image of a laptop side profile. A unimodal RAG system would fail to interpret the image. In contrast, a multimodal RAG system with joint vector embeddings can match the image to similar laptop port diagrams stored in the database and retrieve corresponding product specifications and reviews. This retrieval is only possible because the visual and textual information are both represented as vectors in a shared or aligned space that preserves semantic meaning.

Multimodal vector embeddings also enhance the flexibility of query formulation. Users can input images, text, or even a combination of both, and the system can match them against relevant documents, diagrams, or knowledge chunks. This makes the system more intuitive and inclusive, bridging language barriers and accommodating users who may not have the precise keywords but possess visual or auditory cues.

Furthermore, in RAG systems designed for high-stakes domains like healthcare, legal, or manufacturing, the use of multimodal embeddings ensures a more comprehensive evidence base for answer generation. It reduces the risk of hallucinations by anchoring the generation to real, multimodal data artifacts rather than relying purely on prior model knowledge.

Multimodal vector database

Once multimodal vector embeddings are generated, representing text, images, or both in a shared semantic space, they must be efficiently stored and retrieved to support real-time AI applications. This is where a multimodal vector database becomes essential. It provides a structured, high-performance storage system optimized for similar search across embeddings from different modalities. By organizing these embeddings alongside metadata (e.g., language, timestamp), the vector database enables fast, filtered **approximate nearest neighbor (ANN)** retrieval. This transition from embeddings to a vector database is crucial for powering scalable, cross-modal systems such as multimodal RAG, recommendation engines, and semantic search platforms.

Examples:

- Qdrant, Weaviate, Pinecone, Milvus, and Chroma can all be used as multimodal vector databases, provided:
  - You store both text and image embeddings in the same or logically grouped collections.
  - You normalize embeddings from different modalities into the same dimension (often necessary).
  - You use appropriate metadata tags (e.g., `"type": "text"` or `"type": "image"`) to control retrieval behavior.

You have to touch on some critical design choices when using a multimodal vector database, let us say Qdrant as a vector database for storing and retrieving high-dimensional multimodal embeddings.

Let us understand a few key concepts specifically in the context of Qdrant, a popular vector database. While most vector databases operate on similar principles, detailing each one individually is beyond the scope of this chapter and book.

Collections

A collection is the fundamental organizational unit in Qdrant. It is essentially a labeled group of data points that share a common structure. Each point in a collection is associated with a vector of a fixed size and is compared using a specific similarity metric (e.g., cosine, dot product, Euclidean). All vectors in the same collection must adhere to this uniform dimensionality and distance function. Qdrant also allows multiple vectors to be stored under different names within a single point called **named vectors**, which can individually follow different metric and dimension settings.

Points and point IDs

In Qdrant, a point is an individual entry within a collection. It comprises of the following:

- A unique identifier (point ID).
- One or more vector embeddings.
- Optional metadata known as **payload**.

These points are the basic units that users search against using vector similarity. The point ID is used to retrieve, update, or delete specific records. All point-related operations, including insertions or updates, are first logged to ensure durability and recovery, even in the event of power failure.

Vectors

Vectors (also known as **embeddings**) represent the encoded numerical form of various data types, such as images, text, or audio. These vectors enable the comparison of different data objects in high-dimensional space. The closer two vectors are in this space, the more similar their original objects are considered to be. To generate these embeddings, one typically uses a neural network trained to learn meaningful patterns, often based on contrastive learning from labeled or weakly labeled data. Vectors are the cornerstone of similarity search and are used in clustering, ranking, and retrieval tasks.

Payload

The payload refers to additional metadata stored alongside each vector. This metadata is flexible and can take any JSON-compatible structure. It can describe attributes like language, timestamp, user information, category, or any domain-specific tags. Payloads allow Qdrant to perform filtered searches, letting users restrict similarity searches to vectors with certain metadata properties. For example, retrieving only English-language documents or filtering by date.

Storage and vector store

Qdrant organizes its data into segments within each collection. Each segment maintains its own set of vectors, payloads, and indexes. Segments are optimized for different use cases, like the following:

- Appendable segments support fast inserts, updates, and deletions.
- Non-appendable segments are optimized for static or read-heavy data.

Qdrant supports two storage models, which are as follows:

- **In-memory storage**: Keeps all vector data in RAM for maximum performance, with disk used only for persistence.

- **Memory-mapped storage**: Links disk files to virtual memory, offering a balance between speed and memory usage by leveraging the operating system's page cache.

This architecture ensures that performance and cost can be tuned based on application requirements.

Indexing

In a real-world multimodal GenAI system, efficient data management and retrieval are essential for delivering fast, accurate responses across image and text modalities. Qdrant, a high-performance vector database, enables this by combining vector indexing and payload filtering, ensuring both semantic similarity and structured metadata constraints are handled seamlessly. By leveraging collections, point-level metadata (payloads), and high-dimensional embeddings from models like CLIP or BLIP, Qdrant facilitates hybrid search—retrieving relevant items based on meaning and filters like product category or color. These indexing strategies, including **hierarchical navigable small world** (**HNSW**) and payload indexes, ensure GenAI applications scale reliably while maintaining low-latency performance. Qdrant supports both vector indexing and payload (filter) indexing, allowing efficient hybrid search:

- **Vector indexes** (e.g., HNSW) accelerate similarity searches by organizing vectors into graph structures that reduce the search space.

- **Payload indexes** function similarly to indexes in traditional databases. They allow for fast filtering based on metadata (e.g., language or category fields).

While indexing improves speed and accuracy, it incurs additional memory and processing costs. Users can selectively configure which fields should be indexed based on their expected query patterns and cardinality. Index parameters are defined at the collection level, but the actual index presence in segments depends on optimization rules and data distribution.

Let us integrate all the Qdrant concepts you learned about directly into the context of building a Multimodal GenAI system.

In a practical multimodal GenAI system, managing and retrieving data across modalities, like text and images, is not just about embedding vectors; it is about organizing, filtering, and retrieving them efficiently at scale. This is where concepts like collections, points, vectors, payloads, and indexes, as implemented in vector databases such as Qdrant, become critically important.

At the core of such a system is the vector embedding process. For each input data type, such as a product image or its description, a neural network model (e.g., CLIP or BLIP) converts the input into a high-dimensional vector. These vectors capture semantic meaning, so a caption like a *red sports car* and an image of a red sports car will generate embeddings that lie close to each other in the vector space. These embeddings are then grouped into collections, each representing a logical dataset segment. For example, a single collection may store all vectors related to retail product data, with images and text stored as named vectors under each point.

Each point within this collection represents an individual item, say, a product instance, and is assigned a unique point ID. Alongside the vector(s), a point can include a payload, which stores useful metadata such as language, timestamp, product category, or even the original file source. In a multimodal GenAI setup, this payload becomes crucial when we want to filter results by modality, time range, or other criteria during retrieval.

When a user inputs a query, perhaps a product photo with a textual request like *show similar models available in blue*, the system needs to perform a hybrid search. This means retrieving results not only based on vector similarity but also using constraints defined in the payload (e.g., `color = "blue"`). To enable this, Qdrant supports payload indexing, which allows fast filtering across structured metadata fields, much like indexes in traditional relational databases.

Behind the scenes, the collection is divided into segments, each with its own storage and indexing configuration. Depending on performance requirements, these segments may use in-memory storage for maximum speed or memory-mapped storage to optimize RAM usage while still enabling fast access via the OS-level page cache. For a real-world GenAI application that serves millions of users, segmenting storage this way ensures both scalability and fault tolerance.

Finally, to accelerate vector retrieval, Qdrant supports high-performance vector indexes (e.g., HNSW) that allow the system to quickly approximate the nearest neighbors in high-dimensional space without brute-force comparison. Combined with payload filters, this indexing strategy enables ANN retrieval with precise control, which is vital for real-time multimodal systems.

Implementation comparisons

Two common strategies emerge when storing and searching high-dimensional multimodal embeddings: using a single collection with filters vs. creating multiple collections with localized indexing. These design decisions are especially important when embeddings are updated frequently, such as every day in a production pipeline, and when queries require fine-grained control.

Single collection, partitioned via payload

In this approach, all vector embeddings, whether derived from images, text, or multimodal documents, are stored in a single, unified collection. The differentiation between data types, such as dates or languages, is handled via payload metadata. For example, each point might carry tags like `{"date": "2025-05-09", "language": "en"}`, which are then used as filters during query execution.

This setup is simple and scalable. There is only one collection to maintain, and all embeddings are searchable in a single vector space. Operationally, it is cost-efficient and easy to integrate with downstream systems. However, because no global index is built across subsets (e.g., by date or language), the ANN retrieval accuracy is significantly lower, dropping to around a 50% match rate compared to exact KNN searches.

Filtering embeddings purely through payload without global indexing introduces inefficiencies, especially when the dataset grows or becomes skewed across time and classes. For example, if one date contains disproportionately more data or a specific language dominates, ANN search may lose precision due to uneven vector distribution across the filtered subsets. The following figure depicts a single collection, portioned via a payload approach:

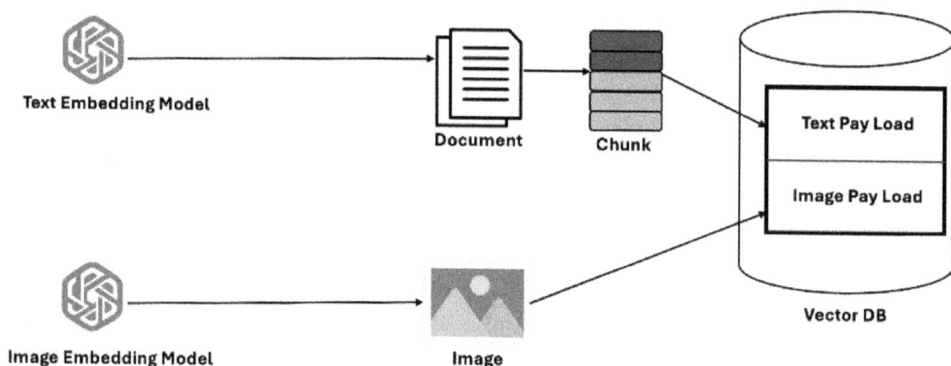

Figure 2.4: *A single collection, partitioned via payload*

Use case: This method is best for environments where ease of maintenance and cost control are prioritized over perfect retrieval accuracy, such as in non-critical retrieval tasks or early-stage prototypes.

Multiple collections with global indexing

The second strategy opts for separating collections by date, creating one collection per day (e.g., **embeddings_2025_05_08**, **embeddings_2025_05_09**). Within each collection, a global vector index (e.g., HNSW) is explicitly built to enable highly optimized ANN retrieval. Each collection can then be partitioned further by language using payload filters.

This approach results in significantly higher precision during ANN-based searches—up to 98% match rate compared to exact KNN—because each collection benefits from localized indexing and a more homogeneous embedding distribution. By narrowing the search space to a single date and filtering only within that segment, the system avoids the dilution of vector clusters that occurs in large, global collections.

However, this model comes at a cost. Maintaining multiple collections increases operational complexity, and the system must manage the indexing cost for each new collection. Additionally, scaling to many collections over time (e.g., per hour or per user) may lead to resource inefficiency and storage overhead.

Use case: This model is ideal when high-accuracy recommendations or precise semantic search are required, such as in product recommendation engines, personalized assistants, or critical analytics pipelines.

The following figure depicts multiple collections with a global indexing approach:

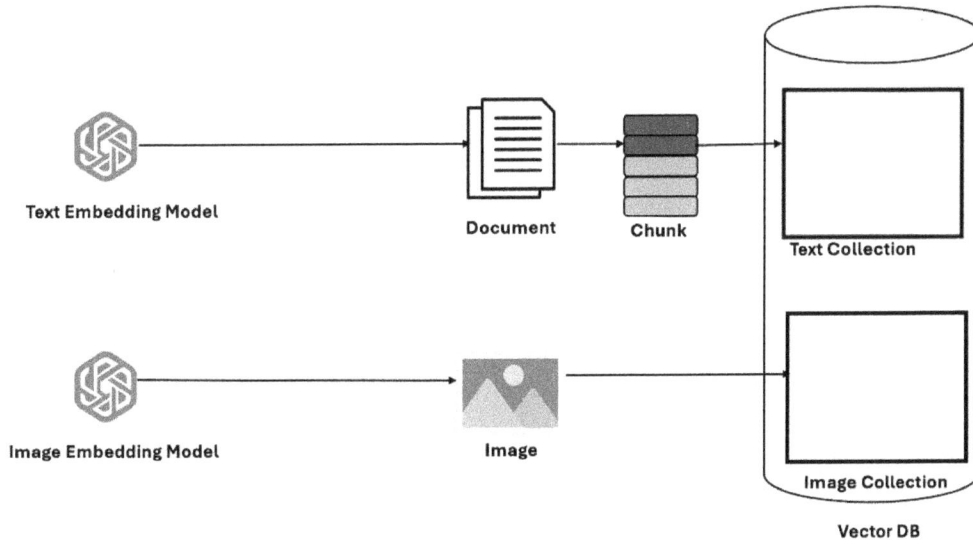

Figure 2.5: Multiple collections with global indexing

Having explored how multimodal vector embeddings are organized, stored, and retrieved using vector databases, we now shift our focus to how these capabilities are applied in end-to-end AI systems. While vector databases serve as the backbone for efficient storage and search across modalities, the architectural choices made on top of this infrastructure, particularly whether to use a multimodal GenAI system or a VLM, can significantly influence performance, scalability, and application fit. In the following section, we examine the fundamental differences between these two approaches and look at when each should be used.

Multimodal generative AI systems vs. VLMs

As AI evolves, the demand for systems that can understand and generate across multiple data modalities, such as text, images, audio, or structured data, has grown significantly. Two approaches have emerged at the forefront of this advancement: VLMs and broader multimodal GenAI systems. While the terms are sometimes used interchangeably, they serve distinct purposes and operate under different architectural principles. This section clarifies their differences and offers guidance on when each is best applied.

Vision-language models

VLMs are a subset of multimodal AI systems that specifically integrate visual and textual modalities. These models are trained to understand and align image features with language features, enabling tasks such as image captioning, VQA, image-text retrieval, and cross-modal reasoning.

VLMs are typically built using architectures that fuse embeddings from two separate neural encoders: a vision encoder (e.g., ViT, ResNet) and a text encoder (e.g., BERT, RoBERTa, or GPT). The fused representation allows the model to reason across both modalities. Some models use cross-attention mechanisms to allow image tokens to attend to text tokens, and vice versa, while others use contrastive learning (e.g., CLIP, ALIGN) to map images and texts into a shared latent space for retrieval.

The following are examples of VLMs:

- CLIP
- BLIP and BLIP-2
- UNITER, LXMERT, VisualBERT
- Flamingo and Kosmos-1 for few-shot multimodal reasoning

VLMs are often pretrained on large image-text datasets, using self-supervised or semi-supervised learning objectives, and can be fine-tuned on downstream tasks requiring vision-language alignment.

Multimodal generative AI systems

In contrast, multimodal GenAI systems are designed to operate across multiple and often arbitrary modalities, not limited to vision and language. These systems combine components for retrieval, reasoning, and generation, often orchestrated through modular architectures.

A key difference is the retrieval-augmented architecture often used in multimodal GenAI systems. Instead of relying solely on a single pretrained model, these systems:

- Retrieve relevant text, image, or structured data from external stores.
- Encode and fuse that information.
- Generate outputs using a language model, image generator, or other modality-specific generator.

Multimodal GenAI systems can incorporate VLMs as subcomponents but are not limited to them. They often support the following:

- Image + text → Structured report
- Audio + text → Summary
- Text → image + Caption
- Image → text + SQL query
- PDF + diagram → Natural language explanation

These systems are typically pipeline-based, combining different models and retrieval layers to perform a task. RAG, orchestration layers (like LangChain or LangGraph), and tool use (via agents) are common.

Let us look at the architectural differences at a glance:

Feature	VLMs	Multimodal GenAI systems
Modalities supported	Vision + text-only	Any modality (text, image, audio, video, tables)
Model structure	End-to-end unified transformer	Modular pipeline with separate retrievers and generators
Typical use case	Captioning, VQA, retrieval	Multimodal chat, document analysis, RAG, complex workflows
Data sources	Pretrained on image-text pairs	Integrates with DBs, APIs, tools, and memory
Retrieval layer	Not always present	Integral part of architecture
Flexibility and customization	Moderate	High
Use of agents or orchestration	Rare	Common (LangChain, LlamaIndex, etc.)
Scalability	Limited by model size	Scalable with retrieval and modularity

Table 2.1: Comparison of VLMs vs. multimodal GenAI systems

Using vision-language models

You should use VLMs in the following cases:

- Your task is tightly coupled with visual and textual alignment, such as:
    - Image classification with text prompts
    - Caption generation
    - VQA
    - Image-text or text-image retrieval
- You need end-to-end performance with low-latency inference and no external retrieval logic.
- You are working with limited modalities and prefer a single-model setup over pipeline orchestration.
- You require models that have been pretrained on large-scale datasets for cross-modal understanding and can be fine-tuned for specialized tasks.
- Your environment favors model inference over dynamic composition, such as mobile applications or edge devices.

In short, VLMs are ideal for controlled, vision-language tasks that benefit from deep cross-modal representation learning in a single-model.

Using multimodal generative AI systems

Use multimodal GenAI systems when:

- You need to combine multiple modalities beyond vision and text, such as:
    - Text + image + tables (e.g., document parsing)
    - Audio + text (e.g., meeting summarization)
    - PDF + chart + question (e.g., scientific paper analysis)
- You require retrieval-augmented reasoning:
    - Search a vector database
    - Retrieve related documents or images
    - Ground the output using external sources
- Your task demands tool use, decision logic, or agent-based orchestration:
    - Querying databases (SQL generation)
    - Invoking APIs
    - Multi-step reasoning (e.g., question decomposition)

- You want a flexible and modular architecture:
  - o Replaceable retrievers
  - o Custom embedding models
  - o Swappable large language models (OpenAI, Ollama, Claude, etc.)
- You need a dynamic knowledge base that updates regularly:
  - o Embedding updates
  - o Multilingual retrieval
  - o Filtered search using metadata (e.g., via Qdrant or Weaviate)

In essence, multimodal GenAI is suited for enterprise-grade, multi-purpose applications that demand high adaptability, live data integration, and sophisticated orchestration of AI components.

Real-world example comparison

Let us take the task of answering a question based on a product manual that includes both text and figures.

- A VLM might be able to caption the image or answer basic visual questions, such as *what color is the switch?*
- A multimodal GenAI system, however, could:
  - o Parse the PDF
  - o Extract diagrams
  - o Use OCR on embedded images
  - o Retrieve relevant product specs
  - o Use a language model to generate a full response like: *to activate the power-saving mode, press the green switch shown in Figure 2.3. The switch controls the secondary circuit.*

This end-to-end capability across text, image, layout, and logic is the hallmark of multimodal GenAI.

Output-based classification of multimodal systems

Multimodal GenAI systems are distinguished not only by their ability to process diverse types of input, such as text, images, audio, or structured data, but also by the variety of outputs they are capable of producing. As organizations deploy AI systems across sectors like e-commerce, healthcare, software development, and knowledge management, it becomes important to classify multimodal systems based on the nature of their output. This classification allows for better architectural design, model selection, and alignment with downstream use cases.

This section introduces a framework for classifying multimodal systems based on the type of output they generate, focusing on six core categories:

- Text-to-image
- Image-to-text
- Text and image-to-image
- Text-to-specifications and image
- Text-to-SQL
- Text-to-code

Each of these categories reflects a unique generation pathway with its own models, challenges, and applications.

Text-to-image systems

Text-to-image generation is a breakthrough capability in multimodal AI, enabling systems to transform natural language prompts into vivid, contextually accurate images. At the heart of this process are powerful generative models like DALL·E 2, Stable Diffusion, Imagen, and Parti, which learn complex mappings between textual semantics and visual features. These systems typically combine transformer-based text encoders with diffusion or autoregressive decoders, sometimes enhanced by super-resolution modules. Applications span creative design, advertising, entertainment, and personalized media. Despite their promise, challenges remain in prompt-image alignment, texture fidelity, and mitigating biases, highlighting ongoing research efforts to improve realism, controllability, and fairness in generated outputs.

Text-to-image generation refers to the process of generating a visual representation (image) based solely on a natural language description. These systems translate descriptive input into detailed and context-aware images using powerful generative models:

- **Core models**: Popular text-to-image models include:
    - DALL·E 2 (OpenAI)
    - Stable Diffusion (Stability AI)
    - Imagen (Google Research)
    - Parti (Google)

    These models use either diffusion techniques or transformer-based architectures to learn mappings between semantic textual inputs and visual outputs.

- **Architecture**:
    - The text encoder (usually a transformer) processes the prompt.

- o   The decoder (e.g., diffusion model) generates an image pixel-by-pixel or through intermediate latent representations.
- o   Optional image super-resolution modules enhance fidelity.

- **Applications**:
  - o   Marketing and advertising creatives
  - o   Product design mockups
  - o   Entertainment and game development
  - o   Personalized content generation

- **Challenges**:
  - o   Ensuring alignment between prompt and image details
  - o   Generating fine-grained textures and spatial arrangements
  - o   Bias in image outputs from training data

Image-to-text systems

Image-to-text generation systems empower machines to interpret and describe visual content using natural language, bridging the gap between vision and language. These systems go beyond basic captioning to deliver rich summaries or structured insights from complex visuals like charts, scenes, or diagrams. Powered by models such as BLIP, MiniGPT-4, and Flamingo, they combine vision encoders with language decoders to generate coherent text from images. Trained on curated or self-supervised datasets, these models support applications in accessibility, content management, and VQA:

- **Core models**:
  - o   BLIP/BLIP-2 (Salesforce)
  - o   MiniGPT-4
  - o   VisualGPT
  - o   Flamingo (DeepMind)

- **Generative image-to-text architecture:**
  - o   A vision encoder extracts visual features from the image.
  - o   A language model decoder translates visual features into coherent, human-readable text.

These models can be trained using supervised datasets like COCO or self-supervised image caption pairs.

- **Applications**:
  - o   Automatic captioning for accessibility

- o   Digital asset tagging and classification
- o   VQA
- o   Descriptive alt-text generation in websites and documents
- **Challenges**:
  - o   Understanding spatial and relational information.
  - o   Handling abstract or artistic content.
  - o   Generalizing across image domains (e.g., medical, aerial, synthetic).

Text and image systems

This class of multimodal systems takes both text and image as input and produces a modified or synthesized image as output. These models often perform guided generation or editing based on the input prompt.

Text and image systems represent an advanced category of multimodal AI where both visual and textual inputs are used to guide image generation or editing. Unlike traditional text-to-image models, these systems condition outputs on an existing image and a descriptive prompt—enabling fine-grained control over modifications. Models like InstructPix2Pix, ControlNet, and Paint by Text leverage dual encoders to extract and merge visual and linguistic features, producing context-aware visual outputs. Applications range from intelligent photo editing and visual personalization to design prototyping. However, challenges persist in balancing prompt fidelity with image integrity—ensuring structural consistency, object preservation, and realistic transformations without over-altering the source image. Let us understand it in detail:

- **Core models**:
  - o   InstructPix2Pix
  - o   ControlNet (used with Stable Diffusion)
  - o   Paint by Text
  - o   Text2LIVE

  These models extend basic text-to-image pipelines by incorporating reference images or conditioning mechanisms.

- **Architecture**:
  - o   An image encoder extracts features from the input image.
  - o   A text encoder captures instructions or prompts.
  - o   A conditioned image generation model merges both modalities to generate an edited or guided image.

- **Applications**:
  - o   AI-assisted photo editing (e.g., *make the sky sunset orange*)

- o Visual personalization
- o Augmenting training data with variations
- o Design iteration based on feedback

- **Challenges**:
  - o Controlling the degree of change from the original image
  - o Preserving object identity and structure
  - o Maintaining visual coherence and realism

Text-only to specifications and image systems

These systems take a text-based prompt, often descriptive or functional in nature, and generate both a structured specification (e.g., a bill of materials, layout plan, or product blueprint) and a corresponding visual output.

This task requires a deep understanding of both the intent expressed in text and the ability to generate multimodal outputs aligned with that intent.

Let us look at some example use cases:

- Generating UI mockups and component specs from textual descriptions.
- Creating architectural blueprints with material listings.
- Product design specs with visual prototypes.
- Robotics or IoT configuration workflows.

  In emerging multimodal systems, text to specs can also be included with image architectures that combine the precision of structured output generation with the creativity of visual synthesis. These systems interpret user prompts to produce both machine-readable specifications (e.g., JSON, YAML) and corresponding images—enabling seamless transitions from concept to design. A language model decodes intent into structured data, while a text-to-image generator visualizes the same concept, often conditioned on shared latent features to ensure alignment. This architecture is key in applications like AI-assisted design, product customization, and digital prototyping, though it faces challenges in maintaining semantic accuracy and synchronizing dual outputs:

- **Architecture**:
  - o A language model interprets the user's intent and generates structured output (in JSON, YAML, etc.).
  - o A text-to-image generator visualizes the outcome based on the same or refined prompt.
  - o In advanced setups, a shared latent representation conditions both outputs to ensure consistency.

- **Applications**:
  - ○ AI-assisted design (Figma plugins, CAD tools)
  - ○ E-commerce product customization
  - ○ Instruction-based digital twins or prototypes

- **Challenges**:
  - ○ Synchronizing structured and visual outputs
  - ○ Ensuring the semantic correctness of specifications
  - ○ Handling ambiguities in natural language prompts

Text-to-SQL systems

Text-to-SQL systems bridge natural language understanding with structured database querying by translating user queries into executable SQL statements. These systems enable intuitive data access without requiring users to know SQL syntax. In advanced multimodal configurations, the models can incorporate additional inputs, such as tables, documents, or images (e.g., scanned invoices), alongside text to generate accurate, context-aware SQL queries. Powered by models like SQLCoder and schema-constrained variants such as PICARD + T5, these systems are evaluated on benchmarks like Spider and CoSQL, pushing the boundaries of database interaction and enterprise analytics automation. Let us look at their details:

- **Core models**:
  - ○ SQLCoder
  - ○ Text-to-SQL LLMs using few-shot prompting
  - ○ PICARD + T5 (schema-constrained generation)
  - ○ CoSQL, Spider as common benchmarks

- **Architecture**:
  - ○ A language model interprets the input prompt.
  - ○ It uses either:
    - ▪ Schema-aware decoding (auto-complete table and column names)
    - ▪ Retrieval of schema from vector DBs
    - ▪ Agentic planning (for multi-turn queries)

In some advanced systems, document embeddings and multimodal signals are used to dynamically guide SQL generation.

- **Applications**:
  - ○ Conversational BI tools

- o   Customer service dashboards
- o   Natural language interfaces for enterprise databases

- **Challenges**:
    - o   Ambiguity in user queries
    - o   Schema alignment and dynamic databases
    - o   Security and query optimization

Text-to-code systems

Text-to-code systems enable the automatic translation of natural language instructions into executable code, streamlining software development and accelerating automation. Leveraging powerful code-focused language models like Codex, Code Llama, and StarCoder, these systems can generate anything from simple functions to full-fledged applications across programming languages. As one of the fastest-growing areas in GenAI, text-to-code technology is reshaping how developers prototype, debug, and build software. With applications in IDE integration, low-code platforms, and developer assistance, these models reduce technical barriers and boost productivity across a wide range of coding tasks. Refer to the following list to build an understanding of text-to-code systems:

- **Core models**:
    - o   Codex (OpenAI)
    - o   Code Llama (Meta)
    - o   StarCoder
    - o   PolyCoder, CodeGen

    These models are trained on large-scale programming corpora (e.g., GitHub) and fine-tuned for instruction-following.

- **Architecture**:
    - o   A language model is fine-tuned to understand developer prompts and produce syntactically valid and functionally relevant code.
    - o   Models can be enhanced with context from:
        - ▪   APIs
        - ▪   Codebases
        - ▪   Documentation

In some multimodal setups, visual diagrams (e.g., flowcharts or **Unified Modeling Language (UML)**) can be paired with prompts to generate code that aligns with visual logic.

- **Applications**:
  - Auto-generating APIs or scripts from functional requirements
  - Creating test cases from documentation
  - Intelligent code completion and bug fixing
  - Low-code/no-code development interfaces

- **Challenges**:
  - Ensuring code correctness and safety
  - Aligning user intent with code functionality
  - Managing versioning and integration into real systems

Classifying multimodal systems based on output type provides clarity on system capabilities, architectural requirements, and deployment readiness. While these six classes are not exhaustive, they represent the most common production-grade use cases emerging today.

Multimodal AI systems can be categorized based on the type of output they generate and the inputs they require. This classification helps in understanding how different combinations of text and image inputs lead to varied outputs such as images, code, SQL, or structured specifications. The following table outlines key output types, their corresponding input modalities, and representative use case categories, ranging from creative design and personalization to data analytics, automation, and accessibility:

Output type	Inputs required	Output generated	Use case category
Text-to-image	Text	Image	Design, marketing, creative AI
Image-to-text	Image	Text	Accessibility, search, indexing
Text + image-to-image	Text + image	Image	Guided editing, personalization
Text to specs + image	Text	Structured output + image	Design automation, engineering
Text-to-SQL	Text	SQL query	Analytics, BI, data search
Text-to-code	Text	Code snippet	Development, automation

Table 2.2: Multimodal systems by output type and use

As multimodal systems continue to evolve, we can expect hybrid models that span multiple output classes. For instance, a system that reads a document (PDF with images), retrieves database context, and produces a code snippet or SQL query is no longer hypothetical, it is already under development in enterprise AI stacks.

Designers of these systems must therefore consider output type as a primary design axis, aligning it with domain needs, user experience goals, and infrastructure capabilities.

Conclusion

In this chapter, we explored the architecture, classifications, and design choices central to building effective multimodal GenAI systems. We differentiated VLMs from broader Multimodal GenAI pipelines, examined their outputs, from text-to-image and image-to-text to text-to-SQL and code, and analyzed implementation strategies using vector databases like Qdrant. Each design, from single collections to retrieval orchestration, impacts scalability, performance, and accuracy. By classifying systems based on output type and aligning them with use case requirements, we gain clarity on when to adopt specialized models versus modular, retrieval-augmented architectures. This understanding forms the foundation for designing scalable, accurate, and efficient multimodal AI applications.

In the next chapter, you will learn how to design and implement a fully offline GenAI system using local LLMs. Focusing on privacy-first and cost-efficient deployments, the chapter guides you through building a RAG pipeline using tools like Ollama, ChromaDB, FAISS, and LangChain, all running locally without reliance on cloud APIs.

You will embed documents, build a retriever, and integrate an LLM for QA using Python. By the end, you will have developed a secure, customizable document-based QA bot capable of operating entirely offline with complete control over data and compute resources.

Join our Discord space

Join our Discord workspace for latest updates, offers, tech happenings around the world, new releases, and sessions with the authors:

https://discord.bpbonline.com

CHAPTER 3

Implementing Unimodal Local GenAI System

Introduction

In this chapter, we embark on building a **retrieval-augmented generation (RAG)** system using local **large language models (LLMs)**, completely offline and free from any dependency on cloud-based **application programming interfaces (APIs)**. This approach is essential for organizations prioritizing privacy, data sovereignty, or operating under strict budget constraints. You will learn how to setup a secure and private **generative AI (GenAI)** pipeline suitable for enterprise or edge deployments.

We will use Ollama to run powerful open-source LLMs locally, ensuring all data remains on your machine. For storing and querying document embeddings, you will choose between **Facebook AI Similarity Search (Faiss)** and Chroma, both optimized for fast, efficient similarity search. The retrieval process will be managed by LangChain, a robust orchestration framework that integrates LLMs, vector stores, and custom logic. LangChain will handle everything from converting user queries into vector representations to fetching relevant documents and prompting the LLM with contextual input.

In addition to hands-on development, we will also examine the failure points of RAG systems, such as poor document chunking, embedding quality issues, and retrieval mismatches, and explore strategies to mitigate them. By the end of this chapter, you will have a fully functional, private unimodal RAG pipeline and a deeper understanding of its design, trade-offs, and limitations.

Structure

In this chapter, we will learn about the following topics:

- GPU in today's generative AI systems
- Using a local GPU
- About Ollama
- Generate a PDF document with Ollama
- RAG implementation
- Challenges in RAG

Objectives

The objective of this chapter is to guide you through building a fully offline, unimodal RAG system using local LLMs. You will learn to run LLMs with Ollama, store and search document embeddings using Faiss or ChromaDB, and manage the retrieval and generation workflow using LangChain. The focus is on creating a secure, private, and cost-effective GenAI pipeline suitable for enterprise or edge environments. Additionally, you will gain insights into common failure points in RAG systems and how to address them to ensure more accurate and reliable AI-generated responses.

GPU in today's generative AI systems

Before we understand the ways of developing a RAG system, as it is important to understand the role **graphics processing units (GPUs)** play in today's GenAI applications.

GPUs play a critical role in accelerating the performance of LLMs and embedding models within a RAG system. However, whether or not you need a GPU depends on several factors, including model size, workload demands, latency requirements, and system architecture. Understanding when a GPU is necessary and when it is optional helps in building efficient and cost-effective GenAI systems, especially in offline or resource-constrained environments.

Let us look at situations that need you to have a GPU:

- **Running large LLMs efficiently**: If your RAG system uses large models like Llama, Mistral, or Mixtral with billions of parameters, GPUs significantly accelerate inference time. These models require substantial memory bandwidth and parallel computation, which GPUs are designed to handle. On **central processing units (CPUs)**, these models may run extremely slowly or not at all due to memory limitations.

- **Low-latency requirements**: For real-time applications, such as chatbots, customer support assistants, or interactive document search, low-latency is essential. A GPU can reduce response times from seconds to milliseconds, greatly improving user experience.

- **Batch processing and high throughput**: In enterprise applications, where many queries are processed simultaneously, GPUs help achieve high throughput. They enable parallel computation for multiple users or documents, making the system scalable.

- **Training or fine-tuning models**: Although most RAG systems focus on inference, some advanced setups require fine-tuning of LLMs or embedding models. This task is practically impossible on CPUs due to massive compute requirements and memory load—GPUs are essential for this phase.

- **Embedding large document sets**: Converting documents into embeddings using models like Sentence Transformers or **Bidirectional Encoder Representations from Transformers** (**BERT**) can be very slow on CPUs. If you are processing thousands of documents, a GPU speeds up the embedding step dramatically.

- **Using small or quantized models**: If your RAG system employs smaller LLMs (e.g., TinyLlama, DistilGPT2) or quantized versions of larger models (like 4-bit or 8-bit quantized Llama), you can run inference reasonably well on modern CPUs. Ollama, for instance, is optimized for such use cases and can run quantized models efficiently without a GPU.

- **Non-real-time applications**: For batch tasks, such as nightly document indexing, report generation, or internal knowledge base querying, where latency is not a concern, CPU-based execution is acceptable. These processes can run slowly without affecting the user experience.

- **Edge or offline deployments with hardware constraints**: In edge devices or secure environments where GPU availability is limited or power consumption is a concern, using CPUs is often the only option. Optimizations like model quantization and efficient retrieval strategies (e.g., pre-filtering embeddings) can help compensate for the lack of GPU acceleration.

- **Proof-of-concept or low-volume use**: For prototyping, academic exploration, or small-scale systems with infrequent usage, CPU execution may suffice. This lowers cost and complexity, making the system easier to deploy and maintain.

While GPUs are essential for accelerating GenAI workloads, the choice between cloud and local deployment impacts both cost and control. Using a local GPU can offer a more economical and efficient solution in many real-world scenarios.

Using a local GPU

LLMs can be broadly classified based on their primary tasks and architectural design goals. Using a local GPU setup can be significantly more cost-friendly than relying on cloud-based GPU services, particularly in scenarios where workloads are predictable, continuous, or privacy-sensitive. Cloud GPU providers, like **Amazon Web Services** (**AWS**), **Google Cloud Platform** (**GCP**), and Microsoft Azure, typically charge by the hour or minute, and costs can escalate quickly, especially for high-end GPUs like the *A100* or *H100*. For teams working on long-running GenAI tasks, such as document processing, real-time RAG systems, or LLM fine-tuning, these charges accumulate rapidly. In contrast, investing in a local GPU workstation, though it may involve a higher upfront cost, can result in substantial savings over time. Once the hardware is paid for, the cost of running models locally is limited mostly to electricity and maintenance.

Moreover, local GPUs offer better control over resource utilization and scheduling, making them more efficient for continuous or iterative development. In cloud environments, users often have to wait for instance availability, deal with session timeouts, or manage additional storage and network fees. Local infrastructure eliminates these inefficiencies, allowing developers to run processes on demand without incurring extra costs. This is particularly beneficial in environments where experiments are run frequently, models are retrained, or batch inference is performed on large datasets. For example, embedding hundreds of documents or running local inference with quantized LLMs can be done without the hourly costs that cloud platforms impose.

Local GPUs support better cost control in privacy-focused or offline deployments. Many enterprises or government institutions have strict data governance policies that prohibit uploading sensitive data to external cloud services. Running GenAI systems with local LLMs on in-house GPUs not only ensures data remains on-premises but also avoids the ongoing cost of compliance-heavy cloud setups. In such cases, cloud GPU usage might require additional security layers, **virtual private clouds** (**VPCs**), and dedicated instances, further increasing costs. A local GPU setup, once in place, provides both a secure and economically sustainable platform for deploying advanced AI systems. For organizations with consistent needs and long-term GenAI goals, local GPUs represent a smart investment with a high return over time.

Running a LLM locally requires balancing hardware capacity, software tools, and model optimization techniques to achieve fast, reliable inference without relying on cloud services. The following steps outlines how selecting the right model size, runtime environment, and deployment strategy, can bring advanced AI capabilities entirely on-device, ensuring privacy, control, and offline availability:

1. **Hardware requirements**: The main factor is model size and whether you use CPU or GPU.

   The following table compares hardware requirements for running LLMs locally at different model sizes, showing the CPU RAM and GPU VRAM needed for smooth inference. It helps you choose the right model size based on your available computing resources.

Model size	CPU RAM (quantized)	GPU VRAM (full precision)	Example models
3–7B	8–16 GB	6–8 GB	Mistral 7B, Llama 2 7B
13B	16–24 GB	12–16 GB	Llama 2 13B
30B+	32–64 GB	24+ GB	Llama 2 33B, Mixtral 8x7B

Table 3.1: Hardware requirements for running LLMs locally at different model sizes

    a.   CPU-only is possible with 4-8-bit quantization (slower but cheaper).

    b.   GPU drastically improves speed (*NVIDIA RTX 3060/4060* and above for 7B models).

2. **Software**:

- **Model runtime**: To load and run the LLM locally.
- **llama.cpp**: A lightweight C++ runner.
- **Ollama**: A simple local model manager.
- **vLLM**: A high-performance GPU inference.
- **Python or API environment**:
    - **Transformers (Hugging Face)**: To load models locally.
    - **Accelerate**: To optimize multi-GPU or mixed precision.
    - **bitsandbytes**: Quantization support for low RAM use.

3. **Model files**:

    a.   Downloaded from Hugging Face or similar.

    b.   Usually `.bin` or `.gguf` files for `llama.cpp`, or PyTorch `.pth` for transformers.

    c.   Quantized versions (4-bit, 8-bit) make local inference practical.

4. **Deployment Patterns**:

    a.   CLI-based | run in terminal for quick tests.

    b.   Local API server | expose endpoints for other apps (e.g., FastAPI, Flask).

    c.   Integrated in apps | call model directly from Python or Node.js scripts.

5. **Performance tips**:

    a.   Use quantization to shrink model size and reduce memory needs.

    b.   Prefer Mistral, Llama, Phi models for efficiency.

    c.   Reduce context length if not needed (fewer tokens | faster inference).

    d.   Store models on SSD for faster load times.

As we explore more efficient and private GenAI deployments, the shift toward local RAG systems becomes increasingly attractive. Tools like Ollama, Unsloth, and lightweight embedding models make it practical to build powerful RAG pipelines entirely on local hardware. We will implement the following architecture shown in *Figure 3.1*.

Architectural components

The following figure represents the architecture of a RAG system, a popular framework in GenAI that combines retrieval-based methods with LLMs to provide accurate, context-aware answers:

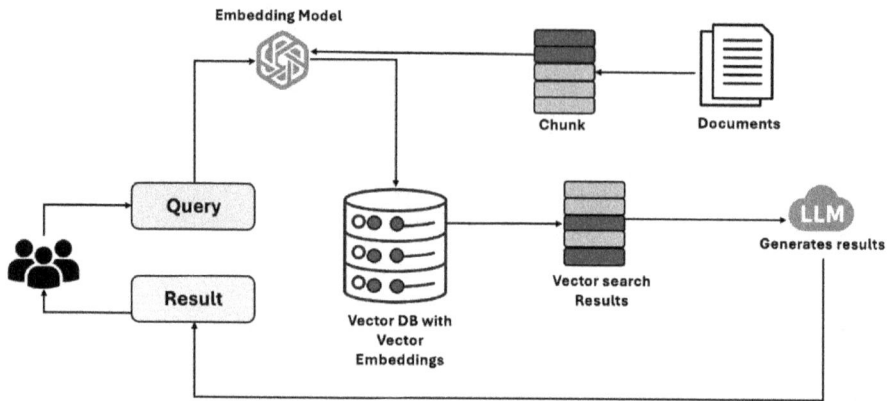

Figure 3.1: *A RAG system which we will be implementing*

As explained in *Chapter 1, Introducing New Age Generative AI,* here is how the preceding figure works:

1. **Document processing**: Raw documents are first ingested and then split into smaller chunks to improve search granularity and retrieval accuracy.

2. **Embedding generation**: These chunks are passed through an embedding model (such as OpenAI or a local alternative), which converts them into high-dimensional vector representations.

    Note: **The chunking is an offline activity; to make it simple, we have shown it in the flow.**

3. **Vector database**: The resulting embeddings are stored in a vector database (e.g., Faiss, Chroma). This database enables fast similarity searches by comparing vectors.

4. **User query**: When a user submits a query, it is also converted into a vector using the same embedding model.

5. **Vector search**: The query vector is matched against the stored document vectors to retrieve the most relevant chunks.

6. **LLM processing**: These retrieved chunks are sent as context to a LLM, which then generates a coherent and informed response.

7. **Result delivery**: The final output is returned to the user.

About Ollama

Ollama is a powerful, yet user-friendly tool designed to simplify the process of running LLMs locally. It provides a clean interface and runtime environment for downloading, managing, and executing models such as Llama, Mistral, and others on your own machine. With just a single command, you can pull pre-configured models and start interacting with them in a secure, offline setting. Ollama handles backend optimizations, including model quantization (e.g., 4-bit and 8-bit), efficient memory usage, and hardware acceleration (GPU/CPU), making it ideal for developers, researchers, and enterprises seeking to build private GenAI applications.

One of Ollama's key advantages is its focus on privacy and simplicity. Since everything runs locally, no data leaves your machine, making it suitable for sensitive or regulated environments. It also supports integration with frameworks like LangChain, making it an excellent choice for RAG pipelines and other GenAI workflows.

Alternatives to Ollama

Several other tools and frameworks provide similar local LLM capabilities, details as follows:

- **LM Studio**: A desktop app that allows you to run and chat with LLMs locally. It includes a GUI and supports model imports from Hugging Face.

- **GPT4All**: Offers a downloadable ecosystem of models and a simple interface for running them locally. It is optimized for consumer-grade hardware.

- **Text Generation Web UI**: A highly customizable browser-based interface for running a variety of LLMs with fine control over parameters and model settings.

- **Unsloth**: Focuses on fast fine-tuning of LLMs using consumer GPUs, making it ideal for custom model training.

- **AutoGPTQ + transformers**: A Python-based setup that allows developers to load quantized models for fast inference without cloud dependence.

Each of these tools caters to slightly different use cases, but all share the goal of democratizing access to powerful LLMs without relying on cloud APIs.

Let us go through a step-by-step guide to install Ollama on your local machine and run the Ollama server:

1. **Check system requirements**: Before installation, ensure you have:
   a. A 64-bit CPU
   b. macOS (M1/M2 or Intel), Linux (Ubuntu/Debian-based), or Windows (via WSL2)
   c. 8GB+ RAM (16GB or more recommended)
   d. Optionally, a GPU (NVIDIA recommended for acceleration)

2. **Install Ollama**:
   a. On macOS (with Homebrew):
      ```
      brew install ollama
      ```
   b. **On Linux**:
      ```
      curl -fsSL https://ollama.com/install.sh | sh
      ```

This will install the Ollama CLI and setup the environment.

3. **On Windows (via WSL2)**:

   a. Install WSL2 with Ubuntu.

   b. Inside WSL terminal, run:

   ```
   curl -fsSL https://ollama.com/install.sh | sh
   ```

4. **Start the Ollama server**: Once installed, start the Ollama server:
   `ollama serve.`

   This runs the Ollama server in the background, ready to load and run models.

5. **Run a model (e.g., Llama 3 or Minstral)**: To download and start chatting with a model:
   `ollama run llama3`

   This will do the following:

   a. Pull the model from Ollama's model registry (first time only)

   b. Start an interactive chat interface in your terminal

6. **Optional step**: Use Ollama with LangChain or API. Ollama exposes a local HTTP API by default at:
   `http://localhost:11434`

   You can now integrate Ollama into applications using REST or libraries like LangChain for local RAG pipelines.

   If you are a Mac user, you will see Ollama:

Figure 3.2: Ollama installation

You can also list all LLMs using the command:
`Ollama list`

Figure 3.3: The image shows a terminal output listing locally installed model in Ollama

The two models shown in the preceding figure are:

- **mistral:latest**, with an **ID f974a74358d6**, a **SIZE** of **4.1 GB**.

- **llama3.2:3b-instruct-fp16**, with an **ID 195a8c01d91e**, **SIZE** of **6.4 GB**.

Both models were modified four weeks ago, indicating recent setup or updates. This confirms that the local environment is prepared to run these models using the Ollama CLI or API for offline LLM inference.

Generate a PDF document with Ollama

Now that you understand Ollama, let us use it to generate a PDF document, which we will later use in our GenAI system.

Here is an end-to-end Python script that:

- Uses the Ollama REST API directly.
- Sends a prompt to the **llama3.2:3b-instruct-fp16** model.
- Generates a document of up to 600 words.
- Saves the output as a PDF file using **reportlab**.

The prerequisites are:

- **Ollama installed and running**:
  ```
  ollama serve
  ```
- **Model pulled**:
  ```
  ollama run llama3.2:3b-instruct-fp16
  ```
- **Python packages installed**:
  ```
  pip install requests reportlab
  ```

With the prerequisites in place, we can now write a Python script that ties everything together.

This script will:

- Send a prompt to the **llama3.2:3b-instruct-fp16** model through the Ollama REST API.
- Generate an informative article (about 600 words).
- Save the generated text as a formatted PDF file using reportlab.

The following is the complete code:

```python
import requests
from reportlab.lib.pagesizes import LETTER
from reportlab.pdfgen import canvas
import textwrap

OLLAMA_URL = "http://localhost:11434/api/generate"
MODEL_NAME = "llama3.2:3b-instruct-fp16"

def generate_text(topic, max_words=600):
    prompt = (
        f"Write an informative article about '{topic}' with
approximately {max_words} words. "
        f"Structure the article with an introduction, body, and conclusion."
    )
    response = requests.post(OLLAMA_URL, json={
```

```python
            "model": MODEL_NAME,
            "prompt": prompt,
            "stream": False
    })
    if response.status_code == 200:
        return response.json()["response"].strip()
    else:
        raise Exception(f"Error: {response.status_code} - {response.text}")

def save_to_pdf(text, filename):
    pdf = canvas.Canvas(filename, pagesize=LETTER)
    width, height = LETTER
    margin = 50
    text_object = pdf.beginText(margin, height - margin)
    text_object.setFont("Times-Roman", 12)

    wrapped_lines = []
    for paragraph in text.split("\n"):
        wrapped_lines.extend(textwrap.wrap(paragraph, width=90))
        wrapped_lines.append("")

    for line in wrapped_lines:
        text_object.textLine(line)
        if text_object.getY() < margin:
            pdf.drawText(text_object)
            pdf.showPage()
            text_object = pdf.beginText(margin, height - margin)
            text_object.setFont("Times-Roman", 12)

    pdf.drawText(text_object)
    pdf.save()

if __name__ == "__main__":
    topic = "The Role of Artificial Intelligence in Modern Education"
    try:
        print(f"Generating article on: {topic}")
        article = generate_text(topic)
        save_to_pdf(article, "ai_education_article.pdf")
        print("PDF generated successfully: ai_education_article.pdf")
    except Exception as e:
        print(str(e))
```

Output: The script will create a PDF file named: **ai_education_article.pdf**:

```
Generating article on: The Role of Artificial Intelligence in Modern Education
PDF generated successfully: ai_education_article.pdf
```

Figure 3.4: The figure confirms successful execution of the script

It shows that an article on the topic **The Role of Artificial Intelligence in Modern Education** was generated using the local Ollama LLM, and the output was saved as a PDF file named **ai_education_article.pdf**. This indicates that the local model ran as expected and the document was created without any errors. You are now ready to open the PDF and review the generated content.

An updated script that generates multiple topic-based PDFs is shared with this book's GitHub repository:

```
generated_articles/
├── the_future_of_renewable_energy.pdf
├── benefits_and_risks_of_artificial_general_intelligence.pdf
├── how_blockchain_is_transforming_financial_services.pdf
├── the_importance_of_mental_health_awareness.pdf
├── climate_change_and_its_impact_on_global_agriculture.pdf
```

Figure 3.5: This figure shows what all synthetic articles are generated after running the script

RAG implementation

Now, that you have learned how to automatically generate documents, we will take the previously created **ai_education_article.pdf** and use it to build a RAG system. This system will include the following components:

- **System prompting with reasoning and acting (ReAct)**: We will use the ReAct prompting technique, which breaks down complex or long-form questions into smaller, manageable sub-queries to improve reasoning and response accuracy.

- **Document chunking**: The PDF will be segmented into smaller chunks to allow for more effective retrieval and contextual analysis.

- **Vector embedding with metadata**: Each chunk will be embedded into a vector representation and stored in a vector database along with relevant metadata for more accurate search and retrieval.

- **Hybrid search module**: The system will use a combination of semantic search (based on vector similarity) and keyword-based search to enhance retrieval performance.

- **LangChain orchestration**: LangChain will serve as the orchestration framework, managing the flow between query parsing, retrieval, context building, and LLM prompting.

- **Conversation buffer**: A conversation memory buffer will ensure continuity in multi-turn conversations, preserving context across user queries.

- **Citation support**: Once an answer is generated, the system will include citations showing exactly which document chunks the answer was derived from.

- **Natural language generation**: Final responses will be generated using the Mistral model via Ollama, ensuring fluent and coherent natural language output.

Figure 3.6 shows a structured layout that exemplifies a clean and scalable RAG pipeline. Each folder represents a critical component, ranging from data ingestion (**source_docs/**), embedding logic (**embeddings/**), and vector storage (**vectorstore/**), to retrieval strategies (**retriever/**), generation logic (**llm/**), and LangChain-based orchestration (**orchestrator/**). The modularity allows for easy customization, debugging, and maintenance. Utility scripts for PDF parsing and citation tracking further enhance functionality, while memory management ensures coherent multi-turn interactions. Such a design not only supports offline deployment using local models like Mistral and Ollama but also encourages reusability and extension across varied RAG use cases. The details are as follows:

- **Modular**: Each responsibility (embedding, retrieval, LLM, etc.) is isolated for clarity and reusability.

- **Scalable**: Easy to extend with more models, data sources, or new retrievers.

- **Debuggable**: Smaller files/functions make it easier to test and maintain.

The following figure illustrates a well-organized directory structure for a modular RAG system. It includes components for document ingestion, embedding, hybrid retrieval, LLM interaction (via Ollama), memory handling, source citation, and orchestration through LangChain. Each module is clearly separated to support scalability, reusability, and clarity in development and deployment.

```
rag-system/
|
|---- main.py                           # Entry point for the RAG pipeline
|---- requirements.txt                  # Python dependencies
|---- config.py                         # Configuration (model names, paths, DB settings)
|
|---- data/
|    |---- source_docs/
|    |    |---- ai_education_article.pdf  # Input PDFs or text documents
|    |---- processed_chunks.json          # Optionally store processed/chunked data
|
|---- embeddings/
|    |---- embedder.py                   # Embedding logic using Ollama-compatible models
|
|---- vectorstore/
|    |---- db_handler.py                 # Logic to create, update, and query vector DB
|    |---- metadata_schema.py            # Metadata schema definitions
|
|---- retriever/
|    |---- hybrid_search.py              # Combines keyword and semantic search
|
|---- llm/
|    |---- generate.py                   # Calls Mistral via Ollama to generate responses
|    |---- react_prompt.py               # ReAct prompting template/logic
|
|---- orchestrator/
|    |---- rag_chain.py                  # LangChain logic to connect retriever, LLM, memory
|
|---- memory/
|    |---- conversation_buffer.py        # Chat memory for context continuity
|
|---- citations/
|    |---- cite_sources.py               # Tracks and returns source references
|
|---- utils/
     |---- pdf_parser.py                 # Extracts and chunks text from PDFs
```

Figure 3.6: *A modular folder structure of a RAG system*

The following code import all the tools from LangChain and Python that you will need for:

- Loading and chunking documents.
- Embedding and storing vectors.
- Performing hybrid retrieval.
- Running a conversational QA chain.
- Interacting with a local LLM.

```
from langchain_community.document_loaders import PyPDFLoader
from langchain.text_splitterC import RecursiveCharacterTextSplitter
from langchain_community.vectorstores import Chroma
from langchain.embeddings import OllamaEmbeddings
from langchain_community.llms import Ollama
from langchain.prompts import PromptTemplate
from langchain.chains import ConversationalRetrievalChain
from langchain.memory import ConversationBufferMemory
from langchain.retrievers import ContextualCompressionRetriever
from langchain.retrievers.multi_query import MultiQueryRetriever
from langchain.retrievers.hybrid import HybridRetriever
from langchain_community.vectorstores import Chroma
from langchain.retrievers import BM25Retriever
import os
```

Load and chunk the PDF document

To begin the RAG pipeline, the PDF document is loaded and segmented into manageable text chunks using LangChain's **PyPDFLoader** and **RecursiveCharacterTextSplitter**. This step is essential for breaking long documents into overlapping text blocks, preserving context while ensuring better retrieval granularity. Chunking with a specified size and overlap allows downstream embedding and retrieval systems to work efficiently without losing the narrative flow. These chunks, as explained in the code and the following list form the foundation of vectorization and search, enabling fine-grained semantic lookup. Proper chunking ensures the system responds with accurate, relevant, and contextually coherent information during user interactions.

```
loader = PyPDFLoader("data/source_docs/ai_education_article.pdf")
documents = loader.load()

text_splitter = RecursiveCharacterTextSplitter(
    chunk_size=500,
    chunk_overlap=50,
    separators=["\n\n", "\n", " ", ""]
```

```
)
chunks = text_splitter.split_documents(documents)
```

- Loads a PDF file and extracts its content.

- Splits the text into overlapping chunks so it is easier to search and retrieve context later.

- `chunk_size = 500` characters; `50` characters `chunk_overlap` ensures smoother transitions between chunks.

While `RecursiveCharacterTextSplitter` is the default and most flexible chunking strategy in LangChain, there are several other chunking methods you can use based on your document type, structure, or use case.

Alternative chunking strategies in LangChain

LangChain supports multiple text splitting strategies beyond the default recursive method. Depending on the structure, language, or domain of your documents, you can choose splitters like `CharacterTextSplitter`, `TokenTextSplitter`, `SentenceTransformersTextSplitter`, `NLTKTextSplitter`, or `SpacyTextSplitter`. Each offers unique benefits—some preserve semantic boundaries, others optimize for LLM token limits, and a few handle structured formats like Markdown. Selecting the right splitter is crucial for maintaining content coherence and optimizing embedding quality, especially for applications like question answering, summarization, or retrieval. This modularity enables precise control over document preparation in a RAG pipeline:

- **CharacterTextSplitter**:

  ```
  from langchain.text_splitter import CharacterTextSplitter
  ```

  o Splits text strictly by character count.

  o Does not use hierarchical separators like a recursive splitter.

  o Simple and fast, but might split in the middle of sentences.

  Use case: When you need consistently sized chunks and do not mind rough breaks.

- **TokenTextSplitter**:

  ```
  from langchain.text_splitter import TokenTextSplitter
  ```

  o Splits text based on token count, not characters.

  o Uses the tokenizer of a specific LLM (e.g., OpenAI, Hugging Face) to avoid prompt size overflow.

  Use case: When working with token-limited models like GPT or Mistral.

- **SentenceTransformersTextSplitter**:

  ```
  from langchain.text_splitter import SentenceTransformersTextSplitter
  ```

- o   Uses sentence boundaries and semantic similarity to split text.
- o   Creates more coherent chunks for better embedding quality.

Use case: When you want semantically meaningful chunks (especially for QA or summarization).

- **NLTKTextSplitter**:

```
from langchain.text_splitter import NLTKTextSplitter
```

- o   Uses the **Natural Language Toolkit** (**NLTK**) to split text into sentences.
- o   Good for well-structured English text.

Use case: Clean sentence-based chunking without manual logic.

- **SpacyTextSplitter**:

```
from langchain.text_splitter import SpacyTextSplitter
```

- o   Uses the spaCy **natural language processing** (**NLP**) library to split based on linguistic features (sentences, paragraphs).
- o   Handles punctuation and sentence boundaries better than raw character-based methods.

Use case: When you want linguistically accurate splitting in multiple languages.

- **MarkdownHeaderTextSplitter**:

```
from langchain.text_splitter import MarkdownHeaderTextSplitter
```

- o   Splits Markdown documents using header levels (e.g., **#**, **##**, **###**) as structural guides.

Use case: For documentation, blogs, or README-style content where headers indicate topic changes.

- **You can also combine splitters**: Use `MarkdownHeaderTextSplitter` first, then `RecursiveCharacterTextSplitter` on each section for precision and structure.

Creating embeddings with metadata

After chunking, each text segment is converted into high-dimensional vectors using embedding models like Mistral via `OllamaEmbeddings`. These embeddings numerically represent semantic meaning, allowing efficient similarity search. Chroma, a local vector database, stores these vectors along with metadata such as document source, enabling traceable retrieval. Persisting this information in the **db** directory allows reuse without re-embedding. Metadata enhances downstream tasks like filtering by source or time. This step as shown in the following code and list transforms unstructured text into structured, queryable memory, making it foundational for intelligent document retrieval in privacy-first, offline deployments:

```
embedding_model = OllamaEmbeddings(model="mistral")
vectorstore = Chroma.from_documents(chunks, embedding=embedding_model,
persist_directory="db")
```

- Uses the Mistral model to convert each chunk into a numerical vector embedding.

- Stores these vectors in a Chroma vector database, along with metadata (like source info).

- The database is saved locally in the **db** folder.

Note: **If you want to reuse an existing index, replace the preceding line with:**

```
if os.path.exists("db/index.sqlite3"):
    vectorstore = Chroma(persist_directory="db",
embedding_function=embedding_model)
else:
    vectorstore = Chroma.from_documents(chunks, embedding=embedding_model,
persist_directory="db")
```

Here are some popular embedding models you can use with **OllamaEmbeddings**, so you can choose the one that best fits your RAG pipeline needs:

- **mxbai-embed-large (~334M params)**: Strong performance for semantic search, often compared to OpenAI's ada-002.

- **nomic-embed-text (~25.8M params)**: High-performance with long context support (2K tokens), recognized for outperforming older commercial models.

- **all-minilm**: A compact Sentence Transformers–style model suited for quick embedding tasks.

- **bge-m3 (BAAI General Embedding, ~567M params)**: Multilingual and versatile embedding model, noted for strong retrieval accuracy and flexibility.

- **snowflake-arctic-embed/snowflake-arctic-embed2**: A family of embedding models with different sizes (e.g., 22M, 110M, 335M) optimized for speed and multilingual support.

- **granite-embedding**: IBM's multilingual embedding models (~30M or 278M parameters), suitable for cross-language contexts.

Using them in code

The following is a quick example showing how to switch between different Ollama embedding models:

```
from langchain.embeddings import OllamaEmbeddings

# Choose one of the models below
model_name = "mxbai-embed-large"
```

```
# model_name = "nomic-embed-text"
# model_name = "all-minilm"
# model_name = "bge-m3"

embeddings = OllamaEmbeddings(model=model_name)
vectors = embeddings.embed_documents(["Sample text to embed"])
print(vectors[0][:5])  # preview of first 5 dimensions
```

Hybrid search with semantic and keyword

Hybrid retrieval combines the strengths of both keyword-based and semantic search. **Best Matching 25 (BM25)** handles exact keyword matches, useful for proper nouns and rare terms, while vector search retrieves contextually similar content. LangChain's **HybridRetriever** fuses both methods, increasing accuracy and recall by addressing both syntactic and semantic relevance. This dual approach ensures robustness across diverse query types, especially in scenarios involving ambiguous or exploratory questions. Configuring **k** (top results) for both retrievers allows fine-tuning of search behavior, making hybrid retrieval an essential component of modern, high-performance RAG pipelines.

BM25 is a ranking function used in information retrieval to estimate the relevance of documents to a search query. It is part of the probabilistic retrieval model and improves upon earlier models by considering term frequency (how often a word appears in a document), inverse document frequency (how rare a word is across all documents), and document length normalization. BM25 assigns higher scores to documents where query terms appear frequently and are rare in the overall corpus, while adjusting for document length. It is widely used in search engines and modern retrieval systems due to its effectiveness and simplicity:

```
bm25_retriever = BM25Retriever.from_documents(chunks)
bm25_retriever.k = 4
vector_retriever = vectorstore.as_retriever(search_kwargs={"k": 4})
hybrid_retriever = HybridRetriever(vectorstore=vectorstore, bm25_
retriever=bm25_retriever)
```

- **BM25Retriever** is for keyword-based search (like traditional search engines).
- **vector_retriever** is for semantic similarity (based on embeddings).
- **HybridRetriever** combines both to improve accuracy.

Aside from **BM25Retriever**, which is great for traditional keyword-based search, LangChain supports several other retrievers that can be used depending on your RAG system's needs. Let us discuss a list of useful retrievers and what they are best suited for.

Other retrievers you can use

LangChain offers advanced retrieval strategies beyond basic vector and keyword search. Tools like **ContextualCompressionRetriever**, **MultiQueryRetriever**, **SelfQueryRetriever**, and **TimeWeightedVectorStoreRetriever** enable summarization, query diversification, and time-aware ranking. Others like **ParentDocumentRetriever** and **EnsembleRetriever** optimize for coherence and weighted strategies across retrievers. Each retriever targets a unique problem, lengthy documents, vague queries, metadata filtering, or temporal priority. By combining or swapping retrievers based on use case needs, you can greatly enhance your RAG system's relevance, flexibility, and performance, particularly in complex, evolving chat or enterprise knowledge environments, details as follows:

- **ContextualCompressionRetriever**:

  ```
  from langchain.retrievers import ContextualCompressionRetriever
  ```

  - Uses an LLM to summarize or compress retrieved content before passing it to the final prompt.
  - Ideal for reducing token size or when documents are very long.

- **MultiQueryRetriever**:

  ```
  from langchain.retrievers.multi_query import MultiQueryRetriever
  ```

  - Generates multiple rephrased versions of the query using an LLM.
  - Retrieves results for each variation, improving coverage and recall.
  - Great for exploratory questions or ambiguous user intent.

- **ParentDocumentRetriever**:

  ```
  from langchain.retrievers import ParentDocumentRetriever
  ```

  - Splits documents into small chunks for vector search but returns the larger parent document to maintain context.
  - Useful for preserving coherence in long documents.

- **SelfQueryRetriever**:

  ```
  from langchain.retrievers import SelfQueryRetriever
  ```

  - Uses an LLM to generate vector search filters based on query content, like metadata-aware retrieval.
  - **Example**: Find documents written after 2020 about AI.

- **TimeWeightedVectorStoreRetriever**:

  ```
  from langchain.retrievers import TimeWeightedVectorStoreRetriever
  ```

  - Prioritizes recent interactions in conversational memory.
  - Useful in chatbot-like systems where recency matters.

- **EnsembleRetriever**:

  ```
  from langchain.retrievers import EnsembleRetriever
  ```

- o Combines multiple retrievers (e.g., BM25 + vector + multi-query) and lets you assign weights to each.
- o Offers more control over retrieval strategy than **HybridRetriever**.

Conversation memory buffer

To maintain context across multi-turn conversations, LangChain introduces **ConversationBufferMemory**. This memory module stores the full chat history, enabling the language model to handle follow-ups and reference earlier queries effectively. It ensures that responses are grounded not only in the current question but also in prior interactions, improving coherence and user satisfaction. This is especially valuable in chatbots and assistants, where continuity is essential. With **return_messages=True**, both user and AI messages are preserved, making the RAG system capable of sustaining rich, ongoing dialogues without losing conversational state.

ConversationBufferMemory is a memory class in LangChain that stores the entire conversation history as a string buffer. It allows a language model (LLM) to remember prior interactions in a chat session, helping the model maintain context across turns, details as follows:

```
memory = ConversationBufferMemory(memory_key="chat_history", return_
messages=True)
```

- Its keeps track of the conversation history to maintain context in multi-turn dialogues.
- Important for chatbots to understand follow-up questions.

LLM configuration natural language generation

The RAG system uses the Ollama interface to load the local Mistral language model, controlling output behavior via parameters like **temperature**. A low temperature value (e.g., **0.2**) results in deterministic, focused responses ideal for factual QA or retrieval tasks. By running locally, the setup ensures privacy and cost-efficiency. This language model interprets retrieved content and user questions, generating structured and informative replies. The following modular configuration allows easy switching between models, aligning output style, speed, and accuracy with your application needs—making it a cornerstone of offline, GenAI deployments:

```
llm = Ollama(model="mistral", temperature=0.2)
```

- Loads the Mistral model locally via **Ollama**.
- **temperature=0.2** means the output will be focused and less random.

ReAct prompt template

ReAct is a prompting strategy that guides LLMs to break down problems into logical steps before answering. The prompt template provides structure: it separates reasoning from the final response, improving transparency and traceability of answers. By explicitly instructing the model to think step-by-step, it aligns LLM output with human-like problem-solving processes. This method boosts performance in knowledge-intensive tasks like retrieval-augmented QA by encouraging the model to synthesize retrieved context meaningfully. ReAct templates enable more explainable, controllable, and trustworthy AI behaviors in RAG systems, details as follows:

```
react_prompt = PromptTemplate(
    input_variables=["context", "question"],
    template=\"\"\"
You are an intelligent assistant using the ReAct (Reasoning + Acting) technique.
Break down the user query into reasoning steps and retrieve relevant information accordingly.

Question: {question}
Relevant Context:
{context}

First, list your reasoning steps clearly.
Then, provide a final answer based on those steps and the retrieved context.

Reasoning Steps:
1.
\"\"\"
)
```

- Instructs the LLM to think step-by-step using the ReAct technique.
- Encourages logical reasoning before generating the final answer.

Building the conversational QA chain

The **ConversationalRetrievalChain** integrates the core components, LLM, retriever, memory, and prompt, to form a complete RAG workflow. It supports multi-turn dialogue by preserving history, retrieves context with hybrid search, reasons with the ReAct prompt, and responds via the Mistral model. This unified chain not only generates high-quality answers but also returns the source documents used, enhancing transparency and citation. It is the backbone of intelligent assistants and document chat systems, enabling dynamic, context-aware responses. This abstraction simplifies orchestration and encourages modular, scalable design in LLM-powered applications:

```
qa_chain = ConversationalRetrievalChain.from_llm(
    llm=llm,
    retriever=hybrid_retriever,
    memory=memory,
    return_source_documents=True,
```

```
        combine_docs_chain_kwargs={"prompt": react_prompt}
)
```

It combines the following:

- The **llm** (Mistral)
- The **retriever** (hybrid search)
- The conversation memory
- The **prompt** for structured reasoning
- Returns both the answer and the source documents (for citation)

User chat loop

The final component is the chat loop, where user input is continuously accepted, processed, and responded to by the RAG system. This loop captures user questions, passes them through the conversational QA chain, and displays both the answer and source citations. It supports real-time interaction and multi-turn memory, making it ideal for chatbots, research assistants, or document QA tools. By integrating all prior components, retrieval, generation, memory, and prompting, the chat loop brings the system to life, turning static documents into an interactive knowledge interface for end users:

```
print("RAG System Ready. Ask a question about the document.")
while True:
    query = input("\nUser: ")
    if query.lower() in ["exit", "quit"]:
        break
    response = qa_chain({"question": query})

    print("\nAssistant:", response["answer"])
    print("\nSources:")
    for doc in response["source_documents"]:
        print("-", doc.metadata.get("source", "[Chunk without source
metadata]"))
```

- Starts an interactive chat with the user.
- Sends the user's question to the RAG system.
- Prints the LLM's natural language answer.
- Also prints which chunks (sources) were used to generate the answer.

In the preceding section, we touched upon a challenge called prompt size overflow, it occurs when the combined length of a prompt, including the user query, context, system instructions, and memory, *exceeds the maximum token limit* of the language model. Each model (like Mistral, Llama, or GPT) has a defined token capacity (e.g., 4,096 or 8,000 tokens), and exceeding this limit causes errors or truncated responses. Overflow often happens in RAG systems when too many large chunks or long conversations are included in a single prompt. To prevent it, you can limit chunk size, truncate older memory, or use token-aware text splitters and compression retrievers to keep input within safe bounds.

Just as prompt size overflow can disrupt the performance of a RAG system, there are several other challenges and potential failure points to be aware of. These issues often stem from how documents are chunked, how embeddings are generated, or how retrieval strategies are configured. If not properly addressed, they can lead to irrelevant results, hallucinations, or poor answer quality. Understanding these pain points is crucial for building robust and reliable RAG pipelines. In the next section, we will explore the most common challenges encountered in RAG systems and discuss how to identify and mitigate them in practice.

Challenges in RAG

The paper, *Seven Failure Points When Engineering a Retrieval Augmented Generation System*, emphasizes that real-world RAG systems need robust runtime validation - you cannot predict failures solely at design time; they must evolve through deployment. It offers valuable insight for practitioners building reliable systems, highlighting where checkpoints and corrective mechanisms are most needed.

Here is how you can address each of the seven RAG failure points from the paper in our current RAG pipeline:

- **Missing content**:
    - ○ **Problem**: The LLM fabricates an answer when the information does not exist in the corpus.
    - ○ **Solution**:
        - ▪ **Add a fallback in the prompt**: If the context is not sufficient to answer, respond with `I don't know based on the given information`.
        - ▪ **Add a confidence threshold**: Use cosine similarity scores from the vector store and reject low-confidence results.
- **Missed top-ranked documents**:
    - ○ **Problem**: Relevant documents are present but not in the top-k retrieved.
    - ○ **Solution**:
        - ▪ Use `MultiQueryRetriever` to generate diverse reformulations of the query.
        - ▪ Increase **k** in:
          `vectorstore.as_retriever(search_kwargs={"k": 8})`
- **Not in context**:
    - ○ **Problem**: Relevant chunks are retrieved but not included due to token/prompt limits.

- o   **Solution:**
    - ▪   **Use ContextualCompressionRetriever:**

      ```
      from langchain.retrievers import
      ContextualCompressionRetriever
      ```

      ```
      retriever = ContextualCompressionRetriever(base_
      compressor=llm, base_retriever=hybrid_retriever)
      ```
    - ▪   Compress or summarize context to fit the model's token window.

- **Not extracted:**
    - o   **Problem:** The LLM fails to extract the answer from context.
    - o   **Solution:**
        - ▪   Improve prompt clarity with explicit instructions and step-by-step reasoning (already done via ReAct).
        - ▪   You can also finetune a smaller LLM specifically for extraction tasks if needed.

- **Wrong format:**
    - o   **Problem:** The LLM ignores formatting instructions (e.g., table, JSON).
    - o   **Solution:**
        - ▪   Modify the prompt with formatting cues:

          Format your answer as a JSON object or bullet list if possible.
        - ▪   You can also use structured output tools like LangChain's Output Parsers.

- **Incorrect specificity:**
    - o   **Problem:** Output is too generic or overly detailed.
    - o   **Solution:**
        - ▪   **Let the user define specificity:** Respond in a high-level summary vs. give detailed technical explanation.
        - ▪   Add prompt templates that accept **response_style** or **detail_level** as a variable.

- **Incomplete answers:**
    - o   **Problem:** The answer includes part of the required info but omits other key facts.
    - o   **Solution:**
        - ▪   Use answer merging logic to extract content from multiple documents.
    - o   Add a checklist-style reasoning step:

1. Identify all relevant facts.
2. Combine and summarize.

What you have learned so far is just scratching the surface of foundational RAG systems. You have built a working pipeline that loads documents, chunks them, generates embeddings, stores them in a vector database, and retrieves relevant context for LLM-based answering. You have also implemented ReAct-style prompting and hybrid search. However, RAG systems are complex, with deeper challenges like prompt optimization, failure detection, scalability, and evaluation. This foundational setup prepares you to explore advanced topics such as tool-augmented agents, knowledge graphs, dynamic routing, and custom retrievers, each offering more control, precision, and flexibility in real-world GenAI applications.

You can now take this RAG system as a foundation and begin exploring its flexibility. As a take-home assignment, try modifying the code to experiment with different chunking/splitting strategies, embedding models, LLMs, and retrieval or search methods. Each of these components is modular and easily swappable, allowing you to tailor the system to specific data types, performance needs, or accuracy goals. This hands-on customization will deepen your understanding of how each layer contributes to the overall performance of a GenAI pipeline.

Conclusion

In this chapter, we explored the essential building blocks of modern GenAI systems. We learned the role of GPUs in accelerating AI workloads and how using a local GPU can be a cost-effective, privacy-friendly alternative. We introduced Ollama as a tool to run local LLMs efficiently and walked through the architecture of RAG systems. You also learned to generate PDF documents using a local LLM, and implemented a complete a RAG pipeline using LangChain, vector databases, and hybrid retrieval strategies. Finally, we examined key challenges in RAG. In the next chapter, we will implement API-based GenAI systems using OpenAI instead of Ollama.

Join our Discord space

Join our Discord workspace for latest updates, offers, tech happenings around the world, new releases, and sessions with the authors:

https://discord.bpbonline.com

## CHAPTER 4

Implementing Unimodal API-based GenAI Systems

Introduction

In this chapter, we build upon the foundation laid in the previous chapter, where we implemented a fully local **retrieval-augmented generation** (**RAG**) system using Ollama and LangChain. While that approach prioritized privacy and offline execution, this chapter shifts focus to cloud-based capabilities by integrating the OpenAI API. This enables us to scale our GenAI applications with access to powerful models like **generative pretrained transformer** (**GPT**) and beyond, allowing for enhanced reasoning, broader knowledge coverage, and more complex query handling. Our goal is to extend the RAG system to support multi-document querying.

We will explore how to design and implement a multi-document GenAI system. By combining OpenAI's API capabilities with thoughtful system design, you will learn how to build more scalable, flexible, and intelligent GenAI pipelines suited for enterprise and cloud-native environments.

Structure

In this chapter, we will learn about the following topics:

- Getting started with OpenAI APIs and models
- Core API endpoints

- Multi-document query
- Implementing modular RAG system with OpenAI
- To do

Objectives

The objective of this chapter is to guide you through building a fully API-based, unimodal RAG system using API-based **large language models** (**LLMs**). You will learn to run LLMs with OpenAI, store and search document embeddings using **Facebook AI Similarity Search** (**Faiss**) and manage the retrieval and generation workflow using LangChain. The focus is on creating a scalable, modular GenAI pipeline suitable for an enterprise.

Getting started with OpenAI APIs and models

OpenAI is one of the leading artificial intelligence research and deployment companies in the world. It is best known for its state-of-the-art generative models such as GPT, DALL·E (text-to-image generation), Whisper (speech recognition), and Sora (text-to-video generation). These models are designed to be accessed via the OpenAI API, which allows developers to build intelligent applications across a variety of domains, including text generation, image synthesis, audio transcription, and more.

This section provides a comprehensive overview of OpenAI, its models, and the different APIs it offers. Whether you are building a RAG system, a chatbot, a summarization tool, or a multimodal application, understanding OpenAI's offerings is essential for choosing the right tools for your project.

OpenAI as a company

Founded in December 2015, OpenAI's mission is to ensure that **artificial general intelligence** (**AGI**) benefits all of humanity. Originally established as a non-profit, OpenAI transitioned into a capped-profit model to attract capital while remaining mission-focused.

The organization is best known for developing powerful language models that are capable of human-like understanding and generation of text. With the release of GPT-2 in 2019, followed by GPT-3 in 2020, and subsequent iterations including GPT-3.5 and GPT-4, OpenAI has consistently set the benchmark in generative AI.

Overview of the OpenAI API

The OpenAI API provides programmatic access to a range of models via RESTful endpoints. This enables developers to integrate powerful AI capabilities into their applications. The API is well-documented and accessible through official **software development kits** (**SDKs**) in languages like Python, Node.js, and others.

The main functionalities covered by the OpenAI API include:

- Text generation
- Chat-based interactions
- Code generation and editing
- Embedding generation
- Image generation and manipulation
- Audio transcription and translation
- Content moderation
- Fine-tuning and custom models

Core API endpoints

The following table summarize the key categories of OpenAI API functionalities, along with their respective endpoints and use cases, highlighting the broad capabilities available for text, image, audio, and model management operations:

Category	Endpoint(s)	Description
Text generation	/v1/completions, /v1/chat/completions	Generate or continue natural language text
Editing	/v1/edits	Modify existing text or code
Embeddings	/v1/embeddings	Generate vector representations for text
Image generation	/v1/images/generations, /v1/images/edits, /v1/images/variations	Create and edit images using DALL·E
Audio processing	/v1/audio/transcriptions, /v1/audio/translations	Convert speech-to-text and translate
Moderation	/v1/moderations	Detect harmful or sensitive content
File handling	/v1/files	Upload and manage files for fine-tuning
Fine-tuning	/v1/fine-tunes	Create custom models using your own data
Model listing	/v1/models	Retrieve available models

Table 4.1: OpenAI API endpoint overview tables

These endpoints provide a robust toolkit for a variety of use cases, from building chatbots and summarizers to developing full-scale AI assistants.

Major OpenAI models

OpenAI offers several families of models, each designed for specific types of tasks. Here is a breakdown of the major models available as of 2025:

- **Text and chat models**: These models are the most used and include:
  - **GPT-3.5 family**:
    - GPT-3.5 Turbo
  - **GPT-4 family**:
    - GPT-4
    - GPT-4o (omni multimodal)
    - GPT-4o-mini
    - GPT-4.1, GPT-4.1-mini, GPT-4.1-nano
  - **O-series (reasoning focused)**:
    - o1, o1-mini, o1-pro
    - o3-mini, o3, o3-mini-high
    - o4-mini, o4-mini-high

Each of these models offers different levels of performance, cost-efficiency, and reasoning capabilities, allowing developers to choose based on their specific application needs.

- **Image models**: OpenAI has also developed powerful models for image generation:
  - **DALL·E series**:
    - DALL·E
    - DALL·E 2
    - DALL·E 3
  - **GPT Image 1 (integrated with GPT-4o)**:

    These models allow users to generate and edit images based on textual descriptions, enabling a wide range of creative and practical applications.

- **Audio models**:
  - **Whisper**: OpenAI's speech-to-text model, capable of transcribing and translating spoken language into text.

- **Video models**:
  - **Sora**: A newer model for text-to-video generation, capable of producing short video clips from textual prompts.

Accessing OpenAI models

To use OpenAI models, developers typically perform the following steps:

1. Create an OpenAI account and obtain an API key.

2. Choose a model appropriate for their task.

3. Call the relevant endpoint using a programming language of their choice.

4. Integrate the responses into their application logic.

Here is an example in Python to list all available models:

```
import openai

openai.api_key = "your-api-key"

models = openai.Model.list()
for model in models.data:
    print(model.id)
```

This helps you dynamically fetch and utilize the models you have access to.

Choosing the right model

When building an application, the choice of model depends on multiple factors, like the following:

- **Performance requirements**: Use GPT-4 or o-series for high reasoning needs.
- **Budget constraints**: Consider using GPT-3.5 or smaller models like GPT-4o-mini.
- **Use case**:
  - **Text generation**: GPT family
  - **Reasoning-heavy tasks**: O-series
  - **Image generation**: DALL·E
  - **Transcription**: Whisper
  - **Video**: Sora

Best practices for beginners

If you are just getting started with OpenAI models, here are some best practices to help you build effectively and avoid common pitfalls:

- **Start with prebuilt models**: Use the base GPT models before venturing into fine-tuning.
- **Monitor usage**: OpenAI provides tools for monitoring token usage and costs.
- **Test extensively**: Prompt engineering is key to performance. Try multiple prompt styles.
- **Stay updated**: OpenAI frequently releases new models and improvements.

OpenAI offers a powerful ecosystem of models and APIs for building AI-enabled applications. With over 20 models across text, image, audio, and video modalities, the platform is robust enough to support a wide range of use cases. Whether you are building a cloud-based RAG system, a multimodal assistant, or an enterprise-level GenAI platform, understanding OpenAI's offerings is the first step toward creating impactful AI solutions.

By mastering the OpenAI API, developers unlock the ability to create intelligent, scalable, and future-ready applications that leverage some of the most advanced AI capabilities available today.

From OpenAI to agentic AI

As OpenAI's models have matured, their capabilities have expanded beyond generating text to performing multi-step reasoning and tool-based task execution. Initially known for models like GPT-3 and GPT-4, which excel at language understanding and generation, OpenAI has evolved its ecosystem to support more autonomous and interactive systems—paving the way for agentic AI.

Agentic AI represents a significant shift from passive text generation to active decision-making, tool use, and autonomous workflows. With the introduction of the Responses API and the Agents SDK, developers can now build intelligent agents capable of reasoning over tasks, invoking tools like web search or file retrieval, and orchestrating complex interactions with minimal intervention.

This transition reflects OpenAI's broader mission to create systems that are not only intelligent but also useful, adaptive, and context-aware. Through frameworks like Operator (for browser tasks) and Codex (for software development), OpenAI enables agents that can act in the real-world, not just simulate conversation.

The following section explores some of the details.

OpenAI's agentic API ecosystem

OpenAI has introduced a powerful set of tools and APIs for building agent-based systems, collectively referred to as the **agentic ecosystem**. These interfaces are designed to support more complex and autonomous workflows where models can reason, invoke tools, perform tasks, and interact with digital environments in a structured manner. This section provides an overview of the core components of OpenAI's agentic infrastructure, including the Responses API, the Agents SDK, Operator, and domain-specific agents like Codex.

Responses API

The Responses API, launched in early 2025, serves as OpenAI's primary interface for building agentic applications. It extends the capabilities of the standard Chat Completions API by enabling a single API call to include not only textual reasoning but also tool invocation and stateful context management. Through the Responses API, developers can orchestrate interactions where the model performs tasks such as file lookups, web searches, or tool-based computations in a coherent sequence.

This API supports integrated reasoning and action loops, making it particularly useful for applications that require dynamic workflows. It is designed to eventually replace assistant APIs, providing a more streamlined and scalable foundation for agentic behavior.

Agents SDK

To support the development of complex workflows and multi-agent systems, OpenAI provides an official Agents SDK. Available in both Python and JavaScript/TypeScript, this SDK offers primitives such as agents, tools, workflows, guardrails, and handoffs. Developers can use the SDK to define agent logic, manage tool interactions, and coordinate actions across multiple AI agents.

The SDK facilitates features such as:

- Tool invocation within reasoning loops
- Guardrails for input/output validation
- Multi-agent collaboration and task delegation
- Native integration with tracing and evaluation tools

For example, using the Python SDK, an agent can be instantiated and executed with minimal setup:

```
from agents import Agent, Runner

agent = Agent(name="Assistant", instructions="You are a helpful assistant")
result = Runner.run_sync(agent, "Write a haiku about recursion")
print(result.final_output)
```

This abstraction allows developers to focus on the business logic while the SDK handles orchestration.

Operator

Operator is an autonomous agent developed by OpenAI for executing web-based tasks. Introduced in 2025, Operator allows AI systems to perform actions such as navigating websites, filling forms, and interacting with graphical user interfaces. It builds on the Responses API to bridge reasoning with real-world action, making it possible for agents to complete workflows that traditionally required human intervention.

This capability is particularly useful for use cases such as order placement, automated customer support, and form-driven workflows, where the agent needs to operate a browser-based interface.

Codex

Codex is OpenAI's agentic AI system designed specifically for software development. Released in May 2025, Codex is capable of generating, debugging, and executing code. It extends beyond simple code generation by enabling agents to run tests, make edits, and interact with existing software systems to fulfill user-defined programming tasks.

Codex is accessible via OpenAI's developer platform and as part of higher-tier subscription plans. It integrates seamlessly with the Responses API and Agents SDK, supporting use cases in software engineering, automation, and DevOps.

Assistants API

Prior to the Responses API, OpenAI provided the Assistants API (Legacy API) to facilitate tool-augmented conversations within a structured thread-based interface. While still available, this API is being phased out in favor of the more flexible and powerful Responses API. Developers are encouraged to transition to the new agentic stack, as future development and support will center around the Responses API and the Agents SDK.

Multi-document query

In earlier chapters, we focused on building systems that query a single document at a time, which is effective for narrow, well-defined tasks. However, real-world applications often require reasoning across multiple-documents to gather context, compare information, or synthesize insights. Transitioning to a multi-document query approach allows our system to handle broader and more complex user intents. This shift involves rethinking how we chunk, embed, and retrieve information, ensuring relevance and coherence across diverse sources. In the following sections, we will explore strategies to support multi-document querying and how to integrate them into a scalable RAG pipeline.

We will use the following code to generate multi-documents:

```
import requests
from reportlab.lib.pagesizes import LETTER
from reportlab.pdfgen import canvas
import textwrap
import os

OLLAMA_URL = "http://localhost:11434/api/generate"
MODEL_NAME = "llama3.2:3b-instruct-fp16"

def generate_text(topic, max_words=600):
    prompt = (
        f"Write an informative article about '{topic}' with approximately
{max_words} words. "
```

```python
        f"Structure the article with an introduction, body, and conclusion."
    )
    response = requests.post(OLLAMA_URL, json={
        "model": MODEL_NAME,
        "prompt": prompt,
        "stream": False
    })

    if response.status_code == 200:
        return response.json()["response"].strip()
    else:
        raise Exception(f"Error: {response.status_code} - {response.text}")

def save_to_pdf(text, filename):
    pdf = canvas.Canvas(filename, pagesize=LETTER)
    width, height = LETTER
    margin = 50
    text_object = pdf.beginText(margin, height - margin)
    text_object.setFont("Times-Roman", 12)

    wrapped_lines = []
    for paragraph in text.split("\n"):
        wrapped_lines.extend(textwrap.wrap(paragraph, width=90))
        wrapped_lines.append("")

    for line in wrapped_lines:
        text_object.textLine(line)
        if text_object.getY() < margin:
            pdf.drawText(text_object)
            pdf.showPage()
            text_object = pdf.beginText(margin, height - margin)
            text_object.setFont("Times-Roman", 12)

    pdf.drawText(text_object)
    pdf.save()

if __name__ == "__main__":
    topics = [
        "The Future of Renewable Energy",
        "Benefits and Risks of Artificial General Intelligence",
        "How Blockchain is Transforming Financial Services",
        "The Importance of Mental Health Awareness",
        "Climate Change and Its Impact on Global Agriculture"
    ]
```

```
    os.makedirs("generated_articles", exist_ok=True)

    for topic in topics:
        try:
            print(f"Generating article on: {topic}")
            article = generate_text(topic)
            safe_title = topic.lower().replace(" ", "_").replace(",", "").
replace(".", "")
            filename = f"generated_articles/{safe_title}.pdf"
            save_to_pdf(article, filename)
            print(f"PDF generated successfully: {filename}")
        except Exception as e:
            print(f"Failed to generate article for topic '{topic}': {str(e)}")
```

Implementing modular RAG with OpenAI

This section provides a detailed walkthrough of a modular RAG system. It combines OpenAI's GPT-4o for QA with Faiss as the vector database for efficient document retrieval. Each component is encapsulated in a separate module for clarity and maintainability.

The following figure illustrates the architecture of a metadata-aware multi-document RAG system using OpenAI's models for both embeddings and answer generation. It highlights how queries are processed through a hybrid retrieval mechanism that combines vector similarity with metadata filtering to ensure accurate, source-specific responses:

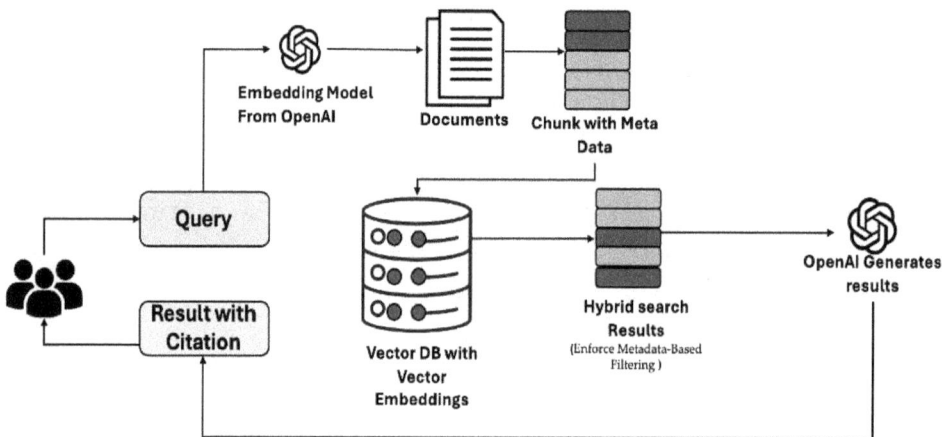

Figure 4.1: Metadata-filtered hybrid RAG architecture using OpenAI

Main controller

This script is the user-facing interface of the RAG system. It loads the RAG chain and enters a continuous loop to accept user questions.

Upon receiving input, it invokes the RAG pipeline to retrieve relevant document chunks and generate a natural language response.

It prints the final answer as well as references to source documents used in the answer generation. This script ensures seamless interaction between the user and the system:

```python
#main.py
from orchestrator.rag_chain import get_rag_chain

print("RAG System Ready. Type 'exit' to quit.")
invoke_rag_chain = get_rag_chain()

while True:
    query = input("\nUser: ")
    if query.lower() in ['exit', 'quit']:
        break

    result = invoke_rag_chain(query)

    print("\nAssistant:", result["answer"])
    print("\nSources:")
    for doc in result.get("source_documents", []):
        print("-", doc.metadata.get("source", "[unknown]"))
```

Configuration

This module centralizes key system constants such as model names, embedding identifiers, API keys, and file paths. It defines the location of source PDFs and the vector database, making it easy to adjust the system setup without editing core logic. By consolidating these values in a single location, the script ensures consistency and facilitates easier debugging and environment portability. It plays a foundational role in making the pipeline easily configurable and modular.

```python
#config.py
MODEL_NAME = "gpt-4o"
EMBEDDING_MODEL = "text-embedding-3-small"
OPENAI_API_KEY = "your-api-key"
VECTOR_DB_PATH = "db"

SOURCE_DOCS = [
    "data/source_docs/ai_education_article.pdf",
    "data/source_docs/how_blockchain_is_transforming_financial_services.pdf"
]
```

Embedding initialization

This script initializes the OpenAI embedding model specified in the configuration. It serves as an abstraction layer to convert raw document text into dense numerical vector embeddings.

These vectors are later used by the retrieval engine to identify relevant chunks semantically close to user queries. The module ensures that embedding generation is reusable, encapsulated, and easy to swap if the backend model changes.

```
#embedder.py

from langchain_openai import OpenAIEmbeddings
from config import EMBEDDING_MODEL, OPENAI_API_KEY

def get_embedding_model():
    return OpenAIEmbeddings(
        model=EMBEDDING_MODEL,
        api_key=OPENAI_API_KEY
    )
```

Vector store setup

This module is responsible for managing the Faiss vector database. It first checks if a vector index already exists locally and loads it if available, avoiding redundant computation.

If the index does not exist, it generates vector embeddings from the document chunks and creates a new Faiss index.

This setup supports persistence and fast retrieval for downstream search components in the RAG pipeline.

```
#db_handler.py

import os
from pathlib import Path
from langchain_community.vectorstores import FAISS
from embeddings.embedder import get_embedding_model
from config import VECTOR_DB_PATH

def get_vectorstore(documents):
    embedding_model = get_embedding_model()

    index_file = Path(VECTOR_DB_PATH) / "index.faiss"
    store_file = Path(VECTOR_DB_PATH) / "index.pkl"

    if index_file.exists() and store_file.exists():
        return FAISS.load_local(
            VECTOR_DB_PATH,
            embedding_model,
            allow_dangerous_deserialization=True
        )

    vectorstore = FAISS.from_documents(
```

```
        documents,
        embedding=embedding_model
    )
    vectorstore.save_local(VECTOR_DB_PATH)
    return vectorstore
```

Metadata tagging

This utility script enriches each document chunk with metadata that tracks its source filename. This metadata is later used to provide attribution and filtering during retrieval and response generation. By tagging the origin of each text chunk, the system can ensure transparency, traceability, and explainability in RAG responses.

This metadata also supports topic-specific filtering and improves user trust by surfacing source information.

```
#metadata_schema.py

def add_metadata_to_chunks(chunks, source_name):
    for chunk in chunks:
        if not chunk.metadata:
            chunk.metadata = {}
        chunk.metadata["source"] = source_name
    return chunks
```

Document loading and chunking

This module handles the ingestion and preprocessing of source PDF documents. It loads each file, extracts the raw text, and then splits the content into overlapping, semantically relevant chunks. Each chunk is further enriched with metadata such as the source filename, enabling better traceability during retrieval. This modular approach prepares the documents for embedding and retrieval while supporting flexible document management.

```
#pdf_parser.py

from langchain_community.document_loaders import PyPDFLoader
from langchain.text_splitter import RecursiveCharacterTextSplitter
from config import SOURCE_DOCS
from vectorstore.metadata_schema import add_metadata_to_chunks
import os

def load_and_chunk_pdfs():
    all_chunks = []
    splitter = RecursiveCharacterTextSplitter(
        chunk_size=500,
        chunk_overlap=50,
        separators=["\n\n", "\n", " ", ""]
```

```
)
for path in SOURCE_DOCS:
    loader = PyPDFLoader(path)
    documents = loader.load()
    chunks = splitter.split_documents(documents)
    source_name = os.path.basename(path)
    enriched_chunks = add_metadata_to_chunks(chunks, source_name)
    all_chunks.extend(enriched_chunks)

return all_chunks
```

Hybrid retriever

This module filters chunks based on topic relevance and combines BM25 and vector retrieval for improved accuracy. Adding a filtering step based on keyword-topic mapping to dynamically restrict chunks by topic before creating BM25 and vector retrievers.

Enforce metadata-based filtering during retrieval

This is done by modifying the retriever logic to filter documents by metadata before scoring and combining them. The following is how you achieve it modularly:

```python
#hybrid_search.py
from langchain.retrievers import BM25Retriever, EnsembleRetriever
def filter_chunks_by_topic(chunks, topic):
    topic = topic.lower()
    if "blockchain" in topic or "crypto" in topic:
        return [c for c in chunks if "blockchain" in c.metadata.get("source",
"").lower()]
    elif "education" in topic or "ai" in topic or "artificial intelligence" in topic:
        return [c for c in chunks if "education" in c.metadata.get("source",
"").lower()]
    else:
        return chunks

def get_hybrid_retriever(chunks, vectorstore, topic=None):
    filtered_chunks = filter_chunks_by_topic(chunks, topic)
    bm25_retriever = BM25Retriever.from_documents(filtered_chunks)
    bm25_retriever.k = 4

    vector_retriever = vectorstore.as_retriever(search_kwargs={"k": 4})

    return EnsembleRetriever(
        retrievers=[bm25_retriever, vector_retriever],
        weights=[0.5, 0.5]
    )
```

Language model

This module initializes the core LLM used for response generation, such as OpenAI's GPT-4o, based on configuration settings. It wraps the model inside LangChain's abstraction to allow easy integration with retrieval chains and memory components. The model is configured with a low temperature to favor deterministic, informative answers. This component serves as the generative backbone of the RAG system, producing human-like responses from the retrieved content.

```python
#generate.py
from langchain_openai import ChatOpenAI
from config import MODEL_NAME, OPENAI_API_KEY

def get_llm():
    return ChatOpenAI(
        model=MODEL_NAME,
        temperature=0.2,
        api_key=OPENAI_API_KEY
    )
```

Prompt template

This module defines the structured prompt that instructs the LLM to follow the **reasoning and acting** (**ReAct**) paradigm. It encourages the model to first list intermediate reasoning steps before providing a final answer. This improves interpretability, reduces hallucination, and ensures the model aligns its reasoning with the retrieved context. It enables a more transparent and auditable answer generation process in complex query scenarios.

```python
#react_prompt.py
from langchain.prompts import PromptTemplate

react_prompt = PromptTemplate(
    input_variables=["context", "question"],
    template="""
You are an intelligent assistant using the ReAct (Reasoning + Acting)
technique.
Break down the user query into reasoning steps and retrieve relevant
information accordingly.

Question: {question}
Relevant Context:
{context}

First, list your reasoning steps clearly.
Then, provide a final answer based on those steps and the retrieved context.
```

```
Reasoning Steps:
1.
"""
)
```

RAG chain assembly

This is the orchestration layer that wires together all components in the RAG system. It loads and preprocesses documents, builds or loads the vector store, configures the LLM and retriever, and binds them into a unified pipeline. It dynamically builds a hybrid retriever based on the user's query to enhance retrieval relevance. The function returns a callable interface that processes user questions end-to-end, generating high-quality answers with source traceability.

```python
#rag_chain.py

from utils.pdf_parser import load_and_chunk_pdfs
from vectorstore.db_handler import get_vectorstore
from retriever.hybrid_search import get_hybrid_retriever
from llm.generate import get_llm
from memory.conversation_buffer import memory
from llm.react_prompt import react_prompt
from langchain.chains import ConversationalRetrievalChain

def get_rag_chain():
    chunks = load_and_chunk_pdfs()
    vectorstore = get_vectorstore(chunks)
    llm = get_llm()

    def invoke_rag_chain(query: str):
        hybrid_retriever = get_hybrid_retriever(chunks, vectorstore, topic=query)
        rag = ConversationalRetrievalChain.from_llm(
            llm=llm,
            retriever=hybrid_retriever,
            memory=memory,
            return_source_documents=True,
            combine_docs_chain_kwargs={"prompt": react_prompt},
            output_key="answer"
        )
        return rag.invoke({"question": query})

    return invoke_rag_chain
```

Conversational memory

This module configures a memory buffer to retain past user queries and assistant responses across multiple turns. It enables the system to carry forward conversational context, making follow-up questions more coherent and contextually aware. By storing interaction history, it transforms the assistant into a truly interactive and conversational agent. This is critical for maintaining continuity in user sessions and improving the overall user experience.

```
#conversation_buffer.py
from langchain.memory import ConversationBufferMemory
memory = ConversationBufferMemory(
    memory_key="chat_history",
    return_messages=True,
    output_key="answer"
)
```

Dependencies

This file lists all required Python packages needed to install and run the RAG system. It includes LangChain modules, OpenAI SDKs, vector database libraries like Faiss, and PDF processing tools. The file allows easy environment bootstrapping using **pip install -r requirements. txt**. Maintaining this file ensures reproducibility, portability, and collaboration across teams or deployments.

```
#requirements.txt
langchain
langchain-community
langchain-openai
faiss-cpu
reportlab
rank_bm25
pypdf
openai
```

Use the following command to install them:

pip install -r requirements.txt

This modular architecture promotes scalability, maintainability, and reusability. Each component has a single responsibility, making it easier to swap out models, change the retrieval mechanism, or update the document pipeline as needed.

You can confidently run your RAG app and expect this:

- Asking *how does blockchain improve payments?* | pulls only from the blockchain PDF.
- Asking *how can AI personalize learning?* | pulls only from the AI education PDF.

To do

In our current implementation, the RAG system is single-tenant, meaning it handles all data and user interactions within a single shared environment. All source documents are embedded into a single vector store, and the retrieval process operates across the same shared document index regardless of which user submits a query.

In contrast, a multi-tenant RAG system must enforce data isolation between tenants, organizations, departments, or individual users. Each tenant would have its own isolated vector store or a namespace within a shared store, ensuring that one user's data and results are never exposed to another. The system must dynamically load the correct vector store and memory context based on the tenant identity during each query.

Use the existing code, available in the GitHub repo of this book, and what specific architectural changes would be required to transform this single-tenant RAG into a secure, scalable multi-tenant system. Focus on vector store separation, memory handling, and request-level routing. Optionally, mention how user authentication or metadata tagging could support these changes.

Conclusion

This chapter offered a concise yet thorough guide to building advanced RAG systems using OpenAI technologies. We began with core concepts and APIs that enable seamless integration of language models into real-world use cases. We then explored the evolution toward agentic AI, autonomous systems capable of reasoning and executing tasks, which marks a shift from static interactions to dynamic, adaptive workflows.

A key focus was multi-document querying, essential for aggregating context from diverse sources. We presented a modular, scalable RAG architecture that combines OpenAI models with Faiss for hybrid retrieval, enabling high relevance, flexibility, and enterprise-grade performance.

In the next chapter, we will understand agentic GenAI with human-AI interaction. It will guide readers through building decision-aware agents that retrieve, reason, act, and interact. This includes integrating tool use, feedback loops, and multi-agent collaboration, extending RAG into dynamic, interactive systems with human oversight.

Join our Discord space

Join our Discord workspace for latest updates, offers, tech happenings around the world, new releases, and sessions with the authors:

https://discord.bpbonline.com

## CHAPTER 5

Implementing Agentic GenAI Systems with Human-in-the-loop

Introduction

As **generative AI (GenAI)** continues to evolve beyond simple query-response paradigms, agentic GenAI emerges as a powerful architectural approach that enables structured, dynamic, and autonomous reasoning. Unlike traditional models that respond in a single-step, agentic GenAI systems are designed to plan, retrieve information, utilize tools, and make decisions across multiple reasoning steps. This chapter introduces readers to the foundational concepts of building such systems, focusing on modular, extensible, and multi-agent architectures. Drawing on real-world patterns, from sequential agents to hierarchical planners, this chapter provides a comprehensive guide to engineering agents that think and act like orchestrators.

You will learn how to use tools like LangChain's ReAct framework, LangGraph, and retrieval components to implement intelligent multi-agent systems. These agents can interact with APIs, query vector databases, utilize memory, and even collaborate with **human-in-the-loop** (**HITL**). Visual frameworks such as aggregator, loop, and router patterns will be mapped to code using Python, giving you practical insight into how these abstract ideas are realized. By mastering these agentic patterns and design principles, you will gain the ability to develop AI systems that do not just generate, but reason, retrieve, and respond with purpose.

Structure

In this chapter, we will learn about the following topics:

- Architecting agentic GenAI systems
- End-to-end human-in-the-loop RAG workflow
- From HITL to multi-agent human-in-the-loop RAG
- Agentic AI vs. AI agents

Objectives

The objective of this chapter is to equip readers with a deep understanding of agentic GenAI systems by exploring their architecture, design patterns, and practical implementations. Readers will learn how to build multi-agent workflows that enable reasoning, tool use, memory integration, and collaboration. The chapter also introduces HITL **retrieval-augmented generation** (**RAG**) systems and contrasts traditional AI agents with agentic AI, emphasizing orchestration and adaptive planning. By the end, readers will be able to design intelligent systems that move beyond single-step responses, laying the foundation for scalable, autonomous AI applications in dynamic, real-world environments.

Architecting agentic GenAI systems

In *Chapter 2, Deep Dive into Multimodal Systems*, we introduced the concept of multi-agent systems—systems where autonomous AI agents collaborate to solve complex tasks. In this section, we explore the design patterns that form the backbone of such systems. These patterns are essential for building intelligent, modular, and scalable GenAI applications. By understanding and applying them, developers can move beyond one-shot generation models and architect truly dynamic, agentic systems capable of planning, reasoning, retrieving, acting, and learning.

Multi-agent systems represent a significant shift from monolithic AI systems to distributed, interactive architectures. Each agent in these systems can be specialized, autonomous, or interdependent, contributing to sophisticated workflows through shared memory, tools, and reasoning paths. In practice, these systems are built by combining reusable design patterns that define how agents interact with one another and the environment. In the following sections, we examine both classical and advanced patterns, ranging from simple sequential flows to collaborative, fault-tolerant, and multimodal reasoning systems.

Parallel pattern

The parallel pattern structures multiple AI agents to operate concurrently on either the same input or different components of a larger input. Each agent performs its task independently, without being influenced by others, and the final result is obtained by merging or aggregating their individual outputs.

Structure and behavior: All agents are triggered simultaneously. They may use the same input (e.g., a shared user prompt) or segmented parts (e.g., split documents). After processing, a merge function aggregates results into a unified output.

Design rationale: This pattern is particularly effective when tasks can be decomposed into independent units of work. It maximizes speed through parallelism and can exploit specialization among agents.

Practical application:

- Running different summarization techniques on a document and selecting the best one.

- Performing multi-language translation simultaneously.

- Running sentiment, intent, and topic analysis in parallel on the same message.

The following figure illustrates a parallel agentic orchestration workflow where a central LLM-based orchestrator distributes input tasks to specialized agents for parallel processing before generating the final output:

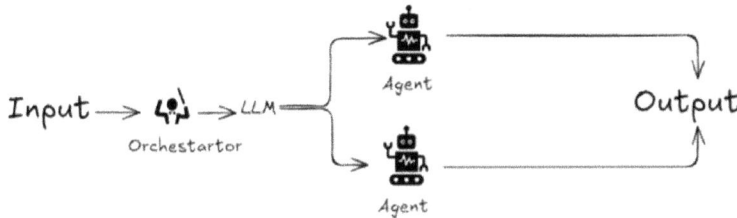

Figure 5.1: LLM orchestrator routes input to agents for collaborative output

Sequential pattern

The sequential pattern connects agents in a pipeline, where each agent's output becomes the next agent's input. This creates a multi-step reasoning or transformation process.

Structure and behavior: Agent A | Agent B | Agent C, forming a clear, ordered chain of execution. Each step builds on the last, often increasing abstraction or refining output.

Design rationale: Useful for workflows requiring layered processing. Each agent can perform a simple task, resulting in manageable, testable, and interpretable steps.

Practical application:

- An agent retrieves data, another summarizes it, and a third formats it.

- Text generation followed by grammar correction and tone adjustment.

- Data extraction | classification | storage.

This figure shows a sequential agent collaboration pattern where an LLM orchestrator routes input through one agent, which delegates part of the task to another agent before producing the final output:

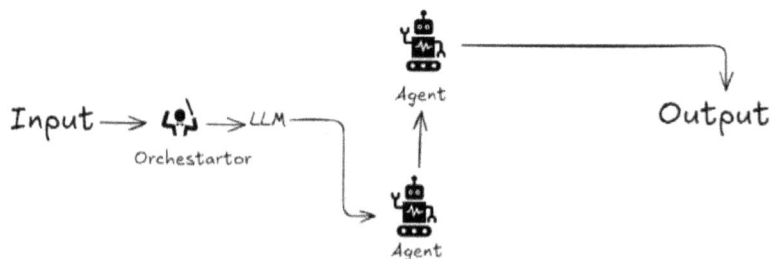

Figure 5.2: *Chained agent collaboration with LLM orchestration*

Loop pattern

In the loop pattern, agents iteratively process an input through a feedback mechanism. The system re-evaluates or refines results in each loop cycle, continuing until a convergence condition is met.

Structure and behavior: Agent A produces output | Agent B evaluates | feedback is returned | repeat until quality threshold is met or loop count ends.

Design rationale: Ideal for tasks involving iterative improvement, optimization, or learning from feedback. Encourages refinement over one-shot generation.

Practical application:

- A writing assistant loops through draft revisions based on critique.
- Generative agent creates responses, while an evaluation agent provides quality feedback.
- Code generation and testing loop until no bugs are found.

This figure represents a looped agent interaction, where agents collaboratively refine results through iterative communication before producing the final output, all under the direction of an LLM orchestrator:

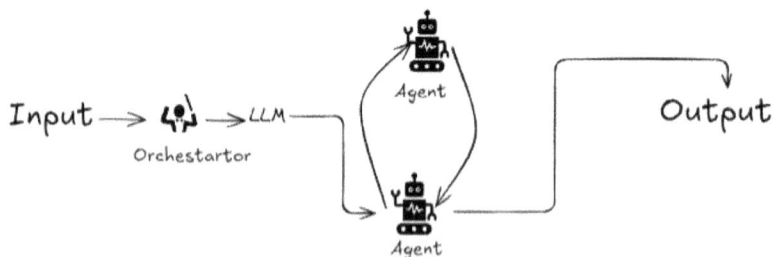

Figure 5.3: *LLM-guided agent loop for iterative task solving*

Router pattern

This pattern introduces a central router agent that dynamically decides which downstream agent should handle an incoming task based on content, context, or metadata.

Structure and behavior: Router receives input | classifies or analyzes | sends to one of many specialized agents | result is returned.

Design rationale: Supports modularity and conditional logic. By separating decision-making from task execution, it promotes reusability and system flexibility.

Practical application:

- Routing finance queries to tax agents, budgeting agents, or investment agents.
- Multimodal input classification (text/image/audio) followed by specialized processing.
- Helpdesk agent routing to technical support or billing systems.

The following architecture introduces a router agent between the LLM orchestrator and downstream agents, enabling smart task delegation based on input characteristics:

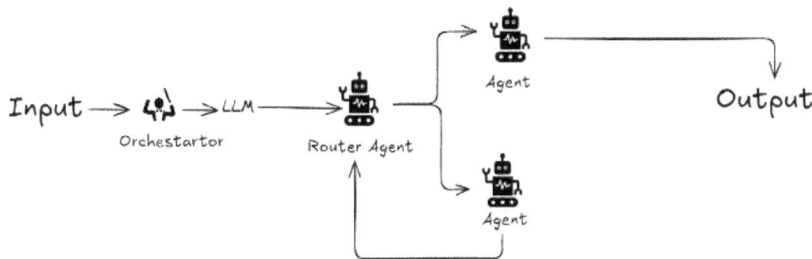

Figure 5.4: Router agent directs tasks to specialized agents for output generation

Aggregator pattern

The aggregator pattern combines inputs or outputs from multiple sources into a coherent result. It focuses not on parallel execution but on synthesis and consolidation.

Structure and behavior: Multiple inputs | aggregator agent | normalizes, merges, or summarizes data | returns single output.

Design rationale: Useful when diverse perspectives or data sources are required for a comprehensive output. Promotes robustness through redundancy.

Practical application:

- Combining answers from different knowledge bases to form a complete response.
- Merging various metric outputs into a single dashboard summary.
- Voting or ensemble models for decision-making.

The following figure depicts an aggregator pattern, where multiple inputs are unified by an LLM-based orchestrator before being passed to an agent for final processing:

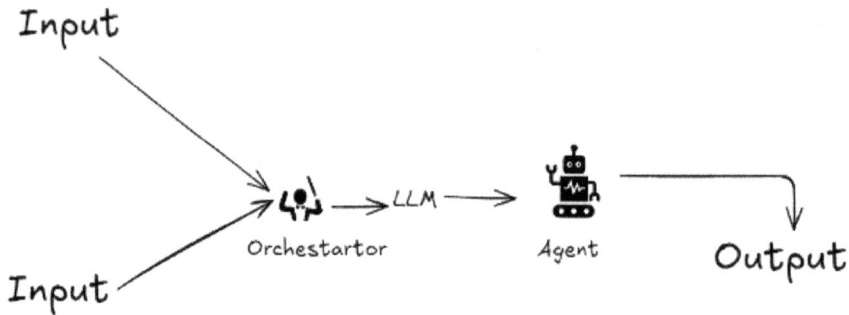

Figure 5.5: Orchestrator aggregates multiple inputs for unified agent execution

Network pattern

In this pattern, agents are fully or partially connected and communicate freely without centralized control. It reflects a decentralized, mesh-like topology.

Structure and behavior: Agents exchange messages with any peer in the network, forming an open, collaborative environment. Coordination is emergent.

Design rationale: Best for complex environments requiring autonomy, adaptability, and peer learning. Suited for distributed problem-solving.

Practical application:

- AI agents representing stakeholders negotiating a contract.
- Autonomous driving simulations with vehicle-to-vehicle communication.
- Distributed consensus on data classification in peer systems.

The following figure illustrates a network pattern where an LLM orchestrator activates a collaborative mesh or network of agents, each contributing to and building upon one another's outputs:

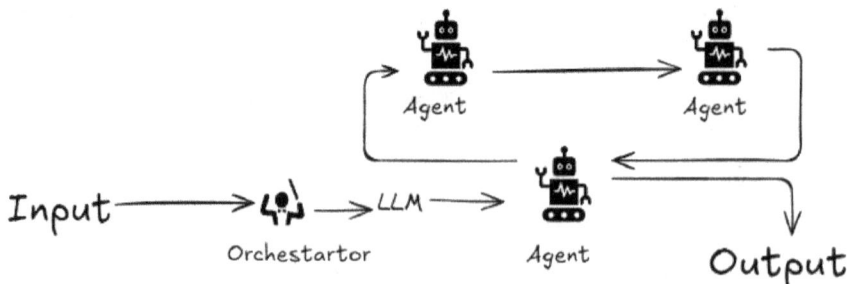

Figure 5.6: Networked agents collaborate for enriched output generation

Hierarchical pattern

The hierarchical pattern organizes agents into layers of abstraction. High-level agents (planners or supervisors) delegate tasks to mid or low-level agents, who execute them.

Structure and behavior: Planner agent | task delegation | worker agents | aggregated output returned up the hierarchy.

Design rationale: Encourages clarity of responsibility and control. Supports task decomposition and team-like collaboration.

Practical application:

- A chatbot manager delegates to knowledge retrieval, formatting, and validation sub-agents.
- Project agent overseeing multiple specialized subprocesses (e.g., translation, summarization, citation).

This architecture represents a hierarchical pattern where an orchestrator routes input through a coordinating agent, which then delegates tasks to specialized agents for parallel outputs:

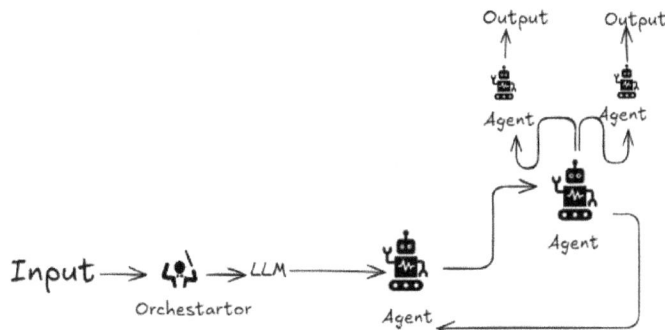

Figure 5.7: Hierarchical agent chain for distributed output generation

Human-in-the-loop pattern

This pattern introduces human decision-making into the system at critical junctures, allowing agents to pause and await user input or validation before continuing.

Structure and behavior: Agent execution halts | human reviews or provides input | execution resumes.

Design rationale: Essential in sensitive domains (legal, healthcare, ethics) where human oversight is required for safety, correctness, or regulation.

Practical application:

- AI drafting a contract clause, then awaiting human approval.

- Human moderation of flagged content.
- Escalating unresolved chatbot queries to human agents.

This figure highlights a HITL agent framework, where the LLM-orchestrated agents generate multiple outputs and the human provides oversight and final judgment:

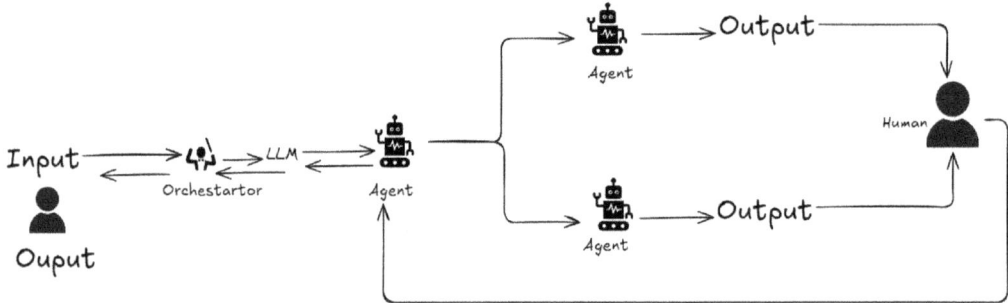

Figure 5.8: Hierarchical agent chain for distributed output generation

Shared tools pattern

Multiple agents access a common toolkit, such as APIs, search engines, or vector databases, to maintain consistency and efficiency across tasks.

Structure and behavior: Agents | shared interface layer | tool/database/API.

Design rationale: Promotes modularity and reduces duplication. Allows centralized updates and monitoring.

Practical application:

- Agents querying a single QA database for different user queries.
- Shared cache or memory system accessed by all agents.
- Unified knowledge graph as a shared backend.

This architecture demonstrates an advanced HITL system where agents not only collaborate but also use shared tools to refine their outputs before human review.

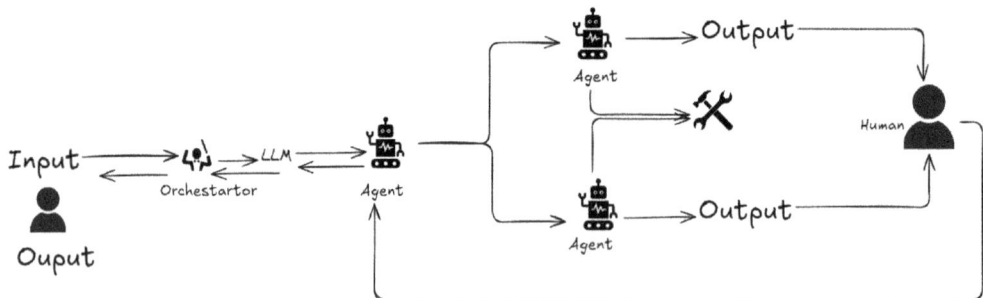

Figure 5.9: Shared tool-augmented agents collaborate under human supervision for optimized output

Database with tools pattern

This pattern surrounds agents with tools and databases that provide, enrich, or persist knowledge in real-time, aiding intelligent decision-making.

Structure and behavior: Agent processes | external tool provides transformation | data stored or fed forward.

Design rationale: Combines computation with structured persistence. Supports complex workflows involving state tracking and enrichment.

Practical application:

- Using a web scraping tool to enrich results before storage in a vector database.
- Data extraction | sentiment enrichment | Save to analytics store.

This architecture showcases agents enhanced with access to external tools like vector databases and web search engines, all coordinated through an LLM orchestrator and guided by human feedback:

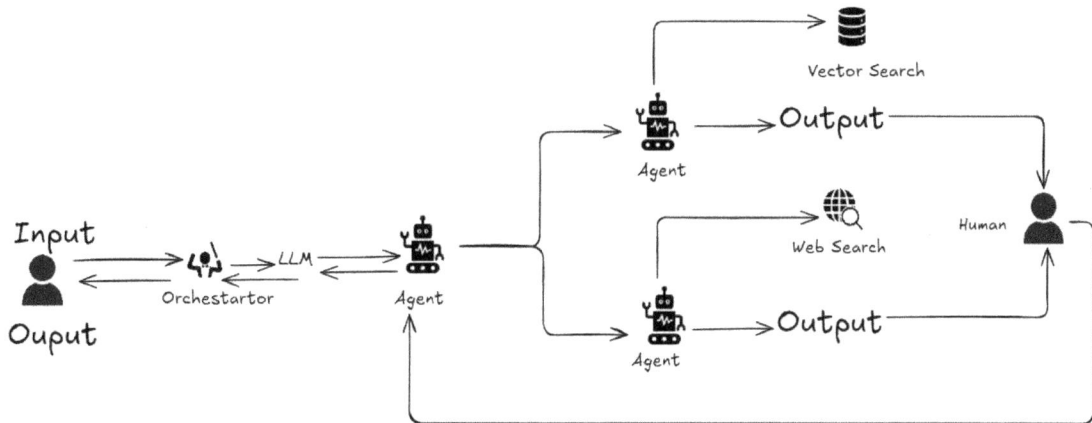

Figure 5.10: *Agents use vector and web search tools to generate enriched, human-verified output*

Memory transformation using tools

In this pattern, agents update memory based on processed insights from tools, enabling learning and personalization across sessions.

Structure and behavior: Agent or tool extracts signal | memory module is updated | future decisions influenced by memory state.

Design rationale: Supports adaptive systems that learn from history, preferences, and interactions over time.

Practical application:

- Chatbots adjusting tone-based on prior conversations.
- Emotional intelligence agents are updating user sentiment profiles.
- Personalized product recommendations based on user behavior history.

This figure illustrates an AI orchestration framework where a user's input is managed by an orchestrator, which uses language models and specialized agents to conduct tasks like vector search, web search, and memory retrieval, facilitating iterative, HITL outputs:

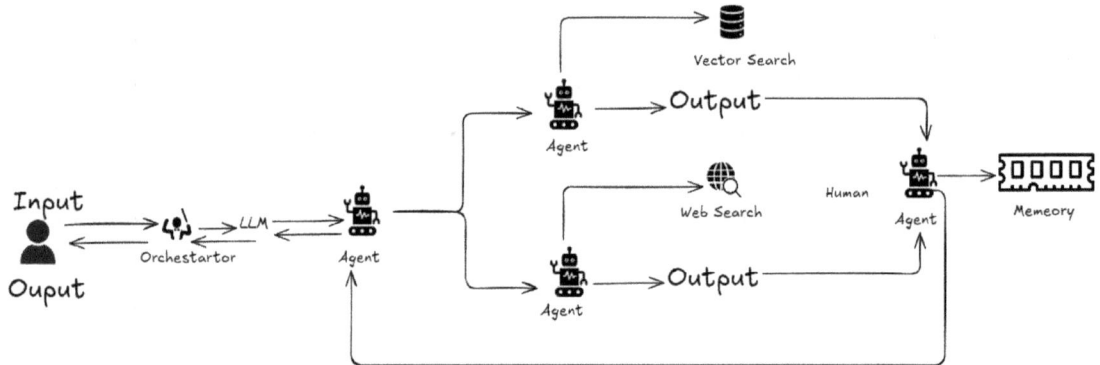

Figure 5.11: AI orchestration architecture

Planner-executor pattern

This pattern divides the system into a planning agent that determines the strategy and one or more executors that carry out actions based on the plan.

Structure and behavior: Planner reasons over goal | forms a plan | executors act step-by-step | feedback returned to planner.

Design rationale: Mimics human cognition (thinking before acting). Enables complex, multi-step reasoning and traceable execution.

Practical application:

- Research agent planning steps for report creation.
- Code generation with pre-planned logic blocks.
- Multi-hop QA with tool use between reasoning steps.

The following figure demonstrates a multi-agent AI workflow, showing how user input is routed via an orchestrator and planner agent to specialized agents for tasks such as vector search and web search, with outputs feeding into memory for iterative improvement:

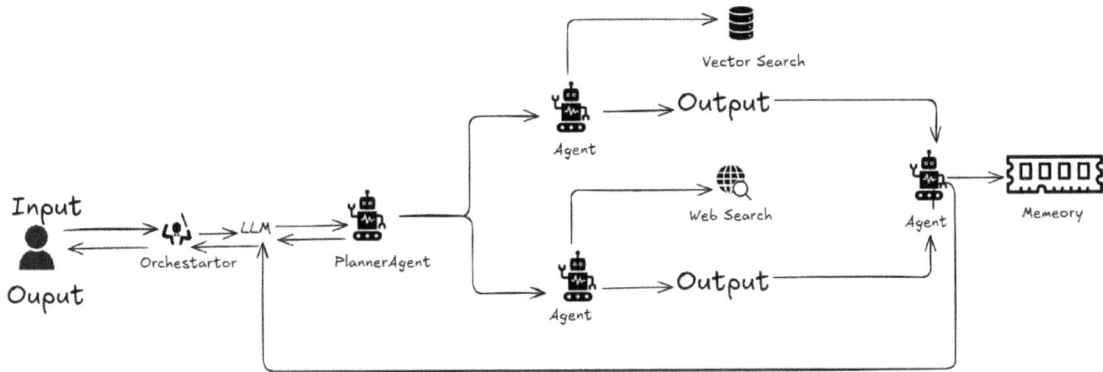

Figure 5.12: *AI multi-agent workflow*

Critic or validator pattern

This pattern includes a validator or critic agent that reviews and either approves or requests revisions of another agent's output.

Structure and behavior: Producer agent | output reviewed by validator | approved or revised | final output.

Design rationale: Improves reliability, reduces hallucinations, and provides quality control. Acts as an internal feedback loop.

Practical application:

- Code suggestion reviewed by a test or lint agent.
- AI writing assistant critiqued for tone or clarity.
- Fact-checker agent validating generated responses.

The following figure illustrates an agent-based AI workflow featuring an orchestrator that processes input and delegates tasks to agents through a critic agent, ensuring quality via feedback loops and agent collaboration:

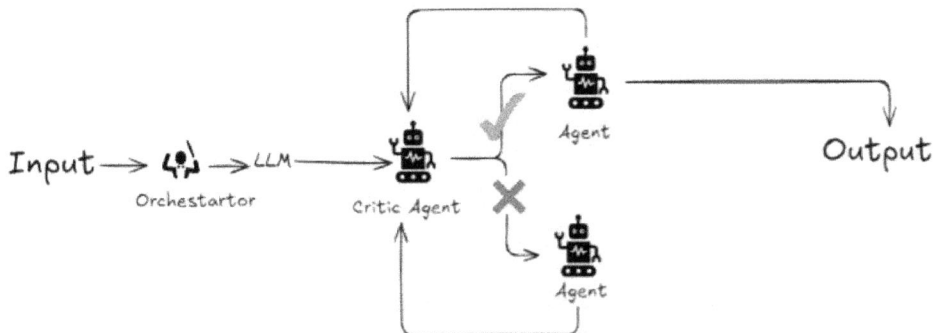

Figure 5.13: *Agent-based AI workflow with critic-mediated task execution and iterative agent feedback*

Negotiator pattern

Agents with differing goals or perspectives communicate iteratively to reach a decision or resolution. This simulates negotiation, compromise, or game-theoretic behavior.

Structure and behavior: Agents exchange offers or proposals | state evolves based on preferences | agreement or failure.

Design rationale: Models real-world stakeholder interaction. Useful in simulations or distributed decision systems.

Practical application:

- AI agents representing the buyer and seller negotiating pricing.
- Team of agents optimizing trade-offs in product design.
- Resource allocation across competing AI subsystems.

This figure depicts a negotiation workflow among AI agents. The negotiator agent issues two signals to each agent: the top agent declines the first signal but accepts the second, while the bottom agent declines both signals. This selective signaling ultimately results in only the top agent contributing to the final output:

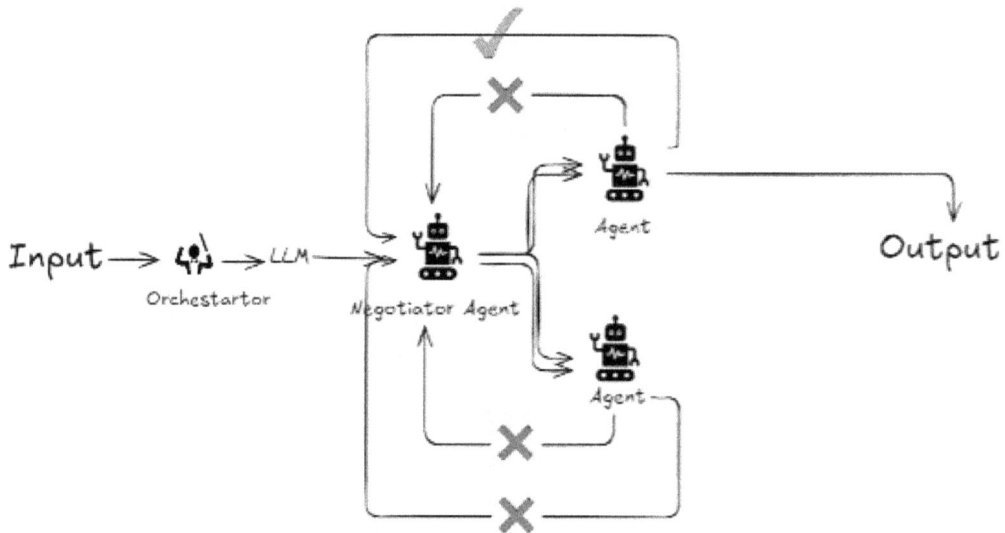

Figure 5.14: Selective output

Multimodal agent pattern

This pattern uses multiple agents to process different types of input or output (e.g., text, image, audio), and combines their insights into a unified result.

Structure and behavior: Input routed based on modality | modality-specific processing | fusion agent combines results.

Design rationale: Enables multi-sensory AI systems that can reason across formats and deliver richer insights.

Practical application:

- AI assistant processes the image and caption, then summarizes in natural language.
- Video-to-text transcription followed by semantic analysis.

The following figure visualizes a coordinated AI system where an orchestrator leverages language models to route user-provided text or images to specialized agents, whose processed outputs are merged for a unified result:

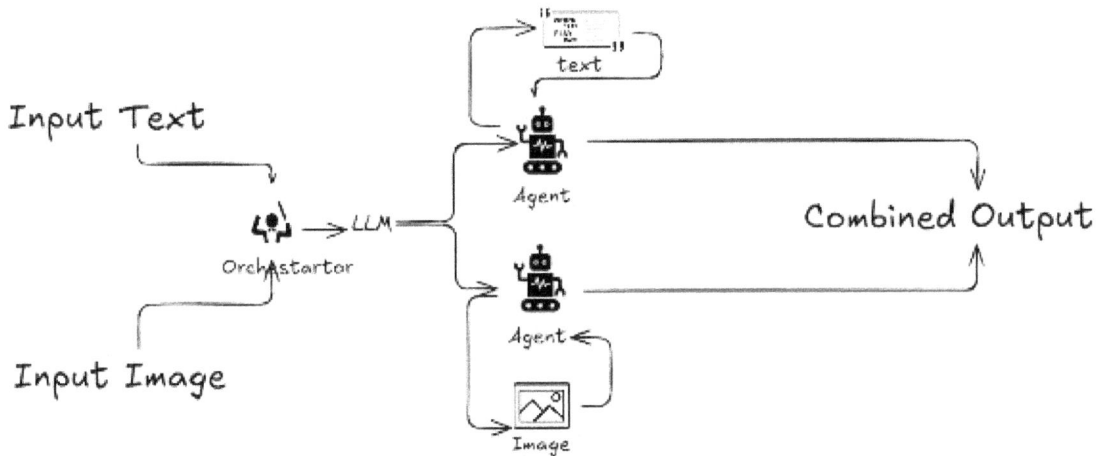

Figure 5.15: Combined output

Voting or consensus pattern

Multiple agents offer answers, and a final result is chosen based on consensus, confidence, or voting algorithms.

Structure and behavior: Agents process in parallel | submit predictions or evaluations | aggregator computes best result.

Design rationale: Boosts reliability and robustness. Reduces bias from a single source of truth.

Practical application:

- Crowd-sourced labeler agents for data annotation.
- Model ensemble voting for classification tasks.
- Redundant summarizers produce a majority result.

The following figure illustrates a multi-agent AI decision-making framework where agents vote on proposed solutions, with the orchestrator selecting the consensus-approved output to ensure high-quality results:

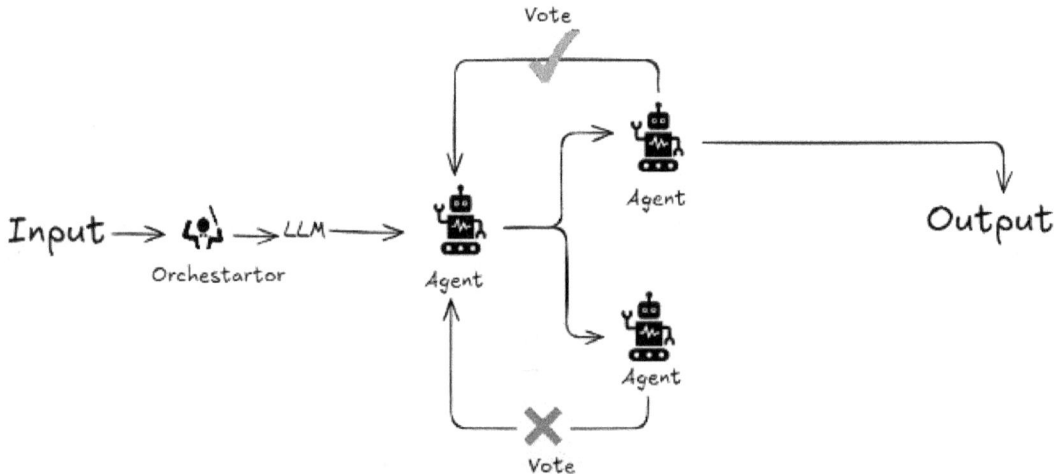

Figure 5.16: Multi-agent AI voting system streamlines decision-making for optimal output

Supervisor-subordinate pattern

The supervisor agent monitors and coordinates a group of working agents, stepping in when needed to guide, correct, or optimize their actions.

Structure and behavior: Worker agents operate autonomously | supervisor observes metrics or behaviors | triggers correction if needed.

Design rationale: Maintains high system integrity while allowing autonomous operation at lower levels.

Practical application:

- Supervisor monitoring chat agents' performance and customer satisfaction.
- Retraining or reconfiguring misbehaving agents dynamically.

This figure represents the supervisor-subordinate pattern common in AI multi-agent systems, where a central supervisor (orchestrator) agent receives the user's input, delegates tasks to multiple specialized subordinate agents, and gathers their outputs. The supervisor centrally controls communication, decision-making, and task assignment, ensuring that work progresses efficiently and reliably. Subordinates focus on executing specific tasks and report back to their supervisor, enabling streamlined coordination, monitoring, and recovery if any agent fails:

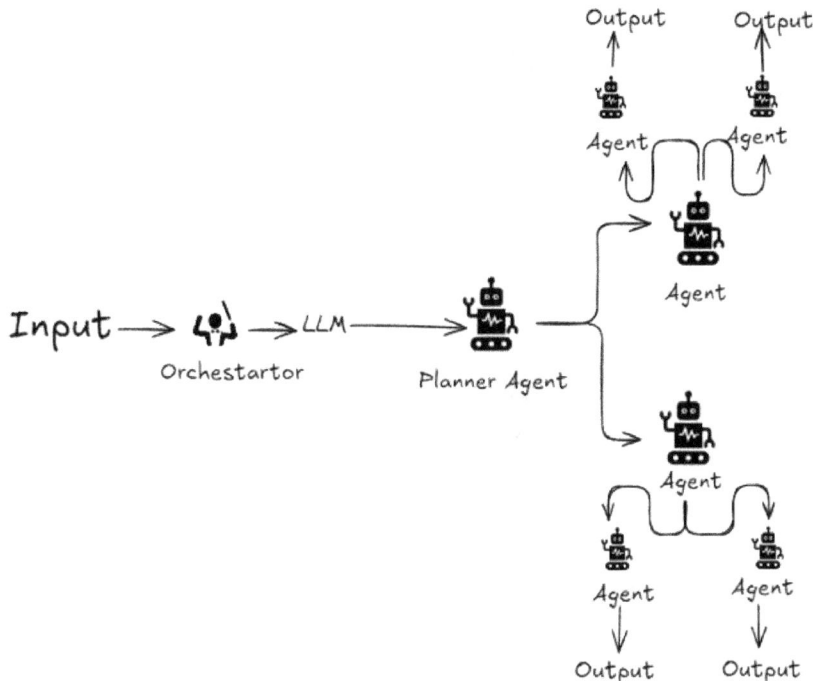

Figure 5.17: Hierarchical AI workflow

Watchdog or recovery pattern

This resilience-focused pattern introduces a watchdog agent that observes system health and initiates recovery if failures or delays occur.

Structure and behavior: Passive monitoring | detect failure or timeout | rerun, escalate, or switch paths.

Design rationale: Improves robustness, uptime, and system recoverability. Crucial in production-grade systems.

Practical application:

- Triggering fallback search if the API is down.
- Reinitializing crashed agents.
- Failing over to redundant workflows during errors.

This figure depicts a robust AI orchestration framework where an orchestrator leverages an LLM to delegate incoming tasks to multiple specialized agents. Each agent is paired with a watchdog module, an autonomous monitor ensuring task reliability and quality:

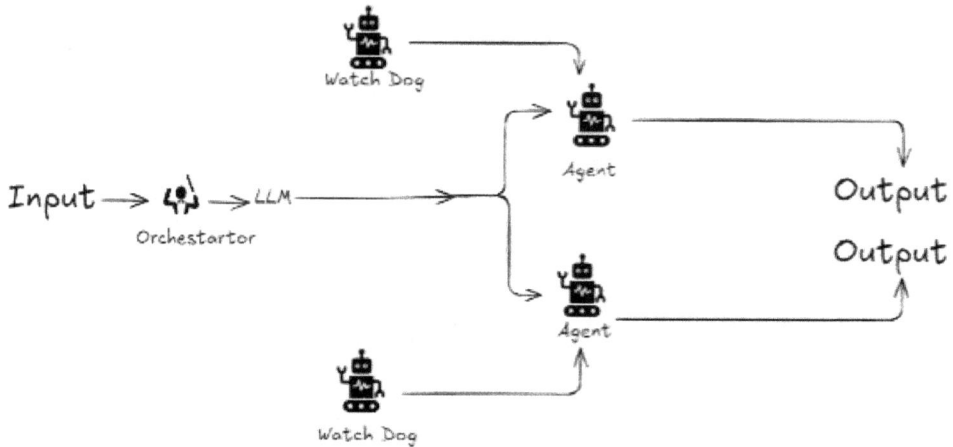

Figure 5.18: AI orchestration with watchdogs

Temporal planner pattern

This variation of the planner-executor pattern incorporates time constraints, scheduling logic, and deadline awareness.

Structure and behavior: Plan includes timestamps or durations | executors run tasks based on schedule | time-based decisions affect flow.

Design rationale: Essential for real-time or delayed execution scenarios. Supports long-horizon planning.

Practical application:

- Scheduling agent for meetings or events.
- Automated reporting agent executes every few hours.
- Time-dependent task prioritization.

The following figure portrays the supervisor-subordinate pattern in AI agent systems, this time emphasizing the temporal dimension: the supervisor issues tasks to subordinate agents across several distinct phases or time steps. At each phase, subordinates execute specific actions and report their outputs; the supervisor assesses progress, updates the strategy, and delegates subsequent tasks based on cumulative results and changing context. This cyclical, time-aware interaction ensures that the system dynamically adapts and coordinates agent efforts throughout multi-stage processes.

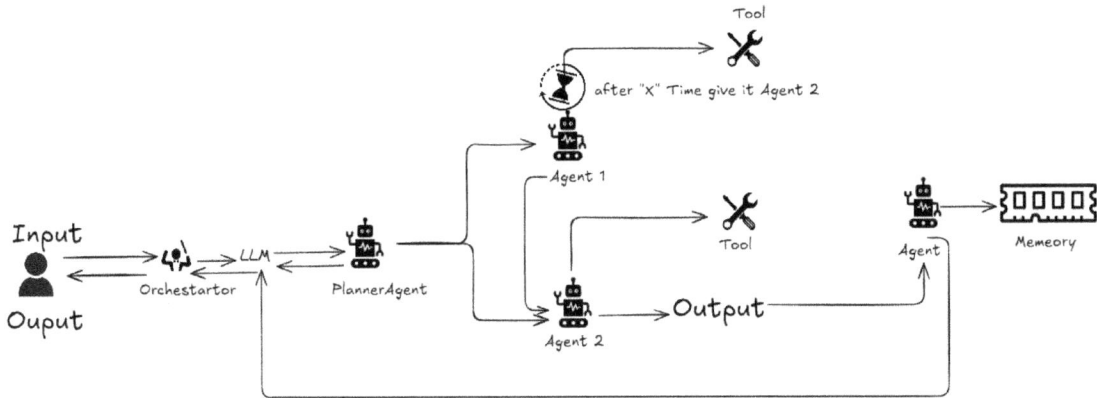

Figure 5.19: *Supervisor agent orchestration*

Having explored the full spectrum of 19 multi-agent system design patterns, from simple sequential chains to complex hierarchical, validator, and consensus-based frameworks, we are now ready to transition from theory to practice. The richness of these patterns is not just academic; it forms the architectural backbone for building intelligent, modular, and scalable GenAI systems.

In this section, we will bring these patterns to life by constructing a real-world, production-ready HITL multi-agent RAG system. This implementation will utilize the StateGraph orchestration capabilities of LangGraph to dynamically route control across agents and tools based on task-specific logic and feedback.

This system will emphasize modularity, extensibility, and full local execution, with no dependency on external APIs or OpenAI services. Instead, we will use the following:

- A local embedding model (e.g., Nomic).

- Chroma as the vector store backend.

- A hybrid retriever combining **Best Matching 25 (BM25)** and semantic similarity.

- ReAct-style prompting for transparent reasoning.

- Integrated PDF parsing to support unstructured knowledge ingestion.

- Source citation tracking for output reliability.

- And crucially, a HITL checkpoint for scenarios requiring human judgment, validation, or intervention.

We will architect the system as a multi-agent workflow, using LangGraph's StateGraph to connect agents with different responsibilities: retrieval, grading, generation, and human oversight. Each component will be built in a modular fashion to enable debugging, customization, and reuse.

What follows is not just a demonstration of agentic reasoning, but a blueprint for how real-world GenAI applications can combine autonomy with accountability, reasoning with reliability, and speed with safety. Let us now walk through the architecture, folder structure, and step-by-step implementation of this intelligent system:

```
rag_hitl_langgraph/

├── main.py                       # Entry point to run the full RAG system
├── config.py                     # Configuration variables (models, paths, flags)
├── requirements.txt              # Python dependencies

├── llm/
│   ├── generate.py               # Local LLM wrapper (e.g., ChatOllama)
│   └── react_prompt.py           # ReAct-style prompt template

├── embeddings/
│   └── embedder.py               # Local embedding model wrapper (e.g., Nomic)

├── vectorstore/
│   ├── db_handler.py             # Vector store initialization and persistence
│   └── metadata_schema.py        # Adds metadata (e.g., PDF source) to document chunks

├── retriever/
│   └── hybrid_search.py          # BM25 + vector retrieval ensemble logic

├── parser/
│   └── pdf_parser.py             # Loads and chunks PDF using text splitter

├── memory/
│   └── conversation_buffer.py    # LangChain memory (e.g., ConversationBufferMemory)

├── grader/
│   ├── doc_relevance.py          # Grades relevance of retrieved documents
│   ├── hallucination.py          # Detects hallucinations in LLM responses
│   └── human_feedback.py         # Interfaces for human-in-the-loop approval

├── orchestrator/
│   └── langgraph_flow.py         # StateGraph definition, agent routing, and orchestratio

├── utils/
│   └── cite_sources.py           # Formats source citations for output

└── data/
    └── source_docs/
        └── ai_education_article.pdf   # Example input document
```

Figure 5.20: The figure shows the folder structure of a RAG with HITL

Human-in-the-loop

One of the most critical design elements in production-grade AI systems is trust, ensuring that the outputs are accurate, grounded, and contextually appropriate. This is especially important in scenarios like education, healthcare, legal research, or enterprise documentation, where an incorrect or misleading response can have serious consequences. To address this, our system integrates a design pattern known as HITL.

In simple terms, HITL means that the AI does not always operate autonomously. Instead, at specific decision points, such as after generating an answer, the system pauses and asks for human validation. This ensures that a person has the opportunity to approve, reject, or request regeneration of the AI's response before it is finalized or acted upon.

In our implementation, the HITL logic is part of the LangGraph workflow. After the RAG agent produces an answer using hybrid retrieval and local LLM reasoning, the system prints the result along with its sources. It then explicitly calls a function that prompts the human user:

```
def human_approval_required():
    return input("\nApprove the answer? (yes/no): ").strip().lower() != "yes"
```

If the user types anything other than yes, the system assumes the answer is unsatisfactory. A retry loop allows up to three regeneration attempts before it halts with a message like *answer rejected after multiple attempts.*

For new AI practitioners, HITL is an essential mechanism to bridge the gap between AI autonomy and human judgment. It brings responsible AI into action, not just as a buzzword, but as a practical safeguard embedded within the system's architecture.

Let us unpack how HITL is implemented in this system:

- **Explicit invocation**: The HITL logic is defined in **grader/human_feedback.py** and is explicitly invoked in the RAG workflow after the answer is generated. The function prompts the user to approve or reject the response:

```
def human_approval_required():
    return input("\nApprove the answer? (yes/no): ").strip().lower() != "yes"
```

- **Retry loop logic**: Within the orchestrator (**orchestrator/langgraph_flow.py**), the function **run_rag_workflow()** includes a retry loop that allows the system to attempt regeneration up to three times if the human does not approve the answer:

```
retries = 3
for attempt in range(retries):
    ...
    if not human_approval_required():
        return result["answer"]
    print("\nRetrying with same question...")
```

- **Graceful fallback handling**: If the human rejects all three regenerated answers, the system exits the loop and returns a clear fallback message:

```
return "Answer rejected after multiple attempts."
```

Let us understand why this matters:

- **Trust**: Ensures human validation in cases where LLM responses may be uncertain or sensitive.
- **Control**: Enables the human operator to reject and regenerate outputs as needed.
- **Safety net**: Prevents misleading outputs from being used without verification.

This HITL feature introduces an extra layer of control and accountability, making the system more suitable for real-world deployment. It transforms a purely autonomous agentic system into a collaborative workflow, where humans and AI work together to produce reliable results.

Now, that we understand the architecture and the role of HITL in ensuring trustworthy AI output, let us explore how this system is implemented in code. The following section walks through the full implementation of each module, step-by-step, highlighting how local embeddings, vector search, hybrid retrieval, ReAct prompting, and LangGraph-based orchestration come together to power an intelligent, controllable, and fully local RAG pipeline.

End-to-end human-in-the-loop RAG workflow

This implementation demonstrates a complete HITL RAG system, orchestrated with LangChain components and designed for full local execution. The system begins by parsing and chunking a local PDF document, then storing those chunks in a persistent vector database (Chroma) using locally generated embeddings.

A hybrid retriever combines BM25 keyword search and vector similarity to identify relevant chunks in response to user queries. The retrieved context is passed to a ReAct-style prompting chain that enables the local language model to reason step-by-step before generating a concise answer.

The system maintains conversational memory, enabling contextual continuity across multiple user inputs. After generating an answer, the system invokes a HITL function that pauses to request user approval. If the response is rejected, the system retries up to three times before gracefully terminating the flow.

This architecture is modular and scalable, making it suitable for enterprise-grade applications where answer accuracy, traceability, and human oversight are essential.

For the complete source code and file structure, refer to the GitHub repository.

From HITL to multi-agent human-in-the-loop RAG

In the previous section, we explored a HITL RAG architecture where the system paused for user validation before finalizing any answer. While this allowed for oversight, the structure was still largely linear and monolithic, with all logic centralized in a single chain.

To truly align with multi-agent design principles, we now decompose the RAG pipeline into modular, interacting agents, each responsible for a specific role. These agents include:

- A retrieval agent for fetching relevant documents.
- A generation agent for synthesizing answers using the ReAct prompting technique,
- A human feedback agent that explicitly asks for approval and loops the system back if the user disapproves.

This design uses LangGraph's StateGraph to orchestrate the workflow, with clear transitions and conditional routing. Unlike the previous implementation, each agent is isolated in logic but coordinated through the graph, ensuring modularity, reusability, and transparency. Retry logic is also embedded: the generation step can re-execute up to three times if the human does not approve the response.

With these structural changes, we now achieve a true multi-agent HITL RAG system, which is both locally deployable and human-controllable.

Figure 5.21 illustrates a HITL RAG architecture enhanced with agentic components. The process begins with a user query, which is matched against a vector database populated with document embeddings. Documents are first chunked with metadata and embedded using an embedding model. A hybrid retrieval agent fetches relevant chunks based on the query, and a result generation agent synthesizes a response. The response then enters a human feedback loop, where a HITL agent either approves the output or triggers a retry mechanism up to three times. If the response remains unsatisfactory, it is rejected; otherwise, it is returned to the user.

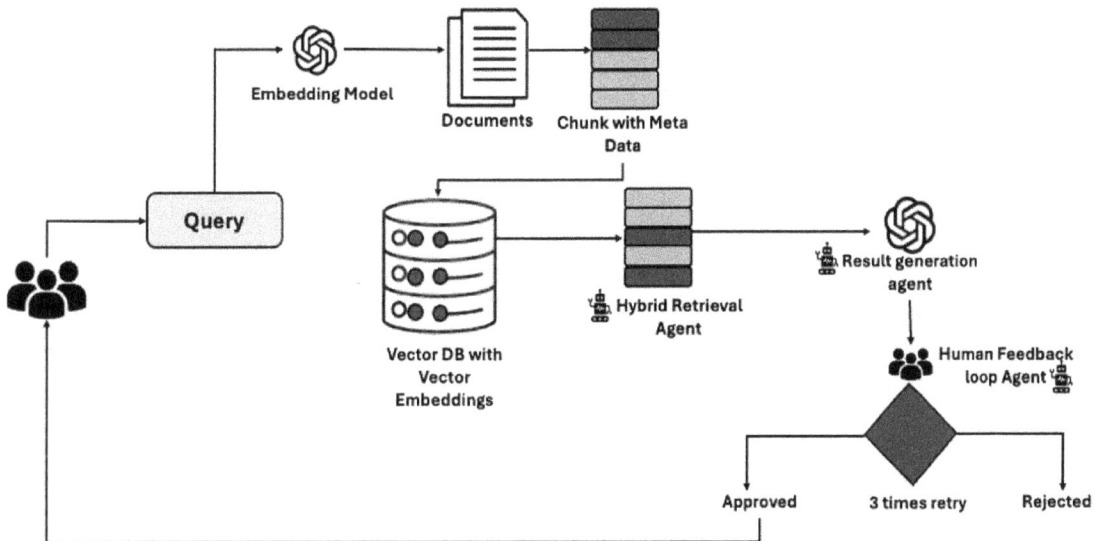

Figure 5.21: End-to-end HITL RAG workflow with agentic feedback loop

For the complete source code and file structure, refer to **Chapter_5_code.ipynb**, multi-agent human-in-the-loop.

The retrieval agent is responsible for fetching relevant document chunks based on the user's question. It uses a hybrid retriever that combines BM25 and vector similarity.

Retrieval agent:
```
def retrieval_agent(state):
    return {"documents": retriever.get_relevant_documents(state["question"])}
```

The generation agent synthesizes a response using a ReAct-style prompting chain, reasoning step-by-step over the retrieved context. It also attaches source citations to ensure traceability and provide transparent grounding for the generated answers.

Generation agent:

```
def generation_agent(state):
    result = rag_chain.invoke({"question": state["question"]})
    return {
        "answer": result["answer"],
        "source_documents": result.get("source_documents", [])
    }
```

The human feedback loop introduces an approval step into the loop. After each generated answer, it prompts for user validation—allowing humans to approve, reject, or request re-generation—enabling controlled oversight and iterative refinement.

Human feedback loop:

```
def human_feedback_agent(state):
    approved = not human_approval_required()
    return {"approved": approved}
```

If the user rejects the answer, the system loops back to the generation agent for a retry, up to a maximum of three attempts. If the user approves, the answer is finalized and returned.

LangGraph's StateGraph manages the flow across agents. It defines a directed graph, and LangGraph orchestrates the entire pipeline using a directed state graph. It sequences agent execution from retrieval to generation to validation, dynamically routing based on human feedback, enabling looped retries and graceful exits based on approval logic.

Orchestration using LangGraph:

```
workflow = StateGraph(GraphState)
workflow.add_node("retrieve", retrieval_agent)
workflow.add_node("generate", generation_agent)
workflow.add_node("validate", human_feedback_agent)

workflow.set_entry_point("retrieve")
workflow.add_edge("retrieve", "generate")
workflow.add_edge("generate", "validate")

workflow.add_conditional_edges(
    "validate",
    lambda state: "end" if state.get("approved") else "generate",
    {
        "end": END,
        "generate": "generate"
    }
)
```

The final graph is compiled and used in the **main.py** file to handle user input interactively.

This architecture exemplifies the agentic design principles discussed earlier in the chapter section: *Architecting agentic GenAI systems*, each agent is isolated, testable, and extensible, enabling a flexible and robust foundation for intelligent retrieval systems. The integration of human validation ensures that the system not only answers, but answers responsibly.

Agentic AI vs. AI agents

To truly appreciate the architectural design patterns we have explored in this chapter, it is essential to distinguish between AI agents and the more advanced paradigm of agentic AI. Although these terms are sometimes used interchangeably, they represent fundamentally different levels of capability, autonomy, and system coordination in AI.

AI agents are autonomous software programs designed to perform specific tasks with minimal human intervention. These systems excel in narrow, well-defined domains such as answering customer service queries, scheduling meetings, or retrieving specific data from APIs. Their behavior is typically reactive, responding to input or triggers, and they often follow a linear, single-step execution pattern. While they can use tools like APIs or databases, their autonomy is generally confined to specific boundaries and does not extend to higher-order planning or collaborative reasoning.

In contrast, agentic AI refers to a more complex system composed of multiple AI agents working collaboratively to solve higher-order problems. These systems go beyond execution and instead focus on goal-setting, advanced planning, and orchestration across multiple steps. Agentic AI embodies characteristics such as multi-agent collaboration, persistent memory for contextual awareness, and adaptive decision-making based on evolving conditions. Unlike traditional AI agents that operate independently, agentic AI systems function as coordinated networks where agents can share information, delegate tasks, and adapt to new goals or contexts dynamically.

One of the key architectural shifts in agentic AI is the movement from isolated task execution to system-level orchestration. Here, a higher-level controller, or an orchestrator agent, coordinates the behavior of specialized agents, enabling the system to decompose complex goals into manageable subtasks. Each specialized agent contributes to a portion of the overall objective, and the orchestrator integrates their outputs to achieve coherent, goal-directed outcomes.

Additionally, while AI agents often rely on rule-based or supervised learning tailored to narrow tasks, agentic AI leverages more sophisticated learning strategies such as *reinforcement learning, meta-learning,* or *hybrid approaches* that allow for adaptation across broader task domains. This adaptability is crucial in applications like supply chain optimization, virtual project management, and enterprise automation, where static responses are insufficient, and dynamic goal-setting and reasoning are required.

Agentic AI also emphasizes persistent memory, a shared context that enables agents to remember previous interactions, track dependencies, and update strategies over time. This form of memory is not just a technical feature but a strategic enabler that allows agents to build upon one another's work, minimize redundant processing, and refine their decisions continuously.

In essence, while AI agents are tools, agentic AI is a system of thinkers—autonomous, interactive, and capable of complex planning. As you move forward with building real-world agentic systems, this distinction will guide your architectural choices, helping you select the right tools, coordination mechanisms, and reasoning strategies needed to scale beyond narrow AI tasks toward general-purpose, autonomous workflows.

Conclusion

In this chapter, we explored the foundational principles of architecting agentic GenAI systems, emphasizing how AI agents evolve from reactive executors to collaborative problem-solvers through structured multi-agent coordination. We examined key design patterns, such as sequential, loop, router, and hierarchical, that enable agents to reason, retrieve, act, and adapt in complex workflows. Building on this, we introduced HITL architectures within RAG, showcasing how humans can guide or validate agentic decisions. Finally, we distinguished between traditional AI agents and Agentic AI, highlighting the latter's focus on multi-step planning, orchestration, and adaptive learning. These concepts lay the groundwork for building dynamic, autonomous systems capable of handling real-world complexity. In the next chapter, we transition from architectural patterns to execution strategies by implementing two-stage GenAI systems enhanced with grading mechanisms, a crucial technique for quality control, response ranking, and robust system evaluation in production-grade applications.

In the next chapter, we will explore interaction mechanisms in dense retrievals and their critical role in two-stage and multi-stage RAG systems. Topics include reranking strategies such as late and full interaction, multi-vector approaches, grading mechanisms, and a practical implementation of a multi-stage RAG workflow with routing and staged reasoning.

Join our Discord space

Join our Discord workspace for latest updates, offers, tech happenings around the world, new releases, and sessions with the authors:

https://discord.bpbonline.com

CHAPTER 6

Two and Multi-stage GenAI Systems

Introduction

As **generative AI (GenAI)** systems have become more prevalent in enterprise, research, and consumer applications, the demand for reliable and trustworthy outputs has never been higher. While **large language models (LLMs)** are capable of generating fluent and contextually appropriate answers, they often suffer from a critical flaw, which is hallucination. These fabricated or inaccurate outputs can undermine user trust and introduce significant risk in high-stakes domains like healthcare, law, finance, and customer support. This chapter introduces a practical and scalable solution: a two-stage generative pipeline that integrates answer grading and reranking as a validation layer before responses are surfaced to users. By systematically evaluating generated answers using a feedback loop, we shift from passive generation to active quality control, laying the foundation for more dependable GenAI systems.

You will implement this architecture using Python, LangChain, and LangGraph, constructing a modular pipeline consisting of a retriever, generator, and grader. The retriever gathers multiple relevant knowledge contexts, the generator proposes candidate answers, and the grader selects the most accurate or appropriate response using custom evaluation prompts or scoring mechanisms. By the end, you will not only understand the theory behind answer validation but also gain hands-on experience in engineering a GenAI feedback system that is both robust and production-ready.

Structure

In this chapter, we will learn about the following topics:

- Concepts of interactions in dense retrievals
- Role of interaction models in two-stage RAG systems
- Reranking with various interaction models
- Two-stage RAG architecture
- Multi-stage RAG
- Grading mechanisms
- Implementation of multi-stage RAG workflow with routing

Objectives

This chapter aims to provide a comprehensive understanding of advanced **retrieval-augmented generation (RAG)** systems, with a focus on the role of dense retrieval interactions and multi-stage processing. It begins by exploring the fundamental concepts of interaction in dense retrieval, followed by an in-depth discussion of two-stage and multi-stage RAG architectures. The chapter then introduces the grading mechanisms used to evaluate retrieval and generation quality. Finally, it presents a practical implementation of a multi-stage RAG workflow with intelligent routing, enabling adaptive query processing using vector search and web search. Readers will gain both conceptual clarity and hands-on insights into building robust RAG systems.

In *Chapter 1, Introducing New Age Generative AI*, we explored the concepts of bi-encoders and cross-encoders, along with the architecture of a two-stage GenAI system as illustrated in *Figure 6.4*. Before we get into the two-stage GenAI architecture, let us first examine the different levels of interactions, specifically, no interaction, late interaction, and full interaction.

Concepts of interactions in dense retrievals

In *Chapter 1, Introducing New Age Generative AI*, we introduced the concept of dense retrieval. In dense retrieval systems, the way queries and documents interact during encoding and comparison plays a central role in determining both retrieval performance and computational efficiency. Broadly, interaction mechanisms fall into three categories, which are no interaction, full interaction, late interaction, and multi-vector representation, each offering unique trade-offs between scalability and semantic matching precision.

No interaction

The bi-encoder architecture represents the most scalable yet coarse-grained approach. Here, the query and the document are encoded independently into fixed-length vector embeddings using separate or shared neural encoders. Once encoded, these vectors are compared using lightweight similarity functions such as cosine similarity or dot product, enabling rapid retrieval using **approximate nearest neighbor** (**ANN**) search. This approach is widely used in large-scale systems due to its speed and efficiency. However, because the query and document tokens do not interact during encoding, the semantic alignment is relatively shallow, often missing finer contextual cues. This method is particularly useful for first-stage retrieval, where speed is prioritized over precision.

The following figure shows no interaction:

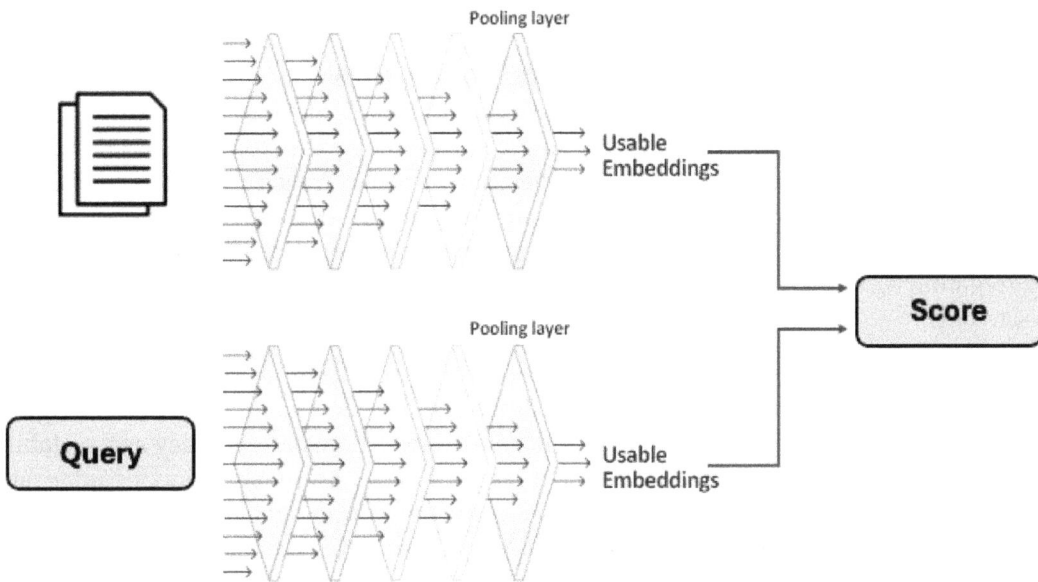

Figure 6.1: *No interaction*

Full interaction

At the other end of the spectrum lies the cross-encoder, or full interaction model. In this approach, the query and document are concatenated and jointly encoded, allowing every query token to interact with every document token via mechanisms like cross-attention. This setup yields highly expressive representations and precise relevance scores, as the model performs deep semantic reasoning across token pairs. However, the trade-off is substantial: Each document-query pair must be evaluated individually at inference time, making this method prohibitively expensive for retrieval from large corpora. Cross-encoders are often reserved for reranking the top-k candidates retrieved by lighter models like bi-encoders.

The following figure shows full interaction:

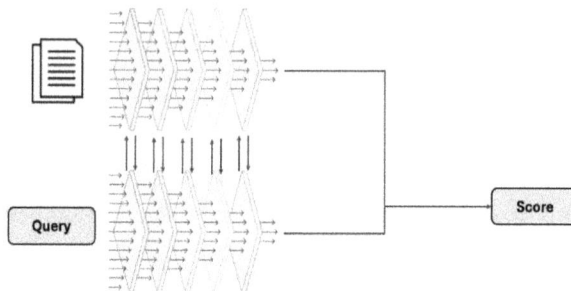

Figure 6.2: Full interaction

Late interaction

Late interaction models such as ColBERT, ColPali, and ColQwen offer a practical middle ground. Like bi-encoders, they encode queries and documents independently. However, instead of collapsing representations into a single vector, they retain token-level embeddings. During retrieval, a fine-grained comparison is performed between each query token embedding and all the document token embeddings using operations such as **maximum similarity** (**MaxSim**) maximum cosine similarity per token. The final relevance score is then computed by aggregating these token-level similarities, often using a sum or average of maximum scores across tokens.

This design enables token-aware matching without the compute burden of full attention. Additionally, because document token embeddings can be precomputed and stored (e.g., in a vector database), these models offer an efficient compromise between accuracy and scalability. Notably, recent variants like ColPali (for text-image fusion) and ColQwen (for integrating LLMs like Qwen) further extend late interaction to multimodal and generative contexts, where embeddings from **vision-language models** (**VLMs**) or instruction-tuned LLMs are aligned in a shared space for cross-modal retrieval and reranking.

The following figure shows late interaction:

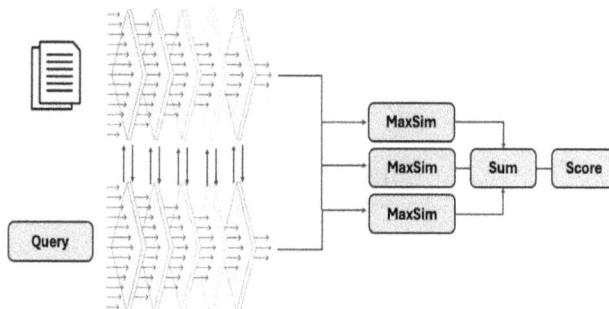

Figure 6.3: Late interaction

The choice between no interaction, late interaction, and full interaction hinges on the application context. No interaction favors speed and indexing; full interaction favors accuracy but scales poorly; late interaction aims for the best of both no interaction and full interaction by preserving rich token-level semantics with practical scalability, making it increasingly popular for dense and multimodal retrieval pipelines in modern AI systems.

Multi-vector representations

Vector representations have become the backbone of modern information retrieval systems, enabling semantic search by embedding documents and queries into high-dimensional continuous spaces. Traditional dense retrieval methods typically represent an entire document as a single vector by pooling token-level embeddings. However, this approach often loses fine-grained semantic information, particularly in the case of long or information-dense texts.

To overcome this limitation, multi-vector representations have been introduced as a mechanism to store and query-document using multiple vectors per entity, often at the token or phrase-level. This design enhances retrieval precision, particularly in scenarios where exact token-level matching is required. Modern vector databases such as Qdrant have introduced native support for multi-vector representations, providing a scalable infrastructure for such fine-grained retrieval mechanisms.

A multi-vector representation is shown in *Figure 6.4*, which refers to the practice of storing multiple vectors for a single logical unit of data, such as a document or paragraph. Instead of compressing all token-level embeddings into a single pooled representation (as in typical dense retrieval), the multi-vector approach retains multiple embeddings per document. These vectors are often derived from token-level or phrase-level outputs of transformer-based encoders.

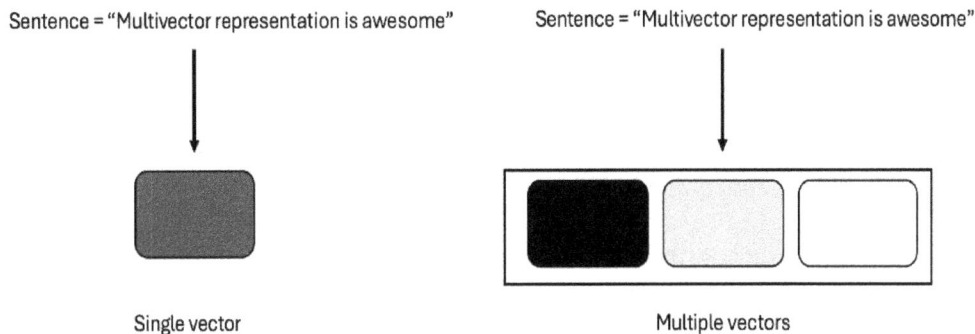

Sentence = "Multivector representation is awesome"   Sentence = "Multivector representation is awesome"

Single vector   Multiple vectors

Figure 6.4: Single vs multi-vector representation

This structure allows more nuanced and context-aware retrieval by enabling query time comparison between query embeddings and the constituent vectors of each document. This is particularly advantageous for tasks such as reranking, where the goal is not just coarse retrieval, but fine-grained scoring based on partial semantic overlaps.

Qdrant offers first-class support for multi-vector representations, allowing each indexed entity to be associated with multiple named vector fields. Each vector field can independently be configured with its own dimensionality, similarity metric (e.g., cosine, dot product), and indexing strategy. A typical configuration involves two vector fields:

- **Dense vector**: It is used for first-pass retrieval via ANN search with **hierarchical navigable small world (HNSW)**.

- **Multi-vector field**: Used for reranking, storing token-level vectors without HNSW indexing to save memory and computational overhead.

Qdrant enables token-aware reranking through a mechanism known as MaxSim, a similarity comparator that computes the MaxSim between each query vector and the set of document vectors. This strategy closely mirrors the reranking logic used in late interaction models and can be configured through the `Multi-vectorComparator.MAX_SIM` setting.

Naively indexing all token-level vectors in an HNSW graph leads to severe performance bottlenecks:

- Increased RAM usage due to maintaining large graph structures.

- Slow insert times because of the complexity of updating the index.

- Redundant compute, since token-level vectors are typically used only during reranking, not during initial retrieval.

To address this, Qdrant allows HNSW indexing to be disabled selectively for multi-vector fields. This optimization enables fast ingestion and lightweight reranking without sacrificing accuracy, as the initial retrieval step is handled via dense vector fields.

Differentiation from late interaction architectures

While multi-vector representations in databases like Qdrant are inspired by late interaction models, the two concepts differ fundamentally in scope and role.

The table provides a comparative analysis between multi-vector representations as implemented in vector databases like Qdrant and late interaction model architectures such as ColBERT. While both approaches aim to leverage token-level embeddings for improved retrieval accuracy, their scope, implementation, and function differ significantly. Multi-vector representations focus on the infrastructure layer, optimizing how token embeddings are stored, indexed, and used during reranking. In contrast, late interaction models define the embedding generation and matching strategy at the model-level, typically during training and inference. The following table highlights key distinctions in their purpose, usage context, indexing strategies, and system dependencies. This comparison clarifies the complementary relationship between the two and underscores the role of vector databases in scaling late interaction-based retrieval pipelines:

Dimension	Multi-vector representations (Qdrant)	Late interaction architectures (e.g., ColBERT)
Definition	Storage and querying mechanism supporting multiple vectors per document.	Model architecture that performs fine-grained similarity at query time.
Purpose	Infrastructure optimization for serving token-level representations.	Semantic modeling and retrieval at the embedding level.
Similarity function	Uses MaxSim or configurable similarity metrics for reranking.	Typically fixed to MaxSim computed between query and document tokens.
Indexing strategy	Allows selective disabling of indexing for multi-vectors.	Indexing is external; document embeddings are stored for matching.
Model dependency	Can use any model outputting multiple embeddings.	Requires specific architectural components (e.g., ColBERT transformer layers).
Usage context	Infrastructure-level support in production vector databases.	Algorithmic design used during training and inference.

Table 6.1: *Comparison of multi-vector and late interaction*

Late interaction refers to the **modeling technique** that retains token-level embeddings and performs interaction at query time, whereas multi-vector support in Qdrant is a retrieval and storage mechanism that enables deployment of such models in an efficient and scalable manner. Late interaction models generate the embeddings; Qdrant's multi-vector infrastructure stores and utilizes them efficiently for reranking.

Multi-vector representations enable fine-grained document retrieval by preserving multiple embeddings per entity, a necessity for modern reranking architectures such as ColBERT. Qdrant's support for multi-vector fields and token-level MaxSim scoring provides a scalable infrastructure for deploying such systems in production environments. While conceptually related to late interaction, multi-vector support operates at the infrastructure-level, complementing model-level innovations by optimizing their deployment and performance characteristics.

Role of interaction models in two-stage RAG systems

In the context of RAG, the type of interaction between query and document representations plays a foundational role in determining both retrieval efficiency and answer accuracy. A two-stage RAG system typically involves an initial retrieval phase to select candidate documents, followed by a reranking phase that refines this list to improve the quality of the generated response. The nature and depth of interaction, whether no interaction, late interaction, or full interaction, directly impact both the architectural design and performance trade-offs of such systems.

Interaction in the retrieval phase

The first-stage of a RAG system generally employs a bi-encoder architecture, also referred to as a **no interaction** model. In this approach, queries and documents are encoded independently into fixed-length vector representations using separate or shared neural encoders. These embeddings are stored and compared using similarity functions such as cosine similarity or dot product, often accelerated through ANN search. This allows for scalable, low-latency retrieval across large corpora, as only the query needs to be encoded at runtime. However, the lack of cross-token attention during encoding may limit semantic granularity, resulting in lower retrieval precision for complex queries.

Reranking with various interaction models

To address the limitations of the bi-encoder, the second-stage of the RAG pipeline incorporates a reranking mechanism that re-evaluates and prioritizes the top retrieved candidates. This is where models with late interaction or full interaction are particularly relevant, details as follows:

- Late interaction models, such as ColBERT, ColPali, and ColQwen, retain token-level embeddings for both queries and documents. During reranking, the model computes fine-grained token-to-token similarity scores (e.g., maximum cosine similarity between each query token and all document tokens), enabling a more nuanced assessment of relevance. While documents are still embedded independently and can be pre-indexed, the reranking operation introduces a form of semantic cross-attention that is computationally efficient compared to full interaction approaches.

- In contrast, full interaction models (cross-encoders) process the query and document jointly by concatenating their token sequences and passing them through a single transformer encoder. This enables full cross-attention, where each query token can attend to every document token, allowing for the highest level of semantic understanding. Although this approach offers the most accurate scoring, it is computationally expensive, and we must evaluate each query document pair individually at runtime. Consequently, it is feasible only for small candidate sets and is unsuitable for large-scale first-stage retrieval.

- Reranking with multi-vector representations enhances retrieval precision by enabling token-level interaction between queries and documents, a capability especially important for complex or fine-grained information needs. In traditional dense retrieval, each document is represented by a single pooled vector, which can obscure nuanced semantic signals and reduce discriminative power. In contrast, multi-vector representations retain multiple embeddings per document—typically at the token or phrase-level—preserving local semantic information.

During reranking, an initial retrieval stage selects a shortlist of candidate documents using fast ANN search over dense vectors. Subsequently, each candidate is reranked by comparing its token-level vectors to the token-level query embeddings using similarity measures such as MaxSim. This process captures more precise alignment between specific query terms and relevant document parts, resulting in improved ranking quality.

Importantly, multi-vector-based reranking does not require indexing the individual token-level vectors, which significantly reduces memory overhead and accelerates document ingestion. By decoupling the coarse retrieval phase from the fine-grained scoring phase, multi-vector reranking provides a scalable mechanism for deploying late interaction models in production systems. This hybrid architecture delivers both speed and retrieval accuracy, making it especially suitable for high-performance semantic search and RAG applications.

Integration into two-stage RAG architectures

In practical RAG architectures, bi-encoders are used to retrieve an initial pool of documents (e.g., top 100 candidates) from a vector database. These candidates are then passed through a reranker that employs either late interaction or full interaction models, depending on the desired trade-off between precision and latency. Late interaction models offer a middle ground by supporting scalable, ANN-compatible storage while improving relevance over pure bi-encoder methods. Full interaction models are ideal when precision is paramount, and computational resources permit per-pair processing.

Thus, understanding and selecting the appropriate interaction paradigm is essential for designing effective two-stage RAG systems. By aligning the retrieval and reranking stages with the appropriate encoder architectures, it is possible to achieve an optimal balance between performance, scalability, and accuracy.

The following figure displays the two-stage RAG architecture:

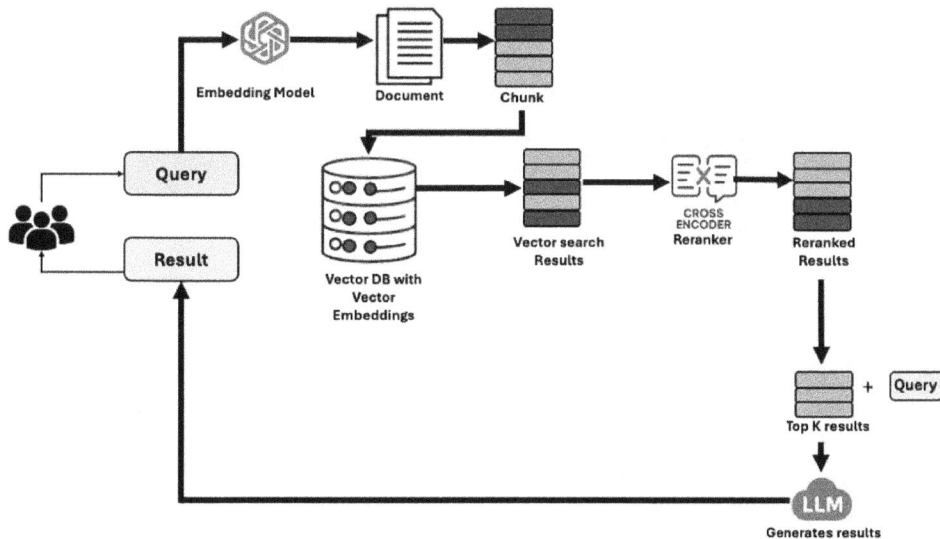

Figure 6.5: *Two-stage RAG architecture*

Two-stage RAG architecture

RAG systems extend the capabilities of LLMs by retrieving and conditioning on relevant external documents. Instead of relying solely on the model's internal parameters for knowledge retrieval, RAG explicitly fetches documents from an indexed corpus to ground the generative response in external, and often up-to-date, information. When reranking mechanisms are incorporated into this pipeline, the architecture evolves into what is commonly termed a two-stage RAG system.

Stage one dense retrievals

The first-stage of this architecture focuses on efficient retrieval from large-scale document corpora. Typically, this is accomplished using dense vector retrieval, where both queries and documents are encoded independently into vector representations. These vectors are indexed in a vector database using ANN search techniques. This allows for scalable and low-latency retrieval, yielding a broad set of semantically relevant documents, often in the range of top fifty to top hundred candidates. However, this stage lacks explicit interaction between the query and the document tokens during encoding. As a result, although the retrieved documents are topically related to the query, their contextual alignment may be shallow, affecting their usefulness in downstream generation tasks.

Stage-two, reranking for semantic precision

The second-stage introduces a reranking component designed to refine the shortlist produced in the first-stage. This is where richer interaction mechanisms are applied between the query and each candidate document. Unlike the initial retrieval, reranking models consider token-level relationships, enabling a deeper semantic alignment. These models may employ token-wise comparisons, attention mechanisms, or partial cross-attention structures that simulate full semantic interaction without incurring the high computational cost of reprocessing the entire corpus. This second pass produces a more accurate relevance score for each document and reorders the shortlist accordingly. The top-ranked documents are then forwarded as the contextual input to the language model for generation.

The strategic role of two-stage design

This bifurcated approach, known as **fast retrieval**, is followed by precise reranking that embodies a strategic trade-off between scalability and accuracy. The first-stage ensures rapid exploration across a vast corpus, prioritizing recall and system responsiveness. The second-stage ensures that only the most contextually appropriate documents are used to condition the LLM, thereby improving generation quality, factual consistency, and topical relevance. Without this reranking stage, the system risks grounding its output in loosely related or suboptimal documents, which can degrade response quality or introduce hallucinations.

So, reranking is not merely an optimization step but a structural enhancement that defines two distinct yet interdependent stages in the RAG pipeline: **retrieval for breadth** and **reranking for depth**. This two-stage configuration ensures alignment between retrieval utility and generation goals, and has become a foundational pattern in modern, high-performance RAG systems, especially those operating in open-domain, enterprise, or high-precision contexts.

Two-stage RAG vs. late interaction

The emergence of late interaction models like ColBERT and ColPali has blurred the lines between traditional two-stage RAG architectures and unified, interaction-rich retrieval systems. These models offer a compelling middle ground between the efficiency of bi-encoders and the precision of cross-encoders. The key question is that *if ColBERT or ColPali is used as the retriever, is a separate reranking stage still necessary?*

Capabilities of ColBERT and ColPali

Unlike standard dense retrievers (e.g., dual-encoder architectures), ColBERT-type models do not compress documents and queries into a single vector. Instead, they preserve token-level embeddings, which are compared during retrieval using operations like MaxSim between query and document tokens. This preserves fine-grained semantic information while still enabling ANN search via indexing of token vectors (e.g., using late interaction indexing schemes).

As a result, ColBERT and ColPali already perform a sophisticated form of reranking at retrieval time. The scoring function considers multiple token interactions, offering far more semantic alignment than traditional bi-encoder retrieval, but without the full computational cost of cross-encoders. In effect, this late interaction serves as an implicit reranking mechanism, making the retrieval stage more precise.

Use of two-stage RAG

However, despite their improved expressiveness, ColBERT-style models may still benefit from a second-stage or two-stage RAG, which uses a reranker in high-stakes or highly nuanced applications. The reasons include:

- **Better ranking fidelity**: Full interaction models (cross-encoders) still outperform late interaction models in certain benchmarks because they model global token dependencies, not just MaxSim heuristics.

- **Generation alignment**: Late interaction scores optimize retrieval ranking, not necessarily the quality of downstream generation. A second-stage reranker can better align retrieval scores with generation utility.

- **Ensemble robustness:** A two-stage pipeline allows the combination of different scoring signals (e.g., late interaction + generative loss + factuality scoring).

In practical systems (e.g., enterprise RAG, long-context retrieval, hybrid multimodal setups), it is not uncommon to use ColBERT for high-recall shortlist generation and follow it with a cross-encoder reranker that focuses only on the top-k candidates.

Multi-stage RAG

RAG systems typically combine retrieval and generation to provide accurate and contextually relevant responses by supplementing generative language models with external knowledge. While commonly described as a two-stage process, retrieving relevant documents and subsequently generating answers from the retrieved content, advanced RAG implementations often involve multiple retrieval, filtering, reranking, and validation stages, collectively referred to as multi-stage RAG.

Beyond two-stage systems

Standard RAG implementations include:

- **Retrieval stage**: Relevant documents or passages are retrieved from a knowledge base using dense embeddings and vector similarity.

- **Generation stage**: A generative model synthesizes retrieved information to provide coherent, contextually appropriate responses.

However, real-world applications often demand additional intermediary stages to enhance performance and accuracy. These stages address challenges such as ambiguity in queries, redundancy in retrieved results, and the potential for generative hallucination.

Components of multi-stage RAG

A multi-stage RAG architecture typically integrates additional steps such as:

- **Query expansion and refinement**: Prior to retrieval, queries can be expanded or refined using pre-trained language models or auxiliary knowledge bases to enhance retrieval accuracy.

- **Multimodal retrieval**: Combining textual embeddings with image, video, or audio embeddings enables richer semantic retrieval, providing context from diverse modalities.

- **Hybrid retrieval**: Incorporating multiple retrieval mechanisms, such as sparse keyword-based retrieval (e.g., **Best Matching 25 (BM25)**) alongside dense semantic retrieval ensures comprehensive coverage and robustness.

- **Reranking stage**: Retrieved documents or passages are reranked based on more computationally intensive cross-encoder models that consider fine-grained interactions between queries and documents, significantly improving the relevance of retrieved items.

- **Validation and fact-checking**: Implementing a dedicated validation step, often using specialized models or rule-based heuristics, reduces inaccuracies by verifying facts or filtering unreliable sources before final generation.

- **Iterative feedback and refinement**: Utilizing intermediate feedback loops, where preliminary outputs from generative models inform additional retrieval or refinement, enables dynamic, iterative improvement of responses.

Benefits of multi-stage RAG

Incorporating multiple stages into RAG architectures can offer several advantages:

- **Improved accuracy and relevance**: Each added stage incrementally refines the retrieval and generation processes, significantly enhancing accuracy and reducing irrelevant or redundant information.

- **Reduction of hallucinations**: Additional validation stages systematically identify and eliminate factual inaccuracies, thus increasing the reliability and credibility of generated content.

- **Enhanced contextual understanding**: Multimodal and hybrid retrieval allow for richer, nuanced contextual interpretation, especially valuable in complex domains requiring integration of textual and visual information.

Types of multi-stage RAG

From the preceding section, you must have understood that RAG systems enhance language models by incorporating external knowledge sources through a combination of retrieval and generation components. While the canonical RAG framework typically involves two-stages, that is, retrieval followed by generation, emerging research and practical implementations demonstrate the efficacy of extending RAG into multi-stage architectures. These advanced configurations address limitations of simple two-stage systems and enable the handling of complex tasks with higher accuracy, contextual understanding, and adaptability.

The following list outlines different types of multi-stage RAGs:

- **Simple RAG**: It represents the foundational architecture wherein the relevant documents are retrieved from a knowledge base using dense vector representations and are subsequently used by a language model to generate a response. This technique is well-suited for straightforward question answering scenarios that benefit from supplemental context but do not require ongoing dialogue or complex reasoning.

- **Simple RAG with memory**: This variant enhances simple RAG by incorporating memory mechanisms to retain context across multiple interactions. Particularly valuable in conversational AI, simple RAG with memory maintains continuity between queries, enabling the system to resolve co-references and follow-up questions effectively. The model leverages prior conversational turns as part of the retrieval or generation process to ensure contextual coherence.

- **Branched RAG**: It introduces multiple retrieval steps, where intermediate outputs inform subsequent retrievals. This structure is instrumental for complex queries that require multi-hop reasoning or synthesis across various information sources. The iterative retrieval mechanism progressively narrows down relevant content, improving the specificity and depth of the final response.

- **Hypothetical Document Embedding (HyDE)**: HyDE modifies the retrieval process by generating a hypothetical ideal document that would likely contain the answer to a given query. This generated document is then embedded and used as a query against the knowledge base. HyDE proves beneficial in cases where the knowledge base may not contain exact matches, such as abstract or underspecified queries, by guiding retrieval toward semantically aligned content.

- **Adaptive RAG**: It dynamically adjusts its retrieval and generation strategies based on the complexity or type of input query. It may choose between sparse or dense retrieval techniques and select different generation models or configurations accordingly. This adaptability enables the system to accommodate a wide spectrum of user intents and data domains, offering a more robust and flexible interface.

- **Corrective RAG (CRAG)**: CRAG introduces a validation loop wherein generated outputs are cross-verified against retrieved content. If discrepancies are detected, the generation is refined through additional retrieval or corrective generation steps. This approach is particularly useful in high-stakes applications such as legal or medical decision-making, where factual accuracy and verifiability are critical.

- **Self-RAG**: It extends the generation pipeline with self-reflection capabilities. After generating an initial response, the model assesses its own output, identifies potential weaknesses, and performs further retrieval to improve the response. This self-improvement cycle aligns with recent developments in reflective and self-consistent reasoning, enhancing overall output quality and depth.

- **Agentic RAG**: It integrates RAG with autonomous agent behavior. The system can plan, reason, and use external tools such as **application programming interfaces (APIs)**, calculators, or databases to execute complex multi-step tasks. This paradigm is well-suited for real-world problem-solving in domains requiring decision-making, workflow orchestration, or interactive tool usage.

The evolution from simple to multi-stage RAG architectures reflects a broader trend toward more adaptive, intelligent, and context-aware AI systems. Each RAG variant addresses specific challenges in information retrieval and **natural language generation (NLG)**, offering tailored solutions for diverse applications ranging from casual conversation to high-stakes analytical reasoning. As RAG continues to mature, hybrid and multi-agent configurations are likely to play an increasingly prominent role in knowledge-intensive AI workflows.

Grading mechanisms

Grading mechanisms are integral in certain RAG variants to evaluate, rank, or select among multiple candidate responses, retrievals, or reasoning paths. This evaluative layer ensures that only the most contextually appropriate and factually accurate outputs are surfaced to the user. Different RAG grading mechanisms are as follows:

- **Agentic RAG**: These systems particularly benefit from grading. Given their autonomy in decision-making, tool invocation, and multi-step planning, these systems often generate multiple hypotheses, action plans, or intermediate outputs. A grading module, often based on a learned scoring function or prompt-based evaluator, is then employed to assess these options based on coherence, factual consistency, relevance, or task-specific criteria. This process helps in selecting the optimal plan or response before final generation or tool execution.

- **Self-RAG**: It may also incorporate grading during the self-reflection phase. After an initial generation, the model may produce alternative versions or corrections. A grader assesses these variations to determine which revision most accurately addresses the user's query, reducing hallucinations and increasing output fidelity.

- **Adaptive RAG**: Grading plays a supportive yet increasingly important role in adaptive RAG systems. Given that adaptive RAG dynamically selects retrieval and generation strategies based on query characteristics, such as complexity, domain, or ambiguity, a grading mechanism can serve as a meta-controller that scores or ranks candidate strategies. This allows the system to evaluate which combination of retrieval method (e.g., sparse vs. dense), retriever depth, or generation configuration yields the most relevant and reliable output for a given context. In practical implementations, this grading may rely on confidence scoring, retrieval quality heuristics, or even LLM-based evaluators. By incorporating a lightweight grading function, adaptive RAG ensures that strategy selection is not just reactive but evidence-based, thus enhancing both precision and generalization across heterogeneous query types.

- **CRAG**: Grading is intrinsic to the process of iterative refinement. After an initial generation is produced, the system evaluates it against retrieved documents to identify inconsistencies, hallucinations, or factual mismatches. This evaluative step functions as a grading mechanism, either rule-based (e.g., keyword matching, entailment checks) or model-based (e.g., a separate LLM scoring factual consistency). The output is assigned a relevance or accuracy score, and if it falls below a defined threshold, the generation is corrected through additional retrieval, rephrasing, or selective regeneration. Thus, grading enables the model to operationalize feedback loops that uphold factual integrity, making it especially suitable for domains where the cost of misinformation is high.

In essence, grading transforms RAG from a purely generative process into a more deliberative and evaluative pipeline, aligning with recent trends in reflective and multi-agent AI systems.

Challenges and considerations

Despite their advantages, multi-stage RAG systems introduce complexity and computational overhead. Critical considerations include balancing performance gains against latency increases, managing resource allocation efficiently, and optimizing inter-stage communication to avoid bottlenecks.

Multi-stage RAG architectures represent a significant advancement over traditional two-stage models. By strategically incorporating additional retrieval, refinement, and validation steps, these sophisticated systems are better suited for high-stakes, real-world applications where accuracy, reliability, and contextual comprehension are paramount.

Token utilization in multi-stage RAG systems

Token utilization is a critical consideration in the design and deployment of multi-stage RAG systems. Each stage of retrieval, reranking, validation, and generation consumes a portion of the available token budget, which is constrained by the context window of the underlying language model. Efficient token budgeting directly impacts both the fidelity of responses and the cost-effectiveness of system deployment.

In multi-stage pipelines, token usage typically escalates due to:

- **Expanded input contexts**: Intermediate stages, such as memory augmentation, branched retrieval, and multi-hop queries, increase the number of documents or prompts passed into the generator.

- **Intermediate summarization or scoring**: Self-RAG, CRAG, and agentic RAG often perform additional passes where candidate outputs are scored or re-encoded, requiring further token expenditure.

- **Long-form generation**: Multimodal inputs or multi-agent plans can lead to longer generated outputs, adding to downstream token consumption.

Token allocation must therefore be strategically managed. Some techniques include selective truncation of low-ranking documents, compression via summarization models, or tiered ranking systems that minimize token-intensive steps unless necessary. Advanced configurations use routing or grading mechanisms to determine which branches of the pipeline warrant deeper token investment.

Ultimately, token optimization in multi-stage RAG systems is essential not only for computational efficiency but also for preserving model accuracy within the token constraints. Thoughtful management of token flow enables the design of scalable, high-precision RAG architectures suitable for enterprise deployment.

Grading types

In RAG pipelines, a second-stage remains essential even when initial retrieval appears sufficient. This is particularly true in scenarios where retrieved documents may be only partially relevant, contain noisy or ambiguous content, or require additional reasoning to determine their usefulness. The second-stage introduces refinement, filtering, or validation mechanisms—typically powered by LLM-based graders—that help ensure only contextually aligned documents are passed to the generation module.

The following outlines a common grading component used in such second-stage setups:

- **Retrieval relevance grader**:
    - **Purpose and role**: The retrieval relevance grader is the first layer of validation in a multi-stage RAG pipeline. Its primary function is to evaluate whether a retrieved document from a knowledge base is semantically relevant to a given user query. This relevance check is foundational, as it determines whether the downstream generative model will be grounded in a pertinent context.
    - **Methodology**: The grader is formulated as an LLM-based binary classifier, prompted with both the user question and a retrieved document. It assesses the document for lexical and semantic alignment with the query. If the document contains terms, concepts, or information that pertain to the question, it is considered relevant.
    - **Prompt design**: The prompt provides a structured input that includes:
        - `The full content of the retrieved document`.
        - `The original user queries`.
        - `Instructions to objectively determine whether the document contains at least some relevant information`.

        The LLM is expected to return a JSON output with a single key:
        - `binary_score, whose value is either "yes" (relevant) or "no" (not relevant)`.
    - **Evaluation format**:
      ```
      {
        "binary_score": "yes"
      }
      ```
    - **Code**:
      ```
      ### Retrieval Grader

      # Doc grader instructions
      doc_grader_instructions = """You are a grader assessing relevance
      of a retrieved document to a user question.
      ```

```
If the document contains keyword(s) or semantic meaning related to
the question, grade it as relevant."""

# Grader prompt
doc_grader_prompt = """"Here is the retrieved document: \n\n
{document} \n\n Here is the user question: \n\n {question}.

This carefully and objectively assess whether the document
contains at least some information that is relevant to the
question.

Return JSON with single key, binary_score, that is 'yes' or 'no'
score to indicate whether the document contains at least some
information that is relevant to the question."""

# Test
question = "What is Chain of thought prompting?"
docs = retriever.invoke(question)
doc_txt = docs[1].page_content
doc_grader_prompt_formatted = doc_grader_prompt.format(
    document=doc_txt, question=question
)
result = llm_json_mode.invoke(
    [SystemMessage(content=doc_grader_instructions)]
    + [HumanMessage(content=doc_grader_prompt_formatted)]
)
json.loads(result.content)
```

- **Hallucination detection grader**:

  o **Purpose and role**: The hallucination detection grader serves a critical verification function by determining whether a generated answer is factually grounded in the source documents retrieved during the RAG process. Hallucination in GenAI refers to fabricated or unsupported information not present in the evidence set. This grader aims to filter such artifacts before the final presentation to the user.

  o **Methodology**: The grader is prompted with two inputs:

    ▪ A corpus of factual documents retrieved earlier in the pipeline

    ▪ A student-generated answer produced by the language model

  The LLM is instructed to verify whether the answer adheres strictly to the content in the provided documents, without introducing external information. The process emphasizes explanation-driven grading, requiring a reasoned judgment rather than a simple binary decision.

- o **Prompt design**: The prompt includes:
  - A labeled section for FACTS (retrieved documents)
  - A labeled section for STUDENT ANSWER (model generation)
  - Clear criteria for judging grounding and hallucination

  The expected output is a JSON object containing:
  - binary_score: "yes" (fully grounded) or "no" (contains hallucination)
  - explanation: a step-by-step justification for the grading decision

- o **Evaluation format**:

```
{
  "binary_score": "no",
  "explanation": "The answer introduces models not found in the document..."
}
```

- o **Code**:

```
### Hallucination Grader

# Hallucination grader instructions
hallucination_grader_instructions = """

You are a teacher grading a quiz.

You will be given FACTS and a STUDENT ANSWER.

Here is the grade criteria to follow:

Ensure the STUDENT ANSWER is grounded in the FACTS.

Ensure the STUDENT ANSWER does not contain "hallucinated"
information outside the scope of the FACTS.

Score:

A score of yes means that the student's answer meets all of the
criteria. This is the highest (best) score.

A score of no means that the student's answer does not meet all of
the criteria. This is the lowest possible score you can give.

Explain your reasoning in a step-by-step manner to ensure your
reasoning and conclusion are correct.

Avoid simply stating the correct answer at the outset."""

# Grader prompt
```

```
hallucination_grader_prompt = """FACTS: \n\n {documents} \n\n
STUDENT ANSWER: {generation}.

Return JSON with two two keys, binary_score is 'yes' or 'no'
score to indicate whether the STUDENT ANSWER is grounded in the
FACTS. And a key, explanation, that contains an explanation of the
score."""

# Test using documents and generation from above
hallucination_grader_prompt_formatted = hallucination_grader_
prompt.format(
documents=docs_txt, generation=generation.content
)
result = llm_json_mode.invoke(
[SystemMessage(content=hallucination_grader_instructions)]
+ [HumanMessage(content=hallucination_grader_prompt_formatted)]
)
json.loads(result.content)
```

- **Answer quality grader**:

  o **Purpose and role**: The answer quality grader evaluates whether the generative response meaningfully addresses the user's original question. Unlike the hallucination grader, which focuses on factual alignment, this grader assesses semantic utility, i.e., whether the answer contributes to resolving the user's intent.

  o **Methodology**: This grader compares the user's question against the model's answer to determine if the response is sufficient, informative, and contextually appropriate. The criteria allow for extra information in the response, provided it helps answer the question.

  o **Prompt design**: The grader prompt contains:
    - `The original QUESTION`
    - `The STUDENT ANSWER`
    - `Instructions that highlight both alignment and completeness`

  The output is a structured JSON object with:
    - `binary_score: "yes" if the answer helps answer the question, "no" otherwise`
    - `explanation: a detailed rationale supporting the score`

  This grader helps differentiate between vague, uninformative answers and those that provide substantial, relevant insights.

o **Evaluation format**:

```
{
  "binary_score": "yes",
  "explanation": "The answer clearly states the Llama 3.2 vision
models and relates them to the question."

}
```

o **Code**:

```
### Answer Grader

# Answer grader instructions
answer_grader_instructions = """You are a teacher grading a quiz.

You will be given a QUESTION and a STUDENT ANSWER.

Here is the grade criteria to follow:

(1) The STUDENT ANSWER helps to answer the QUESTION

Score:

A score of yes means that the student's answer meets all of the
criteria. This is the highest (best) score.

The student can receive a score of yes if the answer contains
extra information that is not explicitly asked for in the
question.

A score of no means that the student's answer does not meet all of
the criteria. This is the lowest possible score you can give.

Explain your reasoning in a step-by-step manner to ensure your
reasoning and conclusion are correct.

Avoid simply stating the correct answer at the outset."""


# Grader prompt
answer_grader_prompt = """QUESTION: \n\n {question} \n\n STUDENT
ANSWER: {generation}.

Return JSON with two two keys, binary_score is 'yes' or 'no' score
to indicate whether the STUDENT ANSWER meets the criteria. And a
key, explanation, that contains an explanation of the score."""

# Test
question = "What are the vision models released today as part of
Llama 3.2?"
answer = "The Llama 3.2 models released today include two vision
models: Llama 3.2 11B Vision Instruct and Llama 3.2 90B Vision
```

```
Instruct, which are available on Azure AI Model Catalog via
managed compute. These models are part of Meta's first foray into
multimodal AI and rival closed models like Anthropic's Claude 3
Haiku and OpenAI's GPT-4o mini in visual reasoning. They replace
the older text-only Llama 3.1 models."

# Test using question and generation from above
answer_grader_prompt_formatted = answer_grader_prompt.format(
    question=question, generation=answer
)
result = llm_json_mode.invoke(
    [SystemMessage(content=answer_grader_instructions)]
    + [HumanMessage(content=answer_grader_prompt_formatted)]
)
json.loads(result.content)
```

You can design multiple types of graders depending on the stage of your RAG pipeline and the evaluation goals (e.g., correctness, factuality, relevance, fluency). Refer to the following table, as it describes comprehensive grader types, their purpose, when to use them, and examples:

Grader type	Purpose	When to use	Example use case
Retrieval relevance grader	Check if the retrieved document is relevant to the query.	After retrieval, before generation.	Ensure only documents relevant to *what is transfer learning?* Are passed to LLM.
Hallucination grader	Check if the generated answer is grounded in retrieved facts.	After generation, before the final output.	Verify if the LLM-generated answer about Llama 3.2 matches the retrieved documents.
Answer quality grader	Judge whether the generated answer meaningfully addresses the query.	Final evaluation stage before display.	Decide if the answer explains *how does gradient descent works?* Correctly and helpfully.
Faithfulness grader	Similar to the hallucination grader, but focused on logical alignment.	Use when LLM may infer unstated conclusions.	Check if the reasoning behind an answer about *causal inference* is backed by sources.
Completeness grader	Judge if the answer covers all required sub-parts of the question.	For multi-part or compound questions.	Evaluate the answer to *what are the benefits and risks of GPT models?*
Coherence grader	Checks whether the answer is logically and grammatically well-formed.	When you want to ensure readability and clarity.	Ensure that a long-form answer flows well and has no contradictions or gaps.
Toxicity or bias grader	Detect harmful, biased, or inappropriate content.	For safety, before deployment or display.	Filter out biased statements in answers about race, gender, and politics.

Grader type	Purpose	When to use	Example use case
Conciseness grader	Ensure the answer is not verbose or off-topic.	When you want short answers (e.g., for summaries or mobile use).	Trim the answer about *quantum computing* to fit within 50 words.
Consistency grader	Check if answers to similar questions are consistent.	For evaluating multi-turn or batch outputs.	Ensure that answers to *what is AI?* and *the definition of AI* are aligned.
Instruction-following grader	Evaluate adherence to specific instructions or constraints.	When prompts contain custom instructions (e.g., list three points only).	Check if LLM follows instructions like *using bullet points* or *avoiding math symbols*.
Evidence attribution grader	Check if the source of an answer is cited properly.	For knowledge-intensive QA or academic applications.	Ensure the answer about a research paper includes a citation like (*Smith et al.*, 2022).

Table 6.2: Types of graders in RAG pipelines

Implementation of multi-stage RAG workflow with routing

In the `Chapter_6.ipynb` there are multiple code implementations of a various multi-stage, retrieval-augmented question answering systems using LangChain, LangGraph, and Ollama-integrated local LLMs (e.g., Llama 3.2). The system retrieves information either from a pre-embedded local vector store or via a live web search, routes queries intelligently, performs generation, and then grades the output for quality and relevance.

It begins by embedding domain-specific documents (e.g., blog posts on agents and adversarial attacks) using `NomicEmbeddings` and storing them in an `SKLearnVectorStore`. Questions are routed through a JSON-mode router model that determines whether to use the vector store or web search via the Tavily API.

Once documents are retrieved, a retrieval grader checks relevance to the query. If the documents are relevant, the system invokes a prompt-based RAG generator. Generated answers are validated with a hallucination grader (to ensure grounding) and an answer quality grader (to assess completeness).

The whole system is orchestrated via a LangGraph state machine, allowing conditional flow through routing, grading, generation, and citation. This design ensures adaptive response synthesis, using both static knowledge and live web data, with integrated quality control mechanisms for reliability and trustworthiness.

The following figure illustrates a multi-stage RAG workflow that incorporates routing logic to determine the most appropriate path for query resolution. This architecture combines traditional retrieval from a vector store, document grading for relevance, and optional fallback strategies such as web search. If the retrieved content is found to be insufficient or not useful, the system invokes a generation phase with retries and conditional exits based on utility. Such a routing-enabled design ensures robust handling of diverse input types and retrieval failures, supporting enhanced accuracy and adaptability in real-world deployments.

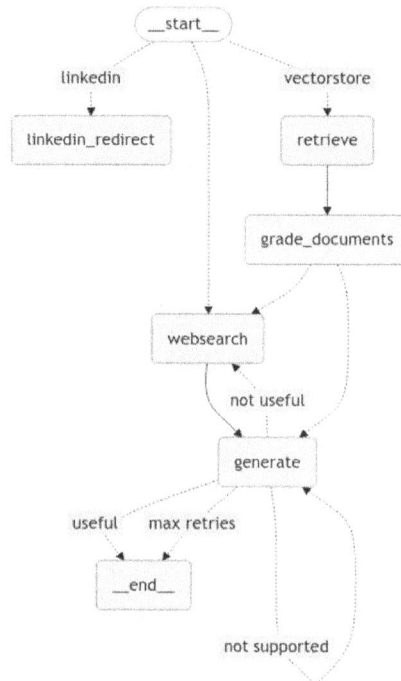

Figure 6.6: *Multi-stage RAG workflow with routing*

Conclusion

In this chapter, we delved into the evolving landscape of RAG systems, emphasizing the shift from basic two-stage models to more sophisticated multi-stage architectures. We explored how dense retrieval interactions underpin relevance matching and how grading mechanisms enhance the trustworthiness of responses by assessing factuality, relevance, and completeness. Through the implementation of a multi-stage RAG workflow with intelligent routing, we demonstrated how retrieval sources and generation pathways can be dynamically selected based on question type and content quality. This modular and adaptive design paves the way for scalable, reliable, and context-aware GenAI systems in real-world applications.

In the next chapter, we will implement a multimodal retrieval system, focusing exclusively on the retrieval component.

## CHAPTER 7

Building a Bidirectional Multimodal Retrieval System

Introduction

In an increasingly visual and interconnected digital world, the ability to search and retrieve information across different modalities, such as text and images, has become a cornerstone of advanced **artificial intelligence** (**AI**) applications. This chapter introduces the concept of multimodal retrieval, where systems are designed to understand and correlate both textual and visual inputs. Unlike traditional search engines that rely solely on textual similarity, multimodal systems use vector representations from both images and text to deliver richer, more contextually aligned results. You will learn how to build such a system by integrating Qdrant as a vector database, **Contrastive Language-Image pre-Training** (**CLIP**) models from *Hugging Face* for generating image embeddings, and LangChain to orchestrate the retrieval process. These tools enable unified access to multiple data formats, allowing users to perform flexible cross-modal searches, such as retrieving descriptions from images or identifying images that match textual inputs.

Throughout the chapter, you will construct dual-index vector stores and develop hybrid retrievers capable of handling diverse query formats. Python-based implementations will guide you through indexing workflows, embedding pipelines, and retrieval logic that switches seamlessly between modalities. Beyond technical architecture, the chapter delves into practical design decisions like similarity scoring, modality prioritization, and custom retrieval logic. By the end, you will have the skills to deploy a production-ready multimodal retriever, a foundation applicable to use cases in e-commerce recommendations, visual content discovery, and semantic search engines. This hands-on approach ensures you not only understand the theory but also gain the ability to implement scalable, real-world solutions.

Structure

In this chapter, we will learn about the following topics:

- Output-based classification of multimodal systems
- Understanding a multimodal retrieval system
- Code implementation and explanation
- To do for the readers

Objectives

The objective of this chapter is to design and implement a multimodal retrieval system capable of handling both text and image inputs. Readers will learn how to preprocess and embed data from multiple modalities using bi-encoders, normalize vector representations, and store them efficiently in a vector database such as Qdrant. The system supports cross-modal queries such as retrieving images from text prompts and textual content from image inputs, enabling semantic search across heterogeneous data types. This chapter lays the technical foundation for building intelligent, modality-aware applications and prepares readers to extend the system further by incorporating generative models in the subsequent chapter.

Output-based classification of multimodal systems

Building upon the foundational concepts introduced in *Chapter 2, Deep Dive into Multimodal Systems,* this section offers an overview of the four key output-based classifications of multimodal systems that are text-to-image, image-to-text, text and image-to-image, and text to specifications and image. These categories define how different combinations of input modalities are used to produce specific output formats, forming the backbone of modern multimodal AI applications. By organizing systems based on their output types, we create a clearer framework for understanding how diverse technologies, from image generation models to captioning tools and specification-driven design engines, function in real-world scenarios. This classification not only reinforces the distinctions made earlier but also provides a structured lens through which the retrieval and generation challenges in upcoming chapters can be better understood and implemented. A quick recap is as follows:

- **Text-to-image**: These systems take a textual prompt and generate a corresponding image. They typically consist of a text encoder that converts the prompt into a latent representation, followed by a generative model like a diffusion or **generative**

adversarial network (**GAN**) based network that decodes this representation into visual content. Models like DALL·E, Imagen, and Stable Diffusion fall into this category. Academically, text-to-image systems are examples of cross-modal generative modeling, mapping language to visuals, and are used extensively for semantic image creation and creative content tasks.

- **Image-to-text**: Here, the system processes an input image and produces a natural language description, caption, or metadata. This involves encoding the image with a visual backbone—such as a **convolutional neural network** (**CNN**) or **Vision Transformer** (**ViT**), and decoding it into text using a language model. Applications include image captioning and visual question answering, where the output ranges from short captions like a *dog playing* to more interactive question and answer responses. These systems enable machines to interpret and articulate visual information in language form.

- **Text and image-to-image**: These hybrid systems accept both text and image as input and output a modified or enhanced image. This includes tasks like conditional image translation, where a user might provide a sketch and a prompt like *make it photorealistic*, or a photo accompanied by text instructions for style adjustments. By merging embeddings from both modalities and feeding them into a conditional image generator, these systems offer semantic visual editing capabilities, useful for creative design and style transformation.

- **Text to specs and image**: The most advanced category combines textual input with the generation of structured specifications and visual renderings. For instance, given a prompt like *design a chair with specific dimensions*, the system outputs both a specification sheet (e.g., dimension tables) and a visual representation of the chair. These systems integrate **natural language processing** (**NLP**) with symbolic reasoning to produce both machine-readable specs and images, ideal for applications in product design, architectural planning, and e-commerce, where precise visual and structural output is needed.

Integration and design implications

Viewed through a theoretical lens, multimodal systems span translation, alignment, and fusion paradigms. Text-to-image and image-to-text systems primarily focus on translating between modalities. The text and image-to-image class demonstrates the fusion of combined multimodal embeddings before image generation. Lastly, the text to specifications and image category blends translation (text to specs), structure generation (specs to image), and fusion, handling both symbolic and visual outputs.

Recognizing these categories is crucial for designing multimodal retrieval systems, such as the hybrid retrievers discussed in *Chapter 6, Two and Multi-stage GenAI Systems*, where indexing, querying, and retrieval must accommodate diverse input/output modalities. Such classification informs how we build vector stores, craft embedding strategies, and define cross-modal search capabilities for tasks like *finding images matching a specification* or *retrieve specs from an image*.

Understanding a multimodal retrieval system

Figure 7.1 illustrates a multimodal retrieval system architecture, where retrieval operates seamlessly across text and image modalities. Academically, this approach leverages embeddings, a vector-based representation capturing semantic relationships within data, generated separately for textual and visual content.

The process initiates with user queries, which may consist of text, images, or both. These inputs are passed to specialized embedding models: a text embedding model for textual queries or documents, and an image embedding model for visual inputs. Documents undergo chunking into smaller units to improve the granularity and efficiency of retrieval, whereas images are directly embedded into the vector representation.

Once embeddings are computed, they are stored in a multimodal vector database designed to handle mixed data types. Upon receiving a query, the system performs vector similarity searches across this database, retrieving results based on semantic proximity rather than exact matches. The returned results, combining textual chunks and images, are then provided back to the user.

In contexts, such multimodal retrieval systems are foundational for advanced applications like cross-modal search, content-based image retrieval, and integrated semantic recommendation systems. The combined use of text and image embeddings enhances the accuracy and contextual relevance of retrieval, supporting richer, more intuitive user interactions.

Technical architecture

The advent of multimodal retrieval systems marks a pivotal advancement in the field of information retrieval, enabling systems to process and semantically align content across distinct data modalities such as text and images. The architectural schematic under discussion illustrates a robust framework that integrates text and image embedding pipelines with a shared or coordinated vector space for high-precision, cross-modal search. This section provides a comprehensive exposition of the technical components, data flow mechanisms, and system design principles underpinning architectures.

The following figure presents the architecture of a multimodal retrieval system that integrates both textual and visual data for unified query processing. User queries, which may include text and/or images, are encoded using separate embedding models tailored to each modality. These embeddings are stored in a multimodal vector database that supports joint retrieval across document chunks and images. Upon querying, the system performs vector similarity search and returns semantically aligned results from both data types, thereby enabling robust and context-rich response generation.

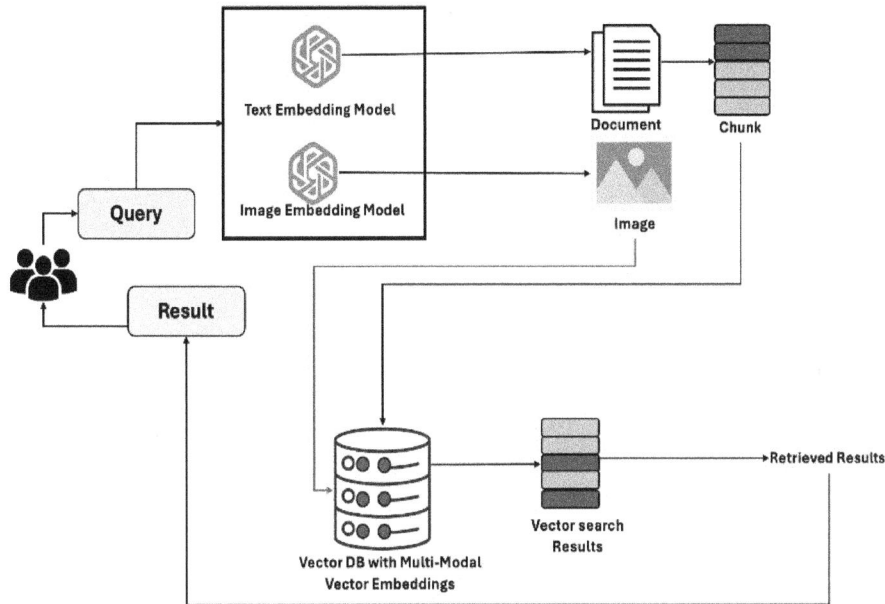

Figure 7.1: *A foundation multimodal retrieval system*

The system's architecture relies on multimodal processing, where user queries can originate from text, images, or a combination of both. To handle this effectively, the pipeline employs specialized embedding models that unify these inputs into a shared semantic space. The key components are outlined in the following list:

- **User interaction and query intake**: The system is initiated through user queries, which may take the form of textual inputs (e.g., descriptions or questions), visual inputs (e.g., product images), or hybrid combinations of both. These multimodal queries reflect real-world information-seeking behaviors and necessitate translation into a common representational format that preserves semantic intent. This is achieved through embedding models that encode raw input into dense vector representations within a latent semantic space.

- **Embedding models for text and image modalities**: At the core of the architecture are dedicated embedding models tailored for each modality:

    o **Text embedding model**: Converts natural language content into high-dimensional vectors. These models are typically instantiated using state-of-the-art transformer architectures such as Sentence-BERT, text-embedding-ada, or similar large-scale language models. They capture syntactic structure and semantic context, enabling fine-grained retrieval at the sentence or paragraph level.

    o **Image embedding model**: Transforms visual content into latent vector representations using pre-trained **vision-language models** (**VLMs**) such as

CLIP. These models are trained to align visual and textual representations in a shared semantic space, allowing direct cross-modal comparison.

The resulting embeddings provide modality-agnostic encodings that facilitate efficient similarity search across heterogeneous data types.

- **Document chunking and embedding preparation**: To ensure compatibility with model token limits and to enhance retrieval granularity, lengthy textual documents are segmented into smaller, coherent units known as **chunks**. Each chunk is individually embedded using the text encoder. Similarly, images, either standalone or extracted from documents, are embedded through the visual encoder. The output of this stage is a structured set of vectorized text and image segments, each linked with relevant metadata such as source identifier, location within the document, and semantic tags.

- **Multimodal vector store integration**: The embedded representations are stored in a vector database designed to support multimodal indexing and search operations. Examples of such systems include Qdrant, Weaviate, and Pinecone, all of which offer high-performance **approximate nearest neighbor** (**ANN**) search via indexing algorithms such as **hierarchical navigable small world** (**HNSW**) graphs.

The vector store must support:

- o **Unified indexing**: A single index accommodating embeddings from both modalities.

- o **Metadata filtering**: Structured filtering based on payload metadata (e.g., timestamps, categories).

- o **Similarity metrics**: Configurable scoring strategies, such as cosine similarity or dot product, to measure semantic proximity between query and stored embeddings.

This architecture may optionally employ dual-index structures, where text and image embeddings are stored and queried separately, with fusion logic applied during post-processing.

- **Query encoding and similarity search**: Upon receipt of a user query, the system dynamically determines the input modality and applies the corresponding embedding model. For hybrid queries, embeddings are generated for both text and image components. The query vectors are then submitted to the vector store to retrieve the top-k most similar embeddings based on vector proximity. Advanced implementations may incorporate the following:

- o **Late fusion strategies**: Combining ranked results from separate modality indexes.

- o **Score normalization**: Aligning similarity scores across heterogeneous embedding distributions.

o **Cross-modal reranking**: Using bi-encoder or cross-encoder architectures to refine initial search results.

This stage yields a ranked list of retrieved vectors, each corresponding to a text chunk or image segment stored in the database.

- **Result mapping and response generation**: The retrieved vector identifiers are mapped back to their original content, be it document snippets or image files, using stored metadata. These are formatted and presented to the user. Optionally, a generative language model (e.g., GPT-based) may be invoked to:

  o Summarize the retrieved content.

  o Generate a natural language answer.

  o Enhance the interpretability of results through multi-turn dialogue.

This final presentation layer bridges the gap between the dense, vector-based internal representation and the user's cognitive expectations, delivering explainable and contextually relevant results.

- **Technical enhancements and design optimizations**: Multimodal retrieval systems may incorporate additional layers of intelligence to optimize performance and accuracy:

  o **Modality routing**: A policy mechanism that detects dominant query modality and routes it to the appropriate retriever.

  o **Embedding caching**: Reduces inference latency by storing embeddings of frequently queried inputs.

  o **Retrieval augmentation**: Supports techniques such as query expansion or pseudo-relevance feedback.

These features collectively contribute to the system's scalability, responsiveness, and effectiveness in real-time applications.

Applications and implications

Such architectures are foundational in a range of AI-driven applications, including but not limited to:

- **Visual product search**: Matching product images to descriptions in e-commerce platforms.

- **Medical imaging retrieval**: Finding annotated radiology reports based on diagnostic images.

- **Multimodal QA**: Retrieving answers based on diagrams and accompanying textual context.

- **Interactive content discovery**: Enabling users to search archives, galleries, or databases using descriptive prompts or reference images.

Code implementation and explanation

So now that you understand that the multimodal retrieval system detailed above exemplifies the convergence of NLP, computer vision, and vector similarity search in a unified architecture. By enabling seamless cross-modal interaction, it provides a powerful framework for real-time, semantically rich retrieval across complex information landscapes. For data science and **generative AI (GenAI)** practitioners, mastering the design and implementation of such systems is essential to advancing the state of multimodal AI applications. Let us understand it using a code example. The code is shared as part of this book.

Requirement

The following Python libraries constitute the foundational software stack required to implement a multimodal retrieval system that integrates text and image embeddings, vector indexing, and real-time interaction. Each package has been carefully selected to support key functionalities such as vector representation learning, semantic search, document parsing, and interactive interface design.

- **Streamlit**:
  - **Purpose**: It provides a lightweight and declarative framework for building web-based user interfaces.
  - **Usage**: Streamlit is employed to create the frontend for multimodal interaction, allowing users to input text or upload images, and receive visual or textual results in real-time.
  - **Context**: It facilitates rapid prototyping of data-centric applications and is widely used in research for the demonstration of machine learning models.

- **QdrantClient**:
  - **Purpose**: A Python client for interacting with the Qdrant vector database.
  - **Usage**: It enables operations such as inserting, querying, and managing embeddings stored as high-dimensional vectors. Qdrant supports efficient ANN search.
  - **Context**: It is suitable for storing multimodal vector embeddings due to its support for payloads, filtering, and multiple collection indexes.

- **LlamaIndex**:
  - **Purpose**: A framework for building **retrieval-augmented generation (RAG)** systems.

o **Usage**: It facilitates indexing, chunking, and document retrieval in combination with language models. Integrates seamlessly with Qdrant and other vector databases.

o **Context**: It enables the construction of scalable RAG pipelines that combine retrieval with generative reasoning for tasks such as open-domain QA and document synthesis.

- **LangChain**:

  o **Purpose**: A powerful orchestration library for chaining together **large language model** (**LLM**) calls, retrieval mechanisms, tools, and user prompts.

  o **Usage**: It manages embedding generation, document retrieval, and LLM-driven post-processing in the multimodal pipeline.

  o **Context**: It is widely used in LLM-centric systems research for constructing agentic workflows and LLM-powered assistants.

- **LangChain Community**:

  o **Purpose**: An extension of the core LangChain library, offering community-contributed integrations and tools.

  o **Usage**: It supports connectors to third-party embedding models, retrievers, and document loaders that may not be in the core package.

  o **Context**: It encourages reproducibility and modular experimentation by enabling access to a broad range of open-source data and model utilities.

- **LangChain and Nomic**:

  o **Purpose**: Integration layer between LangChain and Nomic AI's embedding and indexing tools.

  o **Usage**: It may be used to experiment with alternative embedding backends or advanced visualization of embedding spaces (e.g., via Nomic Atlas).

  o **Context**: It provides additional flexibility for multimodal experimentation and indexing strategies.

- **Sentence Transformers**:

  o **Purpose**: A library for generating high-quality text embeddings using models like all-MiniLM, multi-qa-mpnet, etc.

  o **Usage**: It converts user queries and textual chunks into dense vector representations for similarity-based retrieval.

  o **Context**: It is considered as a standard toolkit for semantic textual similarity, question answering, and document clustering tasks.

- **Transformers**:
  - **Purpose**: Hugging Face flagship library for pre-trained transformer models (e.g., BERT, CLIP, GPT, ViT).
  - **Usage**: It powers both text and image embedding models, such as CLIP for image-text alignment or BERT for textual embeddings.
  - **Context**: It is central to most modern NLP, vision, and multimodal AI research and experimentation.

- **Pillow**:
  - **Purpose**: A Python imaging library for image processing and file handling.
  - **Usage**: It handles uploaded image files, conversion, resizing, and preprocessing prior to embedding.
  - **Context**: It is essential for integrating visual inputs in multimodal systems and preparing them for inference in image encoders.

- **pypdf**:
  - **Purpose**: PDF parsing library for extracting text and metadata from document files.
  - **Usage**: Enables ingestion of PDF-based knowledge sources (e.g., research papers, manuals) into the RAG pipeline.
  - **Context**: Supports document understanding and content indexing, commonly used in automated summarization and search engines.

- **scikit-learn**:
  - **Purpose**: A standard machine learning library for classical algorithms and utilities.
  - **Usage**: Supports clustering, dimensionality reduction e.g., **principal component analysis (PCA)**, and evaluation metrics (e.g., cosine distance) in embedding space analysis.
  - **Context**: Integral to baseline experimentation, preprocessing pipelines, and feature engineering workflows in ML studies.

- **NumPy**:
  - **Purpose**: Fundamental package for numerical computing in Python.
  - **Usage**: Underpins all mathematical operations related to vectors, matrices, similarity scoring, and array manipulation.
  - **Context**: The backbone of numerical computation across AI and data science research, ensuring reproducibility and precision.

Frontend

The following code provides a practical and extensible implementation of a bidirectional multimodal search system, integrating embedding-based semantic understanding with a scalable vector store backend. Its modular design allows for the straightforward extension of additional modalities (e.g., audio, tabular data) and advanced features such as cross-modal reranking, hybrid retrieval, or user feedback loops. It serves as a canonical example of operationalizing multimodal embeddings in real-time applications using lightweight web frameworks and composable AI components.

This streamlit-based application presents a lightweight user interface for performing bidirectional multimodal retrieval, enabling users to search from text-to-image and from image-to-text. The implementation integrates vector embedding, similarity search, and payload-based retrieval, and provides a clear example of how multimodal embeddings can be operationalized through a modern, interactive interface.

The following section breaks down and outlines the key functional components of the multimodal retrieval application, covering initialization, interface design, and query processing for both text-to-image and image-to-text pathways. Each step is crucial in enabling seamless interaction between user inputs, embedding generation, and vector-based semantic search.

- **Environment setup and path configuration**: The code begins by importing core modules: `streamlit` for interface design, **`PIL.Image`** for image handling, and **`os/sys`** for file system and path manipulations.

```
import streamlit as st
from PIL import Image
import sys
import os
```

  The following snippet determines the absolute path of the root directory and appends it to the system path to allow cross-module imports:

```
ROOT_DIR = os.path.abspath(os.path.join(os.path.dirname(__file__), ".."))
if ROOT_DIR not in sys.path:
    sys.path.append(ROOT_DIR)
```

  This ensures that submodules within the project hierarchy (e.g., **`rag.index_builder`**) can be accessed without import errors, promoting modular software design.

- **Index initialization via caching**:

```
from rag.index_builder import build_vectorstores, TEXT_COLLECTION,
IMAGE_COLLECTION

@st.cache_resource(show_spinner="Loading vector index...")
def init_system():
    return build_vectorstores()

client, mm_embed = init_system()
```

Here, **build_vectorstores()** is invoked to initialize the multimodal vector index. The function is decorated with **@st.cache_resource**, which caches the result to avoid reinitializing embeddings or loading vector data on every page refresh. This is particularly important for high-latency operations, such as loading large embedding models or querying vector databases.

- o **client**: The object responsible for interfacing with the vector database (e.g., Qdrant).

- o **mm_embed**: A custom utility that provides modality-specific embedding generation, i.e., **get_text_embedding()** and **get_image_embedding()**.

- o The constants **TEXT_COLLECTION** and **IMAGE_COLLECTION** specify the target vector index or collection for query execution.

- **User interface and mode selection**:

```
st.title(" 🔍 Multimodal Search Demo (Text ↔ Image)")
option = st.radio("Choose your query type:", ["Text → Image", "Image →
Text"])
```

The interface begins with a title, followed by a radio button selection for two modes of interaction:

- o **Text → Image**: The user enters a textual query and receives a matching image.

- o **Image → Text**: The user uploads an image and receives relevant textual content.

This conditional branching drives the remainder of the application flow.

- **Text-to-image retrieval pathway**:

```
if option == "Text → Image":
    query = st.text_input("Enter a text prompt to retrieve relevant
image:")
    if query:
        st.write(f"Searching for image similar to: *{query}*")
        q_vec = mm_embed.get_text_embedding(query)
```

Once the user submits a text prompt, it is embedded into a high-dimensional vector using the **get_text_embedding()** method. This vector representation captures the semantic intent of the input query.

```
        res = client.query_points(
            collection_name=IMAGE_COLLECTION,
            query=q_vec,
            using="image",
            with_payload=["image"],
            limit=1,
        )
```

The embedded query vector is submitted to the vector database **(IMAGE_COLLECTION)** using a semantic similarity search. Only the top-1 match is retrieved. The parameter **with_payload=["image"]** indicates that the associated image filename should be returned alongside the vector match.

```
if res and res.points:
    image_file = res.points[0].payload["image"]
    st.image(f"data/images/{image_file}", caption="Top Match",
use_column_width=True)
    else:
        st.warning("No image match found.")
```

If a result is returned, the payload is used to locate and render the matching image. If no semantically close match exists in the vector store, the user is notified accordingly.

- **Image-to-text retrieval pathway**:

```
elif option == "Image → Text":
    uploaded_img = st.file_uploader("Upload an image to find related
text", type=["png", "jpg", "jpeg"])
```

For the reverse mode, the user uploads an image. The uploaded image is temporarily saved to disk for further processing:

```
    if uploaded_img:
        with open("temp_input_image.jpg", "wb") as f:
            f.write(uploaded_img.read())

        st.image("temp_input_image.jpg", caption="Uploaded Image", use_
column_width=True)
```

Once saved, the image is passed to the get_image_embedding() method:

```
        img_vec = mm_embed.get_image_embedding("temp_input_image.jpg")
```

The resulting vector is then used to query the TEXT_COLLECTION:

```
        res = client.query_points(
            collection_name=TEXT_COLLECTION,
            query=img_vec,
            using="text",
            with_payload=["source"],
            limit=1,
        )
```

The vector search retrieves the most semantically relevant text snippet. The **payload["source"]** contains the retrieved textual content:

```
        if res and res.points:
            source_text = res.points[0].payload["source"]
            st.success("Top matching text:")
```

```
        st.write(source_text)
    else:
        st.warning("No relevant text found.")
```

Results are then rendered on the interface. In case no result meets the similarity threshold, a warning message is issued.

Data directory

The directory structure shown reflects a clean and modular organization for a multimodal retrieval system. The root folder **data** contains two subdirectories: **documents** and **images**. The **documents** folder typically stores textual sources (e.g., PDFs, text, or Markdown files) that are later chunked and embedded using text encoders. The **images** folder contains visual data (e.g., PNG, JPG) to be processed using an image embedding model. This separation supports independent preprocessing and indexing of each modality, facilitating streamlined multimodal embedding, storage, and retrieval workflows in systems built for tasks like search, captioning, or cross-modal question answering.

Figure 7.2: The images folder contains visual data and textual data

The retrieval system

Folder structure of the retrieval system: the following directory showcases the retrieval system and its association represents the core module of a RAG system. It contains Python source files that handle different stages of data processing:

- **loaders.py**: It is responsible for loading documents and images from the filesystem into memory.

- **embedding_utils.py**: It provides utility functions for generating embeddings from text and image inputs using pre-trained models.

- **index_builder.py**: It orchestrates the process of creating and populating vector indexes (e.g., in Qdrant) for multimodal search.

- **__init__.py**: It marks the folder as a Python package, allowing modular imports.

The **__pycache__** directory stores compiled bytecode for performance optimization during execution. This structure reflects good modular design and clear separation of concerns. Let us discuss these in more detail in the following section.

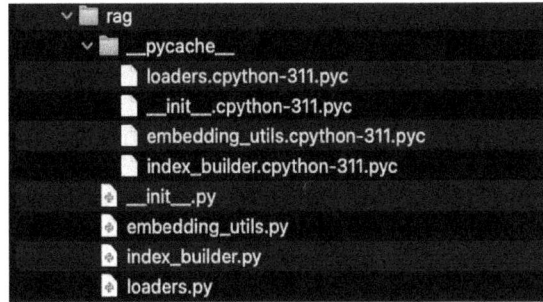

Figure 7.3: *Folder structure of retrieval system*

Loaders

The code defines two utility functions, **load_pdfs_and_texts()** and **load_images()**, to ingest and preprocess textual and visual data, respectively. These functions serve as critical components in a multimodal retrieval system, facilitating the creation of semantically aligned embeddings across document and image modalities. The implementation leverages the LangChain framework for structured document handling and text chunking and adopts a principled approach to prepare raw data for embedding and indexing in downstream vector databases. Let us understand the code in detail:

- **Textual data ingestion and chunking**: This portion imports key utilities from the LangChain ecosystem:

  o **PyPDFLoader**: It is a document loader specifically for parsing PDF files into structured text.

  o **RecursiveCharacterTextSplitter**: It is a robust text chunking utility that preserves semantic boundaries while segmenting long text.

  o **Document**: A structured data class encapsulating content and metadata.

  o **os**: Used for filesystem traversal.

```
from langchain_community.document_loaders import PyPDFLoader
from langchain.text_splitter import RecursiveCharacterTextSplitter
from langchain.schema import Document
import os
```

- **Function: load_pdfs_and_texts(folder_path: str)**: This function is responsible for traversing a directory, identifying **.pdf** and **.txt** files, and processing them into chunked **Document** objects:

```
splitter = RecursiveCharacterTextSplitter(chunk_size=1000, chunk_
overlap=200)
```

  o **Chunk size**: Set to **1000** characters to align with typical token limits of embedding models.

- o **Overlap**: Set to **200** characters to ensure context continuity across adjacent chunks—crucial for preserving semantic coherence during retrieval.

  ```
  for fname in os.listdir(folder_path):
  ```

  Each file in the folder is processed conditionally:

  - **PDF files**: Loaded using **PyPDFLoader**, which returns structured page-level content. The text is then split into chunks using the recursive splitter.

  - **Text files**: Read as a whole string, chunked into overlapping segments, and then wrapped into **Document** objects with the filename stored as **metadata**.

  ```
  Document(page_content=chunk, metadata={"source": fname})
  ```

  This **metadata** enables downstream traceability and source attribution, which are essential in retrieval-based applications where provenance is required.

- **Function: load_images(folder_path: str)**: This function handles the visual modality by scanning a folder for supported image formats and wrapping file paths into **Document** instances:

  ```
  Document(page_content=os.path.join(folder_path, f), metadata={"image": f})
  ```

  - o **page_content** stores the full file path, which will later be passed to an image encoder (e.g., CLIP).

  - o **metadata** contains the image filename, facilitating reverse lookup and UI display post-retrieval.

  This design aligns with LangChain's **Document** schema, ensuring that both text and image inputs are compatible with a unified document-processing pipeline despite originating from different modalities.

- **Design**: These utilities reflect best practices in data preprocessing for vector-based multimodal systems:

  - o They maintain structural uniformity through LangChain's **Document** schema, enabling modality-agnostic handling.

  - o The chunking strategy improves retrieval precision by balancing granularity with semantic preservation.

  - o Metadata tagging enhances retrievability, traceability, and potential for downstream visualization or summarization.

In these settings, such preprocessing routines are foundational to building systems for RAG, semantic search, and cross-modal alignment, where consistent document representations across modalities are critical.

Embedding utils

This code snippet defines a function to initialize a Hugging Face embedding model for multimodal tasks using the **llama_index** library. It imports **HuggingFaceEmbedding** from **llama_index.embeddings**.huggingface and sets the model to **openai/clip-vit-base-patch32**, a popular CLIP model that jointly embeds text and images in the same semantic space. The function **get_mm_embedder()** accepts a device argument (e.g., **cpu** or **cuda**) and returns an embedding interface that can generate vector representations for both modalities. The **trust_remote_code=True** flag allows execution of custom code from Hugging Face repositories, enabling more flexible model loading.

```
from llama_index.embeddings.huggingface import HuggingFaceEmbedding

_MODEL_ID = "openai/clip-vit-base-patch32"

def get_mm_embedder(device: str = "cpu"):
    return HuggingFaceEmbedding(model_name=_MODEL_ID, device=device, trust_
remote_code=True)
```

The CLIP model (**openai/clip-vit-base-patch32**) used in this code functions as a bi-encoder because it independently encodes text and images into vectors using separate neural network branches. Each modality, text and image, is processed in parallel through its respective encoder (a transformer for text and a ViT for images), without direct interaction during inference. The resulting embeddings are projected into a shared latent space, where similarity (e.g., cosine distance) is computed between the two. This architecture is computationally efficient and enables fast retrieval tasks like image-to-text or text-to-image matching by precomputing embeddings for each modality separately.

Index builder

The **index_builder.py** function operationalizes a central tenet of multimodal retrieval systems: encoding disparate modalities into semantically aligned vector spaces and storing them for fast, similarity-based search. By separating collection logic by modality and using cosine-normalized embeddings, the implementation adheres to best practices in vector search architecture. The design is modular, easily extensible to additional modalities (e.g., audio or tabular data), and production-ready for RAG, cross-modal search, and intelligent information access. Let us explore **index_builder.py** further.

The function **build_vectorstores()** constructs and populates two separate vector collections—one for text and one for images—within a local instance of the Qdrant vector database. This enables fast, similarity-based retrieval in multimodal retrieval systems, where user queries may be textual or visual in nature.

The implementation leverages modular components for document ingestion, embedding generation, normalization, and storage, ensuring that the architecture remains scalable, interpretable, and easily extendable. Let us understand them in detail:

- **Module imports and configuration**: These imports enable:
  - Document I/O (**Path, loaders**)
  - Embedding generation (**get_mm_embedder**)
  - Vector normalization (**numpy.linalg.norm**)
  - Qdrant-based vector indexing (**QdrantClient, PointStruct**)
  - Type safety (**List[Document]**)

    ```
    from pathlib import Path
    from typing import List
    from rag.embedding_utils import get_mm_embedder
    from qdrant_client import QdrantClient, models
    from rag.loaders import load_pdfs_and_texts, load_images
    from langchain.schema import Document
    from numpy.linalg import norm
    ```

  Constants are defined to point to storage paths and collection names:

  ```
  DB_PATH = "data/qdrant_mm"
  TEXT_COLLECTION = "vdr_text"
  IMAGE_COLLECTION = "vdr_images"
  ```

- **Vector normalization**:

  ```
  def normalize(vecs):
      return [v / norm(v) for v in vecs]
  ```

  This function performs L2 normalization on all vectors to ensure unit-length embeddings. This is essential when using cosine similarity, which depends solely on vector direction rather than magnitude. Normalization guarantees consistent distance calculations in the high-dimensional embedding space.

- **Document loading and embedding generation**:

  ```
  text_docs: List[Document] = load_pdfs_and_texts("data/documents")
  image_docs: List[Document] = load_images("data/images")
  ```

  Text and image files are ingested from separate directories using pre-defined loaders that wrap each entry into LangChain-style **Document** objects, preserving content and metadata.

  ```
  embedder = get_mm_embedder()
  ```

  The multimodal embedder (typically CLIP-based) is initialized. This embedder provides:

  - **get_text_embedding_batch()**: For encoding multiple text chunks
  - **get_image_embedding_batch()**: For encoding file paths or image tensors

```
text_vecs = normalize(embedder.get_text_embedding_batch([...]))
image_vecs = normalize(embedder.get_image_embedding_batch([...]))
```

Each modality's embeddings are normalized and prepared for insertion into Qdrant.

- **QdrantClient initialization and collection creation**:

```
client = QdrantClient(path=DB_PATH)
```

A local Qdrant instance is initialized with persistent storage located at **data/qdrant_mm.**

```
if not client.collection_exists(...):
    client.create_collection(...)
```

Two separate vector collections are created if they do not exist already:

  o **TEXT_COLLECTION**: For textual chunk embeddings

  o **IMAGE_COLLECTION**: For visual embeddings

  Both use cosine similarity as the distance metric, and the dimensionality (**size=dim**) is inferred from the first embedding vector. This separation of collections ensures optimized retrieval per modality while allowing for hybrid or late-fusion retrieval strategies later.

- **Inserting points into Qdrant collections**:

```
client.upload_points(
    TEXT_COLLECTION,
    [models.PointStruct(id=i, vector=text_vecs[i], payload={"source":
d.page_content}) for i, d in enumerate(text_docs)],
)
```

- **Textual embeddings are stored with**:

  o **id**: An integer index

  o **vector**: The normalized embedding

  o **payload**: Metadata (the original chunk text)

```
    client.upload_points(
        IMAGE_COLLECTION,
        [models.PointStruct(id=i, vector=image_vecs[i],
payload={"image": Path(d.page_content).name}) for i, d in
enumerate(image_docs)],
    )
```

Image embeddings are similarly uploaded, with the image filename stored as metadata. This metadata is critical for subsequent retrieval operations where query results must be rendered back to the user or used for further reasoning.

- **Return values**:

  ```
  return client, embedder
  ```

  The function returns both:

    o The **client**, enabling downstream retrieval operations

    o The **embedder**, allowing query inputs to be transformed into vectors in the same latent space

Process to run the entire code

Ensure the following before executing:

- The **rag/module** (with **index_builder.py**, **embedding_utils.py**, and **loaders.py**) exists and is importable.

- Directories **data/documents/** and **data/images/** contain valid files.

- All required libraries (e.g., **QdrantClient**, LangChain, transformers, etc.) are installed.

This script is typically run once, either during setup or re-indexing of your corpus.

The following code snippet is for executing the entire embedding and indexing pipeline. It begins by importing the **build_vectorstores** function from the **rag.index_builder** module, which is responsible for loading documents and images, generating their embeddings, and storing the resulting vectors in a Qdrant vector database. This function encapsulates all the key components required for preparing a multimodal vector store.

```
from rag.index_builder import build_vectorstores

build_vectorstores()
print(" Embedding complete. Vector stores loaded into Qdrant.")
```

When **build_vectorstores()** is called, the system performs several tasks: it reads textual data from **data/documents** and **images** from **data/images**, uses a shared multimodal embedder (such as CLIP) to generate normalized vector embeddings for both modalities, and initializes the Qdrant database if it has not already been created. It also creates separate collections for text and image vectors (if they do not exist) and uploads the data along with associated metadata for future retrieval.

Finally, the **print()** statement confirms the successful execution of the indexing process. This script is typically executed once during system setup or any time the document/image corpus is updated. Before running the script, ensure that all dependencies are installed and that the required directory structure is in place, along with valid content files.

To do for the readers

While the current implementation establishes a robust multimodal retrieval pipeline, it is important to recognize that it does not yet support generative outputs. The system allows for efficient retrieval of semantically relevant text or images based on a user's query, but stops short of performing **natural language generation** (**NLG**). This design reflects a classical retrieval-only architecture. To evolve this into a full-fledged RAG system, readers are encouraged to extend the pipeline with generative capabilities.

To begin, readers should integrate a LLM—such as GPT, Llama, or Mistral—that can synthesize coherent responses using both the query and retrieved content. This requires constructing a wrapper that couples the retriever with a generation module. Libraries such as LangChain or LlamaIndex offer high-level abstractions like RetrievalQA or RAG chain, which streamline this process. These frameworks allow retrieved documents to be passed directly as context into the LLM, enabling output generation in the form of answers, summaries, or semantic interpretations.

For multimodal scenarios where image embeddings are part of the retrieval results, an additional step may be required. Since most LLMs operate on text, readers should either preprocess retrieved images into captions using image-to-text models or employ multimodal LLMs (e.g., GPT-4V, LLaVA, or Kosmos-2) that natively support image inputs. This enhancement will allow the system to generate contextualized descriptions or insights that span both visual and textual domains.

In summary, readers seeking to extend this project should focus on:

- Integrating a suitable LLM for generative reasoning.
- Wrapping the retriever and LLM into a retrieval-generation pipeline.
- Optionally implementing image-to-text preprocessing for non-textual content.
- Designing prompt templates that instruct the LLM to leverage retrieved documents effectively.

This generative extension not only elevates the system from semantic matching to intelligent reasoning but also aligns it with the current state-of-the-art in multimodal question answering and document understanding.

Conclusion

This chapter guided the reader through the design and implementation of a multimodal retrieval system that integrates text and image inputs using vector embeddings. It demonstrated how to preprocess documents and images, embed them with bi-encoders like CLIP, and store them in a Qdrant vector database for efficient semantic search. The system supports cross-modal querying (text-to-image, image-to-text) and establishes a solid foundation for real-world applications. While the current setup enables retrieval, a future extension involves integrating LLMs for RAG, allowing the system to generate coherent, context-aware outputs across modalities.

In the next chapter, we will implement the missing generative component by building a complete multimodal retrieval and generation system.

Join our Discord space

Join our Discord workspace for latest updates, offers, tech happenings around the world, new releases, and sessions with the authors:

https://discord.bpbonline.com

## CHAPTER 8

Building a Multimodal RAG System

Introduction

In this chapter, we address the one remaining piece, the generative component from *Chapter 7, Building a Bidirectional Multimodal Retrieval Systems,* by extending our multimodal retrieval pipeline into a full **retrieval-augmented generation** (**RAG**) system. Up to now, we have focused on indexing documents and images, embedding them into a shared vector space, and retrieving relevant text or visuals based on user queries. Here, we will integrate a **large language model** (**LLM**) to synthesize coherent, context-aware responses using those retrieved items. We will demonstrate how to wrap the retriever in a generation chain, craft prompt templates that blend the user's query with retrieved context, and handle both text-to-image and image-to-text workflows. By the end of this chapter, you will have a complete, end-to-end multimodal system capable not only of finding relevant content but also of generating insightful answers and summaries.

Structure

In this chapter, we will learn about the following topics:

- Implementation of generation
- Multimodal LLM-based recommender system
- Incorporate grading with OpenAI

- LLM-as-a-judge
- To do

Objectives

This chapter provides a comprehensive overview of advanced evaluation and recommendation strategies in LLM systems. It begins by examining generation techniques, highlighting how LLMs produce context-aware outputs that drive downstream tasks. Building on this, it introduces multimodal recommendation methods that integrate text, image, and other data modalities to improve personalization and user engagement. To ensure the quality and relevance of these generated and recommended outputs, the chapter explores grading mechanisms, automated assessment techniques powered by LLMs that evaluate retrieval accuracy, coherence, and factuality. These grading strategies form the basis for the emerging paradigm of LLM-as-judge, where the LLM is tasked not only with generating responses but also with ranking and validating them. This interconnected view underscores how generation, recommendation, and grading work in concert to support scalable, trustworthy AI systems.

Implementation of generation

Building upon the foundational concepts introduced in *Chapter 7, Building Bidirectional Multimodal Retrieval Systems*, this section offers an implementation of the generative component by extending our multimodal retrieval pipeline into a full RAG system.

In the preceding chapter, we implemented *Figure 8.1*, a multimodal retrieval system architecture, where retrieval operates seamlessly across text and image modalities. Academically, this approach leverages embeddings, a vector-based representation capturing semantic relationships within data, generated separately for textual and visual content.

The process initiates with user queries, which may consist of text, images, or both. These inputs are passed to specialized embedding models: a text embedding model for textual queries or documents, and an image embedding model for visual inputs. The documents undergo chunking into smaller units to improve the granularity and efficiency of retrieval, whereas images are directly embedded into the vector representation.

Once embeddings are computed, they are stored in a multimodal vector database designed to handle mixed data types. Upon receiving a query, the system performs vector similarity searches across this database, retrieving results based on semantic proximity rather than exact matches. The returned results, combining textual chunks and images, are then provided back to the user.

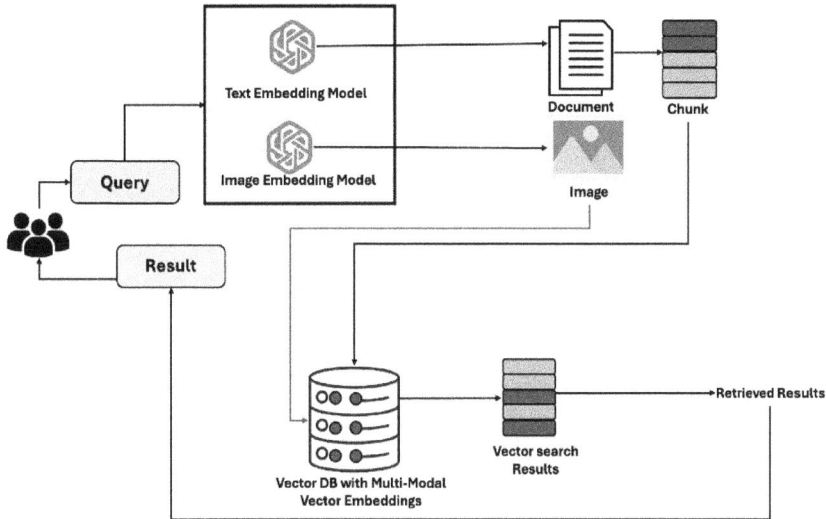

Figure 8.1: *Multimodal retrieval system*

In this chapter, we will implement the generation part of the **generative AI (GenAI)** system as shown in *Figure 8.2*, specifically the portion of the circle. This multimodal RAG pipeline in *Figure 8.2* enables seamless integration of text and image data into a unified semantic search and generation system. The architecture emphasizes modularity and extensibility, making it suitable for a wide range of applications in knowledge retrieval, **visual question answering (VQA)**, and AI-powered document understanding. By utilizing a vector database capable of storing and searching across multiple modalities, the system facilitates richer interaction and more accurate responses, grounded in both textual and visual evidence.

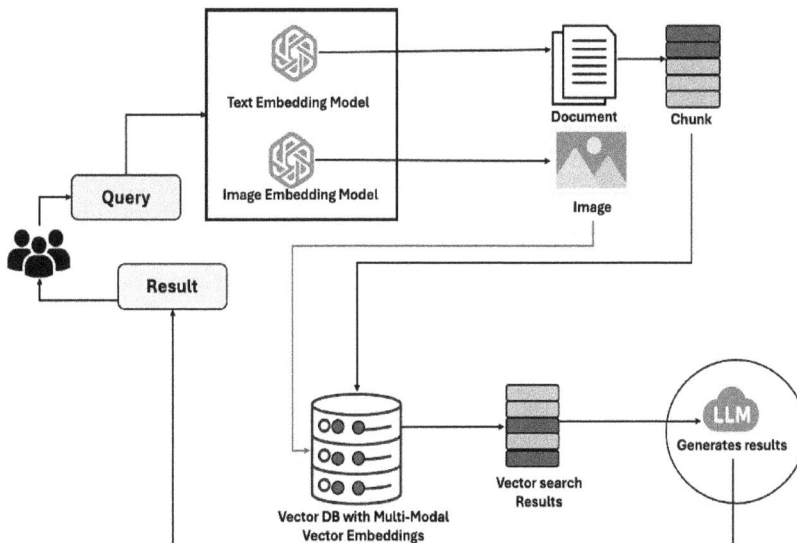

Figure 8.2: *Multimodal RAG system*

Architectural components and workflow

The presented system in *Figure 8.2* outlines a multimodal information retrieval and generation framework that integrates both textual and visual data to support enhanced user interaction. This architecture leverages modality-specific embedding models and a unified vector database to retrieve relevant information, subsequently synthesized into a coherent response by LLM. The design is optimized for applications requiring cross-modal reasoning, such as VQA, document search with image augmentation, or interactive multimodal assistants.

The following section presents a comprehensive end-to-end pipeline for building a multimodal RAG system that seamlessly integrates textual and visual data. Users can submit either text or image queries, which are routed through specialized embedding models to produce unified vector representations. These embeddings are stored in a shared vector database, enabling cross-modal similarity search across both document chunks and image content. Upon retrieval, the top-k relevant results ground the response generation process, powered by a LLM. The final output is a context-rich natural language response reflecting both the query intent and embedded knowledge. The following list outlines all the required modules:

- **User query interface**:
  - Users submit a query, which may be textual or multimodal in nature.
  - This input is routed to the appropriate embedding model depending on the query type.

- **Embedding models**:
  - The system employs two distinct embedding pipelines:
    - A text embedding model, which transforms text-based content (e.g., documents) and text queries into vector representations.
    - An image embedding model, which encodes visual content (e.g., images or screenshots) into a comparable vector space.
  - These embedding models ensure that both documents and images are projected into a unified latent space, enabling cross-modal similarity search.

- **Document and image ingestion**:
  - Documents are first chunked into smaller segments for fine-grained embedding and retrieval.
  - Images are encoded directly without chunking.
  - Both types of content are embedded and stored in a shared vector database capable of handling multimodal vector representations.

- **Vector database with multimodal embeddings**:
  - This database maintains the indexed vector representations of both text and image modalities.

- When a query is embedded, a similarity search retrieves the most relevant entries (text chunks and/or images) from the vector store.

- **Vector search results:**
  - The retrieved results (top-k similar vectors) form the contextual grounding for subsequent generation.
  - This step ensures that only the most semantically relevant documents or images contribute to the final output synthesis.

- **LLM:**
  - An LLM consumes the retrieved context and the original query to generate a comprehensive and context-aware natural language response.
  - The LLM operates on text, but benefits from context that may have originated from either text or image embeddings.

- **Output delivery:**
  - The final response, synthesized by the LLM, is returned to the user.
  - The user receives a context-enriched result that reflects both the query intent and the latent knowledge embedded in the database.

The code of this chapter contains every Python module you need to ingest data, build your indexes, run retrieval, and generate responses. For a detailed understanding of the code blocks, please refer to *Chapter 7, Building a Bidirectional Multimodal Retrieval Systems*, section: *Code implementation and explanation*, a quick checklist is as follows:

- **loaders.py:**
  - **load_pdfs_and_texts()** and **load_images()** to read your raw files

- **embedding_utils.py:**
  - **get_mm_embedder()** wrapping the CLIP-based Hugging Face embedder

- **retriever.py:**
  - **build_vectorstores()** to load, embed, normalize, and upload vectors to Qdrant
  - **retrieve_by_text()**/**retrieve_by_image()** for semantic lookup

- **run_once.py:**
  - One-off script to populate your Qdrant collections before running the app

- **app.py:**
  - Streamlit UI tying everything together

With the retrieval pipeline in place, this section now shifts focus to the generator, which plays a pivotal role in transforming retrieved context into natural language responses. While the rest of the code remains consistent with the earlier setup, the emphasis here is on the **generator. py** module:

- **generator.py**:

  - **init_generator()** and **generate_response()** to wrap an LLM (e.g. GPT-3.5)

This component offers a clean and modular interface for text generation within the RAG workflow, clearly separating model initialization (**init_generator**) from the actual generation logic (**generate_response**). This design promotes reusability, simplifies integration, and aligns well with best practices in prompt engineering and LLM abstraction.

Generator

The rest of the code remains the same; however, the main focus is on the generator part. The **generator.py** module provides a clean and modular interface for text generation in a RAG setup. It separates the model initialization (**init_generator**) from the generation process (**generate_response**), promoting reusability and clarity in design. The architecture aligns with best practices in prompt engineering and model abstraction.

By abstracting the generation logic from retrieval mechanics, the module remains flexible for use across multiple modalities, provided the context can be represented textually. This decoupling is particularly important in multi-agent or multimodal systems where the same generation module can be reused across varied sources of input.

- **Function 1: init_generator()**

  - **Purpose**: This function initializes and returns a LangChain **LLMChain** object for generating responses using an LLM hosted locally via Ollama.

  - **Details**:

    - **ChatOllama** is a LangChain wrapper that enables communication with an Ollama-hosted chat model, such as Llama 3, Mistral, or Llama 2. The **temperature** parameter is set to **0.5**, balancing deterministic and creative outputs.

    - **PromptTemplate** defines a structured prompt that the language model uses to generate its output. This template expects two inputs: query and context.

    - **LLMChain** integrates the prompt with the selected model. It forms an executable unit that can accept inputs and produce corresponding outputs from the model.

  - **Prompt structure**:

    ```
    You are an assistant. Based on the following query and context,
    provide a relevant and coherent answer.
    ```

```
Query: {query}
Context:
{context}
```

Answer:

```
This template is designed to guide the model's behavior by clearly
defining its role (assistant) and the input fields it should consider
before generating an answer. The use of distinct sections for Query
and Context ensures structured input formatting, improving grounding
and coherence in the model's responses.
```

- **Function 2:** `generate_response(llm_chain, query: str, retrieved: list)`

  o **Purpose:** This function uses the pre-initialized language model chain to generate a response by combining a user's query with context derived from a retrieval component.

  o **Details:**

    ▪ The `retrieved list`, which contains context items (such as similar documents or image captions), is concatenated into a single string using newline characters. This aggregated string serves as the contextual input to the model.

    ▪ The `llm_chain.run()` method is called with a dictionary containing the `query` and `context`. LangChain renders the prompt using this input and sends it to the underlying language model for completion.

The end-to-end code can be found in *Chapter 8, Building a Multimodal RAG System*, section: `multimodal_rag_system.py`.

Building on the foundations of multimodal RAG, where LLMs leverage diverse modalities such as text, images, and structured data to enhance information access and synthesis, we now transition to a related yet distinct application: multimodal recommendation systems. While RAG focuses on retrieving and generating contextually rich responses, multimodal recommendation systems use similar cross-modal understanding to predict and suggest relevant content tailored to user preferences. This chapter explores how the same capabilities that empower RAG, embedding alignment, multimodal fusion, and semantic understanding, are adapted to deliver highly personalized, diverse, and context-aware recommendations across industries and platforms.

Multimodal LLM-based recommender system

On an OTT platform, a **multimodal LLM (MLLM)** can revolutionize content recommendation by integrating textual descriptions, promotional images, video thumbnails, user reviews, and viewing history. For instance, if a new user watches trailers with dark cinematography and reads thriller plotlines, the model can infer nuanced genre preferences, such as noir thrillers with psychological elements, despite limited watch history. This enables effective recommendations even in cold-start scenarios, where traditional systems relying on metadata or user similarity may falter. By aligning multimodal signals, LLMs enhance both discovery and engagement, tailoring suggestions to the user's implicit and explicit tastes.

A MLLM can function as a powerful recommendation engine by leveraging its ability to understand and integrate diverse data types—text, images, audio, and even video. Traditional recommendation systems often rely solely on collaborative filtering or structured metadata, which can struggle in cold-start scenarios or fail to capture nuanced user preferences. In contrast, MLLMs extract rich, high-dimensional embeddings from varied content sources and user interactions, enabling more personalized and context-aware recommendations.

For instance, models like CLIP or GPT-4V can understand both product descriptions and visual aesthetics, making them ideal for recommending fashion, home decor, or multimedia content. LLMs can summarize user histories, infer intent from queries, and match them with relevant items across modalities. They also enable explainability, like generating natural language justifications for recommendations, which enhances trust and user satisfaction.

Advanced systems like **MLLMs with Collaborative Filtering Alignment for Enhanced Sequential Recommendation (Molar)**, **LLM-Based Multimodal Recommendation with User History Encoding and Compression (HistLLM)**, and serendipitous MLLM have already demonstrated real-world impact, outperforming conventional approaches in personalization, novelty, and engagement metrics. With hierarchical planning and compressed user histories, these models support scalable and diverse recommendations in real-time. As LLMs continue to evolve, they are poised to become foundational in building next-generation, multimodal recommendation engines across industries.

Emerging architectures such as **LLMs with Graph Augmentation for Recommendation (LLMRec)** expand this paradigm further by embedding LLM-driven reasoning directly into interaction graphs. These systems do not just interpret content, but rather, they actively augment recommendation graphs with inferred relationships, enriched item metadata, and user intent profiles generated by LLMs. By combining LLM capabilities with the structural power of graph-based models, **LLMs for ranking-based recommendation (LlamaRec)** enhance both semantic depth and recommendation accuracy, particularly in sparse data scenarios.

Leading architectures and examples

This section explores leading architectures and recent innovations in multimodal recommendation systems powered by LLMs. It covers models like **Multimodal Recommender System (MMRec)**, Molar, HistLLM, LLMRec, and others that integrate text, image, and behavioral signals to deliver personalized, context-aware, and explainable recommendations. Key design strategies such as multimodal embedding fusion, graph augmentation, history compression, and serendipitous discovery are discussed alongside supporting tools like Ducho 2.0 and ATFLRec (*A Multimodal Recommender System with Audio-Text Fusion and Low-Rank Adaptation via Instruction-Tuned Large Language Model*). The section also outlines a practical implementation roadmap and highlights the advantages of these systems in handling cold-starts, enhancing diversity, and improving engagement. Details are as follows:

- **MMREC**: It extracts embeddings from text and images, unifies them in a shared latent space, and passes them to a deep ranking model. This enables precise, content-aware recommendations and better false-positive control.

- **Molar**: It is designed for sequential recommendation tasks. This model aligns multimodal item embeddings with collaborative filtering signals to personalize content based on evolving user behavior.

- **HistLLM**: It compresses a user's full multimodal interaction history into a single prompt token, enabling faster and more efficient inference with LLMs without losing contextual fidelity.

- **Serendipitous MLLM**: It blends high-level intent detection with hierarchical planning. It delivers recommendations that are novel yet relevant, increasing discovery and user satisfaction.

- **LLMRec**: Augments traditional user-item graphs using LLMs to infer new user interactions, generate rich item attributes, and create textual user profiles. It then applies noise-filtering and feature enhancement techniques to stabilize training and improve robustness across sparse and noisy environments. LLMrec is model-agnostic, meaning it can be integrated with existing **graph neural networks (GNNs)** or **Matrix Factorization (MF)** pipelines.

The following table provides a comparative overview of prominent multimodal recommendation systems, summarizing their core strategies, modalities handled, innovations, cold-start capabilities, system compatibility, and the tools or frameworks used. This comparison highlights the diverse approaches through which LLMs are being integrated with multimodal signals to deliver scalable, personalized, and intelligent recommendation experiences.

Model name	Core strategy	Modality fusion	Key innovation/ strength	Cold-start handling	Compatibility	Tools/ frameworks used
MMREC	Multimodal embedding | deep ranking model.	Text + image	Combines modalities in a shared latent space; strong false-positive control.	Moderate	Deep ranking pipelines.	PyTorch, Transformers, ResNet-50.
Molar	Collaborative filtering alignment with multimodal input.	Text + image + behavior	Aligns item embeddings with user behavior in sequences.	High	Sequential recommender systems.	PyTorch, Hugging Face, **self-attention-based sequential model (SASRec)**.

Model name	Core strategy	Modality fusion	Key innovation/ strength	Cold-start handling	Compatibility	Tools/ frameworks used
HistLLM	History compression using LLM prompt token.	All user interactions	Encodes full user history into a single token for fast inference.	High	LLM-based inference.	OpenAI API, LangChain, Faiss.
Seren-dipitous LLM	Intent modeling with hierarchical planning.	Text + contextual features	Promotes novelty while preserving relevance.	High	Personalized exploration.	Llama, prompt injection, PlannerX.
LLMRec	LLM-driven user graph augmentation + noise-filtering.	Text + graph + attributes	Enhances robust-ness in sparse environments; model-agnostic.	Very high	GNNs, MF hybrid systems.	Neo4j, GraphSAGE, OpenAI, DGL.

Table 8.1: Model comparison overview

MLLM-based recommendation engines represent the next evolution in personalized content delivery. By leveraging the combined strengths of deep multimodal perception and natural language reasoning, these systems offer superior relevance, contextual understanding, and user satisfaction. They are especially useful in handling cold-start scenarios, generating diverse suggestions, and enhancing user engagement through explainable and intuitive recommendations.

Having explored the capabilities and design principles of multimodal recommendation systems, it becomes evident that delivering high-quality suggestions is only one part of the equation. Equally important is the ability to assess, rank, and validate these recommendations in a structured and reliable manner. This brings us to the next critical aspect of intelligent systems: grading. In the following chapter, we shift our focus from generation to evaluation, examining how grading mechanisms, both rule-based and model-driven, can be applied to score responses, rank recommendations, and ensure system outputs meet user expectations and domain-specific standards.

Incorporate grading with OpenAI

As discussed in *Chapter 6, Two and Multi-stage GenAI Systems,* grading plays a critical role in validating and optimizing the output quality of multimodal RAG systems. Without a robust grading mechanism, several issues can compromise system reliability and user trust. First, the absence of quality control may lead to the generation of irrelevant, incoherent, or hallucinated responses, especially when combining diverse modalities like text, images, and video. This degrades user experience and undermines the credibility of recommendations or answers. Second, systems without grading cannot self-assess or improve over time, leading to stagnant or even deteriorating performance as the knowledge base evolves. In safety-critical domains such as healthcare, education, or finance, ungraded outputs can cause misinformation or biased recommendations with serious consequences. Third, the lack of a feedback loop hinders fine-tuning and model alignment efforts, preventing adaptive personalization or performance optimization. Furthermore, the inability to rank candidate outputs weakens multi-candidate selection strategies that could otherwise promote diversity and novelty. Finally, in multi-agent or hybrid RAG setups, where outputs from different retrieval or reasoning modules need to be evaluated for consensus, grading becomes essential for orchestrated decision-making. In summary, grading is not just a post-processing step. It is foundational to ensuring accuracy, trustworthiness, and adaptability in multimodal RAG systems. As shown in *Figure 8.3*, the grading process is situated downstream of the core retrieval and embedding operations and serves as an intelligent evaluation mechanism for both retrieval relevance and generative response quality:

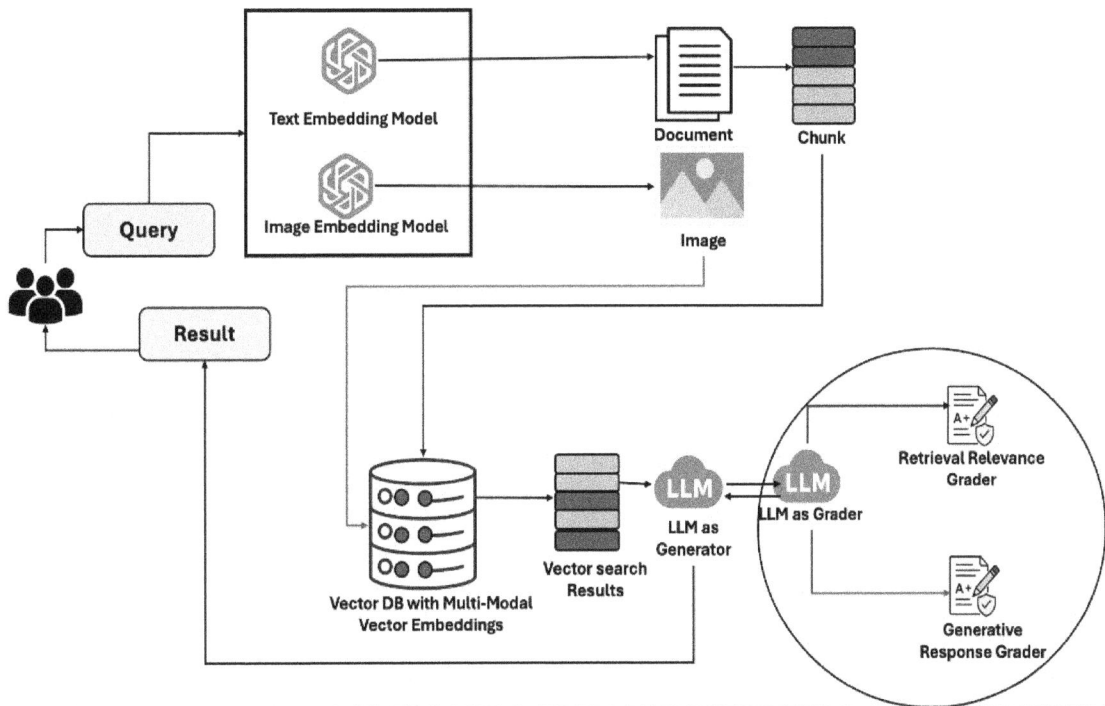

Figure 8.3: Pipeline including grading using a separate LLM

The pipeline begins with a user query, which is simultaneously processed through text and image embedding models. These models generate vector representations of the input, which are then used to query a vector database containing multimodal embeddings derived from both documents and images. Before storage, the documents are segmented into chunks and embedded alongside any associated images to support fine-grained semantic retrieval.

Once the vector database returns a ranked list of relevant results, the grading component is invoked. This component is powered by an LLM operating in a dual role:

- **Retrieval relevance grader**: This module assesses the semantic alignment between the user's query and the retrieved content. It assigns a relevance score to each retrieved item based on contextual fidelity, factual alignment, and task-specific criteria.

- **Generative response grader**: This module evaluates the quality of responses generated based on the retrieved content. It considers factors such as fluency, factual accuracy, informativeness, and user intent alignment.

Together, these grading modules act as a feedback loop, which not only determines which results are presented to the user but also enables fine-tuning of retrieval and generation mechanisms. By leveraging the LLM as a grader, the system ensures that output quality is continually assessed through advanced language understanding capabilities rather than relying on static heuristic rules.

This framework elevates the utility of multimodal RAG systems by integrating intelligent, automated grading, ensuring that users receive the most relevant, high-quality results in both retrieval-based and generative interactions.

The following section provides a breakdown of the components with explanations and embedded code.

Import statements

The script uses LangChain's components for LLMs, prompt templates, and chain orchestration:

```
from langchain.chat_models import ChatOpenAI
from langchain.prompts import PromptTemplate
from langchain.chains import LLMChain
```

These libraries allow integration with OpenAI's GPT models and enable dynamic construction of LLM-based workflows.

Generative responsive grader

This component evaluates how well a generated response answers the user's query based on the retrieved context. It uses a language model to assign a score from one to five, along with a justification, enabling precise assessment of response quality, coherence, and alignment with the original user intent, details as follows:

- **Purpose**: Evaluates how accurately and effectively the generated response answers the query using the given context.

- **Initialization function**:
  ```
  def init_grader():
      llm = ChatOpenAI(temperature=0.3, model="gpt-3.5-turbo")
      prompt = PromptTemplate(
  ```

```
        input_variables=["query", "context", "response"],
        template="""Evaluate the quality of the following generated
response.

Query: {query}
Context: {context}
Response: {response}

Give a score from 1 to 5 and explain why.

Score and Justification:"""
    )
    return LLMChain(llm=llm, prompt=prompt)
```

- o A **ChatOpenAI** model is initialized with a low **temperature=0.3** to ensure relatively deterministic and concise scoring.

- o A **PromptTemplate** defines the input format and instructs the LLM to evaluate a generated response on a scale of one to five, along with justification.

- o The chain returned by LLMChain links the prompt and the LLM for later invocation.

- **Execution function**:

```python
CopyEdit
def grade_response(grader_chain, query: str, context: str, response:
str):
    return grader_chain.run({
        "query": query,
        "context": context,
        "response": response
    })
```

- o This function takes the initialized **grader_chain** and passes a specific query, context, and response to it.

- o It returns a scored evaluation with justification.

Retrieval relevance grader

The following list outlines the purposes, initialization, and execution functions:

- **Purpose**: Assesses whether a retrieved document contains relevant information in relation to the user's query.

- **Initialization function**:

```
def init_retrieval_grader():
```

```
llm = ChatOpenAI(temperature=0, model="gpt-3.5-turbo")
prompt = PromptTemplate(
    input_variables=["question", "document"],
    template="""You are a grader assessing relevance of a retrieved
document to a user question.

If the document contains keyword(s) or semantic meaning related to the
question, grade it as relevant.

Here is the retrieved document:
{document}

Here is the user question:
{question}

Carefully and objectively assess whether the document contains at least
some information that is relevant to the question.

Return a JSON object with a single key, binary_score, that is either
'yes' or 'no'."""
)
return LLMChain(llm=llm, prompt=prompt)
```

- o The **temperature** is set to **0**, ensuring consistent, reproducible binary output (**yes** or **no**).
- o The prompt is more rule-based and structured for objective grading.
- o It expects a JSON output for binary classification.

- **Execution function**:

```
def grade_document_relevance(grader_chain, question: str, document:
str):
    return grader_chain.run({
        "question": question,
        "document": document
    })
```

- o This function executes the grading chain, determining if the document is semantically or topically relevant to the user's question.
- o This module enables plug-and-play evaluation components for any system that uses LLMs for retrieval and generation. It helps ensure:

- Quality control of generated responses, rated on a one to five scale with justification.
- Precision in retrieval, via binary scoring of document relevance.

These graders are crucial for developing intelligent and self-evaluating RAG systems where feedback loops help improve reliability, explainability, and user satisfaction.

Grading and generation models

Grading and generation are fundamentally distinct tasks in natural language systems and therefore require specialized models or chains to achieve optimal performance. Generation involves creating fluent, contextually relevant, and user-aligned responses based on input prompts or retrieved context. It prioritizes creativity, coherence, and intent satisfaction. In contrast, grading is an evaluative task that demands objectivity, consistency, and critical reasoning to assess the quality, correctness, or relevance of a response or retrieved content. Using the same model for both tasks can introduce conflicts: a generative model may exhibit confirmation bias by favoring its own outputs when acting as a grader, thus undermining fairness in evaluation. Additionally, prompts optimized for generation typically encourage verbosity and hypothesis formation, whereas grading prompts require precision, brevity, and analytical rigor. From a systems design perspective, separating these two roles allows task-specific prompt engineering, temperature settings, and scoring criteria. This modularity enhances explainability, enables benchmarking of generation performance, and allows independent updates or model selection per task. As shown in *Figure 8.4*, consequently, using distinct LLMs or chains for grading and generation aligns with best practices in responsible AI system design and ensures more robust, transparent, and accountable recommendations in RAG workflows.

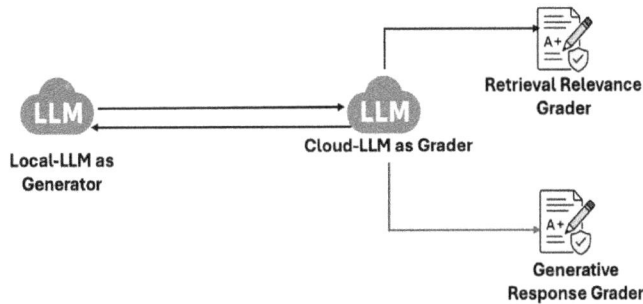

Figure 8.4: Grading with separate LLMs

Cloud LLMs for grading

Grading using cloud-based LLMs offers significant advantages over local deployments, especially in the context of reliability, scalability, and performance. Cloud LLMs, such as OpenAI's GPT-3.5 or GPT-4, benefit from continuous fine-tuning, access to extensive training data, and infrastructure optimizations that are difficult to replicate on-premise. These models are regularly updated to align with the latest linguistic trends, reasoning improvements, and safety filters, resulting in more consistent and accurate evaluations of query-response quality or document relevance. Furthermore, cloud LLMs are typically deployed on high-performance hardware that allows for rapid inference at scale, which is essential for real-time or large-batch grading tasks in production environments. In contrast, local LLMs are often constrained by limited GPU resources and outdated weights, which can degrade grading fidelity. Additionally, implementing version control, bias mitigation, and prompt safety measures on local models requires significant engineering effort. For academic and enterprise systems where robustness and accuracy of evaluation are critical, leveraging cloud-based LLMs as graders ensures higher trustworthiness, up-to-date linguistic knowledge, and greater standardization, making them a superior choice despite cost considerations.

You can find the code in the GitHub repository of *Chapter 8, Building a Multimodal RAG System* under `Chapter_8_multimodal_rag_system_Grader.py`, including grading with local LLM.

By examining *Figure 8.4*, you may begin to recognize an emerging concept known as **LLM-as-a-judge**, and if so, there is an understanding that has been established.

LLM-as-a-judge

LLM-as-a-judge refers to the use of an LLM to evaluate, grade, or rank the outputs of other AI systems, especially in tasks like generation, retrieval, summarization, or reasoning. Instead of using hard-coded rules or human raters, the LLM is prompted to act as an intelligent evaluator.

Figure 8.5 illustrates a best practice architectural pattern where grading and generation are handled by separate LLMs, each optimized for a distinct purpose. A local LLM is used for content generation tasks, ensuring fast, cost-efficient, and offline operation. In parallel, a cloud-hosted LLM acts as an impartial judge, responsible for evaluating both the retrieval relevance and response quality. This separation of roles enables more objective assessment, improves feedback loop integrity, and avoids bias from self-evaluation. The use of cloud LLMs for judgment ensures consistent, high-quality grading aligned with broader semantic understanding, especially for complex or nuanced evaluations required in downstream tasks.

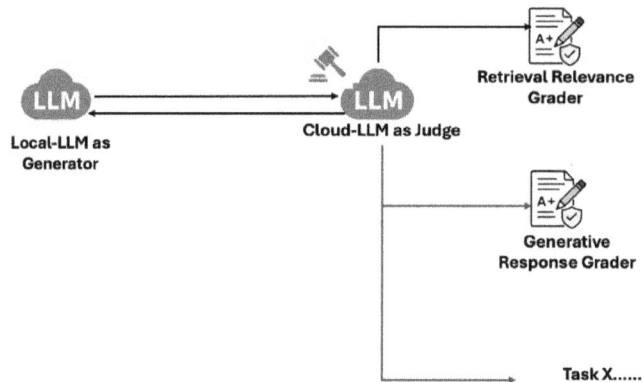

Figure 8.5: LLM-as-a-judge

Rationale and functionality

LLM-as-a-judge operates, as shown in *Figure 8.5,* by prompting a capable LLM (e.g., GPT-4 or GPT-3.5 Turbo) with an explicit rubric, such as relevance, accuracy, clarity, or consistency, and asking it to evaluate or compare outputs based on these criteria. Three common approaches include:

- **Single-output scoring**: The LLM assigns a numeric score (e.g., 1-5) by assessing a single response against rubric criteria, optionally with or without a reference answer.

- **Pairwise comparison**: Given two or more candidate outputs to the same query, the LLM selects the better one. Studies using benchmarks like MT-Bench and Chatbot Arena have demonstrated over 80% agreement between LLM judgments and human evaluations.

- **Reference-based scoring**: The LLM compares generated output to a reference (or retrieved context), increasing score consistency and alignment with human preferences.

The following describes how it is applied to our system.

In our system:

- The response grader evaluates the quality of an LLM-generated answer.

- The retrieval relevance grader judges whether retrieved documents (or captions for images) are relevant to a query.

Both are classic examples of LLMs acting as evaluators, making subjective or semantic judgments using natural language prompts and structured outputs.

To do

The current implementation of the retrieval relevance grader in **grader.py** is limited to evaluating textual content. Specifically, the prompt expects a document, assumed to be a text chunk, and a question, then determines whether the document is relevant to the query based on semantic or keyword overlap. This approach is effective for evaluating text retrieved from a corpus, but does not apply to visual content such as images.

To extend the grading system to support image relevance evaluation, the reader should consider implementing one of the following enhancements:

- **Image captioning as a preprocessing step**: Incorporate an image captioning model (e.g., BLIP, ViT-GPT2, or any Hugging Face-based captioning pipeline) to automatically generate a textual description of each retrieved image. This caption can then be passed as the document variable to the existing relevance grading prompt. This approach enables consistent evaluation logic while remaining within the constraints of text-only LLMs like Llama or GPT-3.5.

- **Multimodal language models for direct image input**: Alternatively, leverage an MLLM such as GPT-4V, LLaVA, or MiniGPT-4 that accepts both images and text as input. These models can directly evaluate the relevance of an image in the context of a query without requiring intermediate captioning. This approach is more powerful but requires appropriate infrastructure and runtime support for multimodal input.

Implementing either of these enhancements would make the relevance grading system more robust and inclusive of multimodal content, aligning it with the broader goals of end-to-end RAG in real-world multimodal AI systems.

Conclusion

In this chapter, readers explored the integration of core components essential for building intelligent, human-aligned AI systems. Starting with generation, the chapter demonstrated how LLMs can produce contextually relevant responses. This was extended into the realm of multimodal recommendation, where text and visual inputs jointly informed retrieval and personalization. Readers also learned how to incorporate grading mechanisms using OpenAI models, enabling automatic, scalable evaluation of both retrieved content and generated outputs. The chapter culminated with the concept of LLM-as-a-judge, emphasizing the role of LLMs in semantically rich, human-aligned evaluation processes.

Having established a strong foundation, the next chapter will extend this architecture by introducing a reranking layer, a critical enhancement that further refines retrieval quality before generation. Readers will understand how rerankers selectively prioritize top candidates based on semantic relevance, factual grounding, or user preferences. This addition plays a vital role in multimodal RAG pipelines, ensuring that the content fed into the LLM for generation is not only relevant but optimally ranked. Through this, we move closer to designing robust, explainable, and high-utility AI systems capable of dynamic reasoning across modalities.

Join our Discord space

Join our Discord workspace for latest updates, offers, tech happenings around the world, new releases, and sessions with the authors:

https://discord.bpbonline.com

CHAPTER 9

Building GenAI Systems with Reranking

Introduction

In an increasingly visual and interconnected digital world, the ability to search and retrieve information across different modalities, such as text and images, has become a cornerstone of advanced **artificial intelligence** (**AI**) applications. This chapter introduces the concept of multimodal retrieval, where systems are designed to understand and correlate both textual and visual inputs. Unlike traditional search engines that rely solely on textual similarity, multimodal systems use vector representations from both images and text to deliver richer, more contextually aligned results. You will learn how to build such a system by integrating Qdrant as a vector database, **Contrastive Language-Image Pretraining** (**CLIP**) models from Hugging Face for generating image embeddings, and LangChain to orchestrate the retrieval process. These tools enable unified access to multiple data formats, allowing users to perform flexible cross-modal searches, such as retrieving descriptions from images or identifying images that match textual inputs.

Throughout the chapter, you will construct dual-index vector stores and develop hybrid retrievers capable of handling diverse query formats. Python-based implementations will guide you through indexing workflows, embedding pipelines, and retrieval logic that switches seamlessly between modalities. Beyond technical architecture, the chapter delves into practical design decisions like similarity scoring, modality prioritization, and custom retrieval logic. By the end, you will have the skills to deploy a production-ready multimodal retriever—a foundation applicable to use cases in e-commerce recommendations, visual content discovery, and semantic search engines. This hands-on approach ensures you not only understand the theory but also gain the ability to implement scalable, real-world solutions.

Structure

In this chapter, we will learn about the following topics:

- Reranking
- Reranking in information retrieval and RAG systems
- Reranking using cross-encoder in multimodal RAG
- Cross-encoder architecture in multimodal settings
- Multi-index embedding in RAG systems
- Code implementation and explanation
- To do

Objectives

This chapter explores reranking in information retrieval and multimodal **retrieval-augmented generation (RAG)** systems. It introduces key reranker categories, with a special focus on cross-encoders for refining retrieved results. Readers will understand the architecture of cross-encoders, multi-index embedding in multimodal contexts, where both images and text are involved, and how these models enhance semantic precision. A practical code walk-through demonstrates how to implement and integrate a cross-encoder-based reranker in a multimodal RAG pipeline. The chapter concludes with a hands-on to do, challenging readers to complete missing components and solidify their understanding through active implementation.

Reranking

Building upon the foundational concepts introduced in *Chapters 1, Introducing New Age generative AI, 6, Two and Multi-stage GenAI Systems,* and *8, Building a Multimodal RAG System,* let us understand *Figure 9.1,* which illustrates a two-stage RAG architecture that incorporates a cross-encoder reranker for enhanced result precision. The workflow begins with a user query that passes through input before proceeding to the retrieval pipeline. Simultaneously, documents in the corpus are chunked and passed through an embedding model, such as a transformer-based encoder, to generate dense vector representations. These are stored in a vector database.

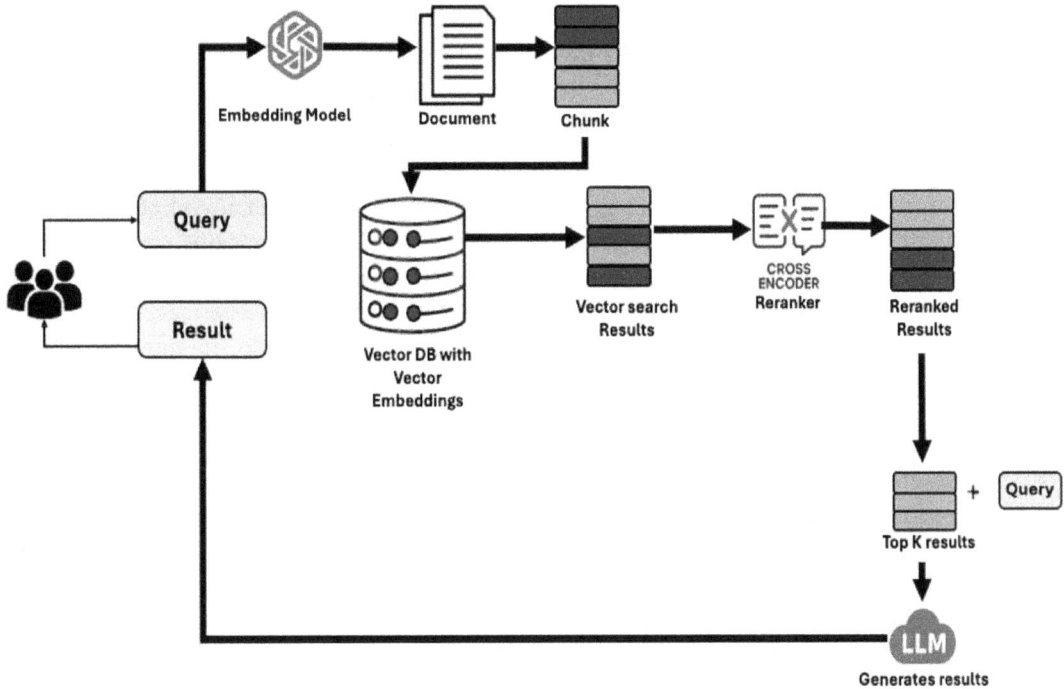

Figure 9.1: Cross-encoder reranking in RAG

At query time, the user query is encoded into a vector and compared against the stored document embeddings using **approximate nearest neighbor** (**ANN**) search, retrieving the top-k most similar candidates. These vector search results are then forwarded to a cross-encoder reranker, which jointly processes the original query and each candidate document to compute fine-grained similarity scores via full token-level interaction. The reranker reorders the results based on semantic relevance, producing a more accurate set of top-k reranked documents.

These reranked documents, along with the original user query, are passed into the **large language model** (**LLM**) for synthesis. The LLM generates the final answer, which is returned to the user. This two-stage design balances scalability (via bi-encoder retrieval) with precision (via cross-encoder reranking), resulting in both efficient and high-quality response generation.

Reranking in information retrieval and RAG systems

Rerankers are pivotal components in both traditional information retrieval systems and modern RAG pipelines. In general information retrieval, rerankers refine an initial list of candidate documents retrieved by a fast, often approximate method. This second-stage reranking is crucial for ensuring that the most semantically or contextually relevant results are surfaced first. With the rise of neural search and large-scale vector databases, rerankers have become even more important as they bridge the gap between high-recall retrieval and high-precision semantic understanding.

In the context of RAG systems, rerankers take on an even more critical role. A typical RAG pipeline involves retrieving passages or documents relevant to a user query and then feeding those to a language model to generate grounded responses. If the retrieved content is only loosely relevant or noisy, the final generation may contain hallucinations or inaccuracies. Rerankers help solve this problem by reordering the retrieved candidates based on a deeper semantic evaluation, often using powerful language models. This ensures that only the most relevant and contextually appropriate passages are forwarded to the generative stage, improving the accuracy and reliability of the system.

The categories of rerankers are as follows:

- **Cross-encoder rerankers**: Cross-encoders represent one of the most precise forms of reranking. In this architecture, the query and each document are concatenated and jointly processed by a transformer-based model such as **Bidirectional Encoder Representations from Transformers (BERT)** or **Text-To-Text Transfer Transformer (T5)**. This allows full token-to-token interaction and deep contextual alignment between the query and the candidate document. As a result, cross-encoders often achieve state-of-the-art performance in semantic search benchmarks. However, this comes at a high computational cost: each query-document pair must be processed individually, making it impractical for large-scale reranking unless the candidate set is already narrowed down.

  Commercial offerings such as *Cohere's Rerank* **application programming interface (API)** exemplify this approach. These services allow developers to submit a query and a list of retrieved documents, returning a rescored and reordered list based on deep semantic matching. Cross-encoder rerankers are ideal when precision is more important than speed or cost, such as in legal search, academic research, or QA systems with relatively small candidate pools.

- **Late interaction rerankers**: Late interaction models, such as ColBERT and its variants, strike a balance between efficiency and precision. Unlike cross-encoders, they pre-encode documents into token-level embeddings and only encode the query at runtime. During reranking, each token in the query is compared with every token in the candidate document embeddings using similarity operations such as MaxSim. This allows token-wise matching while avoiding the need for full joint encoding.

  Late interaction models offer significantly better scalability than cross-encoders and are well-suited for large collections. Variants like ColBERTv2 use advanced techniques such as vector quantization and dimensionality reduction to reduce storage costs while maintaining high retrieval accuracy. Although late interaction models are not as precise as cross-encoders, they often outperform traditional bi-encoders and single vector retrieval approaches in both effectiveness and efficiency.

- **Hybrid reranking approaches**: Hybrid rerankers integrate multiple signals, typically sparse lexical signals like **Best Matching 25 (BM25)** and dense semantic signals from vector models. One common method is score fusion, where relevance scores from different retrieval strategies are combined, either linearly or via algorithms such as **Reciprocal Rank Fusion (RRF)**. Another pattern involves combining ranked lists from multiple sources and using a reranker to determine final ordering.

  A two-stage hybrid approach is especially common in enterprise search and RAG systems. An initial candidate pool is retrieved using a fast lexical or vector-based method, and then a more powerful reranker, often a cross-encoder, is applied to reorder the top-N results. This setup combines the recall strength of the first-stage with the precision of the second, enabling both scalability and semantic depth. In some systems, reranking is even used in a third stage after applying business logic or user-specific constraints.

- **Learning-to-rank models**: Traditional ML methods such as LambdaMART or RankSVM also function as rerankers. These models combine multiple features, like keyword match score, document popularity, recency, or even neural scores, to learn an optimal ranking function. Though less common in modern NLP-centric systems, these models still play a role in hybrid pipelines, especially in production environments where performance tuning is critical.

- **LLM-based rerankers**: A recent development is the use of LLMs for reranking. These can be either fine-tuned models (like T5 or GPT variants trained on relevance tasks) or zero-shot prompting approaches where an LLM is given a query and a list of passages and asked to rank them. This offers high flexibility and interpretability, allowing reranking based on complex or dynamic criteria. However, the cost and latency of LLM-based reranking make them best suited for small-scale or high-value applications.

Reranking in RAG pipelines

In RAG pipelines, reranking significantly improves the quality of document retrieval before generation. For example, a vector search might retrieve fifty documents based on cosine similarity, but the top-ranked ones might not always be the most relevant. A reranker, whether a cross-encoder or late interaction model, can reorder these candidates, ensuring that only the most relevant ones are passed into the LLM's context window. This not only improves generation accuracy but also reduces hallucinations by grounding the output in semantically aligned information.

Rerankers thus serve as a semantic filter in RAG, compressing and distilling the document pool into a focused, high-precision context for generation. Many modern RAG implementations, including those in LangChain and LlamaIndex, now include reranking as a built-in or optional module. Vector databases like *Qdrant*, *Weaviate*, and *Pinecone* also support over-fetching and reranking workflows, allowing developers to easily combine fast retrieval with accurate semantic sorting.

Reranking using cross-encoder in multimodal RAG

In multimodal RAG systems, retrieval fidelity is critical to ensure the relevance and alignment of retrieved context with the input query, be it text, image, or a combination of modalities. While initial retrieval is often handled by bi-encoders or dual encoders for computational scalability, the coarse similarity scores produced at this stage may lack fine-grained semantic alignment. This introduces the need for an intermediate reranking stage, which evaluates candidate documents with greater expressiveness and precision.

One of the most effective reranking strategies involves the use of cross-encoders, which are models that jointly encode both the query and each candidate document to compute a more accurate relevance score. In contrast to bi-encoders, where embeddings for queries and documents are computed independently and compared using cosine or dot product similarity, cross-encoders perform full token-level interaction between the two inputs. This design allows for rich cross-attention mechanisms and deeper semantic reasoning, resulting in higher-quality rankings.

Cross-encoder architecture in multimodal settings

In a multimodal RAG context, where either the query or documents (or both) may consist of text and image pairs, a cross-encoder must be capable of fusing visual and textual inputs. This is typically achieved through **vision-language models** (**VLMs**) such as CLIP, **Bootstrapping Language-Image Pre-training** (**BLIP**), Flamingo, or newer transformer-based architectures like GIT, OFA, or Qwen-VL. These models encode image and text jointly, enabling the model to reason over multimodal inputs.

For reranking, a common pipeline involves:

- **Stage 1-initial retrieval (bi-encoder)**: A fast dense retriever fetches the top-k documents/images using ANN search on vector embeddings.

- **Stage 2-cross-encoder reranking**: For each retrieved candidate, the query and candidate are fed together into a cross-encoder. The model computes a relevance score based on joint attention between query and candidate tokens across modalities.

- **Stage 3-top-N selection**: Candidates are ranked using cross-encoder scores, and the top-N (where $N < k$) are passed to the generator.

Cross-encoders vs. late interaction rerankers

While late interaction models like ColBERT, ColPali, and ColQwen also provide token-level scoring, they maintain independent encoding of query and document tokens, deferring fine-grained comparison to the scoring stage. In contrast, cross-encoders process both sequences simultaneously, enabling global token-to-token interactions via cross-attention layers. This makes cross-encoders more expressive but computationally expensive, as they must encode each query-document pair individually.

Table 9.1 compares three common architectures used for retrieval and reranking in RAG systems: bi-encoders, late interaction models, and cross-encoders. Each approach offers a different trade-off between scalability and accuracy, based on how query-document pairs are encoded and compared. Bi-encoders prioritize speed and scalability by independently encoding inputs, making them ideal for large-scale first-stage retrieval. Late interaction models introduce token-level comparisons post-encoding, striking a balance between performance and cost. Cross-encoders, though computationally intensive, deliver the highest accuracy by jointly encoding and deeply interacting with both inputs, making them the preferred choice for precision reranking over small candidate sets.

Feature	Bi-encoder	Late interaction	Cross-encoder
Encoding	Independent	Independent	Joint
Interaction	None	Token-level (post-encode)	Full (within encoder)
Scalability	High	Moderate	Low
Accuracy	Moderate	High	Highest
Use case in RAG	First-stage retriever	Light-weight reranker	Precision reranker (small N)

Table 9.1: *Comparison of architectures for retrieval and reranking in RAG systems*

Applications in multimodal retrieval

In multimodal use cases, such as product search, medical imaging, **visual question answering** (**VQA**), and interactive assistants, a query might consist of a question paired with an image, or the system might retrieve relevant text from a document corpus using an image as the input. Cross-encoders play a vital role in these setups by ensuring that retrieved documents exhibit semantic and modality-aware alignment with the query. For example, when a user submits an image of a laptop with a query, *which model has HDMI and USB-C?* A cross-encoder can jointly attend to both the image and product descriptions to rerank the most relevant matches.

Despite their accuracy, cross-encoders are computationally expensive, especially in multimodal scenarios where images require high-dimensional encoding and preprocessing. Several strategies are adopted to mitigate the following:

- Use of cross-encoders only on top-k candidates retrieved by bi-encoders.
- Model distillation, where a lightweight model is trained to approximate cross-encoder scores.
- Caching relevance scores for frequently asked queries or popular items.

- Query-aware pruning, where only documents with overlapping metadata are passed to the cross-encoder.

In multimodal RAG systems, cross-encoder-based reranking acts as a high-precision filter, refining coarse retrieval outputs before they are passed to the language model for generation. By allowing full interaction between query and candidate tokens, including across image and text inputs, cross-encoders significantly enhance semantic matching. Although computationally heavier than other reranking approaches, their deployment on a small number of candidates makes them feasible and valuable for improving retrieval quality in real-world applications.

Commercial reranker

Several technology providers now offer hosted reranking solutions that can be easily integrated into search or RAG pipelines without the need for developing and maintaining in-house models. Among the most prominent is Cohere's Rerank API, a powerful transformer-based cross-encoder that takes a query along with a list of candidate documents and returns them reordered by semantic relevance, each with an associated confidence score. This model processes the query and each document jointly, enabling deep contextual understanding and precise matching. The latest versions of the service support long documents, multilingual capabilities, and various content types, including code and semi-structured data, while maintaining improved latency and efficiency compared to earlier releases.

Other cloud providers offer similar reranking capabilities. Microsoft's Azure Cognitive Search includes a semantic reranking feature that enhances the relevance of top-k results using transformer-based models from the Turing series. This semantic reranking can optionally generate highlights and explanations for the ranked results, making it suitable for enterprise search applications.

Amazon provides multiple reranking options through services like Amazon Kendra and Amazon Bedrock. Bedrock users can access hosted rerankers such as Cohere's API directly within the **Amazon Web Services** (**AWS**) ecosystem, enabling high-accuracy semantic reranking on top of existing vector or keyword search outputs.

Open-source ecosystems also support integration with hosted rerankers. For example, *OpenSearch* and *Elasticsearch* can be configured to use external APIs as second-stage rerankers. Some open-source tools, such as *Answer.AI*'s reranker library, provide unified Python interfaces to a variety of reranking models, allowing developers to plug in alternatives like cross-encoders or late interaction models with minimal effort. These integrations make it feasible to upgrade standard search pipelines with sophisticated neural reranking models that significantly improve final result quality.

Recap of cross-encoder

A cross-encoder, as explained in *Figure 9.2* and *Chapter 1, Introducing New Age Generative AI*, is a neural model architecture commonly used in tasks requiring fine-grained interaction between a pair of inputs, most notably in semantic similarity, ranking, and QA. It is distinguished from bi-encoders by the fact that it processes both the query and the candidate (e.g., document) jointly, allowing token-level cross-attention throughout the entire transformer stack.

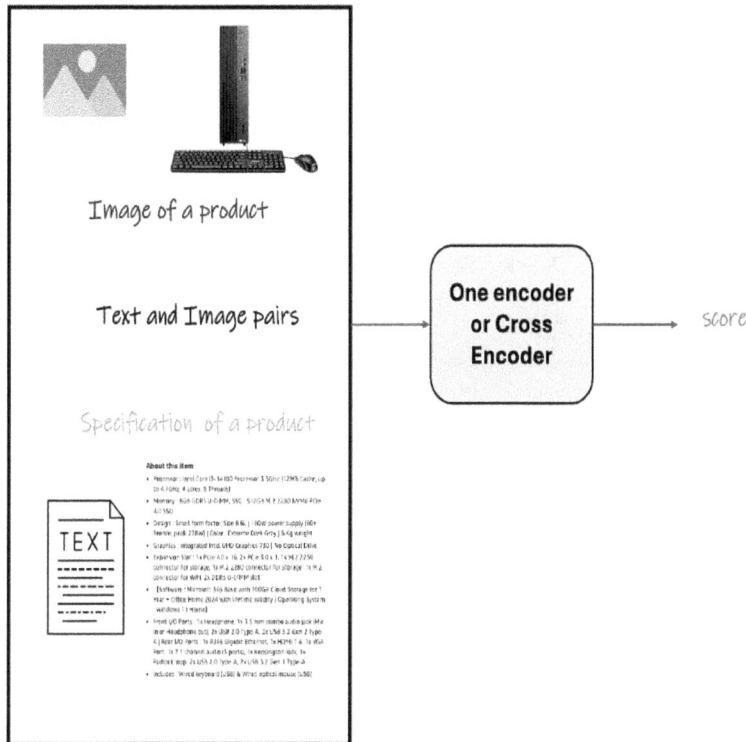

Figure 9.2: Cross-encoder

Cross-encoders and their role in embedding

In the context of retrieval systems and RAG architectures, it is essential to distinguish between bi-encoders and cross-encoders, particularly regarding their embedding capabilities and indexing functionality.

A cross-encoder is a model architecture that jointly processes a pair of inputs, typically a query and a candidate [e.g., (query, document) or (query, image) pair]. Unlike bi-encoders, which generate standalone embeddings for queries and documents independently, cross-encoders do not produce reusable, indexable embeddings. Instead, they compute a single relevance score (e.g., a similarity logit) by encoding both inputs together through a shared transformer model. This score quantifies how well the query matches the candidate, but it does not result in a persistent vector representation of either input.

As a result, cross-encoders are not suitable for indexing. They do not generate vector representations that can be stored in vector databases (e.g., **Facebook AI Similarity Search**

(**Faiss**), Qdrant, ChromaDB) or used for nearest neighbor search. Instead, they are employed in reranking scenarios, where a small set of candidates (retrieved via bi-encoders or keyword search) is rescored for finer semantic accuracy.

To understand the practical differences between encoder architectures, it is useful to examine their support for indexable embeddings and how that impacts their role in retrieval workflows. While bi-encoders generate reusable vector representations suitable for large-scale search, cross-encoders operate directly on query-document pairs, enabling high-accuracy semantic reranking without producing standalone embeddings. This fundamental architectural difference is summarized in the following table:

Encoder type	Indexable embeddings	Primary use
Bi-encoder	Yes	Vector search and retrieval
Cross-encoder	No	Semantic reranking

Table 9.2: Comparison of bi-encoder and cross-encoder architectures

So, cross-encoders are optimized for scoring, not storage. Their reliance on joint input encoding precludes them from producing detached query or document vectors. Therefore, in RAG systems, they serve a complementary role to bi-encoders by enhancing precision during the reranking stage, but not during the initial retrieval or indexing phases.

In RAG systems, multi-index embedding enables modular and modality-aware information retrieval by maintaining separate vector indexes for different data types such as text, images, or code. Each index is constructed using embeddings generated from modality-specific models, facilitating precise retrieval tailored to the nature of the query. This strategy is particularly effective in multimodal applications, allowing for flexible routing and hybrid retrieval from diverse sources. In contrast, cross-encoders do not generate indexable embeddings. Instead, they process a query and candidate pair jointly and output a single scalar relevance score. This score reflects semantic alignment but cannot be reused or stored for vector-based search. As a result, cross-encoders are exclusively applied in the reranking phase, where a small set of candidates retrieved via multi-index embeddings are re-evaluated for final selection. Together, these approaches offer a robust architecture: multi-index embeddings ensure breadth and modality coverage, while cross-encoders enhance semantic precision at the final step of the pipeline. So cross cross-encoders do not create multi-index embeddings. Let us understand what a multi-index embedding is.

Multi-index embedding in RAG systems

Multi-index embedding refers to the construction and utilization of multiple vector indexes within RAG architectures. This approach enables systems to retrieve semantically relevant information from heterogeneous data sources, improving the precision, contextual alignment, and multimodal reasoning capabilities of the generative model. To build an understanding, refer to the following list:

- **Definition and rationale**: In traditional RAG systems, a single vector index is employed to encode and retrieve data. However, this approach often lacks flexibility when dealing with diverse data modalities (e.g., textual specifications, images, structured tables, or code). Multi-index embedding addresses this limitation by maintaining multiple semantically specialized vector stores, each tailored to a particular modality, domain, or embedding model.

- **Applications and benefits**:

    o **Modality-specific retrieval**: Separate indexes can be constructed for textual documents (using models like text-embedding-3-large), images (e.g., via CLIP), and code (e.g., via CodeBERT), allowing targeted retrieval from each modality.

    o **Model optimization**: Indexes can leverage different embedding models optimized for their respective content types, thereby enhancing retrieval accuracy.

    o **Flexible query routing**: During inference, queries may be directed to relevant indexes either independently or in parallel, with results aggregated and optionally reranked.

    o **Improved interpretability**: The use of multiple indexes allows fine-grained analysis of retrieved sources, aiding in explainability and validation of outputs.

- **System workflow**:

    o **Index construction**: Multiple embedding pipelines are used to construct indexes for distinct data sources or modalities.

    o **Query processing**: A user query is embedded and routed to one or more indexes based on modality relevance or pre-defined rules.

    o **Aggregation and reranking**: Retrieved documents from each index are merged and optionally reranked using a cross-encoder or scoring mechanism to improve relevance.

    o **Answer generation**: The top-ranked documents are passed to the language model for synthesis into a natural language response.

    Multi-index embedding introduces modularity and precision into RAG systems by allowing differentiated treatment of diverse content types. It supports hybrid and multimodal retrieval strategies, which are essential for developing robust AI systems capable of reasoning across varied data landscapes.

- **Technical architecture**: At the core, a cross-encoder is based on transformer models (e.g., BERT, RoBERTa, DeBERTa). Unlike bi-encoders, which compute embeddings for each input independently, a cross-encoder concatenates the inputs and feeds them together into a shared transformer.

- **Input formatting**: The input is formatted as a single sequence:

  `[CLS] Query tokens [SEP] Document tokens [SEP]`

  The transformer processes this sequence, and the output is typically taken from the `[CLS]` token, which aggregates the contextualized representation of the entire input.

- **Mathematical explanation**: Let the following be:

  - $Q = \{q_1, q_2, ..., q\_m\}$ be the tokenized query
  - $D = \{d_1, d_2, ..., d\_n\}$ be the tokenized document
  - Let $T = [CLS], q_1, ..., q\_m, [SEP], d_1, ..., d\_n, [SEP]$ be the combined input sequence
  - Let $H^0 \in \mathbb{R}^{\{(m+n+3)\times d\}}$, be the initial embedding matrix of the input tokens (where d is the hidden dimension), derived via word embeddings and positional encodings.

  At each transformer layer l, the representation is updated as:

  $$H^{\{l\}} = TransformerLayer(H^{\{l-1\}})$$

  Where *TransformerLayer* applies multi-head self-attention across all tokens in Q and D together, allowing for full cross-interaction.

  At the final layer l, a pooling strategy is used:

  Often, the final output vector $z \in \mathbb{R}^d$ is the representation of the `[CLS]` token, denoted $z = H^L\_0$

  This vector is passed to a scoring head (e.g., a feed-forward layer followed by a sigmoid or softmax) to predict:

    - A similarity score
    - A binary label (relevant / not relevant)

Example: Relevance scoring

The final output score s between a query Q and document D may be computed as:

$s = sigmoid\ (w^T z + b)$ Where:

- $z \in R^d$ is the embedding
- $w \in R^d,\quad b \in R$ are learned parameters

In training, this score can be supervised using binary labels (relevant or not), using loss functions such as:

- **Binary cross-entropy** (**BCE**) for pointwise ranking.
- Hinge loss or pairwise ranking loss for pairwise training.

Cross-encoders form the second-stage in many retrieval systems (like two-stage RAG), where a bi-encoder or vector search retrieves candidate documents and a cross-encoder refines the ranking based on semantic richness. Their computational cost is justified by their high fidelity in relevance modeling.

Code implementation and explanation

The following code implements a modular Multimodal RAG pipeline to retrieve and generate laptop specifications based on image, text, or hybrid inputs. Leveraging CLIP-based image-text embeddings, ChromaDB for vector search, and an Ollama-based LLM for generation, the system offers multiple query modes: image-only, text-only, image + text, and generative answer completion.

This section outlines the full architecture and implementation details of a modular, multimodal assistant system built using a RAG pipeline. It begins with centralized configuration management in **config.py** and moves through CLIP-based embedding functions, data loaders, and ChromaDB-based index creation for both text and image content. It supports multiple retrieval modes and enables vector fusion for joint queries. To enhance precision, a cross-encoder-based reranker is applied before the final output. The system also integrates Ollama-based text generation and a Streamlit UI offering four interactive modes. Together, these components demonstrate a scalable and extensible RAG implementation for real-world multimodal search and question answering, details as follows:

- **Configuration management**: The configuration file config.py centralizes key parameters for maintainability and reuse. This includes ChromaDB directories, model names, and folder paths for images and texts:

```
CHROMA_PERSIST_DIR = "chromadb_storage"
CHROMA_IMAGE_COLLECTION = "laptop_images"
CHROMA_TEXT_COLLECTION = "laptop_texts"
IMAGE_FOLDER = "data/images"
TEXT_FOLDER = "data/documents"
EMBED_MODEL_NAME = "clip"
MODEL_NAME = "llama3"
```

- **Embedding functions using CLIP**: **embedding_utils.py** defines reusable functions to embed text and image inputs using the CLIP model. The CLIP processor and model are initialized once globally to avoid redundant loading:

```
clip_model = CLIPModel.from_pretrained("openai/clip-vit-base-patch32")
clip_processor = CLIPProcessor.from_pretrained("openai/clip-vit-base-patch32")
```

Embedding is handled by:
```
def embed_text_ollama(text):
    inputs = clip_processor(text=[text], return_tensors="pt",
```

```
        padding=True, truncation=True)
        ...
        return outputs[0].tolist()
def embed_image_ollama(image_path):
    image = Image.open(image_path).convert("RGB")
        ...
        return outputs[0].tolist()
```

These functions produce vector representations used for retrieval in the ChromaDB vector store.

- **Data loaders for indexing**: The `loaders.py` module defines utility functions for reading **.txt** files and loading **.jpg**/**.png** image paths:

```
def load_text_documents(folder):
        ...
        return docs
python
CopyEdit
def load_image_paths(folder):
        ...
        return [os.path.join(folder, f) ...]
```

- **Index building with ChromaDB**: The `index_builder.py` script populates ChromaDB with embeddings and metadata for both text documents and images. It creates or recreates two separate collections:

```
text_collection = client.create_collection(name=CHROMA_TEXT_COLLECTION)
image_collection = client.create_collection(name=CHROMA_IMAGE_
COLLECTION)
Each item is embedded and added using:
text_collection.add(documents=[content], embeddings=[emb],
ids=[str(idx)], metadatas=[{"file": fname}])
image_collection.add(documents=[""], embeddings=[emb], ids=[str(idx)],
metadatas=[{"file": os.path.basename(path)}])
This step is orchestrated via run_once.py:
from rag.index_builder import build_index
if __name__ == "__main__":
    build_index()
```

Our code is performing multi-index vector creation. two separate indexes, one for text and one for images, within ChromaDB:

- In **index_builder.py**, the system creates:

    o **CHROMA_TEXT_COLLECTION**: An index for text documents, using **embed_text_ollama** to convert each document into a vector representation.

- o **CHROMA_IMAGE_COLLECTION**: an index for image files, using **embed_image_ollama** to embed each image.

- These two collections are distinct and modality-specific:

  - o One is used for text-based embeddings.

  - o The other is for image-based embeddings.

  - o In **app.py**, the assistant queries these indexes separately, depending on the user's selected mode (e.g., text-only query, image-only query, or combined input).

  - o The system creates and maintains two separate vector indexes—one for text and one for images—each tailored to a specific modality. Depending on the user's input (text, image, or both), the system selects and queries the appropriate index (or fuses them), enabling flexible, modality-aware retrieval.

    Note: **You can create a single long vector by combining multiple embeddings (e.g., image + text), and our code already does this in the image + text → specs mode:**

    ```
    joint_vec = [(i + j) / 2 for i, j in zip(image_vec, text_vec)]
    ```

    This is a simple average fusion of two same-length vectors.

- **Other options for one long vector**:

  - o If you want to create a **single concatenated vector**, you can do:

    ```
    joint_vec = image_vec + text_vec  # results in a longer vector
    (e.g., 1024 if each is 512)
    ```

  - o This is called **vector concatenation**, and is valid if:

    - ▪ Your vector database (like ChromaDB) supports higher dimensions.

    - ▪ You use the same strategy during both indexing and query time.

- **Cross-encoder reranking**: The reranker.py module introduces a **CrossEncoder** model for reranking retrieved documents:

  ```
  cross_encoder = CrossEncoder('cross-encoder/ms-marco-MiniLM-L-6-v2')
  ```

  Given a query and candidate metadata, the reranker scores and ranks results based on semantic similarity:

  ```
  def rerank(query, metadatas):
      pairs = [(query, doc.get("file", "")) for doc in metadatas]
      ...
      return [doc for doc, _ in ranked]
  ```

  This improves the precision of top results returned by ChromaDB.

- **Language generation with Ollama**: The new **generation.py** module introduces a callable method to invoke an Ollama LLM with a fixed temperature setting:

```
def get_llm():
    return Ollama(model=MODEL_NAME, temperature=0.2)
```

This is useful for generating human-readable specifications or summaries beyond simple retrieval.

- **Streamlit-based user interface**: The **app.py** module presents a user-friendly frontend using Streamlit. The assistant offers four modes:

  o **Image to specs**: Embeds image, retrieves similar images, and fetches associated specs.

  o **Image + text to specs**: Averages text and image vectors, retrieves and reranks.

  o **Text-to-image + specs**: Pure text query, retrieves the spec document and matches with image.

  o **Text to generated answer**: Sends the query to the LLM for a generative response:

```
if mode == "Text → Generated Answer":
    query = st.text_input("Ask something about laptops")
    if query:
        llm = get_llm()
        response = llm.invoke(query)
        st.text_area("LLM Response", response, height=300)
```

Each mode interacts with the respective ChromaDB collection and performs reranking to ensure the most relevant response is shown.

This modular, multimodal assistant system exemplifies a real-world implementation of a RAG pipeline. By cleanly separating configuration, embedding, retrieval, reranking, and generation, the system remains highly extensible and easily maintainable. Future enhancements may include document summarization, multilingual support, or a memory mechanism for chat-based interaction.

To do

While the current implementation establishes a robust multimodal retrieval pipeline, it is important to recognize that it does not yet support generative outputs.

In the current state of the project, two key items are intentionally left incomplete to encourage hands-on practice and deeper understanding.

- **generation.py**: Your task is to implement the generation module.

  At this point, the **rag/** folder does not yet include a fully functional **generation.py**.

Your task is to create this module based on the intended functionality:

- ○ This module will use the Ollama language model (via LangChain) to generate natural language responses from user queries.

- ○ You should import the model name from **config.py**, initialize the LLM using **langchain_community.llms.Ollama**, and define a **get_llm()** method.

- ○ Once completed, this module will enable the **Text** → **Generated Answer** mode in **app.py**.

   Note: **This addition will allow your multimodal RAG assistant to not only retrieve specs but also generate fluent explanations or summaries of laptop features.**

- **run_once.py**: Your task is to move and use this script properly.

   The file **run_once.py**, which builds your ChromaDB index from all available laptop images and specification documents, should be moved into the **scripts/** folder (if not already).

   - ○ This organization improves modularity and keeps utility scripts separate from core logic.

   - ○ Make sure you can still run it correctly using:

      ```
      python -m scripts.run_once
      ```

      Once **run_once.py** is in place and **generation.py** is implemented, your full multimodal RAG system will be complete and production-ready.

Setup instructions

Here are the complete setup instructions to get your multimodal RAG system with generation up and running from scratch:

1. **Environment requirements**: Ensure that you are using:

   a. Python 3.9 or later

   b. Pip or conda

   c. Internet access (to download models)

2. **Directory structure**: Setup your folder like shown in the following figure:

```
multimodal_rag_demo/
├── chromadb_storage/
│   └── ...
├── data/
│   ├── images/
│   │   └── <laptop>.jpg
│   ├── documents/
│   │   └── <laptop>.txt
│   └── temp_image.jpg
├── frontend/
│   ├── __init__.py
│   └── app.py
├── rag/
│   ├── __init__.py
│   ├── config.py
│   ├── embedding_utils.py
│   ├── index_builder.py
│   ├── reranker.py
│   ├── loaders.py
│   └── generation.py        ☑ Add this
├── scripts/
│   └── run_once.py          ☑ Suggested move
├── requirements.txt
├── README.md
```

Figure 9.3: *Final folder structure*

3. **Install dependencies**: Create a virtual environment and install required packages:

```
python -m venv venv
source venv/bin/activate  # On Windows: venv\Scripts\activate

pip install --upgrade pip
pip install streamlit torch torchvision transformers sentence-
transformers chromadb langchain
```

4. **Download pretrained models (Optional: First time only)**:

   a. Your first run will download:

      i. **openai/clip-vit-base-patch32 for image/text embedding**

      ii. **cross-encoder/ms-marco-MiniLM-L-6-v2 for reranking**

      Make sure you have a stable internet connection.

5. **Prepare your data**: Place your **.txt** spec documents and **.jpg** laptop images in:
```
data/documents/
data/images/
```

a. Ensure the text and image filenames correspond (e.g., **dell_inspiron.jpg** and **dell_inspiron.txt**).

b. **Build index (Initial)**: Run once to create ChromaDB collections:

```
python run_once.py
```

This embeds all text and images into Chroma and stores them persistently.

c. **Launch the app**: Start the Streamlit app:

```
streamlit run app.py
```

Access in your browser at: **http://localhost:8501/**

d. **Requirements.txt (Optional)**:

```
streamlit
torch
transformers
sentence-transformers
chromadb
langchain
Pillow
```

e. Then, run the following commands:

```
bash
CopyEdit
pip install -r requirements.txt
```

Conclusion

In this chapter, you explored the role of reranking in enhancing information retrieval within multimodal RAG systems. By categorizing rerankers and focusing on the powerful cross-encoder approach, you learned how to improve the quality of results retrieved from both textual and visual data. You examined the architecture and logic behind cross-encoders in multimodal contexts and implemented a working reranker to refine image-text retrieval pipelines. To solidify your understanding, a set of practical to dos challenged you to fill in missing code and structure. In the next chapter, we will explore various retrieval optimization techniques.

Join our Discord space

Join our Discord workspace for latest updates, offers, tech happenings around the world, new releases, and sessions with the authors:

https://discord.bpbonline.com

CHAPTER 10

Retrieval Optimization for Multimodal GenAI

Introduction

Effective retrieval optimization is critical to building robust and responsive **generative AI (GenAI)** systems, particularly in multimodal and **retrieval-augmented generation (RAG)** scenarios. In practical deployments, merely embedding and retrieving data is insufficient; optimizing the retrieval pipeline significantly impacts the accuracy, efficiency, and relevance of generated responses.

In this chapter, we systematically explore key retrieval optimization techniques such as multi-index embedding, modality-based routing, and hybrid retrieval. We not only define each method conceptually but also provide clear, executable Python code examples that illustrate their implementation and practical utility. By applying techniques like query expansion, embedding normalization, and adaptive index refresh, readers will learn to enhance system recall, precision, adaptability, and critical attributes in production-level GenAI systems.

The importance of this chapter lies in its detailed, hands-on approach to improving retrieval effectiveness, a foundational capability for any robust GenAI pipeline. Through optimization, retrieval components can significantly elevate a system's ability to provide contextually accurate, timely, and meaningful responses, thereby directly influencing the user experience and trustworthiness of AI outputs.

Structure

In this chapter, we will learn about the following topics:

- Retrieval optimization techniques
- Drawbacks retrieval systems
- Retrieval optimization techniques mitigating the limitations
- Enhancing multimodal RAG with adaptive refresh
- To do

Objectives

The objective of this chapter is to equip readers with a comprehensive understanding of retrieval optimization techniques essential for building high-performance information retrieval systems. Focusing on strategies like modality-based routing, query expansion, hybrid retrieval, and cross-encoder reranking, the chapter aims to enhance both recall and precision in search tasks. Readers will learn how to implement these techniques through practical code examples, enabling them to build retrieval pipelines that are accurate, adaptive, and efficient. These skills are crucial for improving the foundational retrieval layer of modern AI systems, particularly in multimodal and RAG workflows.

Retrieval optimization techniques

We have already implemented reranking using cross-encoders and multi-index embedding. In this chapter, we now turn our attention to exploring additional retrieval optimization techniques that further improve relevance, efficiency, and multimodal adaptability.

At query time, the user query is encoded into a vector and compared against the stored document embeddings using **approximate nearest neighbor** (**ANN**) search, retrieving the top-k most similar candidates. These vector search results are then forwarded to a cross-encoder reranker, which jointly processes the original query and each candidate document to compute fine-grained similarity scores via full token-level interaction. The reranker reorders the results based on semantic relevance, producing a more accurate set of top-k reranked documents.

These reranked documents, along with the original user query, are passed into the **large language model** (**LLM**) for synthesis. The LLM generates the final answer, which is returned to the user. This two-stage design balances scalability (via bi-encoder retrieval) with precision (via cross-encoder reranking), resulting in both efficient and high-quality response generation.

Drawbacks retrieval systems

Retrieval systems in multimodal RAG face several critical drawbacks that limit their effectiveness in real-world applications. First, traditional retrieval pipelines often treat modalities independently, leading to suboptimal fusion of textual and visual information. They also rely heavily on static embeddings, which can fail to capture evolving user intent or contextual nuances. Cross-modal relevance scoring is another challenge, often resulting in irrelevant or mismatched outputs. Furthermore, latency increases significantly when dealing with large-scale, multimodal datasets.

Refer to the following list to understand the limitations that hinder both the accuracy and efficiency of multimodal RAG systems, necessitating more adaptive, intelligent, and unified retrieval mechanisms for future advancements:

- **Poor recall vs. precision trade-offs**: A fundamental limitation in information retrieval is the inverse relationship between recall and precision. Systems tuned for high recall often retrieve many items (ensuring fewer relevant documents are missed) at the cost of including more irrelevant results (lower precision), whereas tuning for precision returns only highly relevant hits but risks missing some answers. For example, a semantic embedding search might catch conceptually related documents (improving recall) but also pull in tangential content, whereas a strict keyword search might return only exact matches (high precision) while overlooking paraphrased answers. Balancing this trade-off is challenging, and no single setting optimizes both metrics simultaneously for all queries. As a result, retrieval systems must compromise between completeness and accuracy of results.

- **Limited semantic understanding**: Traditional text search engines rely on lexical matching and lack deep semantic comprehension of queries and documents. They treat queries as bags of words, so if a user's phrasing does not exactly match the wording, relevant documents can be missed. This leads to poor recall in cases where synonyms or contextually related terms are used (e.g., a query about financial earnings might not retrieve a document mentioning quarterly revenue without semantic modelling). Even dense vector retrieval models, while better at semantic matching, have limits; they can capture general meaning but may still fail on nuanced context or rare, domain-specific keywords (e.g., a generic embedding model might miss an exact error code that a lexical search would catch). In multimodal contexts, the semantic gap is even wider: understanding the meaning of an image or aligning it with a text query requires robust cross-modal semantics, which many retrieval systems struggle with. Overall, limited semantic understanding means the system does not truly grasp intent or context, resulting in omissions or irrelevant hits when exact cues are absent.

- **Modality mismatch in multimodal retrieval**: When dealing with multiple data types (e.g., images and text together), retrieval systems face the challenge of comparing and combining different modalities. An image query and text documents live in very different feature spaces, and measuring similarity between them is non-trivial. Naively projecting them into a single index can lead to mismatches: the system might not align visual concepts with textual descriptions accurately. This cross-modal alignment problem is a known drawback; multimodal systems require either separate embedding spaces for each modality or a joint space learned to compare them. Without proper alignment, an image + text retrieval system might return items of the wrong modality (e.g., a text snippet when an image was expected) or fail to retrieve relevant cross-modal results. In essence, differences in how modalities represent information (pixels vs. words) can cause retrieval failures if not carefully handled, limiting the system's effectiveness when queries and targets span images, text, audio, etc.

- **Index staleness (outdated index)**: Retrieval systems depend on an index of the content (documents, embeddings, etc.), which can become outdated if not refreshed. A static index does not automatically incorporate newly added documents or updates to existing data, so over time it stales, meaning the search results might omit recent information or still reflect removed/changed content. Index staleness is a significant drawback, especially for dynamic corpora: the system's knowledge freezes at the last indexing point. For example, a news search engine that is not frequently reindexed will fail to surface yesterday's articles or reflect corrections to past articles. Similarly, in a RAG setting, if the vector store is not updated, the language model may retrieve outdated facts. This issue is compounded if the embeddings themselves drift (e.g., if an updated embedding model is used for new data, old embeddings become incompatible). In short, an out-of-date index can degrade both recall (missing new relevant items) and precision (returning content that is no longer relevant or accurate).

- **Ranking inefficiencies**: Even after retrieving a set of candidate documents, ordering them by relevance is not always done optimally due to efficiency constraints. Many retrieval systems use fast but approximate ranking techniques in the first-stage (e.g., simple vector similarity or **Best Matching 25 (BM25)** scores), which may not perfectly correlate with true relevance. Truly optimal ranking might require more complex analyses (like deep neural scoring or cross-attention between query and document), but applying those to every candidate is computationally expensive. There is thus an inherent inefficiency: the most precise ranking models (e.g., cross-encoders) are too slow for large collections, while faster methods may place some relevant items lower than they deserve. For instance, a first-stage dense retriever might retrieve the right document in the top 100 but not rank it first because it cannot fully understand the query's context or the document's nuances. As a result, relevant results can be buried, and irrelevant ones may appear high, unless additional reranking steps are taken, introducing latency or complexity. This highlights a gap between efficient retrieval and effective ranking, a notable shortcoming of many retrieval pipelines.

- **Lack of contextual awareness**: Retrieval algorithms traditionally treat each query in isolation and each document as an independent chunk of text, which can lead to context-insensitive results. In textual search, if a query is ambiguous or too short, the system has no memory of the user's intent beyond that query, often returning contextually off-target results. In RAG systems and document **question answering (QA)**, breaking documents into chunks can exacerbate this issue: small passages lose the broader context of the source. Therefore, a retrieved chunk might be factually relevant but uninterpretable or misleading when taken out of context. Anthropic highlights this *context conundrum* in traditional RAG. For example, a snippet stating *the company's revenue grew by 3% over the previous quarter* is hard to use if it is unclear which company or timeframe is referenced. The retriever, lacking awareness of the surrounding context, might fetch such fragments that answer a question on the surface but fail to provide clarity. Similarly, a multimodal system might retrieve an image without understanding the narrative context that a user implied. The lack of contextual awareness means retrieval results can be technically relevant to keywords but practically unhelpful or even misleading when context is not preserved.

The following table outlines common drawbacks encountered in information retrieval systems, mapping each limitation to its corresponding impact on retrieval performance. Understanding these challenges highlights the trade-offs and complexities involved in optimizing recall, precision, semantic comprehension, multimodal alignment, index freshness, ranking effectiveness, and contextual awareness in modern retrieval architectures.

Drawback	Impact
Poor recall vs. precision trade-offs	Retrieval systems must compromise between completeness (recall) and accuracy (precision), making it challenging to optimize both simultaneously. This may cause the retrieval of irrelevant results or missing relevant documents.
Limited semantic understanding	Systems fail to grasp deep meaning or intent, leading to missed relevant documents when phrases differ or context is nuanced, causing omissions or irrelevant hits, especially in semantic or multimodal retrievals.
Modality mismatch in multimodal retrieval	Incorrect alignment between different data types (e.g., images and text) results in retrieval failures, such as returning wrong modality items or missing relevant cross-modal results, reducing system effectiveness.
Index staleness (outdated index)	Outdated indexes omit recent information, include obsolete content, and degrade both recall and precision, making retrieval results less accurate and less timely.
Ranking inefficiencies	Fast but approximate ranking may bury relevant documents and elevate irrelevant ones, reducing the effectiveness of result ordering unless slower, complex reranking is applied at added cost and latency.
Lack of contextual awareness	Results can be contextually misleading or unhelpful because retrieval treats queries and documents in isolation, losing broader user intent and narrative context, especially in fragmented or multimodal data.

Table 10.1: Mapping retrieval system limitations to their practical impacts on search quality and user experience

Retrieval optimization techniques mitigating the limitations

To mitigate the preceding limitations, modern retrieval systems employ a range of optimization techniques. The following methods enhance recall, precision, and relevance across textual, multimodal, and RAG scenarios by addressing specific drawbacks.

Multi-index embedding

Instead of representing each document with a single vector or in a single index, multi-index embedding or multi-vector representations techniques use multiple embeddings per item or multiple indexes specialized by content. One common approach is multi-vector indexing, where a long document is segmented into multiple parts, each indexed by its own embedding. This ensures that different topical aspects of a document are captured, improving the chances that at least one segment will match a relevant query. The result is higher recall and finer semantic matching for complex or lengthy documents; the system no longer misses information just because it was buried in a long text. Moreover, considering multiple vectors per document can improve precision by giving a more nuanced representation; each vector covers a specific context, so irrelevant parts of a document are less likely to cause false matches. In practice, multi-index embedding improves semantic coverage and context retention by capturing different facets of content, and it enhances retrieval accuracy and understanding. For example, a technical paper might have separate embeddings for its abstract, methods, and conclusion. A question about the paper's method will directly hit the method embedding segment, rather than relying on a single vector that might dilute this detail. In RAG pipelines, multi-vector schemes similarly allow long knowledge articles to be queried effectively without losing pertinent details, thereby addressing poor recall on long documents and mitigating the loss of context within those documents.

Modality-based routing for multimodal queries

To tackle modality mismatch, retrieval architectures introduce modality-based routing, which means that queries are directed to modality-specific indexes or models. Rather than forcing all data types into one homogeneous representation, the system maintains separate pipelines optimized for text, images, audio, etc., and then combines the outputs. For example, a multimodal search engine might have one vector index for text passages and another for image embeddings; if a query contains both an image and text, it routes each part to the appropriate index. This way, each modality is handled with the best-suited retrieval method, e.g., **Contrastive Language–Image Pretraining (CLIP)** embeddings for images, **Bidirectional Encoder Representations from Transformers (BERT)** based embeddings for text, without one modality's noise confusing the other. By isolating modalities, the system avoids direct comparisons of incomparable features and thus reduces cross-modal error. In practice, one can query multiple indexes in parallel and then perform a late fusion of results, ensuring that the top results from each modality are considered. If a user asks a question with an image example attached, the image can be used to fetch similar images while the text query retrieves relevant documents; the results can then be merged. Another strategy is joint embedding spaces (a form of routing at the model level): using models like CLIP, which learn a shared vector space for text and images so that an image query and a caption can be directly compared. This aligns modalities to speak a common language of vectors, greatly alleviating the modality mismatch problem. Modality-based routing (whether via separate indices or joint embeddings) ensures that each data type's unique characteristics are respected, thereby improving precision and recall in multimodal retrieval by addressing the cross-modal alignment challenge.

Query expansion

Query expansion is a classic technique to improve recall and bridge lexical-semantic gaps in textual retrieval. The idea is to expand the user's query with additional terms or phrases that have similar meaning, including synonyms, related concepts, or alternate formulations. By automatically broadening the query, the system retrieves documents it might otherwise miss due to wording differences. For instance, a query on *global warming effects* could be expanded with terms like *climate change impacts* so that documents using either term are considered. This directly addresses the poor recall aspect of the recall-precision trade-off: expansion increases the number of relevant results found (at some cost to precision). In practice, modern systems use thesauri, language models, or even LLMs to generate expansions. In the context of RAG, query expansion can feed the retriever multiple reformulations of a question, yielding a richer set of context passages for the generator. While this may introduce a few more irrelevant hits (since the query is broader), it significantly reduces the chance of missing pertinent information hidden behind different terminology. Smart expansion strategies (e.g., only adding highly relevant synonyms, or using feedback from initial results to expand further) help maintain precision while boosting recall. By covering more semantic ground, query expansion mitigates the limited semantic understanding of strict keyword search and improves the system's ability to find relevant data despite vocabulary mismatches.

Embedding normalization

Embedding normalization is a low-level but crucial optimization in vector-based retrieval. It addresses an often-overlooked issue: vector embeddings can vary in length (magnitude), which can skew similarity computations. For example, if one document's embedding has a larger norm than another's, it might score higher on a dot product similarity with a query even if the direction (semantic content) is less aligned. Normalization (typically L2 normalization to unit length) ensures that all vectors lie on the same hypersphere, so that similarity is determined purely by angle (cosine similarity) rather than vector length. This improves the semantic fidelity of retrieval—documents are retrieved for being truly similar in content, not just because their embedding has a larger magnitude. Normalized embeddings also bring numerical stability and consistency: maximizing inner product becomes equivalent to maximizing cosine similarity, making the retrieval metric well-behaved and comparable across queries.

In practice, many embedding models already output normalized vectors or have an option to do so; if not, vector databases often allow flagging that data should be treated as normalized. By preventing any single vector from *dominating due to length* anomalies. normalization yields a more reliable ranking of results (addressing a subtle ranking inefficiency). It is especially important in multimodal settings or when merging results from different models, as their embedding scales might differ. Ensuring a uniform scale removes one source of error, letting the retrieval focus on true semantic similarity. In summary, embedding normalization fine-tunes the retrieval engine's mathematical underpinning to enhance precision and consistency in results.

Hybrid retrieval

Hybrid retrieval combines the strengths of keyword (lexical) search and vector (semantic) search to overcome each method's weaknesses. Rather than relying on one approach, a hybrid system performs both a lexical match (e.g., BM25 or TF-IDF index) and a semantic similarity search (via embeddings) and then merges the results. This technique directly confronts the limited semantic understanding of pure keyword search and the complementary issue that pure semantic search can miss exact or rare terms. By using both, the system can balance precise term matching with broader semantic coverage. For example, consider a technical query containing a specific error code and a general problem description: the BM25 component will ensure documents containing that exact error code are retrieved, while the embedding component will fetch documents about the general problem even if they phrase it differently. Rank fusion or reranking of the combined candidate list then yields a final ranking that is more comprehensive and relevant than either method alone. Modern RAG pipelines frequently use this approach; first, gather a set of top-N passages by lexical search and top-M by vector search, then deduplicate and rerank them together. The result is significantly improved recall and precision, as evidenced by *Anthropic's* example, where using both methods returns more applicable chunks for generation. Hybrid retrieval also mitigates context loss: lexical matches can provide the exact contextual identifiers (like names or numbers) that an embedding might overlook, anchoring the semantic results in concrete details. Overall, this optimization addresses recall/precision trade-offs by effectively combining two scoring signals, yielding a retrieval that is both accurate and semantically aware.

Score normalization

Hybrid retrieval systems merge the outputs of keyword-based (lexical) search and semantic (vector) search, but a major technical challenge lies in combining their fundamentally different scoring schemes into a unified ranking. Lexical models like BM25 produce scores based on term frequency and document statistics, while vector search provides similarity measures, often cosine or Euclidean distance, which are not directly comparable or even on the same numeric scale.

To address this, score normalization techniques are applied before merging results. The normalization process transforms scores from each method into a common scale (often or standardized z-scores), allowing fair combination and fusion. Typical strategies include:

- **Min-max normalization**: Each set of scores (BM25 and embedding) is scaled so its minimum becomes 0 and maximum becomes 1, preserving ranking within each group while enabling direct comparison.

- **Z-score normalization**: Scores are standardized based on their distribution, centering them and allowing outliers to be managed appropriately.

- **Rank-based fusion**: Instead of merging raw scores, items are ordered within each method, and fusion is done by interleaving or summing their ranks.

- **Learned or weighted fusion**: Training a model or using heuristics to optimally weigh or combine the normalized scores based on relevance feedback.

For example, in a typical hybrid pipeline, top-N results from BM25 and top-M from embedding search are first selected. Their scores are then normalized, duplicate hits are merged (often keeping the best score per method), and the final list is reranked using the fused (combined or weighted) scores. This process ensures that precise keyword matches (e.g., for IDs or rare terms) are not overshadowed by semantically similar but less precise content, and vice versa.

Score normalization is essential for hybrid retrieval to avoid one modality dominating due to numerical scale differences, ultimately enabling the system to leverage the strengths of both lexical precision and semantic breadth for the best possible retrieval performance.

Reranking with cross-encoders

We have already built an understanding of reranking with a cross-encoder. However, let us understand it more thoroughly. To tackle the ranking inefficiency of first-stage retrieval, systems often employ a reranking step with cross-encoders (or other powerful rerankers). A cross-encoder is a transformer model that takes a query and a candidate document together as input and produces a relevance score, effectively performing a deep semantic comparison with full context. This is far more accurate than the independent encoding used in bi-encoder models (where query and document are embedded separately). The drawback, of course, is that doing this for every possible document is infeasible; however, doing it for a small set of top candidates (say, top 50 or 100 from the initial retriever) is usually manageable. The strategy, therefore, is to use a fast retriever to get a candidate pool, then apply a cross-encoder to rerank those candidates with high precision. This two-stage approach addresses the earlier trade-off by combining speed and accuracy. The cross-encoder corrects the mistakes of the first-stage. For instance, it can be noticed that a top-ranked passage is only superficially matching the query and not relevant, demoting it below a truly relevant passage that maybe the initial stage had a lower rank. Empirically, adding a cross-encoder reranker significantly boosts metrics like **Mean Reciprocal Rank** (**MRR**) or precision@k, as it filters out false positives and reorders results based on a richer understanding of query context and document content. In a RAG system, improved reranking means the LLM gets more relevant grounding passages, directly improving answer quality. The cost is extra computation, but optimizations exist (e.g., using smaller cross-encoders or only reranking a subset). Overall, cross-encoder reranking is a targeted fix for ranking inefficiency as it injects a high-context, high-precision judgment just where it is needed, at the final ranking of top candidates to ensure the results are as relevant and contextually appropriate as possible.

Prefiltering thresholds

Prefiltering thresholds are a practical optimization used in multi-stage retrieval systems to reduce the computational latency of reranking with cross-encoders. Since evaluating a cross-encoder on every candidate document is prohibitively slow, prefiltering thresholds help ensure that only the most promising candidates (i.e., those likely to be relevant) are passed on for costly reranking. Here is how this works and why it is effective:

- **Prefiltering thresholds** are criteria applied to the initial candidate pool (produced by a fast retriever, such as BM25 or a bi-encoder) to exclude low-scoring or obviously irrelevant candidates before reranking.

- The threshold can be a score cutoff (*only rerank candidates with a score above X*) or a top-N cutoff (*rerank only the top 50 or 100 candidates by initial score*), or even a hybrid (e.g., all documents above a high score plus up to N total).

The importance of Prefiltering thresholds is as follows:

- **Reduces reranking latency**: Cross-encoders are computationally expensive because they process the query and document together in a deep model. Prefiltering shrinks the candidate set, so fewer items need to be reranked, making the second stage much faster.

- **Maintains high-quality results:** With a carefully set threshold, most truly relevant documents still make it into the reranking stage, so final accuracy does not suffer, and you avoid wasting compute on likely-irrelevant documents.

- **Balances precision and efficiency**: By tuning the threshold (e.g., increasing N or lowering the score cutoff), systems can find the best trade-off between result quality and response time, adjusting for available compute or latency budgets.

The following is an example of implementation:

- Suppose your first-stage retriever (BM25 or vector search) retrieves 1,000 candidates. You set a prefiltering threshold of top-64 by score (*N=64*).

- Only these 64 are sent to the cross-encoder reranker. The cross-encoder produces a highly accurate relevance order, and only the top-k (say, 5 or 10) are returned to the user or LLM.

- Optionally, you can use both a score and rank threshold to further tighten the pool, e.g., *BM25 score > 5.0 AND top 100 by rank.*

The following are the benefits:

- **Significant speedup**: Dramatically reduces the number of slow, expensive reranking computations per query.

- **Flexibility**: Thresholds can be tuned for specific use cases to optimize latency, quality, or cost depending on requirements.

- **Quality control**: Ensures only reasonable candidates are considered for the final results, decreasing the chance of low-quality answers.

Prefiltering thresholds act as a smart filter between fast retrieval and slow, accurate reranking by cross-encoders, ensuring only the most promising documents are reranked. This approach enables you to enjoy the high precision of a cross-encoder—but without incurring prohibitive inference cost or latency for every candidate—by reducing the reranking workload to a manageable, high-likelihood subset.

Adaptive index refresh

Finally, to combat index staleness and embedding drift, retrieval systems implement adaptive index refresh policies as shown in *Figure 10.1*. This means the index is not a once-and-done static structure but is updated on a schedule or in response to changes. One aspect is incremental indexing: as new documents arrive or existing ones change, they are added to (or reindexed in) the search index continuously or periodically, rather than waiting for a complete reindexing. This keeps the content fresh and ensures recall of up-to-date information. In practice, production systems have an index update pipeline that feeds new data and uses background processing to keep the vector store current. Another aspect is adapting to changes in the embedding model itself. If the system's vector encoder is retrained or replaced (for example, a newer language model is deployed), the stored embeddings may no longer be compatible or optimal. Adaptive refresh entails re-embedding the corpus when models are updated or when significant drift is detected. Monitoring can be used to decide when re-embedding is necessary (e.g., if similarity scores start degrading or recall@k drops). By re-computing embeddings on the latest model and swapping them into the index, the system maintains alignment between query embeddings and document embeddings, preventing the relevance mismatches that arise from embedding drift. In sum, adaptive index refresh addresses the staleness drawback by ensuring the retrieval index remains a living reflection of both the data and the model's understanding. This results in more accurate and timely retrieval: new knowledge is searchable, and the similarity comparisons remain valid over time. Techniques in this vein include scheduled reindexing, real-time indexing for streaming data, and hybrid approaches where recent data is searched live (fallback to slow search) if not yet indexed. Together, these practices guarantee that the retrieval system's knowledge stays current and its vector space stays consistent, thus upholding retrieval performance in the face of evolving content and models.

So, modern retrieval systems, whether pure document search, multimodal search, or RAG are far from static keyword-matchers. They are complex, evolving systems that must overcome fundamental limitations in recall, precision, semantic understanding, cross-modal alignment, and context handling. By applying the above optimization techniques, such systems markedly improve in robustness and relevance: multi-vector representations enrich what is indexed, modality-specific handling aligns disparate data types, query expansion broadens the search horizon, embedding normalization and hybrid search refine the matching process, rerankers inject intelligent ordering, and continuous index refresh keeps the system up-to-date. Each technique targets specific drawbacks, and together they enable retrieval pipelines to provide high-quality, context-aware results in increasingly diverse and demanding applications. The interplay of these methods exemplifies how conceptual innovation (rather than just mathematical complexity) can drive substantial improvements in information retrieval performance and reliability.

Retrieval optimization techniques

In high-performance retrieval systems, especially those supporting multimodal inputs and RAG, optimizing the retrieval process is essential for achieving high precision, recall, and contextual relevance. This section details the implementation of core retrieval optimization strategies using Python and Qdrant, with embeddings generated via Sentence Transformers. Each technique is motivated by a real-world challenge and substantiated with modular, reusable code; details as follows:

- **Modality-based routing**:
    - **Challenge**: In multimodal systems, different data types like text, images, and audio require specialized processing. A unified vector space often fails to capture the distinct semantics of each modality.
    - **Solution**: Modality-based routing directs the user query to the appropriate index (textual, visual, etc.) based on the detected input modality or intent:

    ```
    def route_query(query: str, modality: str = "text") -> str:
        routing_table = {
            "text": "text_index",
            "image": "image_index",
            "multimodal": "hybrid_index"
        }
        return routing_table.get(modality, "text_index")
    ```

    This function ensures that each query is processed by the most relevant sub-index, avoiding modality mismatch and improving retrieval precision.

- **Query expansion**:
    - **Challenge**: Lexical mismatches (e.g., *car vs. automobile*) limit recall in both sparse and dense retrieval systems.

o **Solution**: Query expansion increases semantic coverage by adding related terms to the original query:

```python
def query_expansion(query: str) -> list:
    synonym_dict = {
        "climate": ["environment", "weather"],
        "car": ["vehicle", "automobile"]
    }
    words = query.split()
    expanded = set(words)
    for word in words:
        if word in synonym_dict:
            expanded.update(synonym_dict[word])
    return list(expanded)
```

By expanding climate to include environment and weather, the retrieval system is more likely to return conceptually relevant documents that use alternate terminology.

- **Embedding normalization**:

  o **Challenge**: In vector retrieval systems, unnormalized embeddings can result in similarity scores biased by vector magnitude, not actual semantic closeness.

  o **Solution**: Normalize all embeddings to unit length (L2 norm) to ensure consistent cosine similarity calculations:

```python
def normalize_embedding(embedding: np.ndarray) -> np.ndarray:
    norm = np.linalg.norm(embedding)
    return embedding / norm if norm != 0 else embedding
```

This function guarantees that all embeddings lie on a unit hypersphere, ensuring semantic similarity is judged by angular distance alone, thus improving scoring reliability across indexes.

- **Weighted embedding fusion**:

  o **Challenge**: In multimodal fusion, naive averaging of text and image embeddings can dilute the dominant signal of one modality.

  o **Solution**: Weighted embedding fusion combines embeddings using domain-specific weights:

```python
def weighted_embedding_fusion(text_emb: np.ndarray, image_emb:
np.ndarray, text_weight: float = 0.6) -> np.ndarray:
    fused = text_weight * text_emb + (1 - text_weight) * image_emb
    return normalize_embedding(fused)
```

This fusion technique allows biasing towards more reliable modalities (e.g., text in legal documents, image in e-commerce), and ensures the resulting vector is still normalized for similarity search.

- **Score fusion and aggregation**:
  - ○ **Challenge**: When retrieving from multiple indexes (e.g., text + image), combining results naïvely can lead to suboptimal rankings.
  - ○ **Solution**: Use **Reciprocal Rank Fusion** (RRF) to aggregate results fairly based on rank-position rather than raw score:

```python
def score_fusion(results_a: list, results_b: list, method: str =
"reciprocal_rank") -> list:
    def reciprocal_rank(score, rank):
        return 1 / (rank + 1)

    fused_scores = {}
    for rank, item in enumerate(results_a):
        fused_scores[item.id] = fused_scores.get(item.id, 0) +
reciprocal_rank(item.score, rank)
    for rank, item in enumerate(results_b):
        fused_scores[item.id] = fused_scores.get(item.id, 0) +
reciprocal_rank(item.score, rank)

    merged = [{"id": k, "fused_score": v} for k, v in fused_
scores.items()]
    return sorted(merged, key=lambda x: x["fused_score"],
reverse=True)
```

This technique mitigates modality bias by ensuring that results highly ranked in either list are promoted fairly in the merged output.

- **Contextual filtering**:
  - ○ **Challenge**: Retrieval systems often return technically relevant but contextually inappropriate results, e.g., outdated documents or low-credibility sources.
  - ○ **Solution**: Apply contextual filtering based on metadata (e.g., source type, year, region):

```python
from qdrant_client.http.models import Filter, FieldCondition,
MatchValue

def filter_by_metadata(source: str = None, year: int = None) ->
Filter:
    conditions = []
    if source:
        conditions.append(FieldCondition(key="source",
match=MatchValue(value=source)))
    if year:
        conditions.append(FieldCondition(key="year",
match=MatchValue(value=year)))
    return Filter(must=conditions)
```

Qdrant allows filtering at query time via such metadata. This function can be used to prioritize documents from reliable sources or within a relevant timeframe.

- **Adaptive index refresh**:
  - **Challenge**: Indexes grow stale as documents change or embedding models improve. Without refreshing, retrieval accuracy degrades.
  - **Solution**: Adaptive index refresh re-embeds documents and rebuilds the vector index:

```
from qdrant_client.http.models import VectorParams, Distance,
PointStruct
def refresh_index(collection_name: str, data: list, encoder,
vector_size: int, qdrant_client):
    qdrant_client.recreate_collection(
        collection_name=collection_name,
        vectors_config=VectorParams(size=vector_size,
distance=Distance.COSINE)
    )
    points = []
    for item in data:
        text = item.get("text") or item.get("desc")
        vector = normalize_embedding(encoder.encode(text))
        points.append(PointStruct(id=item["id"], vector=vector.
tolist(), payload=item["metadata"]))
    qdrant_client.upsert(collection_name=collection_name,
points=points)
```

This function allows periodic or event-driven reindexing, ensuring alignment between stored data, metadata, and evolving models.

- **Retrieval optimization using genetic algorithms**:
  - **Challenge**: Selecting optimal combinations of retrieval configurations such as modality weights, query expansion strategies, filter thresholds, and reranking parameters often involves manual tuning, which is both time-consuming and suboptimal. Moreover, the retrieval landscape is non-convex and multi-objective, making traditional optimization techniques less effective.
  - **Solution**: **Genetic algorithms (GAs)** provide a population-based search method inspired by biological evolution, suitable for optimizing retrieval pipelines over multiple parameters simultaneously. A GA evolves candidate configurations through selection, crossover, and mutation, guided by a fitness function, typically defined by retrieval performance metrics (eg, **normalized discounted cumulative gain (NDCG)**, MRR, precision@k).

GA implementation for optimizing modality

To effectively harness the potential of genetic algorithms for retrieval optimization, it is essential to translate theoretical concepts into practical, reproducible code. The following section demonstrates how to simulate the evolutionary process in a retrieval context by defining a fitness function that evaluates configuration performance, and by establishing mechanisms to represent, initialize, and manipulate candidate solutions. Through this approach, we can iteratively refine retrieval pipelines, allowing for automated discovery of superior parameter combinations. This hands-on implementation lays the groundwork for scalable, data-driven optimization, reducing manual intervention and enabling rapid experimentation in complex search environments.

```python
import random
import numpy as np

# Sample fitness function (you'd replace this with actual retrieval evaluation)
def evaluate_config(text_weight, use_query_expansion) -> float:
    # Placeholder: simulate a fitness score based on hyperparameters
    score = 0.7 * text_weight + (0.2 if use_query_expansion else 0)
    noise = np.random.uniform(-0.05, 0.05)
    return score + noise

# Encode individuals as [text_weight, query_expansion_flag]
def initialize_population(size=10):
    return [[random.uniform(0.3, 0.9), random.choice([0, 1])] for _ in
range(size)]

def mutate(individual):
    if random.random() < 0.5:
        individual[0] = min(1.0, max(0.0, individual[0] + random.uniform(-0.1,
0.1)))
    else:
        individual[1] = 1 - individual[1]  # toggle query expansion
    return individual
def crossover(p1, p2):
    return [(p1[0] + p2[0]) / 2, random.choice([p1[1], p2[1]])]
def select(pop, scores, k=4):
    return [pop[i] for i in np.argsort(scores)[-k:]]
def genetic_optimization(generations=20, pop_size=10):
    population = initialize_population(pop_size)
    best_config = None
    best_score = -np.inf

    for gen in range(generations):
        scores = [evaluate_config(*ind) for ind in population]
```

```
    top_individuals = select(population, scores)
    new_population = top_individuals[:]
    while len(new_population) < pop_size:
        p1, p2 = random.sample(top_individuals, 2)
        child = mutate(crossover(p1, p2))
        new_population.append(child)
    population = new_population

    gen_best = max(scores)
    if gen_best > best_score:
        best_score = gen_best
        best_config = population[np.argmax(scores)]

    print(f"Gen {gen+1}: Best Score = {gen_best:.4f}")

print("\nOptimal Parameters Found:")
print(f"Text Weight: {best_config[0]:.2f}, Query Expansion: {'On' if best_
config[1] else 'Off'}")
return best_config
```

Explanation

This GA-based retrieval optimization method addresses the challenge of parameter interaction across retrieval stages (modality fusion, query reformulation, contextual scoring). Unlike gradient-based methods, GAs do not require a differentiable loss and can navigate discrete and continuous search spaces simultaneously. In our implementation:

- Each individual encodes a retrieval configuration vector: [*text_weight* ∈ *[0, 1]*, *query_ expansion_flag* ∈ *{0,1}*].

- The fitness function evaluates performance using a mock retrieval score, though in practice, this would compute NDCG@k or recall@10 on a validation query set.

- The evolutionary process over N generations converges toward the best-performing parameter combination without exhaustive search.

By integrating GAs into the retrieval pipeline, systems can self-optimize over time, adapting to domain-specific needs (e.g., placing more emphasis on image embeddings in fashion search vs. textual metadata in legal corpora).

Multimodal RAG system with adaptive index refresh

Setting up a multimodal RAG system from scratch involves orchestrating multiple components to enable intelligent QA across both text and image data. This guide provides a step-by-step walkthrough for building a fully functional multimodal RAG pipeline, integrating CLIP-based embedding, ChromaDB for vector storage, and LangChain for response generation. A key feature of this system is adaptive index refresh, which ensures the retrieval index remains up-to-date with evolving content or embedding models. Whether you are starting with raw files or adding new data dynamically, this setup equips your system for scalable, context-aware, and accurate multimodal search and generation.

Follow the setup instructions given in *Chapter 9, Building GenAI Systems with Reranking,* with minor changes.

The following figure illustrates the architecture of a multimodal RAG system that supports both text and image inputs. A user submits a query, which is encoded using either a text or image embedding model, depending on modality. Documents and images are preprocessed and chunked into embeddings that are stored in a vector database. The index is periodically refreshed to maintain alignment with updated content. During retrieval, the query is matched against stored embeddings, and top results are passed to an LLM, which generates a contextually informed response that is returned to the user as the final output which is also explained in the following steps.

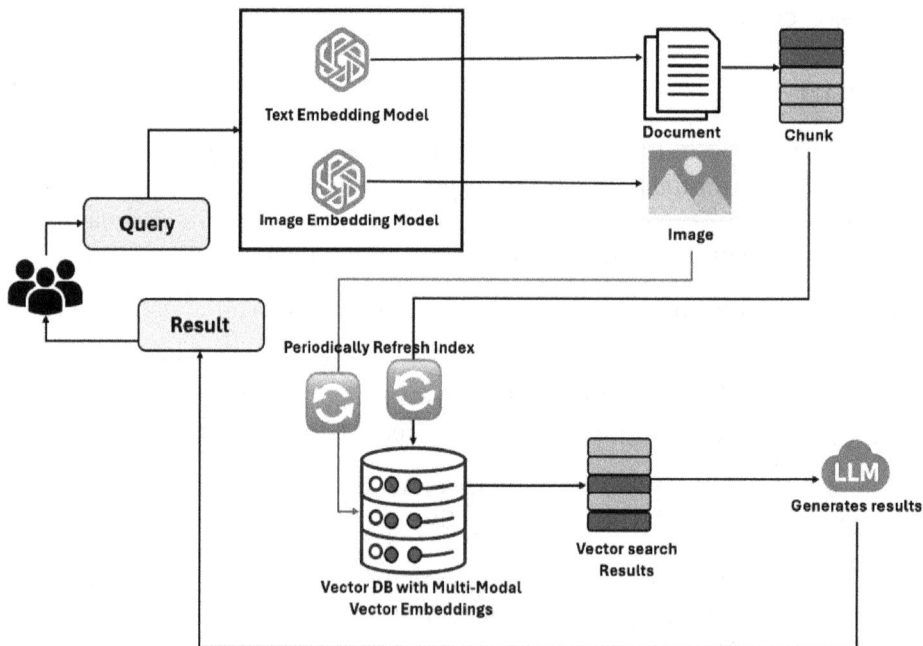

Figure 10.1: Multimodal RAG system with adaptive index refresh

1. **Refresh the index (anytime or on demand)**: To refresh all indexes (e.g., new files added, or model updated):

```
python run_refresh.py
```

Or use the **Refresh Indexes** button in the app UI.

2. **Directory structure**: Setup your folder as shown in the following figure:

```
project_root/
├── app.py
├── run_once.py
├── run_refresh.py
├── rag/
│   ├── __init__.py
│   ├── config.py
│   ├── embedding_utils.py
│   ├── loaders.py
│   ├── index_builder.py
│   ├── refresh.py
│   ├── reranker.py
│   ├── generation.py
├── data/
│   ├── documents/    # contains .txt spec files
│   └── images/       # contains .jpg/.png laptop images
├── chromadb_storage/ # auto-created by Chroma
```

Figure 10.2: Folder structure of the project

The following list is the complete end-to-end code for your multimodal RAG system with adaptive index refresh, organized into clean, modular **.py** files:

- The **config.py** defines global constants and configuration settings used across the project. This includes directory paths for ChromaDB persistence, image and text collection names, data folders, and model names for embedding and LLM inference.

```
####rag/config.py
CHROMA_PERSIST_DIR = "chromadb_storage"
CHROMA_IMAGE_COLLECTION = "laptop_images"
CHROMA_TEXT_COLLECTION = "laptop_texts"
IMAGE_FOLDER = "data/images"
TEXT_FOLDER = "data/documents"
EMBED_MODEL_NAME = "clip"
MODEL_NAME = "llama3"  # For Ollama LLM
```

- The **embedding_utils.py** provides utility functions to generate vector embeddings for both text and image inputs using the CLIP model. These embeddings are essential for populating and querying the vector database with consistent feature representations.

```
####rag/embedding_utils.py
from transformers import CLIPProcessor, CLIPModel
import torch
from PIL import Image
clip_model = CLIPModel.from_pretrained("openai/clip-vit-base-patch32")
```

```
clip_processor = CLIPProcessor.from_pretrained("openai/clip-vit-base-
patch32")
def embed_text_ollama(text):
    inputs = clip_processor(text=[text], return_tensors="pt",
padding=True, truncation=True)
    with torch.no_grad():
        outputs = clip_model.get_text_features(**inputs)
    return outputs[0].tolist()

def embed_image_ollama(image_path):
    image = Image.open(image_path).convert("RGB")
    inputs = clip_processor(images=image, return_tensors="pt")
    with torch.no_grad():
        outputs = clip_model.get_image_features(**inputs)
    return outputs[0].tolist()
```

- The **loaders.py** contains functions to load textual documents and collect valid image file paths from specified folders. It is used during both initial indexing and adaptive refresh operations to read the raw input data.

```
###rag/loaders.py
import os
def load_text_documents(folder):
    docs = {}
    for file in os.listdir(folder):
        if file.endswith(".txt"):
            with open(os.path.join(folder, file), "r", encoding="utf-8")
as f:
                docs[file] = f.read()
    return docs
def load_image_paths(folder):
    return [os.path.join(folder, f) for f in os.listdir(folder) if
f.lower().endswith(('.jpg', '.jpeg', '.png'))]
```

- The **index_builder.py** implements the logic for constructing the initial indexes in ChromaDB. It deletes existing collections, processes all documents and images, generates embeddings, and stores them along with their metadata into separate text and image collections.

```
###rag/index_builder.py
import os
import chromadb
from .embedding_utils import embed_text_ollama, embed_image_ollama
from .config import *
```

```
from .loaders import load_text_documents, load_image_paths
def build_index():
    client = chromadb.PersistentClient(path=CHROMA_PERSIST_DIR)

    # Text Collection
    if CHROMA_TEXT_COLLECTION in [c.name for c in client.list_
collections()]:
        client.delete_collection(name=CHROMA_TEXT_COLLECTION)
    text_collection = client.create_collection(name=CHROMA_TEXT_
COLLECTION)
    texts = load_text_documents(TEXT_FOLDER)
    for idx, (fname, content) in enumerate(texts.items()):
        emb = embed_text_ollama(content)
        text_collection.add(documents=[content], embeddings=[emb],
ids=[str(idx)], metadatas=[{"file": fname}])
    # Image Collection
    if CHROMA_IMAGE_COLLECTION in [c.name for c in client.list_
collections()]:
        client.delete_collection(name=CHROMA_IMAGE_COLLECTION)
    image_collection = client.create_collection(name=CHROMA_IMAGE_
COLLECTION)
    images = load_image_paths(IMAGE_FOLDER)
    for idx, path in enumerate(images):
        emb = embed_image_ollama(path)
        image_collection.add(documents=[""], embeddings=[emb],
ids=[str(idx)], metadatas=[{"file": os.path.basename(path)}])
```

- The **refresh.py** enables adaptive index refresh functionality. It deletes outdated text and image collections and rebuilds them using the latest files in the **document** and **image** folders, ensuring the system remains up-to-date with new or modified content.

  ####rag/refresh.py

```
import os
import chromadb
from .embedding_utils import embed_text_ollama, embed_image_ollama
from .config import *
from .loaders import load_text_documents, load_image_paths
def refresh_text_index():
    client = chromadb.PersistentClient(path=CHROMA_PERSIST_DIR)
    if CHROMA_TEXT_COLLECTION in [c.name for c in client.list_
collections()]:
```

```
        client.delete_collection(CHROMA_TEXT_COLLECTION)
    collection = client.create_collection(name=CHROMA_TEXT_COLLECTION)
    texts = load_text_documents(TEXT_FOLDER)
    for idx, (fname, content) in enumerate(texts.items()):
        emb = embed_text_ollama(content)
        collection.add(documents=[content], embeddings=[emb],
ids=[str(idx)], metadatas=[{"file": fname}])
    print(f" Text index refreshed with {len(texts)} documents.")
def refresh_image_index():
    client = chromadb.PersistentClient(path=CHROMA_PERSIST_DIR)
    if CHROMA_IMAGE_COLLECTION in [c.name for c in client.list_
collections()]:
        client.delete_collection(CHROMA_IMAGE_COLLECTION)
    collection = client.create_collection(name=CHROMA_IMAGE_COLLECTION)
    images = load_image_paths(IMAGE_FOLDER)
    for idx, path in enumerate(images):
        emb = embed_image_ollama(path)
        collection.add(documents=[""], embeddings=[emb], ids=[str(idx)],
metadatas=[{"file": os.path.basename(path)}])
    print(f"Image index refreshed with {len(images)} images.")
def refresh_all_indexes():
    refresh_text_index()
    refresh_image_index()
```

- The **reranker.py** uses a cross-encoder model to re-evaluate and reorder retrieved results based on semantic similarity with the query. This reranking step improves the precision of final results by leveraging richer contextual comparisons.

```
####rag/reranker.py
from sentence_transformers import CrossEncoder

cross_encoder = CrossEncoder('cross-encoder/ms-marco-MiniLM-L-6-v2')
def rerank(query, metadatas):
    pairs = [(query, doc.get("file", "")) for doc in metadatas]
    scores = cross_encoder.predict(pairs)
    ranked = sorted(zip(metadatas, scores), key=lambda x: x[1],
reverse=True)
    return [doc for doc, _ in ranked]
```

- The **generation.py** initializes and returns an Ollama-based language model for use in generative tasks. It is specifically called when the system needs to produce a synthesized natural language response to a user query.

```
###rag/generation.py
from langchain_community.llms import Ollama
from .config import MODEL_NAME
def get_llm():
    return Ollama(model=MODEL_NAME, temperature=0.2)
```

- The **run_once.py** executes a one-time full index build using the functions in **index_builder.py**. It is typically run when setting up the system for the first time or when a complete reindexing is required.

```
##### run_once.py
from rag.index_builder import build_index
if __name__ == "__main__":
    build_index()
```

One-time or scheduled index refresh script

The following are the different kinds of scripts:

- The **run_refresh.py** triggers the adaptive index refresh process defined in **refresh.py**. It is designed to be executed manually or scheduled periodically to keep the indexes in sync with updated image or document content.

```
####run_refresh.py
from rag.refresh import refresh_all_indexes
if __name__ == "__main__":
    refresh_all_indexes()
```

- **Refresh button**: The **app.py** implements the Streamlit-based user interface for the RAG assistant. It supports multiple query modes (image, text, hybrid), retrieves and reranks results, displays matched content, and includes a button to manually refresh the indexes.

  Note: **You may create your own UI; the following is a sample example.**

```
#### app.py
import streamlit as st
import os
import chromadb
from rag.embedding_utils import embed_text_ollama, embed_image_ollama
from rag.reranker import rerank
from rag.config import *
from rag.generation import get_llm
from rag.refresh import refresh_all_indexes

client = chromadb.PersistentClient(path=CHROMA_PERSIST_DIR)
```

```
st.title("Multimodal RAG Laptop Assistant")
mode = st.radio("Choose Mode", ["Image → Specs", "Image + Text → Specs",
"Text → Image + Specs", "Text → Generated Answer"])

if st.button("Refresh Indexes"):
    refresh_all_indexes()
    st.success("Indexes refreshed successfully!")

# ... (same content as the Chapter_8 and 9 `app.py` query handling logic
here) ...
```

This setup integrates adaptive index refresh into your existing multimodal RAG pipeline.

Enhancing multimodal RAG with adaptive refresh

This comprehensive approach enhances the capabilities of your multimodal RAG pipeline by integrating cutting-edge methods for both representation and retrieval. By combining adaptive index refresh, multi-vector embeddings, and a unified vector database, the system is able to handle a wide range of input modalities and query types with efficiency and precision. Through careful orchestration of text and image embeddings, as well as sophisticated reranking techniques, the architecture serves as a robust foundation for building advanced AI assistants. The following sections further detail the underlying pipeline, storage architecture, and retrieval mechanisms that power this system.

The end-to-end code can be found in the GitHub repository of the book. Please refer to the multi-vector representation concept listed in *Chapter 6, Two and Multi-stage GenAI Systems*. This system integrates dense and multi-vector text embeddings along with image embeddings into a unified vector database using Qdrant. It supports multimodal retrieval and token-level reranking and leverages an adaptive embedding refresh mechanism to ensure data consistency. The architecture exemplifies a practical implementation of a hybrid RAG pipeline with late interaction, multimodal context, and local LLM reasoning.

The following figure illustrates a robust RAG pipeline designed to efficiently process and respond to user queries using both text and image inputs. By leveraging dedicated embedding models for each modality and storing them in a unified vector database, the system supports hybrid semantic search and retrieval. Periodic index refreshes ensure that newly ingested documents and images are reflected in the database. Retrieved results undergo multi-vector-based reranking before being passed to an LLM for final answer generation, enabling accurate and context-aware multimodal responses.

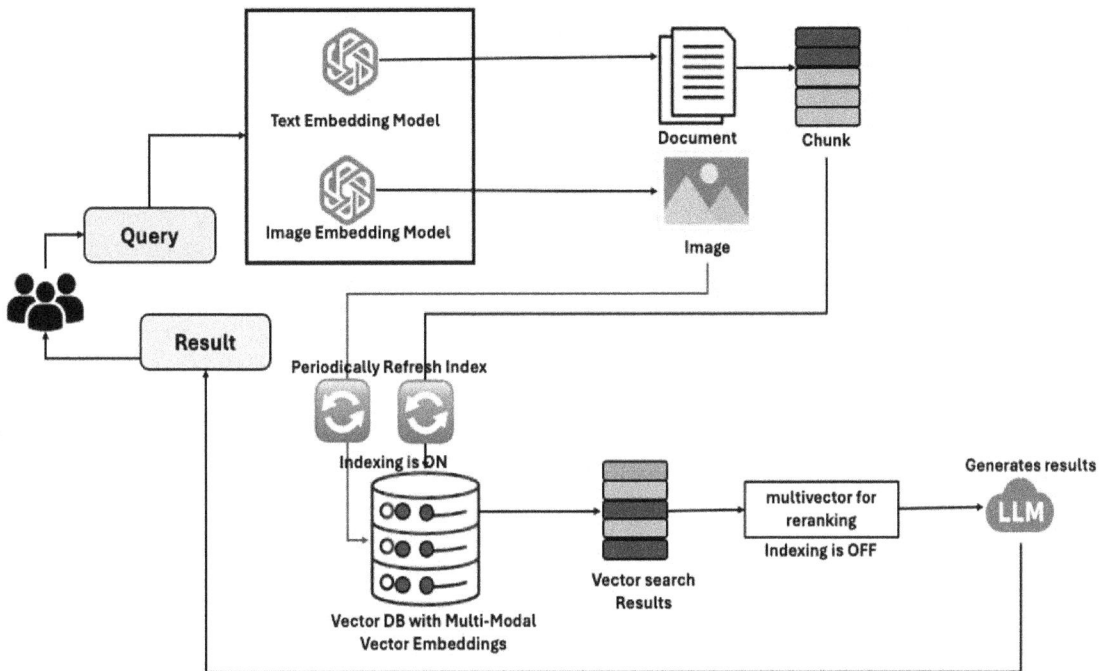

Figure 10.3: Multimodal RAG with reranking flow

Vector embedding pipeline and storage in Qdrant

The system generates and stores three types of vector representations for each paired text and image document:

- **Dense text embedding (dense_text)**: The textual content is first embedded using the BAAI/bge-small-en model, implemented via Sentence Transformers. This produces a single 384-dimensional vector representing the overall meaning of the text. These dense vectors are used for the initial stage of retrieval, where speed is prioritized.

- **ColBERT multi-vector embedding (colbert_text)**: In addition to dense vectors, the system generates token-level embeddings using the colbert-ir/colbertv2.0 model through `LateInteractionTextEmbedding`. Unlike traditional approaches that collapse an entire document into a single vector, this multi-vector approach retains a vector for each significant token or phrase. These vectors are stored in Qdrant using a multi-vector configuration (`MultiVectorConfig` with `MAX_SIM` comparator) that enables late interaction reranking. Each document is therefore represented by a set of 128-dimensional token vectors.

- **Image embedding (image)**: The associated image file is embedded using the CLIP model (`openai/clip-vit-base-patch32`), which converts the visual content into a 512-dimensional vector. This allows for similarity-based image retrieval.

- **Insertion into a unified collection**: All three types of embeddings, dense text, multi-vector text, and image, are inserted into a single Qdrant collection under separate vector fields. Each record is uniquely identified using a **Universal Unique Identifier** (**UUID**) and contains metadata such as the filename and raw text.

This design results in a unified vector store that supports multimodal retrieval (text and image) and multi-vector reranking (token-level precision).

Two-stage retrieval and multi-vector reranking

The retrieval process is divided into two-stages to balance speed and accuracy:

- **Stage 1, dense retrieval**: The initial retrieval is performed using the **dense_text** vectors. The query is embedded into a single dense vector using the same BAAI/bge-small-en model, and a fast similarity search is executed using the HNSW index in Qdrant.

```
prefetch = models.Prefetch(query=dense_query, using="dense_text")
```

- **Stage 2, multi-vector reranking**: In the reranking stage, the same query is embedded at the token-level using the ColBERT model. This token-level embedding is compared with the stored **colbert_text** multi-vectors using the **MAX_SIM** operator, which selects the best matching document tokens for each query token. This enables fine-grained reranking of the initial candidate set.

```
query=colbert_query,
using="colbert_text",
```

- **Optional, image-based retrieval**: If an image vector is provided, a separate similarity search is executed using the **image** vector field. This enables retrieval based on visual similarity alone or in combination with text.

Context assembly and language generation

Once the top-ranked documents are selected, their textual content is extracted and concatenated to form a context string. This context is passed, along with the original query, to a local LLM (Mistral via Ollama) using a ReAct-style prompt in LangChain:

```
python
CopyEdit
response = chain.run({"query": query_text, "context": context})
```

The LLM synthesizes the context and returns a natural language response.

Adaptive embedding refresh mechanism

The system includes an adaptive refresh function that scans a specified **text** and **images** folder. It detects valid **.txt** and **.jpg** file pairs, generates all necessary embeddings, and upserts them into Qdrant.

This process is adaptive in the following ways:

- It reflects the current contents of the data folders.
- It automatically generates embeddings for new files.
- It avoids reprocessing if a required image file is missing.
- However, it currently does not deduplicate or overwrite based on file names. Each insert uses a new UUID.

This refresh mechanism ensures that Qdrant stays up-to-date with the latest dataset, making it suitable for environments where documents change regularly (e.g., weekly updates).

Indexing behavior

The collection is configured with different indexing strategies per vector type:

- **dense_text**: HNSW indexing is enabled for fast retrieval.
- **colbert_text**: HNSW indexing is disabled to support precise reranking using **MAX_SIM**.
- **image**: HNSW indexing is enabled for similarity-based image search.

This configuration is optimal for a two-stage retrieval system that relies on fast preselection and accurate late interaction reranking.

To do

After completing the adaptive index refresh integration, you are encouraged to extend this system by implementing additional retrieval optimization techniques. Start by incorporating query expansion to improve recall using synonyms or paraphrasing. Add modality-based routing to dynamically direct queries to the appropriate index based on input type. Implement embedding normalization before similarity comparisons and experiment with weighted embedding fusion to balance multimodal inputs. Integrate score fusion and aggregation for combining results from multiple sources. Finally, enhance contextual filtering using metadata such as timestamps or reliability. These additions will significantly improve the relevance, robustness, and adaptability of your system.

Conclusion

This chapter provided a comprehensive overview of retrieval optimization techniques, addressing the fundamental drawbacks of traditional and modern retrieval systems. We explored how targeted strategies, such as modality-based routing, query expansion, score fusion, and adaptive index refresh, mitigate these limitations. Through detailed design principles and modular Python implementations, we demonstrated how to implement adaptive index refresh. A fully functional codebase featuring ChromaDB, CLIP embeddings, and a Streamlit interface was presented, culminating in an adaptive indexing pipeline. Readers are now equipped with both conceptual understanding and practical tools to extend this framework with additional optimization techniques for real-world applications. In the next chapter, we will implement multimodal GenAI systems with voice as input.

Join our Discord space

Join our Discord workspace for latest updates, offers, tech happenings around the world, new releases, and sessions with the authors:

https://discord.bpbonline.com

## CHAPTER 11

Building Multimodal GenAI Systems with Voice as Input

Introduction

This chapter explores adding speech as a primary input mode to multimodal **generative AI (GenAI)** systems. Traditionally reliant on text or visual input, such systems are increasingly embracing voice to enhance accessibility, natural interaction, and user engagement. The illustrated pipeline introduces a seamless flow where user queries—via keyboard or voice—are routed through a **retrieval-augmented generation (RAG)** chatbot. Voice input undergoes a **speech-to-text (STT)** transformation before integration. The system then checks a vector database for relevant context. If found, the context is passed to a Mistral **large language model (LLM)** for answer generation. If not, the pipeline dynamically falls back on a web search to provide sufficient grounding for response synthesis. Finally, generated answers are optionally converted to speech, closing the multimodal loop with a voice-based output. This architecture highlights the growing sophistication of GenAI interfaces, unifying speech, text, retrieval, and generation into a robust, user-centric interaction model.

Structure

In this chapter, we will learn about the following topics:

- RAG beyond image and text RAG
- Concepts

- Integrating speech interfaces into RAG architecture
- Code implementation of the voice-enabled RAG system

Objectives

The objective of this chapter is to design and implement a voice-enabled multimodal RAG system that integrates speech, document retrieval, web search fallback, and local LLM-based response generation. By enabling both STT and **text-to-speech** (**TTS**) capabilities, the system aims to create a more natural, accessible, and context-aware conversational interface. The solution combines modular LangChain components, LangGraph orchestration, Ollama-hosted LLMs, and Streamlit UI to deliver grounded responses from local **Portable Document Format** (**PDFs**) or the web. This chapter demonstrates how speech can serve as a primary input modality in advanced RAG architectures, enhancing usability across real-world, multimodal applications.

RAG beyond image and text RAG

RAG has emerged as a powerful paradigm for grounding LLMs in external knowledge. While early implementations of RAG systems predominantly operated in the textual domain and subsequently evolved to incorporate visual modalities such as images, recent advancements call for an expansion toward a broader spectrum of modalities. A truly multimodal RAG system integrates diverse data types, including but not limited to audio (speech), video, sensor data, tabular inputs, and structured knowledge graphs, enabling richer and more contextually grounded generation across domains.

In this broader multimodal RAG framework, queries can originate from various input channels: speech (converted to text), gesture (interpreted via pose estimation), spatial data (via **light detection and ranging** (**LiDAR**) or **Internet of Things** (**IoT**) sensors), or user interactions in real-time environments (e.g., **augmented reality and virtual reality** (**AR/VR**) settings). The retrieval mechanism must therefore operate over heterogeneous index structures—embedding databases, graph databases, or structured warehouses, each representing a different modality-specific embedding space. This requires either modality-aware retrievers or cross-modal alignment techniques to ensure semantically coherent retrieval.

The generation module, typically powered by a foundation model (e.g., Mistral, GPT, or Gemini), then integrates these retrieved contexts, potentially across modalities, using fusion techniques such as attention-weighted late fusion, embedding concatenation, or contextual scoring. Such architectures enable applications ranging from multimodal conversational agents and intelligent tutoring systems to autonomous agents in physical environments. Thus, expanding RAG beyond image-text fusion unlocks new frontiers for grounding LLMs in complex, real-world information ecosystems.

At query time, the user query is encoded into a vector and compared against the stored document embeddings using **approximate nearest neighbor** (**ANN**) search, retrieving the top-k most similar candidates. These vector search results are then forwarded to a cross-encoder reranker, which jointly processes the original query and each candidate document to compute fine-grained similarity scores via full token-level interaction. The reranker reorders the results based on semantic relevance, producing a more accurate set of top-k reranked documents.

These reranked documents, along with the original user query, are passed into the LLM for synthesis. The LLM generates the final answer, which is returned to the user. This two-stage design balances scalability (via bi-encoder retrieval) with precision (via cross-encoder reranking), resulting in both efficient and high-quality response generation.

Concepts

STT and TTS technologies serve as foundational components in the development of voice-enabled multimodal AI systems. By enabling natural language interaction through spoken input and auditory output, these technologies significantly enhance accessibility, hands-free operation, and user engagement, especially in environments where visual or tactile input may be constrained.

Let us understand the core components that power voice-enabled conversational systems STT and TTS. These technologies form the bidirectional bridge between human speech and machine intelligence, enabling natural, intuitive interactions. STT transcribes spoken input into machine-readable text, acting as the auditory gateway to downstream AI models. TTS, in turn, gives voice to the system's responses, synthesizing human-like speech from generated text. Together, they enable seamless, end-to-end voice interaction in modern conversational AI pipelines. Details are as follows:

- **STT**: The systems leverage **automatic speech recognition** (**ASR**) models to convert spoken language into machine-readable text. Modern ASR models are built upon deep neural networks, often incorporating attention-based encoder-decoder architectures or conformer models, allowing them to capture temporal dependencies and accommodate various accents, speech rates, and acoustic environments. STT acts as the first-stage enabler in voice-based query systems, allowing natural spoken language to be routed into downstream components such as RAG-based LLMs.

- **TTS**: It transforms the model-generated textual response into natural-sounding speech using neural vocoders (e.g., WaveNet, HiFi-GAN) or end-to-end transformer-based models (e.g., FastSpeech). TTS systems aim to optimize intelligibility, prosody, and emotional expressiveness, ensuring output speech feels human-like and contextually appropriate.

Together, STT and TTS form a closed feedback loop, converting user speech into actionable machine input and delivering synthesized voice output, thereby completing the auditory interface cycle in conversational AI.

Integrating speech interfaces into RAG architecture

The integration of STT and TTS technologies into RAG pipelines extends the capabilities of generative systems beyond traditional text-based interfaces, enabling more natural and multimodal human-computer interaction. This voice augmentation is particularly impactful in applications such as virtual assistants, accessibility systems, and embodied AI agents operating in real-world environments.

In a voice-enabled RAG pipeline, STT modules serve as the entry point, transcribing spoken user input into structured text. This transcribed text is then routed through the core RAG pipeline, where it is used to perform semantic retrieval against a vector database or other knowledge source. Retrieved documents are concatenated with the input query and passed to an LLM, such as Mistral, GPT, or Llama, which generates a contextually grounded response.

Following response generation, TTS systems are employed at the output stage to synthesize natural speech from the textual output of the LLM. This completes the voice-based interaction loop, delivering conversational responses in a human-auditory format.

This bidirectional speech integration not only enhances user experience but also introduces challenges in latency, streaming inference, and real-time error correction. Addressing these requires careful orchestration of asynchronous **input/output (I/O)**, fast STT/TTS inference engines, and fallback mechanisms for low-confidence speech recognition or generation outputs.

The following figure illustrates a multimodal voice-enabled RAG pipeline designed to handle both keyboard and voice inputs in an intelligent **question answering (QA)** system:

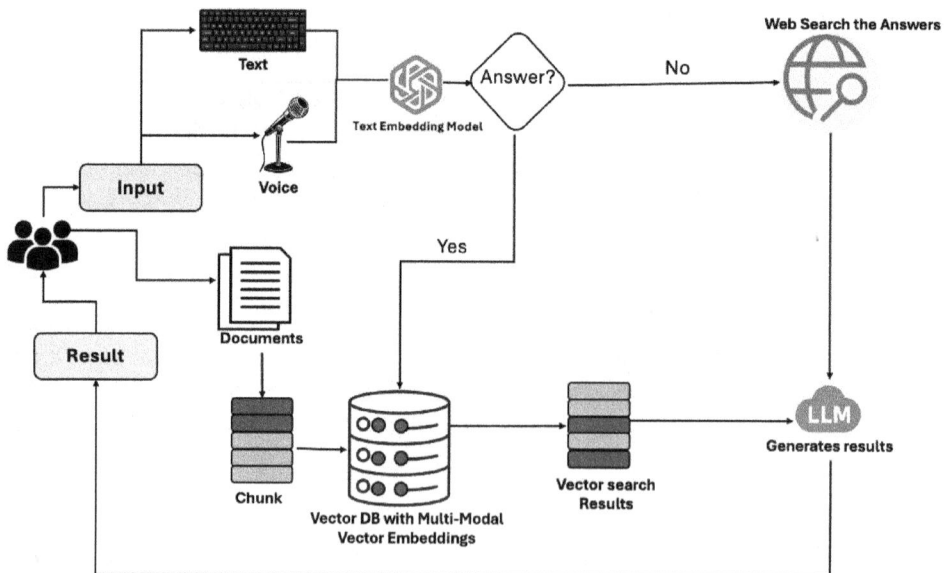

Figure 11.1: Voice-enabled multimodal RAG pipeline integrating speech

The process begins with user input, which can be entered either through a keyboard or captured via voice. For spoken queries, the system first performs STT conversion, transcribing the spoken words into textual form. Regardless of input modality, the question routing module ensures that all inputs are normalized and sent downstream in a unified format.

Next, the query is handled by the RAG chatbot, which performs a vector database lookup to check whether relevant contextual knowledge is already embedded and retrievable. If context is found, it is passed directly to the Mistral LLM, which uses this context to generate a grounded response. If no relevant context is located, the system defaults to web search-based retrieval, ensuring the LLM still receives sufficient grounding information.

The generated answer, produced by the Mistral LLM, can then optionally be converted back into audio using TTS synthesis, providing a spoken output that aligns with the original input modality. This closed-loop pipeline exemplifies how modern multimodal systems can integrate retrieval, generation, and speech technologies to deliver intuitive, accessible conversational AI experiences.

Code implementation of the voice-enabled RAG system

Figure 11.2 presents the high-level project directory structure for a voice-enabled multimodal RAG chatbot system. The architecture modularizes key functionalities such as language modeling, vector retrieval, prompt engineering, and voice processing. This organization supports extensibility and clear separation of concerns, ranging from document ingestion and embedding to real-time speech interaction and frontend deployment.

```
rag_chatbot_with_speach/
├── rag/
│   ├── ollama_llm.py
│   ├── graph_workflow.py
│   ├── prompts.py
│   ├── vectorstore.py
│   ├── embeddings.py
│   ├── loaders.py
│   ├── tavily_search.py
│   ├── router.py
│   └── utils.py
├── voice.py
├── run_once.py
├── frontend/
│   └── app.py
├── data/
│   ├── documents/          # Place PDFs here
│   └── structured.db       # Optional SQLite data
├── .env                    # Env variables (Tavily key)
├── requirements.txt
```

Figure 11.2: Voice-enabled multimodal RAG bot structure

Tech stack overview

The system leverages a carefully curated technology stack designed to support modular, local-first, and speech-enabled RAG workflows, as outlined in the following table:

Component	Description
LangChain	Serves as the backbone for RAG, enabling prompt templating, document loading, and LLM orchestration in a modular pipeline.
LangGraph	Provides a graph-based execution model to manage conditional flows (e.g., fallback to web search) and dynamic routing of query paths. Ideal for managing complex query states.
Ollama	Hosts local LLMs such as Mistral or Llama, enabling fast, offline inference without external **application programming interface (API)** calls. Supports custom model integration and GPU acceleration.
Streamlit	Powers the web-based frontend UI, enabling users to interact with the chatbot via a clean, reactive interface. Supports real-time voice and text inputs.
Tavily API	Acts as a live web search fallback when no relevant context is found in the local vector database, ensuring responses remain grounded in up-to-date external knowledge.
Nomic Embeddings	Used to convert ingested documents into high-dimensional vector representations suitable for similarity search in the vector database.
pyttsx3	Enables TTS conversion on the client side, generating audible responses from LLM outputs in a fully offline, platform-agnostic manner.
SpeechRecognition	Captures and transcribes voice input into text using local microphone streams, acting as the system's STT engine.

Table 11.1: Key components of the voice-enabled multimodal RAG chatbot

This integrated stack supports an end-to-end multimodal conversational AI pipeline that is capable of local inference, dynamic retrieval, real-time speech interaction, and fallback augmentation.

Frontend

The system features a minimalist Streamlit-based frontend that enables users to interact with the multimodal RAG chatbot using either keyboard input or real-time voice queries. The interface displays transcribed speech, dynamically retrieves relevant context, and presents grounded answers with source attribution.

The frontend interface, as shown in the following figure, is a multimodal RAG chatbot that is implemented using Streamlit, providing users with a web-based **user interface (UI)** to interact with the system via either keyboard or voice. The script (**app.py**) integrates various backend modules and coordinates user input, retrieval, generation, and speech functionalities in a modular, real-time workflow.

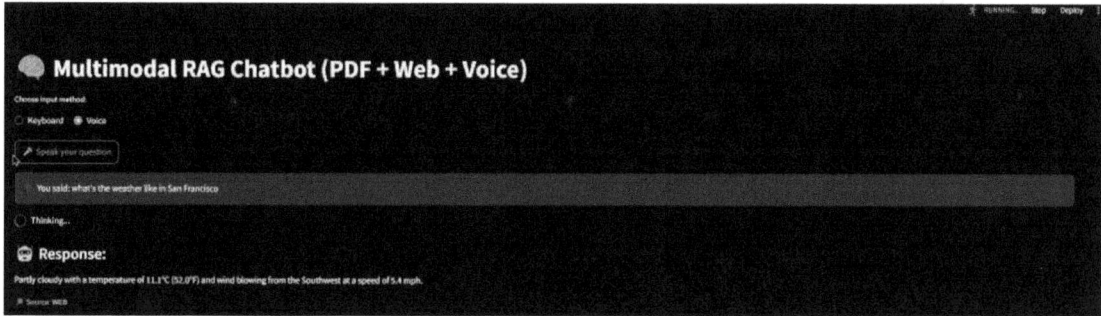

Figure:11.3: Voice-enabled chatbot UI

To understand the core execution flow of the voice-enabled multimodal RAG chatbot. This Streamlit-based application integrates local LLM inference, speech processing, and dynamic document retrieval. From environment setup and module imports to real-time interaction via keyboard or microphone, the pipeline orchestrates LLM invocation, graph-based reasoning, and speech synthesis to deliver a seamless user experience. Here, we break down the major steps that enable multimodal interaction in this system:

1. **Environment setup and imports:** The script begins by resolving the module path and importing dependencies:

   ```
   sys.path.append(os.path.abspath(os.path.join(os.path.dirname(__file__),
   "..")))
   from rag.ollama_llm import get_llm
   from rag.graph_workflow import graph
   from rag.voice import listen_from_microphone, speak_text
   ```

   This setup ensures access to internal RAG modules and encapsulated logic for LLM invocation (**get_llm()**), graph-based reasoning (**graph.invoke()**), and speech interaction.

2. **Page initialization:** The Streamlit page is initialized with a title and layout:

   ```
   st.set_page_config(page_title="RAG Chatbot with Voice", layout="wide")
   st.title("Multimodal RAG Chatbot (PDF + Web + Voice)")
   ```

3. **Input mode selection**: A radio button allows users to choose between **Keyboard** and **Voice** input:

   ```
   input_mode = st.radio("Choose input method:", ["Keyboard", "Voice"],
   horizontal=True)
   ```

4. **Keyboard interaction flow:** For text input, the query is submitted via a **st.text_ input()** field and processed upon clicking the **"Ask"** button:

```
query = st.text_input("Type your question:")
if query.strip() and st.button("Ask"):
    with st.spinner("Thinking..."):
        state = graph.invoke({...})
```

The **graph.invoke()** function controls the RAG pipeline, retrieving documents and web content if necessary. The prompt is constructed dynamically using retrieved context:

```
prompt = f"""{prefix}
You are a helpful assistant. Use ONLY the information in the CONTEXT below...
"""
```

The response is generated by the local Ollama-hosted LLM and returned to the user via st.markdown(...), while also being converted to speech:

```
response = llm.invoke([HumanMessage(content=prompt)])
speak_text(final_answer)
```

5. **Voice interaction flow**: In the **"Voice"** mode, clicking **"Speak your question"** triggers real-time microphone capture:

```
query = listen_from_microphone()
```

The captured voice is transcribed via the **SpeechRecognition** module. The transcribed query follows the same logic path as text: passing through retrieval, prompt assembly, generation, and final response rendering. Again, **speak_text(final_answer)** ensures audio output:

```
st.success(f"You said: {query}")
final_answer = response.content.strip()
speak_text(final_answer)
```

Exception handling is incorporated to report runtime errors:

```
except Exception as e:
    st.error(f" Voice error: {e}")
```

This frontend orchestrates a complete multimodal loop, accepting voice/text, performing retrieval with LangGraph, invoking LLMs via LangChain, and returning responses both visually and auditorily. The modularity and clarity of design make it well-suited for real-time RAG interactions with multimodal capabilities.

Main voice-enabled pipeline

To understand the internal workings of the multimodal RAG chatbot, it is essential to explore how the system is modularized across its core Python components. Each script in the **rag/** directory is responsible for a specific function, ranging from document ingestion and vector indexing to prompt construction, query routing, and LLM inference. The following explanation builds an understanding of these modules in a logical execution order, highlighting how they collaborate to enable end-to-end RAG with voice and web search capabilities. The system begins by loading PDF documents (**loaders.py**) and transforming them into vector embeddings (**embeddings.py**), which are stored in a vector database (**vectorstore.py**). When a user query arrives, the system first tries to retrieve relevant documents locally. If no context is found, it queries the web using Tavily (**tavily_search.py**). The **router.py** module decides between these two sources. Context is then formatted into a structured prompt (**prompts.py**) and passed to a local LLM using Ollama (**ollama_llm.py**). The execution flow is managed by **graph_workflow.py** using LangGraph, while **utils.py** supports formatting and preprocessing throughout the pipeline.

This section delineates the foundational components and operational logic underlying the voice-enabled multimodal RAG framework. It systematically explores the document preprocessing pipeline, embedding strategies, vector indexing mechanisms, LLM-based query routing, and graph-driven control flow, thereby illustrating a cohesive architecture for grounded, speech-integrated information retrieval.

PDF loading and chunking **load_pdfs()** functions are as follows:

- The **load_pdfs()** function is designed to automate the ingestion and preprocessing of PDF documents for downstream embedding and retrieval in a RAG pipeline. It performs two critical tasks: document loading and text chunking.

  ```
  from langchain_community.document_loaders import PyPDFLoader
  from langchain.text_splitter import RecursiveCharacterTextSplitter
  import os
  ```

  o **Function overview**:

  ```
  def load_pdfs(folder_path):
      documents = []
      splitter = RecursiveCharacterTextSplitter(chunk_size=1000,
  chunk_overlap=200)
  ```

  - Initializes an empty list document to collect all processed chunks.

  - Instantiates a **RecursiveCharacterTextSplitter** with a **chunk_size** of **1000** characters and a **chunk_overlap** of **200** characters. This overlap ensures semantic continuity between adjacent chunks, which is beneficial for context-aware retrieval.

  o **File traversal and loading**:

  ```
  for filename in os.listdir(folder_path):
      if filename.endswith(".pdf"):
          loader = PyPDFLoader(os.path.join(folder_path, filename))
          docs = loader.load()
  ```

  - Iterates through all files in the given **folder_path**.

- For each **.pdf** file, creates a **PyPDFLoader** instance from LangChain's document loader module.

- The **load()** method extracts raw text content, typically separated by page.

o **Splitting and aggregation**:

```
documents.extend(splitter.split_documents(docs))
return documents
```

- Each loaded document is split into overlapping text chunks using the **RecursiveCharacterTextSplitter**.

- These chunks are appended to the cumulative documents list and returned as a list of structured text segments ready for embedding.

o **Role in the pipeline**: This function is typically called during the indexing phase, where documents from the **data/documents/** folder are preprocessed into retrieval-ready units. These units are then passed to an embedding model (e.g., in **embeddings.py**) and stored in a vector database (e.g., in **vectorstore.py**).

- **Embedding initialization**: The **get_embeddings()** function encapsulates the instantiation of a locally hosted embedding model, specifically from the LangChain–Nomic integration, for use in document vectorization within a RAG pipeline.

```
from langchain_nomic.embeddings import NomicEmbeddings
```

This **import** statement loads the **NomicEmbeddings** wrapper, which provides a standard LangChain-compatible interface to the **nomic-embed-text-v1.5** model, a high-performance embedding model optimized for semantic search and document retrieval tasks.

o **Function definition**:

```
def get_embeddings():
    return NomicEmbeddings(model="nomic-embed-text-v1.5",
inference_mode="local")
```

- **model="nomic-embed-text-v1.5"** specifies the embedding model version to be used. This model supports dense vector representations for textual data and is tuned for information retrieval tasks.

- **inference_mode="local"** indicates that the embedding computation will run on the local machine rather than through remote APIs. This enables faster, offline embedding and eliminates dependency on external services.

o **Role in the RAG pipeline**: This function is typically called in the document indexing or query vectorization stage (often inside **vectorstore.py**). It returns an embedding object that can be passed into LangChain's vector store abstraction for both storing and searching against document chunks.

By encapsulating the embedding logic in **get_embeddings()**, the system ensures a plug-and-play architecture, facilitating easy model replacement or configuration changes without modifying downstream code.

- **Vector index construction**: The **create_vectorstore()** function is responsible for transforming embedded document chunks into a searchable vector index using **LangChain's SKLearnVectorStore**, a lightweight in-memory vector store built on top of scikit-learn's nearest neighbor algorithms.

```
from langchain_community.vectorstores import SKLearnVectorStore
```

This import brings in the **SKLearnVectorStore** implementation from LangChain's community module. It is particularly well-suited for local, prototyping environments where persistent or large-scale vector storage (e.g., Qdrant, Faiss) is not required.

- **Function definition**:

```
def create_vectorstore(docs, embedding):
    return SKLearnVectorStore.from_documents(docs, embedding)
```

- docs: A list of document chunks, typically preprocessed via a splitter (e.g., **RecursiveCharacterTextSplitter**) and returned from the loader pipeline.

- embedding: An embedding model object, such as the one returned by **get_embeddings()** (e.g., using Nomic Embeddings), which converts each text chunk into a high-dimensional vector representation.

The **from_documents()** method performs two operations:

- Embeds all the document chunks using the specified **embedding** function.

- Constructs an internal index using scikit-learn's nearest neighbor search (e.g., **NearestNeighbors** with cosine or Euclidean distance).

- **Role in the RAG pipeline**: This function is typically invoked during the indexing phase, where loaded and split documents are converted into vector form and indexed for retrieval. At inference time, this vector store enables semantic similarity search between user queries and the indexed documents.

Due to its in-memory nature, **SKLearnVectorStore** is ideal for development and testing but may not scale for production use where persistent or distributed indexing (e.g., via Qdrant or Pinecone) is needed.

- **Web retrieval fallback**: The **search_tavily()** function interfaces with the Tavily Search API to retrieve live, up-to-date content from the internet when the local vector database fails to return to the relevant context. It acts as a web search fallback module within a RAG pipeline, ensuring robustness in cases where indexed documents are insufficient or outdated.

```
import os
import requests
from langchain.schema import Document
from dotenv import load_dotenv
```

This function imports environment variables, network request tools, and the **Document** schema from LangChain to maintain compatibility with the rest of the RAG architecture.

- o **Environment configuration and API setup**:

  ```
  load_dotenv()
  api_key = os.getenv("TAVILY_API_KEY")
  ```

  - Loads the Tavily API key from a local **.env** file using **python-dotenv**.
  - Ensures secure credential management outside of the codebase.

- o **Web search request and error handling**:

  ```
  url = "https://api.tavily.com/search"
  headers = {"Authorization": f"Bearer {api_key}"}
  payload = {"query": query, "num_results": max_results}
  ```

  - Constructs a POST request to the Tavily API with the search query and an optional **max_results** parameter (default: **3**).
  - Uses a bearer token for secure authentication.

  Robust exception handling ensures graceful degradation in case of network errors or unexpected responses:

  ```
  response = requests.post(url, headers=headers, json=payload)
  response.raise_for_status()
  ```

- o **Response parsing and output conversion**:

  ```
  data = response.json()
  results = data.get("results", [])
  return [Document(page_content=entry["content"]) for entry in
  results if "content" in entry]
  ```

  - Extracts the response JSON and formats each result into a LangChain **Document** object.
  - If no results are found, a fallback message is returned:

    ```
    return [Document(page_content="Tavily returned no results.")]
    ```

- o **Role in the RAG pipeline**: This function is typically invoked within the query router or fallback logic, often in **router.py** or **graph_workflow.py**. When the vector search fails (e.g., low relevance or empty results), **search_tavily()**

fetches fresh web content that can be incorporated into the prompt fed to the language model.

This enables live knowledge augmentation, especially critical for time-sensitive, fact-based queries not covered by static document corpora.

- **Query routing logic-route_question_and_get_source()**: The **route_question_and_ get_source()** function plays a pivotal role in adaptive query handling within a multimodal RAG system. Its purpose is to dynamically decide whether a given user query should be answered using locally embedded documents (**"pdf"**) or by performing a live web search fallback (**"web"**), based on the judgment of a language model.

```
from langchain.schema import HumanMessage, SystemMessage
from rag.ollama_llm import get_llm
from rag.prompts import router_instructions
from rag.utils import safe_json_parse
```

This setup imports LangChain-compatible message schemas, an LLM interface, pre-defined routing instructions as system prompts, and a utility function for robust JSON parsing.

- **Function definition and LLM-oriented decision making**:

```
def route_question_and_get_source(question: str) -> str:
```

- Accepts a natural language question as input.

- Returns a source decision: **"pdf"** (vectorstore-based retrieval) or **"web"** (Tavily API fallback).

- **Prompt construction and LLM invocation**:

```
messages = [
    SystemMessage(content=router_instructions),
    HumanMessage(content=question)
]
response = llm_json_mode.invoke(messages)
```

The function sends a two-turn conversation to the LLM:

- A system message loaded from **router_instructions**, which guides the LLM on how to make the routing decision.

- The human message containing the user's actual query.

This approach leverages LLM-driven control flow, where the model returns a structured JSON output indicating the preferred data source.

- **Safe JSON parsing and decision logic**:

```
result = safe_json_parse(response.content)
datasource = result.get("datasource", "vectorstore").lower()
```

- The LLM's response is parsed using a fault-tolerant utility **safe_json_parse()** to handle unstructured or malformed outputs gracefully.

- If the LLM suggests **"websearch"**, the function returns **"web"**; otherwise, it defaults to **"pdf"**.

```
return "web" if datasource == "websearch" else "pdf"
```

In the event of a failure (e.g., parsing error or unexpected content), the system defaults to using the local document **vectorstore**:

```
except Exception as e:
    print(f"[ROUTER] JSON parsing failed: {e}")
    return "pdf"
```

- **Role in the RAG pipeline**: This routing function is typically invoked prior to retrieval, acting as a gating mechanism to:

  - Use vector-based retrieval for questions likely to be answered from the indexed corpus.

  - Use web search fallback (e.g., Tavily) for time-sensitive, out-of-domain, or general knowledge queries.

  This design introduces dynamic adaptability in response sourcing, ensuring higher response relevance without manual rule-based routing.

- **Prompt engineering for control and accuracy in RAG systems**: Prompt engineering is critical in steering LLMs within RAG systems. The following two prompts are **router_instructions** and **rag_prompt**, they serve specific, tightly scoped functions: query routing and grounded response generation, respectively.

  - **Routing prompt**:

```
router_instructions = """
You are a router deciding whether a question should be answered
using the user's private PDFs or from a web search.

If the question is about LangChain, prompt engineering, or other
topics covered in the provided documents → use 'vectorstore'.

If the question is about recent events, weather, people,
locations, or real-world data → use 'websearch'.

Return ONLY a JSON like:
{ "datasource": "websearch" }
or
{ "datasource": "vectorstore" }
"""
```

- o **Purpose**:
    - This prompt is used to control the decision-making process of an LLM acting as a router agent.
    - It classifies incoming queries into two categories: for PDF-based document retrieval, **vectorstore**, and for fallback to real-time online search via Tavily, **websearch**.

- o **Design considerations**:
    - Binary classification using constrained output (**"datasource": "..."**) ensures predictable downstream logic.
    - It leverages domain-specific cues (e.g., LangChain, prompt engineering) vs. open-domain, real-world questions (e.g., weather, recent events).
    - This method allows the RAG system to dynamically adapt its retrieval strategy using LLM-based control flow, reducing hard-coded rules.

- o **Answer generation prompt**:

```
rag_prompt = """
You are a helpful assistant. Use ONLY the information in the
CONTEXT below to answer the QUESTION.
If the CONTEXT does not contain the answer, respond exactly with:
"I don't know based on the context."

---
CONTEXT:
{context}
---
QUESTION:
{question}
---
INSTRUCTIONS:
- Do NOT use prior knowledge.
- Do NOT make up any answers.
- ONLY use information in the context above.
- Answer in 2-3 concise sentences.
- Say "I don't know based on the context" if unsure.
---
Answer:
"""
```

- o **Purpose**:
    - This prompt instructs the LLM to generate an answer strictly grounded in the retrieved context from vector search or web search.

- It enforces hallucination prevention by disallowing use of prior knowledge or speculation.

    o **Design features**:

    - **Clear output boundaries**: Separators (`---`) structure the context, question, and rules.

    - **Fallback safety net**: Explicit instruction to reply with **I don't know based on the context** mitigates the risk of unsupported claims.

    - **Conciseness**: Limit responses to two to three sentences for brevity and focus.

    o **Role in the pipeline**:

    - The `router_instructions` prompt is used early in the pipeline, prior to retrieval, to guide data source selection.

    - The `rag_prompt` is used after retrieval, during the LLM response generation phase, to ensure that answers remain contextually accurate and verifiable.

    Together, these prompts ensure both intelligent routing and grounded generation, two foundational components of trustworthy RAG systems.

- **LLM Initialization**: The `get_llm()` function provides a standardized interface to instantiate a locally hosted LLM using LangChain's **ChatOllama** wrapper. This enables model invocation without reliance on external APIs, supporting offline and private deployments of RAG systems.

```
from langchain_community.chat_models import ChatOllama
```

The **import** references the community-supported **ChatOllama** integration, which connects LangChain with models served via the Ollama runtime, a popular framework for running lightweight LLMs locally on CPU or GPU.

    o **Function definition**:

```
def get_llm():
    return ChatOllama(model="mistral")
```

    - `ChatOllama(model="mistral")` launches or connects to the Mistral model, a performant open-weight LLM optimized for fast inference and strong reasoning capabilities.

    - Returns a LangChain-compatible chat model object that supports `.invoke()` and `.stream()` methods for interactive completion tasks.

    o **Role in the RAG pipeline**: This function is used throughout the pipeline wherever LLM-based reasoning is required:

    - **Routing decisions**: Interprets user queries to decide between **vectorstore** and web fallback (**router.py**).

- **Answer generation**: Constructs responses using retrieved document context (**graph_workflow.py**).

- **Prompt templating**: Accepts structured prompts from **prompts.py** and produces context-grounded answers.

By wrapping the model instantiation inside **get_llm()**, the design follows dependency injection best practices, allowing easy substitution of models (e.g., switching from Mistral to Llama 2) without changing the core logic.

- **Graph-based RAG workflow with LangGraph**: The **graph_workflow.py** module defines the logic and control flow of a RAG system using LangGraph, a framework for constructing LLM-integrated state machines. The system supports hybrid retrieval (PDFs + web), summarization, prompt generation, and quality control through a structured, state-driven execution plan.

  - **Core components and initial setup**:
    ```
    llm = get_llm()
    docs = load_pdfs("data/documents")
    retriever = create_vectorstore(docs, get_embeddings()).as_
    retriever(search_kwargs={"k": min(3, len(docs))})
    ```

    - Loads local PDF documents, embeds them using Nomic Embeddings, and builds a retriever using **SKLearnVectorStore**.

    - Instantiates the local LLM (Mistral) via Ollama.

  - **State schema**:
    ```
    class GraphState(TypedDict):
        question: str
        generation: str
        web_search: str
        max_retries: int
        answers: int
        loop_step: Annotated[int, operator.add]
        documents: List[Document]
    ```

    The following list defines the state variables passed between graph nodes:

    - **question**: The user query

    - **documents**: Retrieved docs

    - **web_search**: Flag indicating data source

    - **generation**: Final or intermediate answer

    - **loop_step**: Iteration count for retry logic

- o **Graph nodes (functional units)**:

```
retrieve(state)
def retrieve(state):
    return {
        "documents": retriever.invoke(state["question"]),
        "web_search": "No"
    }
```

  - ▪ Retrieves top-k relevant documents from the local vector store based on semantic similarity.

```
web_search(state)
def web_search(state):
    docs = search_tavily(state["question"])
    return {
        "documents": docs,
        "web_search": "Yes"
    }
```

  - ▪ Fetches real-time web results via the Tavily API and wraps them as **Document** objects.

```
generate(state)
def generate(state):
    # summarize if from web
    # format context into rag_prompt
    # call LLM to get answer
```

  - ▪ If results are from the web, use a summarization prompt to condense them before final generation.
  - ▪ Formats context + question into the structured RAG prompt.
  - ▪ Produces the final answer via **llm.invoke()**.

- o **route_question(state)**: Calls the LLM-based router **(route_question_and_get_source)** to decide whether to use **"websearch"** or **"retrieve"**.

- o **grade_documents(state)**: Pass-through node that maintains document state. Placeholder for future document scoring.

- o **decide_to_generate(state)**: Logic to determine whether to generate directly or switch to web search:

```
Return "generate" if state["web_search"] == "No" else "websearch"
```

- **grade_generation_v_documents_and_question(state)**: Currently hard-coded to **"useful"**, but reserved for evaluating LLM output quality against context and question.

- o **Graph construction:**

```
workflow = StateGraph(GraphState)
workflow.add_node("retrieve", retrieve)
workflow.add_node("generate", generate)
workflow.add_node("websearch", web_search)
workflow.add_node("grade_documents", grade_documents)
```

  Defines the nodes and how data flows between them. The **set_conditional_ entry_point()** allows the graph to dynamically choose its starting node (**retrieve** or **websearch**) based on LLM routing.

- o **Conditional edges drive the logic**:

  - ▪ After document retrieval | grade | decide whether to generate or fall back to web.

  - ▪ After generation | grade output | either end, retry, or fallback.

```
workflow.add_conditional_edges("generate", grade_generation_v_
documents_and_question, {
    "useful": END,
    "not useful": "websearch",
    "not supported": "generate",
    "max retries": END
})
```

- o **Final graph compilation:**

```
return workflow.compile()
```

- o **The graph is compiled into an executable object and exposed as**:

```
graph = build_graph()
```

- o **Role in the system**: This module integrates all prior components:

  - ▪ Document ingestion

  - ▪ Embedding and retrieval

  - ▪ Query routing

  - ▪ Web search fallback

  - ▪ Prompt construction

  - ▪ LLM invocation

  - ▪ Answer quality gating

It ensures dynamic, context-aware, and adaptable execution, supporting retries, fallback, and summarization through a structured, extensible pipeline.

Robust JSON parsing utility: The **safe_json_parse()** function is a fault-tolerant utility designed to extract and parse JSON-formatted content from LLM-generated text. LLM, even when prompted to return structured data, can sometimes produce additional natural language output or malformed JSON. This utility ensures that downstream components receive clean, machine-readable JSON objects, thereby maintaining reliability in automated workflows such as query routing. The details are as follows:

- **Source code:**

```python
import json
import re

def safe_json_parse(text):
    try:
        match = re.search(r'{.*?}', text.strip(), re.DOTALL)
        if match:
            return json.loads(match.group(0))
        else:
            raise ValueError("No JSON found in LLM output")
    except Exception as e:
        raise ValueError(f"JSON parsing failed: {e}\nRaw Text:\n{text}")
```

- **Function logic: Regex extraction:**

```python
match = re.search(r'{.*?}', text.strip(), re.DOTALL)
```

  o Uses a regular expression to extract the first JSON object embedded in the LLM output.

  o The **re.DOTALL** flag ensures multiline matches, useful if the JSON spans multiple lines.

- **JSON decoding:**

```python
return json.loads(match.group(0))
```

  o If a JSON object is found, it is parsed using Python's built-in **json** module.

  o The result is returned as a Python dictionary.

- **Error handling:**

  o If no match is found or **json.loads()** raises an exception, the function raises a **ValueError** with both the error message and the raw input text for debugging.

```python
raise ValueError(f"JSON parsing failed: {e}\nRaw Text:\n{text}")
```

  o **Role in the RAG pipeline:** This utility is primarily used in modules where structured JSON output is expected from the LLM, particularly in:

    ▪ **router.py** — when parsing LLM output to determine whether to route a query to **"websearch"** or **"vectorstore"**.

    By acting as a defensive programming layer, **safe_json_parse()** mitigates the risk of downstream crashes due to malformed or noisy LLM responses, enabling a more reliable and production-ready pipeline.

- **One-time document indexing script**: The **run_once.py** script serves as a one-time execution utility for ingesting, embedding, and indexing documents before real-time query processing in the RAG pipeline. It modularly invokes key functions from the **rag/** package to prepare the local **vectorstore** used for semantic retrieval.

  o **Functional walkthrough:**

  ```
  from rag.loaders import load_pdfs
  from rag.embeddings import get_embeddings
  from rag.vectorstore import create_vectorstore
  ```

  These imports modularly encapsulate document loading (**load_pdfs()**), embedding initialization (**get_embeddings()**), and vector index creation (**create_vectorstore()**).

  o **Main pipeline execution**:

  ```
  def main():
      print("  Loading documents from data/documents...")
      docs = load_pdfs("data/documents")
      print(f"Loaded {len(docs)} documents.")
  ```

  - Loads all **.pdf** files from the **data/documents/** directory.

  - Splits them into overlapping text chunks suitable for embedding and semantic retrieval.

    ```
    print("  Creating vectorstore...")
    vectorstore = create_vectorstore(docs, get_embeddings())
    ```

  - Instantiates an embedding model (e.g., **nomic-embed-text-v1.5**) and computes dense vector representations of each chunk.

  - Stores the embeddings in an in-memory vector index (e.g., **SKLearnVectorStore**).

    ```
    print(f"Embedded {len(docs)} documents into vectorstore.")
    ```

  - Confirms the completion of the indexing process.

    ```
    if __name__ == "__main__":
        main()
    ```

  - Ensures the script executes only when run directly, not when imported.

  o **Purpose and role in the system**:

  - This script is not part of the live inference pipeline; rather, it prepares the knowledge base that will be queried by the chatbot at runtime.

  - It ensures that document ingestion and **vectorstore** construction are executed once, making it ideal for batch processing or development initialization.

o **Usage context**:

Run this script:

```
python run_once.py
```

To populate your **vectorstore** before deploying the frontend or invoking the LangGraph workflow.

This system began with a simple premise: to augment RAG with voice as a primary input modality, making interaction more natural, accessible, and user-centric. Through careful modular design, the project evolved into a robust multimodal AI assistant, capable of ingesting local documents, intelligently routing queries, retrieving context via vector search or web fallback, and generating grounded, reliable responses using a locally hosted LLM.

We started by enabling STT input and TTS output, seamlessly integrating human voice into the RAG feedback loop. We then introduced a graph-based orchestration layer using LangGraph, allowing conditional flows such as summarizing web content, retrying queries, and gracefully handling document coverage gaps.

Each Python module was purpose-built; **loaders.py** for document ingestion, **embeddings.py** for vectorization, **router.py** for LLM-based source routing, and **graph_workflow.py** for state-driven control. A minimalist yet effective frontend was built using Streamlit, allowing users to interact via voice or text with a consistent backend execution flow.

This system not only showcases the potential of voice-enabled RAG architectures but also provides a foundation for further extension into image, video, or real-time multimodal applications. In doing so, it bridges the gap between human communication and grounded AI reasoning—efficiently, ethically, and interactively. The end-to-end code is available at **Chapter_11, code.Zip**.

Conclusion

This chapter explored the evolution of RAG systems beyond traditional image and text inputs, emphasizing the integration of voice as a core modality. We examined the conceptual and architectural foundations of a voice-enabled multimodal RAG pipeline, detailing how STT and TTS interfaces can enhance natural interaction. The system dynamically routes queries between local vector search and web-based retrieval, ensuring grounded, context-aware responses. We also dissected the full implementation—from document ingestion to LangGraph-based orchestration and frontend deployment, demonstrating how modular code design supports real-time, speech-driven AI experiences. Together, these components illustrate how voice augments RAG systems for richer, more accessible applications.

The following chapter delves into reasoning and reranking techniques, offering insights into their roles in enhancing response quality within RAG systems.

## CHAPTER 12

Advanced Multimodal GenAI Systems

Introduction

As **generative AI** (**GenAI**) continues to evolve, the ability to simply retrieve and generate content is no longer enough. Truly intelligent systems must be able to reason, interpret diverse modalities like text and images, and select the best response from many possible outputs. This chapter pushes the boundaries of multimodal GenAI by introducing you to **chain of thoughts** (**CoT**) prompting combined with reranking, enabling your models to think step-by-step and choose wisely.

In this chapter, you will explore how to architect systems where models do not just respond but rather deliberate. You will learn to guide models through explicit reasoning steps, integrating context from both retrieved documents and image-based information, and then apply multi-pass reranking to refine answers based on quality, relevance, or task-specific constraints.

Through hands-on implementation using LangChain, Ollama, and custom CoT templates, you will build unified multimodal flows where text and image signals converge to support robust decision-making. Topics include few-shot CoT strategies, dynamic prompt construction, and context-aware reranking, all of which culminate in the development of powerful, reasoning-augmented multimodal applications.

By the end of this chapter, you will have constructed a sophisticated GenAI system capable of performing visual **question answering** (**QA**), multimodal document analysis, and step-by-step contextual decision-making, paving the way for next-generation AI that can reason as well as it retrieves.

Structure

In this chapter, we will learn about the following topics:

- The critical role of reasoning in generative AI systems
- Reasoning in GenAI and their types
- Tool-based reasoning and ReAct agents
- About reasoning benchmarks

Objectives

This chapter is theoretical in nature, so that you can understand the core concepts of reasoning in GenAI systems. It explores why reasoning is essential for building intelligent, reliable, and explainable AI models. We examine various types of reasoning, including deductive, inductive, abductive, analogical, commonsense, causal, mathematical, spatial, temporal, tool-based, and multimodal reasoning, and explain how each contributes to improved performance and decision-making. You will also learn how modern techniques like CoT prompting and **reasoning and acting** (**ReAct**) agents enable models to reason step-by-step. This foundation will prepare you to design and implement more capable and context-aware AI systems in later chapters.

The critical role of reasoning in generative AI systems

GenAI has rapidly evolved from generating text, code, or images to supporting complex decision-making tasks. At the core of this evolution lies the integration of reasoning capabilities, the ability of a model to not just generate outputs, but to understand, plan, and explain them. As the landscape of GenAI applications expands into multimodal domains and high-stakes environments, reasoning becomes the differentiating factor that transforms a reactive model into a reliable, intelligent system.

From generation to deliberation

Most traditional GenAI models rely on surface-level pattern recognition. Given a prompt, they generate a response based on statistical likelihood. While this is effective for simple tasks (e.g., drafting an email, generating a poem), it often falls short in scenarios where:

- Multiple valid answers exist
- Ambiguities must be resolved

- Logical sequences are required
- Accuracy and accountability are paramount

Reasoning fills this gap by enabling models to *think out loud,* evaluating intermediate steps, simulating decisions, and justifying outcomes. This is essential when working with complex, multi-hop queries (e.g., *which department has the highest budget among those where employees earn over $90,000?*). Without reasoning, the model may guess or skip steps; with reasoning, it can break down the query, identify subtasks, and solve them sequentially.

Trust and explainability in AI systems

A key challenge in GenAI adoption is trust. In business, law, medicine, and education, users demand systems that are not only correct but also explain their decisions. Reasoning improves explainability by:

- Making thought processes transparent (e.g., through CoT or ReAct-style outputs).
- Allowing human users to audit intermediate steps.
- Supporting validation against known rules or constraints.

For example, in legal document analysis, a GenAI model should not only summarize a contract clause but explain why a clause is considered risky, step-by-step. This level of accountability is only possible through reasoning.

Handling ambiguity and disambiguation

In real-world language and vision tasks, ambiguity is common. The same term may refer to different things based on context (*Apple as a company vs. a fruit; a name in an employee vs. a department table*). Reasoning enables the following:

- Disambiguation based on schema, visual clues, or surrounding context.
- Clarification-seeking behavior (e.g., *do you mean the employee's name or the department's name?*).
- Safe defaults or probabilistic ranking when ambiguity cannot be resolved with certainty.

In multimodal GenAI, this becomes even more critical. For example, if a model is answering a question about a chart or an image, it must combine visual cues with textual intent and use logic to infer what the user likely means.

Multimodal integration requires logical composition

The true power of GenAI lies in its ability to handle multimodal inputs—text, images, documents, code, tables, and even audio. However, these modalities come with diverse structures and semantics. Reasoning is essential for:

- Aligning modalities (e.g., linking an image caption with a specific region of interest).

- Composing multi-step interpretations (e.g., interpreting a diagram and referencing a textual explanation).

- Making deductions that span multiple modalities (e.g., comparing data in a chart with conditions stated in a policy document).

A model that simply embeds and retrieves multimodal data cannot go far without the capacity to reason across formats and infer missing links.

Prompt engineering and CoT reasoning

Advanced prompting strategies like CoT and ReAct are direct implementations of reasoning in GenAI. These prompts encourage the model to:

- Decompose tasks into logical steps.

- Solve sub-problems before combining answers.

- Justify actions before execution.

For instance, when converting a natural language query into SQL, a CoT-enabled model can first reason about which tables and columns are relevant, then construct the query. This dramatically improves correctness and reduces hallucinations.

Moreover, few-shot CoT prompting shows that even **large language models** (**LLMs**) benefit from seeing examples of step-by-step reasoning. This mirrors human learning and reinforces the idea that reasoning is not just a technique; it is a cognitive scaffolding that improves performance.

Reranking and meta-reasoning

In practice, GenAI systems often generate multiple candidate responses. Without reasoning, choosing the best one becomes arbitrary or embedding-based. With reasoning + reranking, systems can:

- Evaluate the answer's plausibility or factuality.

- Score answers based on internal consistency.

- Apply constraints (e.g., *is this answer consistent with retrieved facts?*).

This meta-reasoning, reasoning about generated responses, is critical for reducing hallucinations and improving reliability. It is especially important in high-stakes decision-making systems, such as AI assistants in healthcare or finance.

Learning generalizable strategies

Reasoning helps models generalize to novel tasks. A model trained to reason can often:

- Apply familiar problem-solving frameworks to new questions.

- Use analogical reasoning (*this is like that other problem...*).
- Adapt to instructions or goals that have not been seen before.

Without reasoning, the model is limited to surface memorization. With reasoning, it begins to approximate problem-solving intelligence—a hallmark of true general-purpose AI.

Human-AI collaboration

Reasoning not only helps the machine; it also helps the human collaborating with it. When GenAI models explain their steps, users can:

- Identify mistakes early.
- Provide corrections or nudges.
- Gain insights into complex problems.

This is particularly useful in co-pilot scenarios where AI assists a domain expert. For example, in data science, a GenAI agent that can reason through **exploratory data analysis** (**EDA**) steps helps analysts speed up discovery while staying in control.

Foundation for agentic AI

As we move toward agentic systems—AI agents that plan, act, and reflect autonomously—reasoning becomes the foundation. These agents must:

- Form plans
- Select tools
- React to outcomes
- Retry or revise based on context

Every one of these actions depends on a reasoning layer. Without it, agents are random trial-and-error engines, but with reasoning, they become adaptable, intelligent assistants.

In an era where GenAI systems are increasingly integrated into workflows, decision-making, and user interactions, reasoning is not optional; it is essential. It transforms passive generators into active problem-solvers. It brings clarity, accuracy, adaptability, and trustworthiness into AI interactions. Whether through CoT prompting, ReAct loops, or multimodal reasoning chains, this capability enables AI to handle ambiguity, plan actions, explain decisions, and collaborate meaningfully with humans.

As we build more advanced GenAI systems, reasoning is the bridge between generation and intelligence. And crossing that bridge is what unlocks the next frontier of AI.

Reasoning in GenAI and their types

GenAI systems, especially LLMs and AI agents, are increasingly being designed to *think* through problems rather than just produce surface-level text. Modern LLMs like GPT-4 and PaLM can mimic various reasoning patterns (from strict logic to commonsense) to draw conclusions or make decisions. However, while they excel at pattern recognition and fluent imitation, *true reasoning* (logically connecting information, inferring unseen facts, solving novel problems) is still a challenge. Researchers are actively enhancing LLM reasoning via techniques like CoT prompting, ReAct agents, and multimodal fusion architectures to make AI's thinking more human-like and robust. An overview of key types of reasoning in GenAI has been thoroughly explained in the following section, and it covers what they are, examples of each, and how current systems implement them to improve performance, decision-making, disambiguation, and robustness.

Deductive reasoning in AI

Deductive reasoning is the process of drawing specific, logically certain conclusions from general premises or rules. If the given premises are true, a deductive conclusion must also be true. For example, from *all whales are mammals* and *Orca is a whale*, a deductive system concludes *Orca is a mammal*. LLMs can emulate deductive logic by following if-then rules and performing step-by-step inference. In practice, CoT prompting often instils a deductive style; the model is prompted to break a problem into logical steps and derive the answer systematically. This has been effective for tasks like formal logic puzzles or arithmetic, where the solution follows inevitably from the premises. By explicitly generating intermediate steps, an LLM's answer is more likely to be *logically valid* and traceable to the input facts, which improves reliability in domains like math proofs or code reasoning. Deductive reasoning contributes to robust decision-making by ensuring conclusions are consistent with given facts, reducing mistakes in tasks that demand rigorous correctness.

Implemented in GenAI: CoT prompts are a direct way to elicit deductive thinking. For instance, given a math word problem or a logical riddle, models like GPT-4 are encouraged to list premises and infer each step before finalizing the answer, much like a proof. This method significantly boosts accuracy on multi-step logic and math tasks. Some neuro-symbolic systems even combine LLMs with automated theorem provers to double-check deductive steps, blending statistical and formal reasoning for extra rigor.

Inductive reasoning in AI

Inductive reasoning involves generalizing from specific instances or evidence to broader rules or conclusions. The outcome is probable rather than guaranteed; it is essentially pattern learning from examples. In human terms, if you observe *the past 10 code builds that succeeded after adding a certain patch,* you might inductively conclude that *this patch generally fixes the build.* LLMs are inherently strong inductive reasoners because of the way they are trained: They ingest millions of examples and learn to predict patterns. Few-shot learning in prompts is a prime example; an LLM is given a handful of **input/output** (**I/O**) examples (specific cases), and it infers the general pattern to apply to a new query. In-context learning in LLMs is often described as inductive reasoning, as the model abstracts a rule from the prompt examples and extends it to solve a novel instance. This contributes to generalization and adaptability. For example, if shown a couple of formatted date conversions, the model can induce the formatting rule and convert a new date without explicit programming. Inductive reasoning improves creative generation and pattern recognition, but it can also introduce uncertainty—the conclusions are plausible but not certain, so models must sometimes verify inductive guesses with additional checks.

Implemented in GenAI: LLMs implement induction largely via learning from data and few-shot prompting. Rather than a special prompting technique, induction is a natural by-product of training on vast text and adjusting to given examples. For instance, GPT-style models can infer a list sorting rule or grammatical pattern from a few demonstrations and then continue it, showcasing inductive generalization. Self-consistency techniques can augment induction by having the model-generate multiple plausible answers and then choose the most common or consistent one, effectively considering several inductive hypotheses and selecting the best.

Abductive reasoning in AI

Abductive reasoning is reasoning to the best explanation, forming a plausible hypothesis given incomplete observation. It is the kind of reasoning a detective uses. *If we see footprints by the window and the safe open, the best explanation is a burglary.* Unlike deduction, abductive conclusions are not guaranteed to be true; they are educated guesses. LLMs can perform abductive reasoning in tasks where they must fill in gaps or infer hidden causes. For example, given a partial story, an AI might guess a character's motive that best explains their actions. Abductive reasoning is valuable for commonsense inference and troubleshooting, where multiple explanations exist and the system must pick the most likely. In GenAI, one way to implement this is via a propose-and-verify CoT. The model first posits a hypothesis, then internally checks if it fits the evidence. Studies show that LLMs can benefit from this approach: for instance, treating a multiple-choice question as an abductive task, hypothesizing an answer, and then seeing if it makes sense in context often yields better results. Humans naturally switch to abductive reasoning when direct deduction is hard, and LLM agents are starting to mimic that flexibility. By incorporating abductive reasoning, AI systems become more robust to ambiguity, as they can handle incomplete information and still offer a reasonable solution.

Implemented in GenAI: Researchers have explored prompts that explicitly tell the LLM to think of possible explanations. For example, given a riddle or a diagnostic question, the model might be guided to enumerate potential reasons and then conclude with the most plausible one. Some agent frameworks implement abductive strategies by generating a hypothesis and using a tool (like a knowledge lookup) to verify it before finalizing the answer, a process akin to hypothesize, then test. This approach is useful in diagnosis tasks (medical or technical) where the AI suggests a cause for symptoms and then checks consistency with known facts, improving decision-making under uncertainty.

Analogical reasoning in AI

Analogical reasoning involves drawing parallels between similar situations or structures to infer a conclusion. In essence, the AI uses an analogy that if two things share some relationships, then knowledge about one can inform understanding of the other. A classic example is solving analogies like *bird is to sky as fish is to ___?* The model must see the relation it lives in and find that fish live in water. LLMs can handle simple analogies because they have seen many word relationships (synonyms, categories, etc.) during training. For instance, GPT-4 can complete *knife is to cut as pen is to ___*, with write by recognizing the functional analogy. Beyond word puzzles, analogical reasoning lets AI apply known solutions to new problems by recognizing structural similarity. An LLM agent might approach a new task by recalling a scenario it knows that is analogous, then mapping the solution over. This contributes to creative problem-solving and disambiguation. *f* an instruction is unclear, the AI might recall an analogous example from its prompt or memory to interpret it correctly. However, analogical reasoning can be challenging when the analogy is abstract or requires real-world experience. Current GenAI systems implement analogies mostly implicitly (through learned language patterns), but research is emerging to make this more explicit. One approach directs the model to identify the relationship in one pair and then apply it to another, thereby forcing an analogical CoT.

Implemented in GenAI: It is not commonly highlighted as other reasoning types, but analogical reasoning is present in tasks like metaphor understanding or **Scholastic Aptitude Test** (**SAT**)-style analogy questions. Prompting strategies can encourage analogy by asking, *how is this situation similar to a known scenario?* Some experimental methods give the LLM examples of analogies to follow. For example, a prompt might show: `Paris is to France as Tokyo is to Japan (country-capital relationship)`, and then ask the model to apply that relation to a new pair. By doing so, the model explicitly searches for the analogous relationship. Encouraging analogies helps in knowledge transfer. For instance, a multimodal agent could reason that holding a pencil is analogous to holding a paintbrush to transfer motor skills, or an LLM could solve a puzzle by recalling a similar puzzle's solution format. Recent work even trains meta-models to pick the best reasoning style (deductive vs. abductive vs. analogical) for a given problem, illustrating that adding analogical thinking can expand the range of solvable tasks.

Commonsense reasoning

Commonsense reasoning is the ability of an AI to use everyday world knowledge and obvious logic that humans take for granted. This includes basic facts (water is wet), spatial-temporal common sense (people do not walk through walls), social norms, and cause-and-effect in typical situations. It is crucial for understanding implicit meanings and avoiding nonsensical answers. LLMs learn a great deal of common sense from their training text, but they may not always apply it reliably. For example, a naive model might answer the question, *can an elephant fit through a doorway?* The answer can be *yes*, if it squeezes, demonstrating a lack of commonsense physical reasoning. With proper techniques, generative models can reason that an elephant is too large for a standard door, so the answer should be no. One successful approach is using a CoT to inject commonsense, such as by walking through a scenario step-by-step, the model can be reminded of common knowledge at each step. Indeed, CoT prompting has been found to improve performance on commonsense QA tasks by letting the model articulate cause-and-effect and world knowledge before answering. For example, given that *it is raining and John left his umbrella at home. What will happen when he walks outside?* A CoT might explicitly note that it is raining, and without an umbrella, John will get wet, leading to the answer that John will get soaked. Commonsense reasoning greatly aids disambiguation; it helps an AI choose interpretations that make sense in context (e.g., understanding idioms, resolving pronouns by plausible intent). Modern LLMs also leverage external knowledge bases or tools used for commonsense: if unsure, an agent can query a fact database (like asking if elephants fit through doors) to avoid silly mistakes. By building in commonsense, AI systems become more robust and aligned with human expectations, improving their decision-making in open-ended real-world scenarios.

Implemented in GenAI: Commonsense reasoning is often enhanced by prompt engineering and fine-tuning on specialized data. Datasets like CommonsenseQA or StrategyQA train models on everyday reasoning questions, improving their internal grasp of physical and social logic. In prompts, developers might include statements of obvious facts (*Reminder: elephants are bigger than doors*) to cue the model. CoT is helpful as models like GPT-4 can be prompted to explain a scenario (*the cup fell off the table, so it likely broke because cups are fragile*) before answering, ensuring they consider general knowledge. Another approach is retrieval-augmentation: if a question needs commonsense knowledge (e.g., *do elephants fit through doors*), an LLM agent can use a search tool to check typical elephant sizes or known facts. This tool-augmented reasoning mimics how humans recall facts or consult references, leading to answers that are both correct and make sense. By combining innate model knowledge with external information and explicit reasoning steps, current AI systems handle commonsense queries much better than earlier generations.

Causal reasoning

Causal reasoning is the ability to understand cause-and-effect relationships by identifying what leads to an event or predicting its outcomes. For example, an AI capable of causal reasoning can infer that *a glass falling on a hard floor | shatters*, or conversely, reason that *it rained | the street is wet*. This type of reasoning is vital for planning and prediction tasks. In GenAI, causal reasoning comes into play when models need to reason about why something happened or what-if scenarios. LLMs can sometimes infer causal links by relying on patterns (rain leads to wet streets is common in text), but true causal inference is hard because correlation in data is not always causation. To improve this, CoT prompting can be used to have the model explicitly consider causal chains: e.g., *X happened, which would cause Y, which in turn causes Z*. By enumerating these links, the model can avoid logical leaps. One interesting benefit of decision-making is that an agent with causal reasoning will foresee the outcome of its actions (useful in planning tasks or game environments). For instance, a robot-planning LLM might reason: *if I knock over the vase, it will break and upset the user, so I should avoid that.* This forward simulation is causal reasoning at work. It also aids disambiguation; consider a question like, *the lawn is wet in the morning. What might be the cause?* A causal reasoning LLM can propose, *maybe it rained overnight, or the sprinkler ran*, intending to apply real-world knowledge of typical causes. Some specialized benchmarks (e.g. CLadder, CausalQA) test LLMs on cause-effect understanding, and results show that larger models with reasoning prompts can identify causal relations more often than chance. Still, purely text-based models can be fooled by surface cues, so researchers integrate causal diagrams or structured knowledge to solidify this ability. Causal reasoning ultimately contributes to an AI's robustness by ensuring its actions and answers follow logically from causes, and it can handle what-if questions more reliably.

Implemented in GenAI: Current systems enhance causal reasoning through a mix of prompting and architecture. On the prompting side, techniques like counterfactual prompts ask the model to imagine different causes and check consistency (*If X had not happened, would Y still happen?*). This encourages the LLM to distinguish mere correlation from actual dependency. CoT can explicitly prompt: *let us analyze the causal chain step-by-step.* On the architecture side, some approaches convert text into structured forms like causal graphs and then reason over them. For example, an LLM can be guided to read a paragraph and extract events and their temporal order or causal links, forming a mini knowledge graph. It might then reason over this graph (either with an internal module or by generating a logical explanation) to answer a question or make a decision. Such a method was used to improve temporal and causal reasoning by translating text into a timeline graph and then performing reasoning with the help of CoT on that graph. Additionally, tool-augmented agents can do causal reasoning by querying cause-effect databases or running simulations. For instance, an AI might use a physics engine tool to predict outcomes of physical actions, thereby grounding its causal predictions in reality. All these implementations aim to ensure the AI not only knows that something happens, but why, thereby making its behavior more reliable and interpretable.

Spatial reasoning

Spatial reasoning is the capacity to reason about space, geometry, and physical layouts: understanding relationships like left-right, above-below, distances, or how objects fit together. In humans, this underpins tasks from packing a suitcase to navigating a route. For AI, spatial reasoning can mean reading a textual description of a scene and determining spatial relations or looking at an image and understanding object arrangements. LLMs on their own (with only text input) often struggle with complex spatial problems described in language. For example, a text-based puzzle might say *the red ball is two spots to the left of the blue ball, which is not at the leftmost position,* and ask which spot the red ball is in. Without a diagram, the model must simulate a mental map. Generative models have had difficulty with such tasks because keeping track of multiple relative positions is challenging in pure language form. However, researchers developed prompting strategies to help. One effective method is **Chain-of-Symbol (CoS)** prompting, which has the model convert spatial descriptions into a simplified symbolic representation (like a grid or list of coordinates) before reasoning. By using symbols (e.g., abbreviations for objects and positions), the model can internally draw a mental map and then answer questions about it. This approach greatly improved accuracy on spatial tasks such as planning and navigation instructions. For instance, in one example, the model was asked about a list of items and had to figure out how many were vegetables (requiring it to identify items and count them). By representing the items as a dictionary of categories, the LLM could count vegetables and arrive at the correct answer (7) in a step-by-step manner. Spatial reasoning is crucial for multimodal agents (like robots or **vision-language models** (**VLMs**)) because they must interpret real-world layouts. It contributes to robust performance by preventing absurd outputs (an AI with spatial sense will not say the cat is inside the closed box if not possible) and allowing better planning (knowing an object's location relative to another).

Implemented in GenAI: Spatial reasoning is implemented both through specialized prompting and multimodal model design. On the text side, as noted, CoT can incorporate symbols: e.g., the prompt can instruct, *let us use coordinates, mark positions of each object, and then answer.* This was shown to save tokens and boost accuracy on complex spatial puzzles. For navigation or pathfinding, LLM-based agents can output step-by-step directions by internally simulating movements on a map described in text. In the multimodal realm, VLMs (like GPT-4V or PaLM-E) inherently perform spatial reasoning by processing images. These models use fusion architectures that combine visual and textual features, allowing them to, say, look at an image of a room and answer spatial questions (*is the chair to the left of the table?*). Some advanced systems even allow the LLM to manipulate images as part of reasoning, for example, *Visual ChatGPT* or *OpenAI's Visual CoT* can rotate or zoom into an image to better inspect details. This is akin to a human tilting their head to understand a scene. Such tool-assisted visual reasoning enables the AI to handle spatial tasks with greater accuracy. Overall, by integrating spatial representations (either via symbols or via visual inputs), GenAI becomes much more capable at tasks that mirror our physical world understanding.

Temporal reasoning

Temporal reasoning is reasoning about time, the order of events, durations, frequencies, and temporal relationships (before/after, while, until, etc.). For AI, temporal reasoning is needed to interpret stories, schedule tasks, or understand processes. For example, an AI should infer from a narrative that *Alice finished breakfast before going to work,* which implies *breakfast happened earlier than work.* While this sounds simple, LLMs can get confused with complex time-based logic, especially when events are described out of chronological order or involve implicit time jumps. Temporal reasoning also includes understanding durations (e.g., if told *John took a 2-hour nap starting at 1 PM,* the AI should conclude *he woke at 3 PM*). In GenAI systems, robust temporal reasoning ensures consistency in stories (no character magically knowing something that has not happened yet), correct answers in questions about sequences, and proper planning for agents. Research indicates that LLMs still struggle with temporal logic and often require augmentations to handle it. For instance, one study noted that temporal reasoning tasks require a combination of skills, logical ordering, basic arithmetic (for dates or durations), and commonsense knowledge of typical timelines. To improve LLM performance, a technique has been to use an intermediate temporal representation, such as a timeline or **temporal graph** (**TG**). In a recent approach, text describing events is converted into a TG, a structured timeline, and then the LLM reasons over that graph using CoT steps. By explicitly mapping events to a timeline, the model more easily answers questions like *what happened just before X?* or *did Y happen after Z?* This method yielded more reliable reasoning steps and answers than letting the LLM free-form its internal timeline. In interactive agents, temporal reasoning allows planning over time (e.g., figuring out an order of execution: *first heat the oven, then mix ingredients, because the oven needs preheating*). It also helps with disambiguation, if two similar events are mentioned, understanding which came first can clarify context (as in stories or historical questions). Overall, temporal reasoning adds to an AI's robustness and coherence, ensuring that the dimension of time is handled in a human-like way.

Implemented in GenAI: Improvements in temporal reasoning come from explicitly teaching models about time. One strategy is temporal CoT, where the prompt guides the LLM to list events in order or compute time differences step-by-step. For example, a prompt might say: *Let us sort these events by when they happened,* before answering a question about them. Another strategy is integrating tools: an LLM agent might call a calendar API or a date calculator to handle tricky date arithmetic (like *what day of the week will it be 45 days from Tuesday?*) to avoid mistakes. As mentioned, converting text to a temporal graph is like giving the model an internal timeline to consult. After building such a graph (nodes as events, edges as temporal relations), the AI can either query it with a logical module or traverse it with learned reasoning steps. Also, specialized training data can help, e.g., fine-tuning a model on stories with annotated event timelines or on math word problems about time (so it learns concepts like elapsed time). In summary, GenAI systems are increasingly addressing temporal reasoning by combining language models with structured time representations and by prompting them to *think chronologically*, which leads to a more accurate understanding of when things happen and in what sequence.

Mathematical reasoning

Mathematical reasoning refers to the ability to solve mathematical problems and perform correct calculations or symbol manipulations. This ranges from basic arithmetic (*what is 12 × 9?*) to complex word problems or even proving theorems. Historically, pure neural language models were notorious for making arithmetic errors or failing at multi-step math problems because they tended to guess answers based on pattern recognition. However, with techniques like CoT, LLMs have shown remarkable improvements in math problem-solving. The key is that math requires *deductive, stepwise reasoning*, exactly what CoT prompting encourages. For example, consider a word problem: *Roger has five tennis balls. He buys two cans of three tennis balls each. How many balls does he have now?* If asked naively, a model might output a wrong guess, but with a CoT prompt, it will do: *He had 5. Two cans of 3 each means 6 more. 5 + 6 = 11.* and then conclude *11.* By externalizing each step (instead of trying to do it all in the hidden layers), the model dramatically reduces errors. Mathematical reasoning is not just arithmetic; it includes algebraic reasoning (solving for *X*), geometric reasoning (about shapes), and even logical puzzles like Sudoku. LLMs still have limits here, especially without tools; they might falter on very large numbers or long proofs because of length and precision limits. To bolster performance and accuracy, AI systems often incorporate tool-based approaches for math. An LLM agent can call a calculator or a Python interpreter for exact computation, ensuring no simple arithmetic mistakes. This kind of tool use has been shown to essentially eliminate calculation errors while the LLM focuses on setting up the problem correctly. The synergy of the LLM's reasoning and the tool's precision yields both correct and explainable solutions. The model explains the reasoning in words, and the tool provides the numeric answer. Mathematical reasoning in AI leads to improved performance on benchmarks (like GSM8K, a math word problem set) and is a good indicator of an AI's ability to handle systematic logical tasks.

Implemented in GenAI: Cot prompting is the main paradigm shift that unlocked much better mathematical reasoning in LLMs. Developers include worked examples with step-by-step solutions in the prompt or instruct the model to think step-by-step for math questions. This has enabled even models like GPT-3.5 to solve many grade-school math problems correctly, where they previously failed. For higher-level math or longer calculations, integrating external tools is common. For instance, OpenAI's code interpreter allows ChatGPT to write and run Python code; a user can ask a complex math question, and the model will generate a small script to compute the answer, combining logical setup from its reasoning with flawless computation by the machine. In agent frameworks like ReAct, a math question might trigger the LLM to issue an action, *Calculator[expression]*, get the result, and then continue the reasoning with that number. There are also specialized neuro-symbolic models (like *AlphaCode* for coding or *MetaMath* for theorem solving) that blend neural networks with formal math solvers. These systems treat math problems by generating hypotheses (potential solutions) and formally verifying them, much like a human might test an equation solution. In summary, mathematical reasoning is implemented through careful prompt design that encourages logical breakdown, sometimes combined with symbolic modules or tools that execute the grunt work of math, allowing the AI to achieve both correctness and clear justification in its answers.

Tool-based reasoning and ReAct agents

Tool-based reasoning in AI refers to an agent's ability to use external tools or APIs (such as search engines, calculators, databases, or even other AI models) as part of its reasoning process. Instead of relying solely on its internal knowledge, the AI recognizes when a tool can help and then acts to fetch information or perform an operation, and then reasons with the result. The ReAct framework is a leading paradigm that formalizes this process. In ReAct agents, the LLM does not just output an answer; it interleaves thoughts (CoT reasoning) with actions like tool calls. For example, consider a complex question: *what is the capital of the country that won the FIFA World Cup in 2018?* A tool-using agent will think that *the question asks for the capital of the country that won in 2018. That country was France (won the 2018 World Cup). The capital of France is Paris.* However, to be sure, it might perform actions: search for the **2018 World Cup winner** (gets France), then search for the **capital of France** (gets Paris), and then answer Paris. During this process, the agent's reasoning trace might look like:

```
Thought: I need to find the World Cup 2018 winner.
Action would be search(2018 World Cup winner)
Observation: France won in 2018.
Thought: Now find the capital of France.
Action would be search(capital of France)
Observation. The capital is Paris.
Thought would be, So the answer is Paris.
```

This framework improves accuracy and robustness because the model can fetch up-to-date or precise information rather than guessing (reducing hallucinations). It also helps with disambiguation, like if the question is unclear, the agent can do a quick lookup or ask a clarifying question as a tool. According to the ReAct paper, such agents showed superior performance on knowledge-intensive tasks and reduced errors that come from the model's uncertainty. Essentially, tool-based reasoning lets AI systems overcome their training limitations. If an LLM does not know something (e.g., a very recent event or a tricky calculation), a tool call can supply that knowledge, and then the LLM's reasoning can integrate it into the answer. This synergy mimics how humans think; we use notepads for calculation, search engines for facts, etc., resulting in more reliable and trustworthy AI outputs.

Implemented in GenAI: Modern LLM-based agents (e.g., those built with frameworks like LangChain, or OpenAI's Function calling API) operationalize tool use with structured prompts. A typical ReAct prompt might include examples like:

```
Thought: I need to know X
I will use Tool Y. Action: Y(query).
Observation.
Thought: Based on that, next I will... and so on.
```

The agent continues this loop until it can formulate a final answer (**finish[answer]**). Tools can be anything: a web search (for knowledge), a calculator (for math), a translation API, a database lookup, or even image recognition in a multimodal agent. The prompt engineering ensures the LLM knows the tools available and how to format actions. Because the LLM's CoT is explicitly connected to actions, the system can handle very complex tasks by decomposing them: the reasoning decides what needs to be done and in what order, and the acting fetches results or effects changes. This greatly improves decision-making in unfamiliar situations. For instance, an AI home assistant faced with *my internet is down, what should I do?* It might not have that answer in its training, but with tool use, it can run through steps: ping a server, read a troubleshooting guide, etc., then give a solution. Multimodal agents also use tool-based reasoning: an example is an agent that can see an image and then use an OCR module as a tool to read text in the image, then reason about it. Tool-based reasoning frameworks like ReAct have been pivotal in moving AI beyond static QA to interactive problem-solving. They contribute to robustness (fewer incorrect answers since the model can verify facts) and enable continuous learning, in a sense, because the model can always fetch updated info, and it is less constrained by the fixed training data. In sum, tool-based reasoning equips GenAI with a form of augmented intelligence, combining the model's textual reasoning with the precise capabilities of external tools to achieve far better performance on complex, real-world tasks.

Multimodal reasoning and fusion in AI systems

While many of the above reasoning types are discussed in the context of text, multimodal agents extend reasoning across various data types, e.g., images, audio, video, and text together. In such systems, reasoning involves fusing information from multiple modalities and potentially using one modality to disambiguate or confirm information from another. For instance, consider an AI that sees an image of a messy room and is asked, *can the vacuum reach the crumbs under the couch?* It must combine visual spatial reasoning (from the image) with physical commonsense to answer. Multimodal reasoning is enabled by architectures that perform alignment and fusion of modalities. Alignment means linking corresponding elements (e.g., matching a caption sentence to a region in an image), and fusion means jointly processing the inputs to produce a unified understanding. Models like GPT-4 Vision and Google's PaLM-E use transformers that accept both text and visual embeddings, so the model effectively sees and reads in one combined representation. This allows it to do things like identify an object in an image and then reason about it with world knowledge. Notably, OpenAI's recent research demonstrated models that think with images in their CoT, meaning the model can perform internal visual processing as part of step-by-step reasoning. For example, the model might internally decide to zoom into a part of an image or rotate it to read text, all as intermediate steps in solving a problem. This is essentially a multimodal ReAct: the model treats image manipulations as tools within a CoT reasoning process. The result is a significant improvement in tasks like **visual QA (VQA)**, image-based troubleshooting, or spatial reasoning from pictures. By fusing visual and textual reasoning, these systems achieve state-of-the-art performance on benchmarks that require understanding both modalities. For instance, an AI can read a diagram (image) and a related text paragraph together, reason about them, and answer a complex science question that needs both modalities, something neither text-only nor image-only models could easily do alone. Multimodal fusion contributes to disambiguation (the image can clarify what the text refers to and vice versa) and to robustness (the AI is less likely to hallucinate about visual details because it sees them). It also opens advanced applications: a multimodal agent can plan actions in a physical environment (vision gives it the current state, language reasoning gives it planning ability) or provide richer explanations (pointing to parts of an image while verbally reasoning).

Implemented in GenAI: At the architecture level, multimodal transformers incorporate modalities through techniques like cross-attention, where, say, text tokens attend to image feature maps. There are generally two patterns: a two-tower model encodes each modality separately, then combines at a later stage (e.g., via concatenation or a small fusion network), and a one-tower model that, from the start, processes mixed modality input in one network. The one-tower (fully fused) approach is what models like GPT-4 Vision use, essentially treating image patches like tokens alongside text tokens. This tight integration enables nuanced reasoning, like referencing a specific object in the image when generating text. On the software side, frameworks like *HuggingGPT* and others orchestrate multiple expert models (one for vision, one for language) in a reasoning loop; the language model decides when to call the vision model (as a tool), and then uses the result. This is a modular way to get multimodal reasoning: the LLM's CoT includes steps like self-questioning; *I have an image, let me ask the vision module for a description, then using that description, I will answer the question.* Such systems have successfully handled tasks like describing an image and then answering follow-up questions about it. Visual CoT prompting is another emerging technique: the model is prompted with not just textual thinking but also to imagine or sketch out a solution. For example, to solve a puzzle about tying knots, the prompt might encourage the model to visualize the steps (some research gets models to produce a pseudo-drawing in ASCII as part of reasoning!). While in the early stages, these approaches point towards AI that can use imagination-like processes. Finally, multimodal reasoning improves comprehensiveness by leveraging complementary strengths of each modality; the AI gets a fuller picture. Empirically, combining modalities often boosts accuracy and generalization. Multimodal GenAI agents can therefore tackle complex tasks (like explaining a meme, which needs vision + language + cultural commonsense) that were previously out of reach, all by integrating the reasoning types discussed (spatial, causal, commonsense, etc.) within a unified multimodal framework.

So, today's GenAI systems intertwine these diverse reasoning types to achieve more human-like intelligence. Each type of reasoning contributes in its own way to making AI outputs more accurate, coherent, and reliable. For instance, deductive logic ensures consistency and correctness given rules, induction and abduction allow creativity and handling of uncertainty, analogies enable knowledge transfer, and strong commonsense, causal, spatial, and temporal reasoning prevent the bizarre mistakes earlier models made about the world. Mathematical reasoning and tool use greatly enhance precision and factual accuracy, addressing key weaknesses of the past. Implementations like CoT prompting have proven that prompting an LLM to think aloud can significantly improve performance across math, logic, and commonsense tasks. Agent frameworks like ReAct go a step further by letting the model act on its thoughts (e.g., browsing or calculating), which makes decision-making more grounded and less prone to hallucination. And as we embrace multimodal fusion, AI can draw on the full richness of visual and textual information, leading to robust understanding and reasoning in complex, real-world scenarios. Crucially, research has shown that no single reasoning strategy is best for all problems—each approach can uniquely solve certain challenges. Therefore, the cutting edge of AI is about combining these reasoning types. By equipping generative models with a toolbox of reasoning skills and the strategies to choose among them, we are moving closer to AI systems that can think through problems as flexibly and reliably as humans do, if not more so.

About reasoning benchmark

Reasoning benchmarks are specialized evaluation tools designed to measure how well LLMs can think through problems, make logical inferences, and arrive at correct conclusions beyond simple pattern matching. Unlike traditional **natural language processing (NLP)** benchmarks that focus on language fluency or factual recall, reasoning benchmarks test multi-step problem-solving, mathematical deduction, causal inference, and planning skills essential for tackling complex, real-world tasks. By providing standardized, challenging scenarios across diverse domains such as science, law, and commonsense reasoning, these benchmarks help researchers objectively assess model performance, identify weaknesses, compare systems, and track progress over time. They are critical for ensuring that LLMs are not only articulate but also genuinely capable of robust, reliable reasoning.

The following table summarizes widely recognized benchmarks used to evaluate the reasoning capabilities of LLMs, highlighting their primary purpose and areas of focus:

Benchmark	Purpose	Focus
Massive Multitask Language Understanding (MMLU), AI2 Reasoning Challenge (ARC), HellaSwag, **Grade School Math 8K (GSM8K)**	General reasoning, commonsense, and math.	Broad reasoning skills.
Google-proof Question and Answers (GPQA), MATH, LogiQA	Advanced reasoning in STEM and logic.	Deep domain-specific reasoning.
R-Bench, OneEval, **Humanity's Last Exam (HLE)**	Multidisciplinary or structured reasoning.	Challenging cross-domain evaluation.
Advanced Reasoning Benchmark (ARB), PlanBench	Complex, specialized reasoning scenarios.	Next-level reasoning depth.
OptiLLMBench	Inference techniques impact.	Reasoning efficiency.
Apple's puzzles	Stress-testing reasoning limits.	Model robustness evaluation.

Table 12.1: Key benchmarks for LLM reasoning evaluation

Conclusion

In this chapter, we laid the theoretical groundwork for understanding reasoning in GenAI systems. By exploring a range of reasoning types, from deductive logic to multimodal integration, we highlighted how each contributes to more intelligent, reliable, and context-aware AI behavior. We examined how reasoning enhances capabilities like disambiguation, planning, tool use, and explanation. With techniques such as CoT prompting and ReAct-style agent design, reasoning becomes a practical tool for guiding AI outputs. This foundational understanding equips you to build advanced GenAI systems that not only generate but also reason through complex, real-world tasks.

In the next chapter, we will implement two types of reasoning in GenAI systems.

Join our Discord space

Join our Discord workspace for latest updates, offers, tech happenings around the world, new releases, and sessions with the authors:

https://discord.bpbonline.com

## CHAPTER 13

Advanced Multimodal GenAI Systems Implementation

Introduction

Having established a thorough theoretical foundation for reasoning in **generative AI (GenAI)**, we now shift focus from *why* reasoning matters to *how* it can be practically implemented. In this chapter, we will understand the architectural design patterns, frameworks, and modular components required to build reasoning-augmented GenAI systems.

You will explore real-world implementations using tools like LangChain, Ollama, and Python, and learn how to combine **chain of thought (CoT)** prompting, **reasoning and acting (ReAct)** style agent workflows, and tool-augmented execution into scalable AI pipelines. Through hands-on code walkthroughs and reusable templates, you will learn how to engineer systems that retrieve, reason, act, and adapt across text, images, and structured data.

Structure

In this chapter, we will learn about the following topics:

- Prompting techniques for reasoning in GenAI systems
- Architecture for reasoning at the reranking stage
- Architecture for reasoning at the recommendation stage

Objectives

This chapter aims to provide a comprehensive understanding of reasoning mechanisms within GenAI systems. It begins by exploring advanced prompting techniques that facilitate structured reasoning in language models. The chapter then delves into architectural frameworks and implementation strategies for integrating reasoning at the reranking stage, where retrieved candidates are evaluated and refined. Finally, it examines reasoning at the recommendation stage, demonstrating how multi-source data and user profiles can be synthesized to generate context-aware suggestions. Through practical examples and design principles, readers will gain insights into building intelligent, reasoning-capable AI systems for both retrieval refinement and personalized recommendations.

Prompting techniques for reasoning in GenAI systems

Before understanding code and architecture, let us have a quick understanding of prompting techniques for reasoning. Prompting is one of the most critical techniques for guiding and extracting reasoning capabilities from **large language models** (**LLMs**). As models grow more powerful, prompting strategies must evolve to support not just pattern recognition, but structured, explainable, and multi-step reasoning. This section begins with foundational prompting strategies like zero-shot and few-shot prompting. Then it progresses towards the advanced methods such as CoT, **tree of thoughts** (**ToT**), ReAct, and others that explicitly scaffold and enrich reasoning processes in GenAI systems.

Basic prompting techniques

This section introduces two foundational prompting strategies, which are zero-shot prompting and few-shot prompting, that are widely used to guide LLMs in generating accurate and context-aware responses. While these techniques offer powerful ways to elicit task-relevant behavior without model fine-tuning, it is worth noting that a broader range of advanced prompting strategies, such as CoT prompting, self-consistency, tool-augmented prompting, and contrastive prompting.

Zero-shot prompting

Zero-shot prompting refers to instructing a model to perform a task without providing any prior examples in the prompt. Instead, the model relies entirely on its pretrained knowledge and the natural language instructions given.

Example:

- **Prompt:** `Translate the following sentence into French: I am happy.`
- **Response:** `Je suis heureux.`

When used in reasoning tasks, zero-shot prompting is often paired with process-oriented cues such as let us think step-by-step, which help elicit implicit reasoning chains. This approach has been shown to improve performance on arithmetic, logic, and commonsense problems by encouraging the model to externalize its thought process.

The benefits are as follows:

- Requires no task-specific examples.
- Easy to deploy across domains.
- Useful for rapid experimentation or broad generalization.

The following are the limitations:

- May underperform on complex tasks without guidance.
- Sensitive to prompt phrasing.
- Cannot demonstrate reasoning format explicitly.

Few-shot prompting

Few-shot prompting involves including a small number of **input/output (I/O)** examples within the prompt. The following are some examples that serve as in-context demonstrations that guide the model in understanding the task format, reasoning style, or domain expectations.

Example (reasoning task):

```
Q: Tom has 3 apples. He buys 2 more. How many does he have?
A: Tom starts with 3 apples. He buys 2 more. So, 3 + 2 = 5. Answer: 5

Q: A bottle holds 1.5 liters. How much in 3 bottles?
A: Each bottle holds 1.5 liters. 1.5 × 3 = 4.5. Answer: 4.5

Q: A car travels at 40 km/h for 2 hours. How far?
A:  The car travels at 40 km/h for 2 hours. So, 40 × 2 = 80 so Answer is 80
```

Few-shot prompting is specifically effective for eliciting CoT reasoning, where the model learns to articulate intermediate steps before arriving at a final answer.

The benefits are as follows:

- Significantly improves accuracy on structured tasks.
- Encourages reasoning patterns via example imitation.
- Does not require model fine-tuning.

The following are the limitations:

- Prompt size is constrained by the context window.
- Requires careful example curation.
- Susceptible to order effects and prompt sensitivity.

Advanced prompting strategies for reasoning in GenAI systems

While zero-shot and few-shot prompting provide the foundation, advanced reasoning tasks, such as planning, tool-use, and multimodal integration, often require explicit scaffolding of reasoning, memory, or search. The following strategies represent emerging best practices for enabling deeper, more interpretable, and more robust reasoning capabilities in LLMs and GenAI agents.

This section provides an overview of advanced prompting paradigms that specifically aim to scaffold reasoning in LLMs and multimodal agents:

- **ToT prompting**: ToT (*Yao et al.*, 2023 or **https://arxiv.org/abs/2305.10601**) extends CoT prompting by enabling the model to explore multiple reasoning paths in a structured decision tree. Each branch represents a distinct intermediate step or idea, allowing the model to generate, evaluate, and select among divergent thoughts. This approach supports deliberation over multiple possibilities and has demonstrated improved performance in tasks requiring search-based problem-solving, planning, and creative ideation.

- **Graph-of-Thoughts (GoT)**: GoT generalizes ToT by allowing non-linear and cyclic reasoning structures. Instead of a strict tree, it models reasoning as a graph, enabling interlinked concepts, backtracking, and multimodal fusion. This structure is particularly useful in multi-hop **question answering (QA)**, dialogue systems, and interactive planning, where reasoning does not follow a single linear path. GoT is often combined with memory modules or agent frameworks to support persistent and contextual reasoning across steps.

- **Self-consistency prompting:** Self-consistency (*Wang et al.*, 2022 or **https://arxiv.org/abs/2203.11171**) improves CoT performance by sampling multiple reasoning traces for the same input and selecting the final answer based on majority vote or probabilistic consensus. This mitigates the variability of single-pass generation and reduces the impact of incorrect reasoning paths. The approach is especially effective in domains such as arithmetic reasoning, logic puzzles, and commonsense inference, where a single incorrect step can invalidate the final output.

- **Chain-of-Symbol (CoS) prompting**: CoS prompting augments CoT by converting linguistic reasoning into a structured symbolic form, such as spatial grids, tables, or key-value maps. This abstraction facilitates intermediate symbolic manipulation and has been shown to significantly improve model performance on spatial reasoning, inventory classification, and diagram-based problem-solving. By using symbols as cognitive scaffolding, models are able to organize better and operate on internal representations of complex inputs.

- **Scratchpad prompting**: Scratchpad prompting instructs the model to maintain and update intermediate variables explicitly during generation. This mirrors how humans write out steps when solving math or logic problems. It is particularly effective in domains such as mathematics, code synthesis, and data transformation, where intermediate state tracking is critical for correctness. The scratchpad acts as both memory and a validation mechanism within the reasoning loop.

- **ReAct prompting**: ReAct (*Yao et al.*, 2022) is a hybrid prompting strategy that interleaves CoT reasoning with tool-use actions. In this framework, models cycle through thought ⎮ action ⎮ observation steps, enabling them to reason, interact with external tools, and update their beliefs based on observations. ReAct has been particularly impactful in the development of agentic LLMs, allowing them to perform interactive problem-solving, **retrieval-augmented generation** (**RAG**), and task completion via APIs.

- **Typed CoT/typed thinker:** Typed CoT enhances standard CoT by assigning explicit reasoning types (e.g., causal, temporal, spatial, mathematical) to each step. This type of scaffolding improves reasoning diversity, modularity, and interpretability, and allows meta-models to select the most suitable reasoning type for a given problem. Recent studies show this approach increases accuracy and clarity, especially in multi-domain and open-ended reasoning tasks.

- **Generate–then–select (reranking-based prompting)**: This two-phase prompting approach involves the following:

  o Generating multiple reasoning paths or answers.

  o Selecting or reranking the outputs based on plausibility, consistency, or scoring heuristics.

    This approach is often used in conjunction with ToT or CoT and improves reliability in tasks where multiple outputs are plausible (e.g., open-ended questions, creative writing, fact-based QA). Reranking can be implemented via LLM self-evaluation, external critic models, or retrieval-guided validation.

- **Multi-agent prompting (debate and socratic reasoning)**: In this strategy, multiple LLM agents adopt different roles (e.g., proposer, skeptic, explainer) and engage in dialogue-based reasoning. The process simulates debate, peer review, or cooperative problem-solving and leads to higher-quality, cross-validated answers. This method promotes exploratory reasoning, conflict resolution, and multi-perspective understanding, and has shown promise in ethical decision-making, policy analysis, and interactive tutoring systems.

- **Automatic-CoT (Auto-CoT generation**: Auto-CoT reduces reliance on handcrafted exemplars by automatically generating CoT examples from existing QA pairs using heuristics or small models. This improves prompt scalability, supports domain adaptation, and enables zero-resource CoT fine-tuning. Auto-CoT can bootstrap reasoning abilities in new domains by systematically exposing the model to decomposed reasoning patterns.

These advanced prompting techniques represent a significant step toward aligning GenAI systems with human-like reasoning capabilities. By incorporating structured, diverse, and tool-enhanced reasoning flows, they enable LLMs to handle complex tasks with greater reliability, transparency, and contextual awareness. As GenAI systems are increasingly integrated into real-world workflows, the use of such reasoning-centric prompting strategies will be central to their robustness and trustworthiness.

Now that we have established a comprehensive conceptual understanding, let us proceed to implement two distinct scenarios:

- **Reasoning at the reranking stage**: This scenario demonstrates how reasoning is applied during the reranking phase using a CoT style reranker within a multimodal GenAI system.

- **Reasoning at the recommendation stage**: In this case, reasoning is employed during the recommendation process, where insights are derived from multiple heterogeneous datasets.

Architecture for reasoning at the reranking stage

The following figure illustrates a hybrid RAG architecture that enhances result relevance through combined reranking using both cross-encoders and LLM-based CoT reasoning. Starting from user input, the system retrieves semantically similar documents using a vector database, then refines the candidate ranking by fusing shallow semantic similarity (via cross-encoders) with deep reasoning-based scoring (via CoT prompts). The top-k reranked results are finally passed to an LLM for response generation, enabling contextually rich, highly relevant outputs tailored to complex user queries.

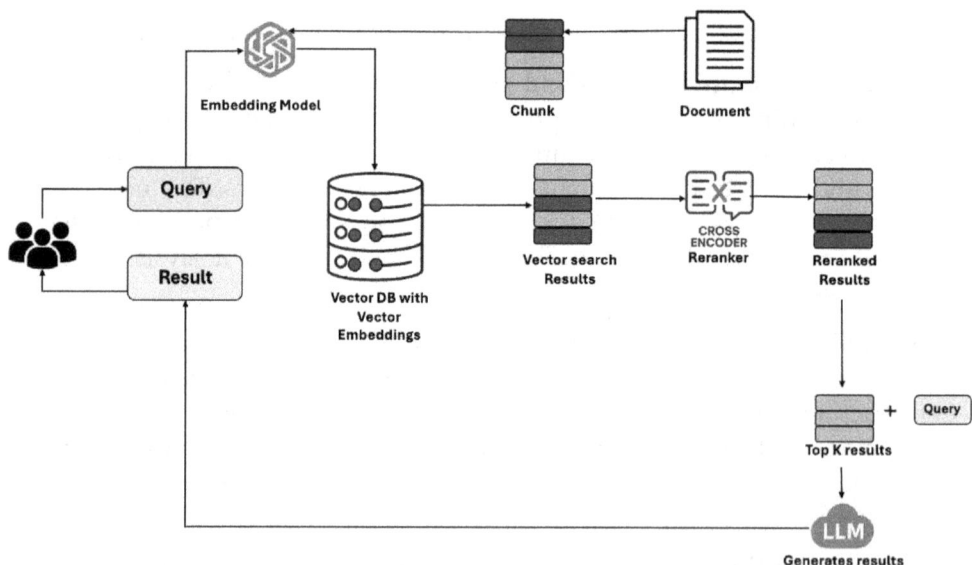

Figure 13.1: Hybrid RAG architecture with reranking for improved relevance

The reranking here combines image similarity (1–distance) and textual relevance scored using a CoT prompt via a language model (LLM). For each candidate spec retrieved using vector similarity, the LLM is prompted to reason step-by-step about how well the specs meet the user query, then assigns a numeric score (0–1). This CoT-generated score is blended with the image similarity score using a weighted average ($\alpha = 0.5$). The candidate with the highest combined score is selected. Thus, CoT enables deeper semantic understanding beyond vector similarity, improving reranking with interpretability and better alignment to user intent.

Let us understand the code in depth. this section provides a systematic explanation of a modular GenAI pipeline implemented in Python, designed for multimodal query handling, specifically matching user queries with laptop specifications using both image and text modalities. The system is built upon key components such as ChromaDB for vector storage, CLIP for image and text embeddings, and LangGraph for agentic execution with CoT-based reranking.

The following directory structure represents the implementation of a multimodal RAG system that incorporates dual-stage reranking, leveraging both cross-encoder scoring and LLM-based reasoning. Designed to support hybrid retrieval with image and text modalities, the architecture integrates core components for embedding, indexing, reranking, and orchestration via LangGraph agents. This modular layout ensures flexibility for experimenting with different reranking strategies and multimodal retrieval workflows.

```
multimodal_rag_demo_Dual Reranker+cross encoder+LLM score+image/
├── __pycache__/
├── chromadb_storage/
├── data/
├── frontend/
├── rag/
│   ├── __init__.py
│   ├── __pycache__/
│   ├── config.py
│   ├── embedding_utils.py
│   ├── index_builder.py
│   ├── langgraph_agent.py
│   ├── loaders.py
├── reranker/
│   └── cross_encoder_reranker.py        ← ☑ New module for reranking
└── requirements.txt
```

Figure 13.2: Folder structure of reasoning at the reranking stage

Module: loaders.py

This module encapsulates I/O utility functions for loading raw data from disk:

- **load_text_documents(folder):** This function recursively scans a specified folder, identifies all **.txt** files, and loads their content into a dictionary:

```python
def load_text_documents(folder):
    docs = {}
```

```
    for file in os.listdir(folder):
        if file.endswith(".txt"):
            with open(os.path.join(folder, file), "r", encoding="utf-8")
as f:
                docs[file] = f.read()
    return docs
```

This function ensures that textual specifications for laptops are appropriately read and prepared for embedding.

- **load_image_paths(folder):** This function identifies image files (with **.jpg**, **.jpeg**, **.png** extensions) from the specified directory and returns their absolute paths:

```
def load_image_paths(folder):
    return [os.path.join(folder, f) for f in os.listdir(folder) if
f.lower().endswith(('.jpg', '.jpeg', '.png'))]
```

This is crucial for preparing image paths for embedding and indexing.

Module: embedding_utils.py

This module provides access to *OpenAI's CLIP* model to embed both text and images into a shared vector space. The model and processor are loaded once globally for computational efficiency:

```
clip_model = CLIPModel.from_pretrained("openai/clip-vit-base-patch32")
clip_processor = CLIPProcessor.from_pretrained("openai/clip-vit-base-patch32")
embed_text_ollama(text)
```

Processes and encodes a given text string into a 512-dimensional embedding using CLIP:

```
def embed_text_ollama(text):
    inputs = clip_processor(text=[text], return_tensors="pt", padding=True,
truncation=True)
    with torch.no_grad():
        outputs = clip_model.get_text_features(**inputs)
    return outputs[0].tolist()
embed_image_ollama(image_path)
```

Encodes an image (loaded from disk) into a 512-dimensional embedding vector:

```
def embed_image_ollama(image_path):
    image = Image.open(image_path).convert("RGB")
    inputs = clip_processor(images=image, return_tensors="pt")
    with torch.no_grad():
        outputs = clip_model.get_image_features(**inputs)
    return outputs[0].tolist()
```

These embeddings allow for semantic comparisons across modalities.

Module: index_builder.py

This script builds the vector index using ChromaDB. It performs the following steps:

1. **Instantiate Chroma client**: To begin the indexing process, we first establish a connection to the persistent Chroma client:

   ```
   client = chromadb.PersistentClient(path=CHROMA_PERSIST_DIR)
   ```

2. **Create or reset collections**: Text and image collections are (re)initialized to avoid stale data:

   ```
   if CHROMA_TEXT_COLLECTION in [c.name for c in client.list_
   collections()]:
       client.delete_collection(name=CHROMA_TEXT_COLLECTION)
   ```

3. **Index text data**: Documents loaded via **load_text_documents()** are embedded and added to the Chroma text collection:

   ```
   text_collection.add(documents=[content], embeddings=[emb],
   ids=[str(idx)], metadatas=[{"file": fname}])
   ```

4. **Index image data**: Similarly, image paths are loaded and embedded, with only metadata (filename) used for reference:

   ```
   image_collection.add(documents=[""], embeddings=[emb], ids=[str(idx)],
   metadatas=[{"file": os.path.basename(path)}])
   ```

   This module ensures that all resources are embedded and stored for downstream retrieval.

Module: reranker.py

This module uses a cross-encoder model for reranking based on semantic similarity between the query and retrieved metadata filenames.

- **rerank(query, metadatas):** Constructs pairwise comparisons between the query and metadata file names and reranks using **CrossEncoder**:

  ```
  cross_encoder = CrossEncoder('cross-encoder/ms-marco-MiniLM-L-6-v2')
  def rerank(query, metadatas):
      pairs = [(query, doc.get("file", "")) for doc in metadatas]
      scores = cross_encoder.predict(pairs)
      ranked = sorted(zip(metadatas, scores), key=lambda x: x[1],
  reverse=True)
      return [doc for doc, _ in ranked]
  ```

  Although not used in **langgraph_agent.py**, it can complement or replace LLM-based reranking depending on the application.

Module: langgraph_agent.py

This module defines a structured agent using LangGraph to execute a multi-step retrieval and reranking process using CoT reasoning. The workflow follows three primary stages: embedding, reranking, and reading.

Agentic characteristics of the langgraph_agent.py module

The `langgraph_agent.py` module exemplifies an agentic system architecture grounded in the principles of structured decision-making, modular planning, and multimodal reasoning. Leveraging the LangGraph framework, the system implements a stateful pipeline to process user queries, retrieve semantically similar candidates, and rerank them using a hybrid scoring mechanism.

The agent's design incorporates several advanced capabilities that collectively enable intelligent, multimodal, and context-aware decision-making. The key architectural features include the following:

- **Stateful execution and modular design**: At the core of the agent is a LangGraph-based state machine, defined using a **StateGraph** that orchestrates node transitions across a linear pipeline comprising embed, rerank, and read stages. Each node transforms and propagates a shared mutable **state** dictionary, supporting agent memory and enabling sequential task execution. This aligns with agentic paradigms wherein decisions are conditioned on the evolving internal state of the system.

- **Reasoning via CoT prompting:** A salient feature of the agent is the use of CoT prompting to guide its reranking behavior. Specifically, the function **llm_score()** invokes a language model to reason step-by-step about the alignment between the user query and candidate laptop specifications. The model is prompted to output both an explanatory rationale and a normalized relevance score. This mimics the internal deliberation process characteristic of cognitive agents.

- **Multimodal decision-making and fusion strategy:** The agent incorporates both image and text modalities through the use of CLIP embeddings. During reranking, it computes a combined relevance score by fusing the image similarity score (derived from vector distance) and the CoT-based text score as shown in the following formula:

$$\text{Combined score} = \alpha \cdot \text{image score} + (1 - \alpha) \cdot \text{text score}$$

This decision policy exemplifies multimodal reasoning, allowing the agent to autonomously determine the most relevant candidate through weighted evidence aggregation.

Agentic attributes and functionality

The system demonstrates key properties of an agentic architecture:

- State management via a mutable dictionary passed across nodes.

- Autonomous decision-making based on learned embeddings and LLM-generated evaluations.

- Task decomposition into modular and reusable graph nodes.

- Explainability through logged reasoning and selected scores.

- Robustness via fallback logic when suitable candidates are not identified.

Although the current design follows a linear execution path without dynamic branching or tool use, the underlying architecture is extensible to support conditional transitions, tool invocation, and more complex agent behaviors. The agent is built upon a LangGraph-based execution flow, where each node performs a specialized function, ranging from embedding inputs to reranking candidates using LLM-based reasoning. The architecture enables interpretable, multimodal decision-making through modular state transitions and structured prompt engineering. The key components include the following:

- **LLM scoring with CoT**: The `llm_score()` function prompts the model to evaluate how well a given spec matches the query. The prompt is designed to elicit step-by-step reasoning followed by a numeric score:

```
def llm_score(query: str, specs_text: str) -> tuple[float, str]:
    prompt = (
        "Evaluate how well these laptop specs satisfy the user
request.\n"
        "First think step-by-step, then output exactly two lines:\n"
        "Reasoning: <your analysis>\n"
        "Score: <single number between 0 and 1>\n\n"
        f"User request: {query}\n\nLaptop specs:\n{specs_text}"
    )
    ...
```

The LLM used here is **ChatOllama** with the **"mistral"** model.

- **LangGraph nodes**: The LangGraph agent defines three core nodes, which are embed, rerank, and read, and each is responsible for a distinct step in the multimodal retrieval and decision pipeline, details as follows:

  o **node_embed(state):** Embeds the input query and optionally an image. It computes a vector average if both are present, and queries Chroma for top-5 nearest text specs:

    ```
    vec = [(a + b) / 2 for a, b in zip(text_vec, img_vec)] if img_vec
    else text_vec
    res = client.get_collection(CHROMA_TEXT_COLLECTION).query(query_
    embeddings=[vec], ...)
    ```

  o **node_rerank_llm(state):** Performs a multimodal scoring strategy that combines:

    ```
    image_score = 1 – distance
    ```

```
text_score = llm_score(query, spec)
combined_score = α·image_score + (1-α)·text_score
```

This score is used to select the most appropriate spec:

```
combined = alpha * img_score + (1 - alpha) * text_score
```

The CoT reasoning is also logged for interpretability.

   o   **node_read(state):** Reads the text of the best-ranked spec and its associated image path. If either is unavailable, it handles missing data gracefully.

- **Graph construction**: Using **StateGraph**, the agent flow is defined with explicit transitions:

```
builder.add_node("Embed",  node_embed)
builder.add_node("Rerank", node_rerank_llm)
builder.add_node("Read",   node_read)

builder.set_entry_point("Embed")
builder.add_edge("Embed", "Rerank")
builder.add_edge("Rerank", "Read")
builder.set_finish_point("Read")
graph = builder.compile()
```

- **Agent API**: The final callable method **execute_graph_agent()** initiates the graph with a query and an optional image vector:

```
def execute_graph_agent(user_query: str, image_vec: list[float] | None =
None) -> str:
    res = graph.invoke({"input": user_query, "image_vec": image_vec})
    ...
```

It returns a formatted output that includes the selected specs, image path, and reasoning log.

The codebase presents a well-modularized and extensible system for multimodal information retrieval and recommendation. Notably, **langgraph_agent.py** integrates LangGraph for orchestrating a pipeline with semantic retrieval and CoT reranking, thus allowing the system to produce explainable and robust matches between user queries and multimodal content. The separation of concerns across loaders, embedding modules, indexing, and reranking ensures reusability and maintainability across various domains beyond laptops, such as e-commerce, education, or healthcare.

The full code can be found in the GitHub repository of this book, under the section reasoning at the recommendation stage.

Having explored how reasoning is leveraged during the reranking phase through a CoT reasoning reranker in a multimodal GenAI system, we now shift our focus to a different but equally critical stage in the pipeline, recommendation.

In this next scenario, reasoning plays a pivotal role in synthesizing insights across multiple heterogeneous datasets to generate personalized and context-aware recommendations.

Architecture for reasoning at the recommendation stage

The following figure illustrates the complete flow of a personalized RAG pipeline that integrates structured catalogue data, user preference profiles, and metadata into a unified vector database. All datasets are chunked, embedded using a shared embedding model, and stored in a vector store. At query time, the system performs hybrid retrieval (combining **Best Matching 25 (BM25)** and dense vector search), followed by a cross-encoder-based reranker for fine-grained scoring.

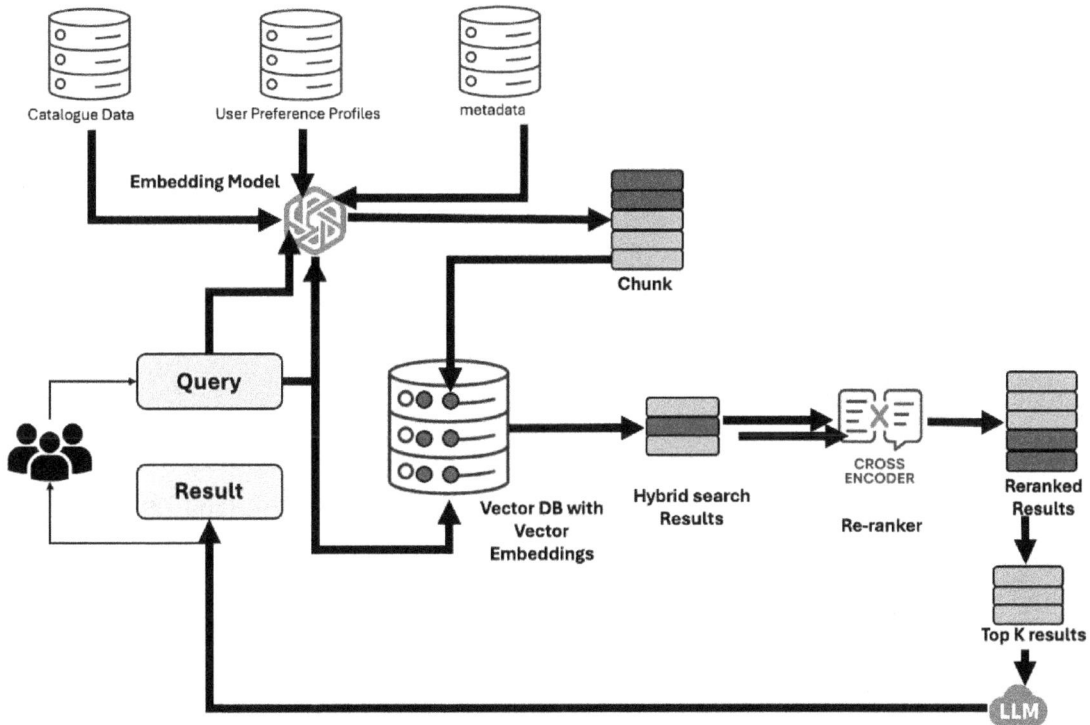

Figure 13.3: Architecture for reasoning at the recommendation stage

The dataset

Three datasets were used in this code, which has been shared along with the code in *Chapter 12, Advanced Multimodal GenAI Systems*, with CoT, reasoning, and reranking Recommendation engine with LLM, code part 2.

The following list outlines the three different datasets:

- **Updated_Synthetic_Dataset__500_Rows_.csv:**

  - **Purpose**: This is the main content database containing 500 rows of synthetic content items.

  - **Use case**:
    - Used to build the vector store (Chroma).
    - Embedded using `OllamaEmbeddings`.
    - Queried and retrieved based on user prompts (e.g., nostalgic mood).

  - **Contents include**: `title`, `genre`, `sub_genre`, `theme`, `live_event_flag`, `content_category`, `age_rating`, etc.

- **User_Preference_Profiles.csv:**

  - **Purpose**: This dataset defines user preferences, i.e., likes and dislikes.

  - **Use case**:
    - Matches incoming queries to users with similar tastes (e.g., user 16, 52, 19).
    - Helps guide filtering logic (e.g., family content, coming-of-age themes).

- **synthetic_dataset_metadata.csv:**

  - **Purpose**: Describes the meaning of each column in the main dataset (metadata dictionary).

  - **Use case**:
    - Acts as a documentation layer for human and LLM interpretability.
    - Can be optionally included in system prompts or for field validation.

The following directory structure outlines the architecture of the `rag_llm_memory_project`, a modular RAG system enhanced with long-term memory, personalized profiling, and multimodal reasoning capabilities. Each folder encapsulates a key functional layer of the pipeline, from embedding and retrieval to orchestration, reasoning prompts, and reranking, enabling scalable, context-aware content recommendations and diverse data modalities.

```
rag_llm_memory_project/
|
├── app/
|   ├── main.py                    # Entry point for the RAG system
|   └── config.py                  # Model names, file paths
|
├── embeddings/
|   └── embedder.py                # Embedding model via Ollama
|
├── vectorstore/
|   ├── db_handler.py              # Embeds and stores documents in Chroma
|   └── metadata_schema.py         # Adds metadata (e.g., source name)
|
├── retriever/
|   └── hybrid_search.py           # Combines BM25 + Vector similarity retriever
|
├── llm/
|   ├── generate.py                # Loads the Ollama LLM
|   ├── system_prompt.py           # Chain-of-thought system-level reasoning prompt
|   └── react_prompt.py            # ReAct-style reasoning prompt template
|
├── orchestrator/
|   └── rag_chain.py               # Orchestrates all modules into a full RAG chain
|
├── memory/
|   └── conversation_buffer.py     # Keeps chat history for personalized dialogue
|
├── profiling/
|   └── profile_parser.py          # Parses User_Preference_Profiles.csv for personalizatio
|
├── utils/
|   └── data_loader.py             # Loads and chunks all 3 CSV datasets as LangChain docs
|
├── data/
|   ├── Updated_Synthetic_Dataset__500_Rows_.csv   # Main content dataset
|   ├── User_Preference_Profiles.csv               # 50 users' likes/dislikes in NL
|   └── synthetic_dataset_metadata.csv             # Metadata descriptions for content
|
├── reranker/
|   └── cross_encoder_reranker.py
└── requirements.txt
```

Figure 13.4: Folder structure for reasoning at the recommendation stage

Goal of the recommendation engine

The goal of this recommendation engine is to deliver contextually appropriate content by interpreting natural language prompts through a CoT reasoning process. The following illustrates a representative execution scenario based on the user prompt:

User input prompt:

`I'm looking for content that matches my mood, which is currently nostalgic, and I want to watch with my 17-year-old daughter.`

The following list outlines the system's reasoning and execution steps:

1. **Mood identification**: The system interpreted the emotional tone of the query and categorized the user's current mood as nostalgic.

2. **Audience analysis**: The assistant recognized that the content must be suitable for both the user and a 17-year-old viewer, thus enforcing family-friendly constraints.

3. **Genre mapping**: The mood nostalgic, was algorithmically associated with the coming-of-age sub-genre, which typically aligns with reflective and emotional themes.

4. **Demographic compatibility**: The assistant prioritized content with cross-generational appeal, targeting narratives resonant with both teenage and adult audiences.

5. **User preference profiling**: The engine referenced a preference database, examining profiles of users aged 16, 52, 19, 77, and 82 to filter for those favoring family and coming-of-age content.

6. **Intersection analysis**: A focused subset of users (IDs: 16, 52, 19) was identified whose preferences aligned with both genre and audience criteria.

7. **Thematic enrichment**: Common thematic preferences across the filtered user group were extracted, highlighting courage, love, and adventure as dominant narrative elements.

8. **Content-type filtering**: The system excluded live event content by applying a logical constraint (`live_event_flag = False`), in accordance with inferred viewing context.

Final retrieval constraints

The system formalized the query as the following structured retrieval specification:

- `content_category = "Family"`
- `sub_genre = "Coming-of-Age"`
- `themes ∈ {Courage, Love, Adventure}`
- `live_event_flag = False`

The following is the final output statement:

`Retrieve non-live Family content with a focus on the Coming-of-Age sub-genre, incorporating themes of Courage, Love, and Adventure.`

Modular codebase breakdown

This system is a modular RAG pipeline designed to deliver personalized content recommendations by integrating structured profile data, hybrid retrieval mechanisms (BM25 + dense vectors), reranking via cross-encoder models, and LLM reasoning. The pipeline is built using LangChain, ChromaDB, Ollama, Transformers, and PyTorch, enabling dynamic retrieval, reasoning, and user-specific memory-based generation.

The following list outlines the modular components forming the backbone of the RAG assistant, each responsible for a specific stage in the retrieval and generation workflow, from data loading and vector indexing to hybrid retrieval, reranking, reasoning, and answer generation:

- **app/main.py**:
    - **Purpose**: Entry point for the RAG assistant interaction loop.
    - **Key responsibilities**:
        - Accepts user queries from the command line.
        - Calls the **rag_chain** via **invoke()** and prints both the answer and source documents.

- **app/config.py**:
    - **Purpose**: Stores global configuration constants.
    - **Includes**:
        - Model names (LLM and embedding models).
        - Paths to vector databases and data sources.

- **embeddings/embedder.py**:
    - **Purpose**: Initializes the embedding model.
    - **Implements**:
        - **OllamaEmbeddings** for converting text chunks into dense vectors using a local embedding model like **nomic-embed-text**.

- **vectorstore/db_handler.py**:
    - **Purpose**: Creates and persists the vector store using ChromaDB.
    - **Details**:
        - Loads documents and embeds them.
        - Stores them in a persistent directory (**VECTOR_DB_PATH**).

- **vectorstore/metadata_schema.py**:
    - **Purpose**: Attaches metadata to each document chunk before vector indexing.
    - **Metadata example**:
        - **"source"** field from the file name to trace results to their origin.

- **retriever/hybrid_search.py**:
    - **Purpose**: Implements hybrid retrieval using BM25 + vector similarity.

- o **Details**:
  - Uses `EnsembleRetriever` to combine sparse (BM25) and dense (Chroma) scores.
  - Helps recall both lexical and semantic matches effectively.

- **reranker/cross_encoder.py**:
  - o **Purpose**: Reranks retrieved passages using a pretrained cross-encoder model.
  - o **Model used**: cross-encoder/ms-marco-MiniLM-L-6-v2
  - o **Workflow**:
    - For each query-document pair, it computes a relevance score using BERT-style scoring.
    - Returns the top-k reranked passages used by the generator.

- **llm/generate.py**:
  - o **Purpose**: Initializes the LLM used for final answer generation.
  - o **Model used**: `Ollama`
  - o **Features**:
    - Local inference, low-latency, configurable temperature, and decoding settings.

- **llm/react_prompt.py**:
  - o **Purpose**: Provides a ReAct-style prompt for reasoning over the retrieved documents.
  - o **Format**:
    - First, ask the LLM to list reasoning steps.
    - Then, to produce an answer based on reasoning and context.

- **llm/system_prompt.py**:
  - o **Purpose**: Defines the system prompt that acts as the instruction guide for the assistant.
  - o **Scenario**:
    - Interprets structured user profiles and adapts recommendations to context (e.g., mood, companion, age appropriateness).

- **orchestrator/rag_chain.py**:
  - o **Purpose**: Integrates all modules into a complete LangChain RAG pipeline.

- **Pipeline**:
  1. Load documents and chunk them.
  2. Embed and store them.
  3. Use hybrid retrieval to fetch relevant chunks.
  4. Apply the cross-encoder reranker.
  5. Run the final generation with a ReAct prompt.
  6. Store conversation memory.
  7. Return the answer and sources.

- **memory/conversation_buffer.py**:
  - **Purpose**: Maintains conversational history across turns.
  - **Used for**:
    - Enabling contextual responses in multi-turn dialogue.
    - Only the assistant's generated response is saved, not the retrieval sources.

- **utils/data_loader.py**:
  - **Purpose**: Loads and parses CSV datasets.
  - **Datasets supported**:
    - `Updated_Synthetic_Dataset__500_Rows_`
    - `User_Preference_Profiles`
    - `synthetic_dataset_metadata`
  - **Function**: Splits rows into chunks and returns LangChain **Document** objects for vectorization.

The output is a structured reasoning trace from a conversational recommender system that tailors film suggestions based on user preferences. Two users are involved; details as follows:

- **User_82** wants 90s coming-of-age and family dramas suitable for a 17-year-old, avoiding genres like Sci-Fi and Comedy, and dislike's themes like friendship and family bonds.

- **User_19** requests light-hearted 80s films (romantic comedies or slice-of-life) suitable for a 13-year-old and their partner.

The following figure depicts the assistant filters, which retrieve and present recommendations accordingly. It suggests classics like *The Goonies, E.T.*, and *Back to the Future* as they align with the nostalgic, family-friendly, and age-appropriate preferences.

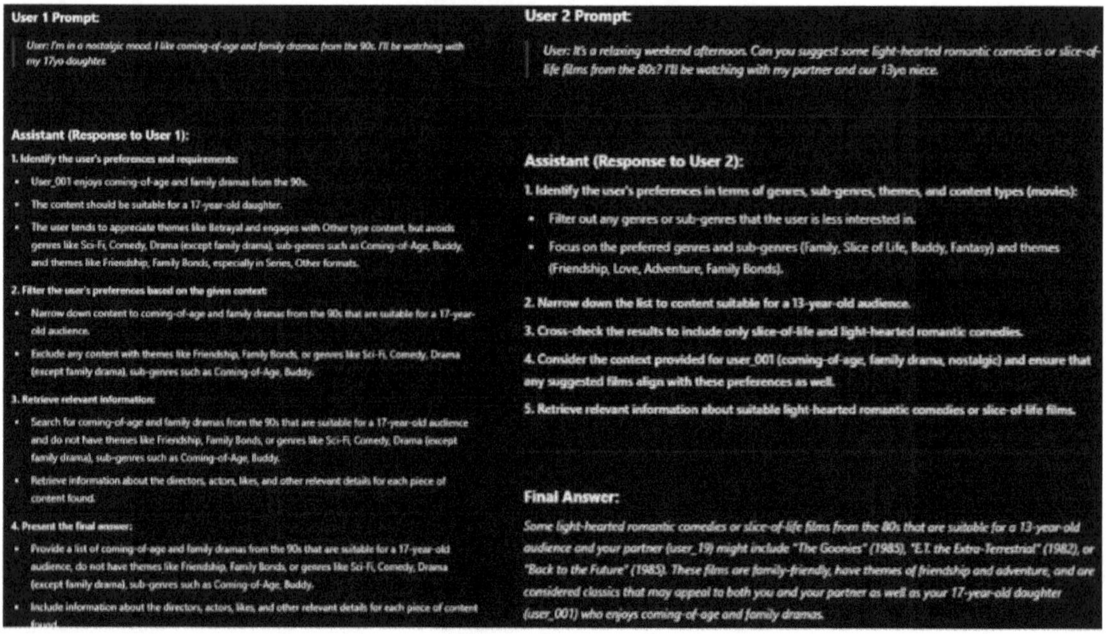

Figure 13.5: Output from the GenAI recommendation engine for two users

This system presents an advanced RAG pipeline that seamlessly integrates profile-based and content-based recommendation strategies, enhancing personalization through the use of hybrid retrieval and cross-encoder reranking for improved relevance. By incorporating conversational memory and ReAct-style prompting, it enables intelligent, context-aware responses tailored to user preferences. Additionally, the architecture is designed for extensibility, allowing future integration with multimodal inputs or real-time streaming data sources.

Conclusion

This chapter has outlined the foundational principles and practical implementations of reasoning within GenAI systems. By examining prompting techniques, we highlighted how structured reasoning can be elicited from language models to enhance decision-making. The discussion on reranking architectures demonstrated how reasoning can improve the selection of relevant outputs, while the exploration of recommendation stage reasoning illustrated the integration of diverse data sources to personalize content effectively. Together, these components form a cohesive framework for developing intelligent systems that go beyond surface-level retrieval, enabling context-aware, user-aligned responses. This understanding sets the stage for designing more robust and interpretable AI applications.

In the next chapter, we will understand other topics like text-to-SQL.

CHAPTER 14

Building Text-to-SQL Systems

Introduction

In the age of data-driven decision-making, the ability to interact with databases using natural language has emerged as a transformative capability. Text-to-**Structured Query Language (SQL)**, a branch of **natural language processing (NLP)**, enables users to translate plain English queries into structured SQL commands, allowing even non-technical users to access complex data insights with ease. This chapter explores the fundamental principles, system design, real-world applications, and practical implementation of text-to-SQL systems, particularly those powered by **large language models (LLMs)**.

We begin by introducing the basic concepts underpinning text-to-SQL, including natural language understanding, schema linking, and SQL query generation. We will then examine the architectural foundations of modern text-to-SQL systems, highlighting the role of schema-aware prompting, LLMs, and tool-based orchestration. The chapter also discusses various applications, from **business intelligence (BI)** dashboards to voice-enabled analytics assistants.

Despite its promise, text-to-SQL poses unique challenges, including handling ambiguous queries, ensuring SQL validity, and aligning natural language with complex database schemas. We conclude with a practical implementation guide, outlining strategies for prompt design, schema integration, validation techniques, and evaluation metrics.

By the end of this chapter, readers will gain a comprehensive understanding of how natural language interfaces can revolutionize database accessibility and empower broader data literacy across organizations.

Structure

This chapter covers the following topics:

- Text-to-SQL a hard problem
- Understanding basic concepts
- Exploration of real-world applications
- Key challenges
- Practical guidance on designing a text-to-SQL system
- Entity extraction using LLM and text-to-SQL system
- Enhance data accessibility and literacy
- Performance metrics and best practices

Objectives

The primary objective of this chapter is to equip readers with a foundational understanding of text-to-SQL systems, enabling them to grasp how natural language inputs can be transformed into executable SQL queries using modern LLM-based techniques. By exploring core concepts, system architecture, practical applications, implementation strategies, and evaluation metrics, this chapter aims to provide both conceptual clarity and practical guidance. Readers will gain the necessary knowledge to design, evaluate, or extend text-to-SQL pipelines within their own domains, preparing them for more advanced, agent-based systems discussed in the next chapter. This sets the stage for intelligent, interactive data access workflows.

Text-to-SQL a hard problem

Despite the rapid advancements in **generative AI (GenAI)**, particularly in NLP and code generation, the task of translating natural language into SQL, commonly referred to as **text-to-SQL**, remains one of the most challenging and nuanced problems in the field. While LLMs such as **Generative Pre-trained Transformer (GPT)** have significantly improved the fluency and contextual understanding of machines, they still struggle with the precise, structured, and domain-specific nature of SQL generation. This difficulty is compounded by a range of practical and theoretical challenges that make widespread deployment of text-to-SQL systems non-trivial, particularly in enterprise settings.

One of the fundamental challenges lies in the misalignment between natural language and structured data schemas. Human language is inherently ambiguous, context-rich, and often incomplete, whereas SQL requires exact, deterministic specifications that match the schema of a particular database. Users may refer to columns or tables in ways that do not directly align with the schema, using synonyms, abbreviations, or business-specific terminology, which requires the model not only to understand the intent but also to map it accurately to the database structure. This issue, known as **schema linking**, remains one of the core bottlenecks in building robust text-to-SQL systems.

Furthermore, not every organization's data is ready for GenAI-based querying. Most enterprise databases are designed for performance and legacy compatibility, not for semantic accessibility. They may lack proper documentation, use inconsistent naming conventions, or contain deeply nested schemas that are hard to interpret even for experienced engineers. Without clean, well-structured, and richly annotated metadata, even the most powerful LLMs struggle to produce valid and contextually accurate SQL queries. This lack of GenAI readiness in corporate data environments severely limits the practical applicability of text-to-SQL systems in many organizations.

Another challenge is the lack of generalizability across domains. While LLMs fine-tuned on benchmark datasets like *Spider* or *WikiSQL* perform reasonably well in academic settings, their effectiveness drops significantly when applied to real-world databases that differ in schema design, data quality, or business logic. Domain-specific nuances often require customization of prompts, fine-tuning on proprietary data, and the inclusion of domain knowledge, which increases development complexity and reduces scalability.

Additionally, ensuring the correctness and safety of the generated SQL poses a significant risk. Incorrect or malformed SQL queries can lead to performance degradation, privacy violations, or even data corruption if write operations are involved. Validating the output of LLMs requires execution-time checks, permission constraints, and ideally a **human-in-the-loop** (**HITL**) system, all of which introduce latency and operational overhead.

In summary, while GenAI has brought unprecedented capabilities to natural language understanding and generation, the structured, context-specific, and high-stakes nature of SQL generation makes text-to-SQL an enduringly difficult problem. The challenges of schema alignment, data readiness, domain generalization, and execution safety must all be carefully addressed before text-to-SQL can achieve widespread, reliable adoption in enterprise environments.

Understanding basic concepts

Text-to-SQL refers to the task of translating natural language queries into SQL statements that can be executed on relational databases. The goal is to enable non-technical users to interact with databases without needing expertise in SQL syntax or a deep understanding of the underlying data schema. This transformation involves several key components, including natural language understanding, schema linking, semantic parsing, and SQL query generation.

Natural language understanding is the initial phase where the system interprets the user's intent conveyed through human language. For instance, if a user asks, *what are the total sales for each region in 2023?* The system must identify entities such as *sales*, *region*, and the *temporal constraint 2023*. This requires both syntactic analysis (e.g., parts-of-speech tagging, dependency parsing) and semantic interpretation (e.g., recognizing that *total* implies an aggregation function).

Schema linking is a fundamental aspect that involves aligning the natural language elements with the database schema components. In practice, this requires mapping phrases like **total sales** to a specific column in a **sales** table, and **region** to either a column in the same table or in a related **regions** table. Effective schema linking often involves synonym resolution, entity recognition, and disambiguation, which are non-trivial in heterogeneous or poorly documented databases. Schema linking can be categorized into explicit (direct matches between query and schema terms), implicit (requiring inference based on context), and fuzzy (handling vague or ambiguous references).

Semantic parsing is the process of converting the interpreted natural language into a structured logical form, such as an abstract syntax tree or logical query plan. This representation captures the semantics of the user's request in a format that can be translated into SQL. Different parsing techniques include rule-based systems, statistical models, and neural approaches such as encoder-decoder architectures with attention mechanisms.

SQL generation involves mapping the logical form into an executable SQL query. This includes determining the appropriate SQL clauses (**SELECT, FROM, WHERE, GROUP BY,** etc.), resolving joins between related tables, applying aggregation functions, and ensuring correct filtering conditions. For example, the natural language question, *which products sold more than 1,000 units in January 2023?* Would be translated into:

```
SELECT product_name FROM sales WHERE units_sold > 1000 AND sale_date BETWEEN
'2023-01-01' AND '2023-01-31';
```

This transformation shows the need for precise mapping between human intent and machine-readable syntax.

Historically, text-to-SQL systems started as rule-based or template-driven methods that relied on handcrafted grammars and limited vocabularies. These systems lacked scalability and adaptability across domains. The introduction of **machine learning** (**ML**), especially deep learning, marked a shift toward more flexible, data-driven approaches. The use of **sequence-to-sequence** (**Seq2Seq**) models, attention mechanisms, and, more recently, LLMs such as GPT and Codex, has significantly advanced the state of the art.

Different types of SQL queries must also be considered. Simple queries involve **SELECT** or **WHERE** clauses, but more complex queries involve joins, aggregations, nested subqueries, window functions, and set operations like **UNION** or **INTERSECT**. Understanding these types is essential to cover a wide range of user intents.

Text-to-SQL systems can be categorized based on the level of supervision in their training: fully supervised systems require paired natural language and SQL examples; weakly supervised systems rely on indirect supervision (e.g., execution results); and unsupervised systems attempt to learn mappings without explicit training examples. Another useful classification is based on the interaction style, single-shot queries vs. multi-turn dialogue systems that support follow-up questions and clarification.

In terms of schema representation, systems must handle various complexities, including flat schemas (single table), hierarchical schemas (parent-child relationships), and relational graphs (multi-table databases with foreign keys). Representing the schema in a way that LLMs can understand, such as serialized table schemas, table-entity graphs, or embeddings, is crucial for accurate query generation.

In modern GenAI contexts, large pre-trained models have proven effective in understanding and generating SQL queries. However, they still depend heavily on prompt quality and schema-awareness. Techniques such as prompt engineering, **retrieval-augmented generation (RAG)**, and tool-based augmentation [e.g., function calling **application programming interface (APIs)**] are commonly used to improve accuracy and generalizability.

Use cases for text-to-SQL span across domains. In finance, users may query transaction volumes or average revenue. In healthcare, physicians might ask for patient data filtered by conditions or timeframes. In education, students can learn SQL by comparing natural language and formal query pairs. In public data access, citizens can ask natural language questions to extract insights from open government databases.

Despite advancements, common errors in text-to-SQL systems include semantic drift (where the generated SQL does not match the original intent), incorrect table or column references, and misinterpretation of filters or constraints. Mitigating these issues requires robust schema linking, strong language understanding, and dynamic validation mechanisms.

Understanding the basic concepts of text-to-SQL involves dissecting the multi-step process of parsing, linking, and translating human language into SQL. As GenAI models evolve, these systems are poised to become more accessible, adaptable, and accurate, but the foundational principles remain critical for successful implementation.

Exploration of real-world applications

The practical value of text-to-SQL systems extends across a wide spectrum of industries, enabling more intuitive and efficient access to data through natural language interfaces. As organizations increasingly adopt data-driven decision-making processes, the need for non-technical stakeholders to interact directly with structured databases becomes critical. Text-to-SQL provides a mechanism for bridging this gap, fostering inclusivity, and democratizing access to insights. The following are the key domains where text-to-SQL is making a significant impact:

- **BI and analytics**: One of the most common applications of text-to-SQL is within BI platforms and analytical dashboards. BI tools like *Power BI*, *Tableau*, and *Looker* are often configured with static SQL queries or filters, requiring technical expertise to modify.

By integrating a text-to-SQL engine, business analysts, product managers, or sales executives can query data repositories using natural language. For instance, a user could ask, *what were the top five products by revenue in Q2 2023?* And receive a visualized table or chart powered by a dynamically generated SQL query. This capability reduces the burden on IT teams and accelerates insight discovery.

- **Conversational interfaces and virtual assistants**: Text-to-SQL serves as a core component in conversational data agents—virtual assistants that allow users to pose questions about data in plain language. These systems are being embedded into enterprise chat platforms (like *Slack*, *Teams*, or custom internal dashboards), where they can respond to real-time data queries. A marketing manager might ask, *how many users signed up through the referral program last week?* And receive an immediate response, backed by a live SQL query executed on the backend.

- **Customer support and operations analytics**: Support teams benefit from natural language interfaces that allow them to monitor performance metrics and customer feedback. Text-to-SQL systems can enable support managers to ask, *show me the average ticket resolution time by agent in the past month*, or *list all unresolved high-priority issues*. These systems eliminate delays that typically arise from waiting for technical staff to write or run SQL scripts.

- **Healthcare and clinical informatics**: In clinical settings, text-to-SQL can assist healthcare providers in retrieving relevant patient data, medical history, or aggregated outcomes. For example, a clinician might query, *list diabetic patients over 60 who had elevated blood glucose in the last 3 months*. In many **electronic health record (EHR)** systems, the underlying data is complex and requires knowledge of both schema and medical terminology. Text-to-SQL bridges this divide, improving accessibility while maintaining data compliance when paired with robust access control mechanisms.

- **Education and SQL learning environments**: Educational tools that incorporate text-to-SQL offer students interactive ways to learn about databases and query formulation. Platforms designed for teaching data science or computer science often allow learners to enter a question in English and observe how it maps to an SQL query. These scaffolds for learning by connecting intuitive thinking to formal logic can also serve as a debugging or reverse-engineering tool.

- **Open government and civic technology**: Public data portals maintained by government agencies often expose datasets through SQL-backed APIs. However, public users frequently lack the expertise to write queries. Integrating text-to-SQL interfaces into civic platforms can allow citizens to pose questions like, *which districts received the most education funding in 2022?* And access curated data without barriers. This enhances transparency, civic participation, and policy analysis.

- **Retail and e-commerce personalization**: In the retail sector, category managers, inventory planners, and marketing teams often require fast access to operational metrics. With text-to-SQL, they can ask, *which SKUs had stockouts in more than three regions last month?* Or, *what was the average basket size for online purchases in Diwali week?* These insights drive campaign design, product placement, and supply chain responsiveness.

- **Financial services and risk monitoring**: Financial analysts and auditors frequently rely on historical data for forecasting, compliance, and fraud detection. Text-to-SQL can assist in querying structured financial systems using prompts such as, *list all transactions over $10,000 flagged as suspicious between January and March 2023*. This lowers entry barriers for auditors or compliance officers who may not be SQL experts but need direct access to timely data.

- **Manufacturing and IoT operations**: With the rise of **industrial IoT** (**IIoT**), manufacturing systems generate vast amounts of structured telemetry data. Engineers and operations managers may use text-to-SQL to investigate performance anomalies or efficiency metrics. For example, *show me all machine failures logged in Plant A with downtime greater than 2 hours last quarter*. This promotes proactive maintenance and reduces downtime.

- **Human resources and organizational planning**: **Human resource** (**HR**) professionals can benefit from text-to-SQL by querying employee data, training history, and performance metrics. Queries like, *how many new hires completed onboarding in Q1?* Or, *what is the average tenure of employees in the sales department?* Help in workforce analytics and planning. These systems also support diversity and inclusion reporting when integrated responsibly.

The real-world applications of text-to-SQL are vast and growing. From empowering internal stakeholders to improving public access to data, these systems are at the forefront of a shift toward more inclusive and intelligent data ecosystems. Their impact is particularly significant in organizations with large, heterogeneous datasets, where the friction of manual SQL scripting hinders decision-making. By embedding natural language interfaces into analytics workflows, organizations can unlock broader usage, deeper insights, and a faster path from question to answer.

Key challenges

While text-to-SQL systems offer a powerful interface between natural language and structured databases, the task remains fraught with substantial technical and practical challenges. These challenges arise from both the inherent ambiguity of natural language and the rigidity of SQL. Understanding these challenges is essential to designing robust, scalable, and enterprise-ready text-to-SQL systems.

The following list explores the most significant obstacles faced in this domain:

- **Ambiguity in natural language**: Natural language is inherently ambiguous and context-dependent. Unlike SQL, which requires precise syntax and semantics, human language often relies on implied meanings, contextual cues, and incomplete expressions. This gap makes accurate translation difficult.

For instance, consider the question, *show me the top-performing regions last quarter.* The term *top-performing* could refer to revenue, profit margin, customer satisfaction, or some other metric. Similarly, *last quarter* must be resolved relative to the current date, requiring temporal context. In the absence of explicit clarification, even advanced LLMs may struggle to generate accurate SQL queries.

Another layer of complexity arises from pronouns and ellipsis in multi-turn dialogues. In a conversation where a user first asks, *list all products sold in Europe,* and then follows up with *which of them had declining sales?* The model must maintain contextual memory and resolve them to the correct entity set, a task that goes beyond syntactic translation and enters into the realm of dialogue modeling and co-reference resolution.

- **Schema alignment and schema linking**: A fundamental requirement in text-to-SQL systems is schema alignment, mapping user language to the specific schema elements of the underlying database. This includes identifying which table and column names correspond to entities and attributes mentioned in the query. The problem is particularly challenging when the schema is large, uses non-intuitive names, or is sparsely documented.

Schema linking involves resolving expressions like the *highest earning employee* to something like `employee.salary` in the database. The complexity increases with the following:

  o Synonyms (e.g., *income vs. revenue*)

  o Abbreviations (e.g., *dept vs. department*)

  o Hidden relationships (e.g., *join paths between tables not immediately obvious*)

  o Multilingual expressions in user queries

This necessitates deep semantic understanding and often requires embedding the schema context into the prompt or model input in a way that supports accurate grounding.

- **Lack of domain generalization**: Text-to-SQL models trained on benchmark datasets often perform well within the scope of those datasets but struggle when applied to domain-specific enterprise schemas. This issue, referred to as domain generalization, becomes more pronounced when the model is exposed to the following:

  o Unseen table names and column structures.

  o Industry-specific terminology (e.g., *claims ratio in insurance*).

  o Highly normalized relational databases.

    Even LLMs such as GPT-4 can falter without schema conditioning or fine-tuning on domain-relevant queries. This limits the out-of-the-box utility of text-to-SQL solutions and necessitates domain adaptation techniques such as RAG, schema pre-embedding, and prompt engineering with domain-specific examples.

- **SQL syntax and logical validity**: Generating syntactically valid SQL is a non-trivial task, particularly when dealing with complex query structures involving multiple joins, nested subqueries, aggregations, and window functions. LLMs, while capable of generating plausible-looking SQL, often produce queries that:

  o Are syntactically incorrect.

  o Reference non-existent columns or tables.

  o Include contradictory conditions in **WHERE** or **JOIN** clauses.

Beyond syntax, logical validity is another challenge. A query might run without error but return incorrect or misleading results. For example, an incorrectly placed **GROUP BY** clause or a missing **HAVING** filter can change the semantics of the query, resulting in analytics errors that may go unnoticed.

- **Query execution constraints**: Even when syntactically and semantically valid, executing the generated SQL poses risks and constraints in production environments. Key challenges include the following:

  o **Performance issues**: poorly optimized queries may strain database resources.

  o **Security**: risk of SQL injection or unauthorized access to sensitive data.

  o **Data freshness**: models unaware of recent schema or data changes may produce outdated or irrelevant queries.

Additionally, query execution requires live database access, which complicates the training, debugging, and deployment of these systems. Offline validation environments or test sandboxes are often required, but they do not always replicate the production schema or data volume accurately.

- **Multi-turn interaction and dialogue context**: In real-world applications, users often engage in multi-turn conversations with data agents. This introduces the challenge of maintaining context across interactions, interpreting follow-up questions, and refining results iteratively.

Consider a dialogue like:

  o *Show me sales for Q1.*

  o *Now break that down by region.*

  o *Exclude products with returns over 10%.*

Each utterance depends on the context established by the previous ones. Maintaining the evolving query structure, filtering criteria, and target table references across turns is a significant architectural and modeling challenge. It requires memory-aware systems capable of maintaining and updating query state or constructing semantic graphs of the conversation.

- **Evaluation and feedback loops**: Evaluating the correctness of text-to-SQL systems is itself a complex task. Execution accuracy (i.e., whether the query returns the correct result) is often preferred over exact string match because multiple SQL formulations can yield the same output. However, execution-based metrics require a live database or simulation environment.

  Moreover, building feedback loops from user corrections, errors, or approval signals remains an open research area. Incorporating **reinforcement learning from human feedback (RLHF)**, confidence scoring, and fallback mechanisms can help improve reliability but introduce further design complexity.

- **Data privacy and governance**: In enterprise environments, access to data via SQL must adhere to strict governance policies. Text-to-SQL systems must be designed to:

  o Respect row-level and column-level access restrictions.

  o Mask sensitive fields (e.g., **personally identifiable information (PII)**, financial data).

  o Log and audit generated queries for compliance.

  Failure to do so could result in data leaks, audit failures, or regulatory violations. This adds another layer of responsibility to system design, beyond just model accuracy.

- **User intent disambiguation**: Understanding what the user truly wants often requires pragmatic inference beyond surface semantics. A query like *show me the best customers last year* leaves open questions:

  o *How is best defined? By revenue, order frequency, or retention?*

  o *Should the model default to one metric or ask for clarification?*

  o Intent disambiguation strategies include the following:

    ▪ Query clarification dialogues.

    ▪ Multiple choice disambiguation prompts.

    ▪ User-defined defaults or profiles.

  These strategies must balance **user experience (UX)** (keeping interactions efficient) with interpretability and correctness.

While text-to-SQL represents a promising interface between human language and structured databases, its implementation in real-world settings is constrained by a host of technical, linguistic, and organizational challenges. From resolving natural language ambiguity to ensuring SQL safety and execution correctness, the path from user question to executable query is fraught with potential failure points. Addressing these challenges requires advances in model design, schema representation, domain adaptation, and user-centered interaction design. Only through a holistic approach that blends AI, data engineering, and UX considerations can robust and trustworthy text-to-SQL systems be developed.

Practical guidance on designing a text-to-SQL system

Implementing a robust text-to-SQL system using modern language models requires careful orchestration of multiple components, ranging from prompt design and schema integration to output validation and system monitoring. While LLMs like GPT-4 have dramatically improved the feasibility of natural language interfaces for databases, their raw outputs must be carefully controlled, conditioned, and evaluated to ensure both correctness and safety in real-world settings. This section provides a comprehensive, step-by-step guide for implementing such systems, with an emphasis on pragmatic strategies grounded in current industry practices.

The following figure illustrates a high-level architecture of a modern text-to-SQL system, highlighting the critical stages from language model prompting to SQL validation and observability. It captures key components such as schema integration, user clarification, fallback mechanisms, multimodal extensions, and feedback loops essential for building robust and reliable natural language to SQL interfaces.

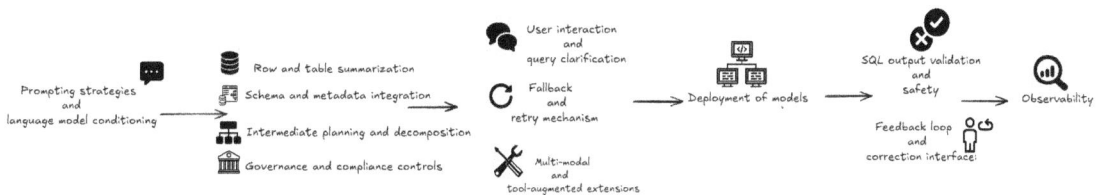

Figure 14.1: End-to-end text-to-SQL pipeline

The following is an explanation of *Figure 14.1*:

1. **Prompting strategies and language model conditioning**: Prompt engineering is a critical part of text-to-SQL implementation. Since LLMs operate within a zero-shot or few-shot paradigm, carefully constructed prompts can significantly influence their ability to translate natural language to correct SQL.

    - **Zero-shot prompting**: This approach assumes the model has been pre-trained on SQL patterns. A basic prompt might simply present the user query and database schema, followed by the instruction: *Generate the corresponding SQL query*.

      Example:

      o **Input**: `List customers who placed more than 5 orders last month`.

      o **Schema**: `Customers (id, name)`, `Orders (id, customer_id, order_date)`

        The model must infer the correct join and time filter from context alone.

- **Few-shot prompting**: Few-shot prompting includes 1-5 manually curated examples in the prompt to illustrate mappings between questions and SQL. This method improves accuracy, especially for complex queries, and allows injection of domain-specific idioms or business rules.

- **Chain of thought (CoT) prompting**: For very complex queries, one may use intermediate reasoning steps in the prompt. For instance: first identify relevant tables, then define filters, then compose joins.

  COT also enables a modular or agentic decomposition approach, particularly useful in enterprise settings with complex schemas.

2. **Schema and meta data integration**: LLMs do not inherently know the schema of a specific database and meta data of the schema unless it is explicitly provided. To bridge this gap, the schema and meta data must be embedded into the prompt or passed as context.

   a. **Flat schema listing**: Tables and columns are simply listed before the prompt. This is effective for small or moderately sized databases.

   b. **Structured schema encoding**: For larger schemas, especially with multiple foreign keys and nested joins, structured representation formats like JSON, annotated schema graphs, or entity-relationship summaries can be more effective.

   c. **Semantic schema mapping**: Advanced implementations use embedding-based semantic matching to relate user query terms with schema labels, identifying synonyms, acronyms, and implicit references. For instance, mapping `staff` to `employe` or `revenue` to `sales_amount`.

3. **Intermediate planning and decomposition**: Some implementations benefit from intermediate planning stages. Instead of generating SQL directly, the system might:

   a. First generate a natural language plan (e.g., *we need to join Orders and Customers, filter by order_date, group by customer_id*).

   b. Then transform that plan into SQL.

   c. This decomposition allows for validation at each stage and makes debugging easier.

4. **Row and table summarization**: Row summarization refers to generating a textual description of a specific row or record in a table. This often involves identifying key values, relationships, or anomalies and expressing them in fluent natural language. Table summarization focuses on producing concise narratives or insights about an entire dataset, such as trends, aggregates, distributions, or outliers across multiple rows and columns.

a. **Row summarization workflow**:

The system first interprets the user's natural language prompt and identifies the target row (via SQL filtering or lookup). Then, a summarization module, either rule-based or powered by LLMs, generates a narrative using selected fields and values.

    i. **Input prompt**: `Summarize the top-selling product in April.`

    ii. **Row output**: `{Product: 'Smartwatch X', Sales: 15,300, Region: 'North America'}.`

    iii. **Summary**: `Smartwatch X was the best-selling product in April, with 15,300 units sold in North America.`

b. **Table summarization workflow**:

After executing a SQL query that returns multiple rows, the system identifies key metrics (averages, trends, modes, and anomalies) and generates a summary.

    i. **Input prompt**: `Give me a summary of quarterly sales.`

    ii. **Summary**: `Sales increased steadily over the quarters, peaking in Q4 with $3.2M in revenue. The North region consistently outperformed other regions.`

5. **SQL output validation and safety**: SQL generated by LLMs can be syntactically or logically incorrect. It is important to validate generated queries before execution.

- **Static analysis**: Apply a SQL parser to check for syntax correctness. Tools like SQLparse or dialect-specific validators can catch basic errors.

- **Schema-aware validation**: Cross-check whether referenced tables and columns exist in the target database schema.

- **Logical validation**: Some systems implement test queries on a sample database or restrict execution to read-only views to prevent unintended side effects.

6. **Multimodal and tool-augmented extensions**: Recent systems explore hybrid architectures where the LLM interfaces with external tools or databases through function-calling APIs or plugins. For instance, an LLM might call a `get_table_info` tool to dynamically retrieve schema metadata or use a vector search module to resolve ambiguous column references. These tool-augmented LLMs blur the line between static language models and interactive agents.

Moreover, multimodal extensions may incorporate tables, charts, or visual dashboards as output formats. While still emerging, architectures that combine text input with visual output (text-to-SQL-to-visualization) are gaining traction in BI settings.

7. **System integration considerations**: Architectural decisions must also consider latency, scalability, and deployment environment. Some systems are cloud-based with real-time API calls to models like *OpenAI's Codex* or *Anthropic's Claude*. Others run locally with open-source models like **LLM Meta AI (Llama)** or **Falcon**, offering better control and privacy. Caching frequently used query results and modularizing the system components ensures both performance and maintainability.

8. **User interaction and query clarification**: Since many queries are ambiguous, the system should support clarification prompts. If multiple SQL interpretations are possible, present choices to the user:

   a. *Did you mean top customers by revenue or by number of orders?* This prevents wrong assumptions and builds trust.

9. **Governance and compliance controls**: In enterprise settings, ensure the system:

   a. Redacts or masks sensitive fields in generated SQL.

   b. Enforces row-level access restrictions.

   c. Validates user credentials and access scope.

   Integrating with existing **identity and access management (IAM)** systems ensures responsible deployment.

10. **Fallback and retry mechanisms in text-to-SQL systems**: As text-to-SQL systems evolve to support natural language access to structured databases, they must deal with a range of ambiguities, errors, and unpredictable user inputs. To ensure reliability and resilience, modern systems implement fallback and retry strategies, essential components for maintaining usability, trust, and accuracy. These mechanisms deal with the following:

    a. Ambiguous queries (e.g., *How many leads closed last quarter?* When *closed* is not clearly defined)

    b. Schema mismatches (e.g., using *revenue* when the table column is *total_sales*)

    c. Model hallucination (e.g., referencing non-existent tables or columns)

    d. Execution errors (e.g., SQL syntax errors, timeouts, or permission issues)

Fallback and retry strategies in text-to-SQL systems can take several forms, each designed to improve reliability and UX when the initial query fails. One approach is natural language clarification, where the system detects ambiguity or missing context and responds with a follow-up question, for example, *did you mean total revenue or net profit?* This encourages a conversational loop that helps disambiguate intent. Another method is retry with prompt refinement, where the system automatically adjusts the prompt using more specific templates, schema hints, or fine-tuned few-shot examples to regenerate valid SQL, typically without exposing this process to the user. In cases where the input is too complex, the system may perform a fallback to a simplified query, reformulating the request into a more basic version that still yields useful insights; for instance, turning a complex query about revenue growth for top SKUs into a simpler *show average revenue by SKU*. When the system cannot interpret the prompt at all, it may fallback to search or documentation, redirecting the user to dashboards, saved queries, or relevant schema references. Another strategy involves using default query templates for common requests, such as *top 10 customers* or *monthly trend*, especially when the intent is clear but exact mapping fails.

A robust retry engine might follow this logic:

```
try:
    sql = generate_sql(natural_query)
    result = execute_sql(sql)
except SQLValidationError:
    sql = regenerate_with_schema_guidance(natural_query)
    result = execute_sql(sql)
except TableOrColumnNotFound:
    sql = retry_with_synonym_mapping(natural_query)
    result = execute_sql(sql)
except Exception:
    return "Sorry, I couldn't find what you're asking for. Could you
rephrase?"
```

11. **Deployment of models**: Implementation can follow different deployment strategies, which are as follows:

    a. **Embedded LLM API**: Using external APIs like OpenAI's GPT or Azure OpenAI with schema-aware prompts.

    b. **Self-hosted model**: Fine-tuned smaller models (e.g., SQLCoder) deployed on local servers.

    c. **Hybrid agentic systems**: LangChain-based orchestration with separate tools for parsing, validation, and reranking.

    Choice of deployment depends on latency requirements, data security policies, and cost considerations.

Implementing a text-to-SQL system using LLMs requires far more than calling an API with a user prompt. It involves thoughtful integration of schema context, careful prompt construction, robust query validation, and user interaction design. When implemented well, such systems can transform how users engage with data—making structured databases accessible to non-technical users and accelerating insight generation across domains. However, reliability and safety must remain core priorities in any practical deployment.

12. **Observability**: As text-to-SQL systems grow in complexity, observability becomes critical for ensuring reliability, transparency, and continuous improvement. Observability refers to the ability to monitor internal states through externally measurable outputs such as query logs, model confidence scores, failure patterns, and latency metrics. Academic and production-grade systems alike benefit from instrumenting each stage of the text-to-SQL pipeline—from natural language parsing to SQL generation and execution—with detailed telemetry. This facilitates error diagnosis, user behavior analysis, prompt optimization, and safe rollback during model updates, ultimately supporting system accountability and responsible AI practices.

13. **Feedback loop and correction interface**: Finally, in enterprise-grade deployments, HITL escalation ensures that unresolved queries are routed to data analysts, who can provide responses and contribute to improving the system through feedback and training data. These layered fallback strategies make text-to-SQL systems more resilient, adaptive, and user-friendly. Users should be able to flag incorrect outputs and suggest corrections. Capturing this data enables retraining, fine-tuning, or rule updates.

    a. **Correction interface**: Allow users to edit generated SQL or select from ranked alternatives. Use this input to adjust future prompt templates or schema mappings.

    b. **Logging and analytics**: Track model confidence, failure reasons, and common query patterns. Over time, this supports system refinement and identifies training gaps.

       Note: Execution environment setup: A reliable execution environment is essential for safe query evaluation:

       - **Run queries against a test sandbox database before production**
       - **Use read-only replicas to prevent write or update operations**
       - **Impose query timeout limits and resource caps**
       - **Enable logging of all queries for audit and error tracking**

Building on the step-by-step guide for implementing a text-to-SQL system, which typically includes components such as schema ingestion, prompt engineering, SQL decoding, and query validation, the next logical focus is on entity extraction. Entity extraction acts as the semantic bridge between unstructured user queries and structured database elements, enabling the system to ground natural language input in the schema vocabulary. Whether as a standalone module or as part of an agent-based orchestration workflow, robust entity extraction enhances interpretability, modularity, and SQL accuracy, laying the foundation for more reliable downstream query generation.

Entity extraction using LLM and text-to-SQL system

This pipeline implements an end-to-end NLP workflow that transforms unstructured product review text into structured tabular data. It achieves this by extracting named entities such as customer names and purchase dates using a local LLM, combining them with existing tabular records, and storing the merged results in an in-memory SQL database for subsequent querying.

The system is modular and agentic in design, leveraging the LangGraph library to define stateful graph transitions and Ollama for LLM inference. This pattern supports scalable, interpretable workflows for enterprise data integration and **question answering** (**QA**).

The following figure visually represents the LangGraph-based workflow for a text-to-SQL preprocessing pipeline. It captures the conditional execution logic between multiple agent nodes responsible for parsing column semantics, generating LLM-based chains, extracting structured data, merging datasets, and populating an SQL-accessible database. The flow begins with a conditional entry point based on the availability of column descriptions and proceeds through a deterministic path of entity extraction and data consolidation. A retry branch ensures robustness, while the final decision node allows the system to either populate the database or terminate gracefully. This modular design enables interpretable, state-aware orchestration of NLP tasks.

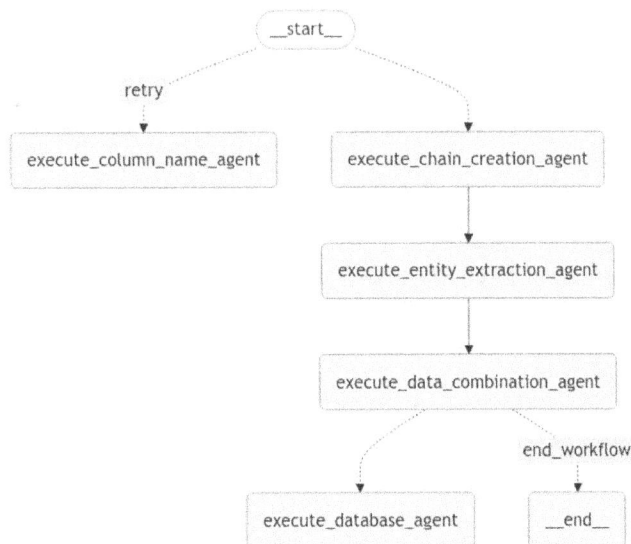

Figure 14.2: *LangGraph workflow for entity extraction using text-to-SQL*

The complete end-to-end code is provided in the GitHub repository, where you can find and understand various architectural approaches to experiment with.

Architecture overview

The implementation is architected as a multi-agent system using the LangGraph framework. The workflow is composed of five main agents, each encapsulating a discrete function, which are as follows:

- **ColumnNameAgent**: It parses and structures user-defined column descriptions.

- **ChainCreationAgent**: It creates an LLM-based extraction chain using structured prompts and a JSON parser.

- **EntityExtractionAgent**: It applies the LLM pipeline to extract data from natural language reviews.

- **DataCombinationAgent**: It merges structured and extracted data using pandas.

- **DatabaseAgent**: It converts merged data into an SQL-accessible format via SQLite and SQLAlchemy.

A graph-based control flow governs the transitions between these agents, supporting conditional branching, retry logic, and full control over execution sequencing.

The following steps outline a detailed walkthrough of the code:

1. **Imports and environment setup**: To begin, all necessary libraries are imported, including LangGraph for workflow orchestration, Ollama for local model interaction, and pandas/SQLAlchemy for data processing and storage, as shown in the following code:

```
import ollama, langgraph
from langchain_ollama import ChatOllama
from sqlalchemy import create_engine
from sqlalchemy.pool import StaticPool
```

The environment combines Ollama for local LLM inference and LangGraph for declarative workflow definition. The **ChatOllama** wrapper interfaces with the model **llama3.2:3b-instruct-fp16**, which serves as the **named entity recognition (NER)** engine.

2. **Defining the shared graph state**: The pipeline uses a mutable, typed graph state to pass structured data and artifacts between agents. This centralized state design supports modular, state-aware transitions, as shown in the following code:

```
class GraphState(TypedDict):
    question: str
    ...
```

The **GraphState** type defines the shape of the shared mutable state. It includes metadata (like the user question), input schema, chain objects, and intermediate outputs. This design adheres to functional programming principles while enabling state mutation across agent transitions.

3. **ColumnNameAgent**: This agent constructs a LangChain pipeline, connecting a prompt, a local LLM, and a JSON parser. The following is the core of the entity recognition process:

```
class ColumnNameAgent:
    def run(self, state):

        ...
```

This agent parses the user-defined **column_name_str** into a structured dictionary **column_names**. Each entry maps a raw column label to a semantic description (e.g., *"Name": "<Name of the customer>"*). These tags guide the LLM in downstream extraction.

4. **ChainCreationAgent**: This agent constructs a LangChain pipeline, connecting a prompt, a local LLM, and a JSON parser. The following is the core of the entity recognition process:

```
class ChainCreationAgent:
    def run(self, state):

        ...
```

a. The LLM is configured with a **PromptTemplate** instructing it to perform named entity recognition. The prompt is crafted in a role-specific tone and demands structured output:

```
template = """You need to act as a Named Entity Recognizer.
```

b. Extract the following column names from the review text:

```
{column_names}
...
STRICTLY respond in JSON format like: {"column_1": "<value 1>",
... }
"""
```

This agent initializes a chain, linking the prompt | LLM | JSON parser.

5. **EntityExtractionAgent**: The model-powered chain is now invoked over a list of review texts, generating structured row-wise dictionaries of extracted values for downstream processing, as shown in the following code:

```
class EntityExtractionAgent:
    def run(self, state):

        ...
```

The chain is applied iteratively over the **ReviewText** column in **df2**. Each LLM output is parsed and collected into **extracted_data**, a list of dictionaries representing structured row-level extractions. This agent essentially operationalizes the LLM as an entity extractor.

6. **DataCombinationAgent**: The extracted fields are merged with the existing tabular data, aligning on key columns. The result is a fully structured dataset with both original and derived information, as shown in the following code:

```
class DataCombinationAgent:
    def run(self, state):
        ...
```

    a.   This stage performs a join between:

        i.   The original structured table **df1**

        ii.   The newly extracted **dataframe extracted_df**

    Join keys are inferred from the structured column definitions. The result is saved as **merged_data** and exported to disk as a CSV file.

7. **DatabaseAgent**: After combining the datasets, this agent writes the output to a memory-resident SQLite database, making it accessible via SQL queries:

```
class DatabaseAgent:
    def run(self, state):
        ...
```

Here, the merged data is persisted in a transient SQLite database. SQLAlchemy is configured with a StaticPool to ensure the in-memory connection remains valid across sessions. This enables downstream LLMs or applications to perform SQL queries without requiring a full **relational database management system (RDBMS)**.

8. **Graph definition and workflow compilation**: Each agent is added to the LangGraph as a node. Conditional edges define execution paths based on data availability and retry logic, as shown in the following code:

```
workflow = StateGraph(GraphState)
...
graph = workflow.compile()
```

Each agent is added as a node in the LangGraph, with conditional transitions between them. Entry point routing and retry logic are controlled by custom functions **decide_entry_point** and **decide_next_step**.

9. **Workflow execution**: A custom runner simulates step-by-step execution of the graph. This loop handles node routing, transitions, and error resolution, as shown:

```
def process_workflow(state):
    ...
```

The **process_workflow** function executes the pipeline sequentially. This is a linearized version of LangGraph's graph traversal. It manually steps through each phase until the end is reached, logging output at each transition.

10. **Initialization and example run**: Finally, sample data is used to initialize the state, and the full workflow is executed. Outputs include the final structured dataset and a live database engine for SQL access, as shown in the following code:

```
initial_state = GraphState(...)
```

   a. Two toy DataFrames (**df1** and **df2**) simulate a customer dataset and corresponding review texts. Upon execution, the final state includes the following:

   i. Extracted entities

   ii. Merged dataset

   iii. Database engine

   This setup facilitates downstream querying, visualization, or LLM-assisted analytics over the structured result.

This workflow demonstrates a composable, interpretable architecture for turning natural language data into SQL-ready form using local LLMs and graph-based orchestration. The modular agent design enhances explainability and error isolation, while LangGraph enables flexible control of overflow logic and retries. Such systems are valuable in customer support automation, e-commerce analytics, and review summarization pipelines.

An end-to-end Multi DB Agentic implementation is available in *Chapter 15, Agentic Text-to-SQL Systems and Architecture Decision-Making*.

Enhance data accessibility and literacy

In the modern data-centric economy, access to actionable information is critical for decision-making, innovation, and operational efficiency. Yet the vast majority of valuable data resides in structured relational databases that are often inaccessible to non-technical users. These users typically lack the expertise to write SQL queries, understand schema complexity, or navigate BI tools with steep learning curves. Text-to-SQL systems, which enable users to interact with structured data using natural language, are poised to transform this landscape by dramatically increasing data accessibility and promoting data literacy across organizational hierarchies.

The following list explores how text-to-SQL systems are transforming the landscape of data accessibility, enabling a more inclusive, agile, and data-literate workforce:

- **Bridging the technical divide**: Traditionally, querying databases has been the domain of data analysts, database administrators, or software engineers. Business users, such as sales managers, product owners, and HR professionals, are typically forced to rely on these technical experts to extract insights from data. This creates bottlenecks and delays in insight generation, limiting responsiveness and innovation.

   Text-to-SQL systems remove this barrier by allowing users to express their queries in plain language. For example, instead of waiting for a data analyst to write a SQL query, a marketing manager could type, *show me all leads from last month who converted into customers*. This input is translated automatically into SQL, executed, and visualized instantly. The result is a faster feedback loop, empowering business users to make data-informed decisions independently.

- **Democratizing data in large organizations**: As organizations scale, data becomes siloed both physically across departments and cognitively across knowledge domains. Different teams may use different terminologies or interpret metrics in unique ways. Text-to-SQL systems help to unify access by presenting a common natural language interface, customized to the enterprise's vocabulary.

  By embedding domain-specific prompts and leveraging schema-aware prompting, these systems can accommodate multiple departments without requiring them to understand the underlying database structure. This democratization promotes transparency, cross-functional collaboration, and a shared understanding of key metrics.

- **Fostering a culture of data literacy**: Data literacy refers to the ability to read, work with, analyze, and communicate with data. It is a vital skill in the digital economy, yet it remains underdeveloped in many organizations due to barriers in tooling and training.

  Text-to-SQL lowers the entry point for engaging with data. By allowing users to formulate and iterate on data questions in natural language, it builds an intuitive understanding of how data is structured and how it can answer business questions. Over time, users begin to develop mental models of the schema, understand joins and filters, and even improve their question formulation skills.

  Additionally, some educational platforms use text-to-SQL as a teaching tool. Learners can input questions in English and see how they map to SQL syntax. This interactive learning process supports comprehension and builds confidence in data exploration.

- **Empowering real-time decision-making**: The speed of decision-making is often constrained by the availability of insights. In fast-paced industries, such as e-commerce, logistics, and finance, waiting for a data request to be fulfilled can result in lost opportunities. Text-to-SQL systems, especially when embedded in dashboards, chat interfaces, or mobile apps, allow frontline workers to obtain insights on demand.

  - **For example**:
    - A warehouse manager can ask, *which items are running low in Zone 3?*
    - A financial planner can ask, *what was the YoY revenue change for Q3?*
    - A healthcare provider can ask, *how many patients with asthma visited in the last 7 days?*

    These questions are transformed into executable queries and delivered instantly, reducing friction and enabling real-time decisions.

- **Enhancing data governance and traceability**: When users manually write SQL, version control and access control become hard to enforce. Text-to-SQL systems centralize query generation, making it easier to enforce:

  o   Role-based access to data.

  o   Logging and auditing of all queries.

  o   Consistent metrics definitions via templates.

  This increases trust in data, reduces the risk of misinterpretation, and supports compliance with internal policies or regulatory standards.

- **Closing the gap between curiosity and capability**: One of the hidden costs in data workflows is the suppression of curiosity. When users know that it is too difficult or takes too long to get a data question answered, they stop asking. Text-to-SQL reactivates this curiosity by enabling fast iteration. Users can ask a follow-up question, rephrase, or drill down without needing to re-engage an analyst or engineer.

  This cultivates a more exploratory, insight-driven mindset across the organization, moving from static dashboards to dynamic querying.

- **Supporting inclusive and global access**: In multilingual or accessibility-aware environments, text-to-SQL systems can support localized inputs or voice queries, broadening data access to a wider range of users. With proper training and interface design, even non-literate or visually impaired users could query databases using speech or translated queries.

  This positions text-to-SQL not only as a technical innovation but also as a key enabler of digital inclusion.

Text-to-SQL technology is more than a technical convenience; it is a strategic enabler of widespread data empowerment. By allowing users to ask questions in their own words and receive reliable answers grounded in structured data, these systems break down longstanding barriers between data and people. They enable self-service analytics, foster a culture of curiosity, and elevate the data literacy of an organization as a whole. In the coming years, the successful adoption of text-to-SQL systems may be a key differentiator for organizations that seek to be truly data-driven in both strategy and execution.

Performance metrics and best practices

Evaluating the performance of text-to-SQL systems is a complex and multifaceted task. These systems do not produce simple labels or continuous values; instead, they generate structured queries that must be both syntactically correct and semantically aligned with the user's intent. Moreover, there is often more than one correct way to express a query in SQL, which complicates evaluation further. This section introduces key evaluation metrics used in text-to-SQL research and practice, providing detailed definitions and guidance on their use, followed by best practices for real-world deployments.

Exact match accuracy

Exact match accuracy measures the percentage of generated SQL queries that match the reference (ground truth) queries exactly, including all elements such as clauses, table names, aliases, and formatting. This is a strict metric where even a minor variation (such as a different join order or use of an alias) is considered an error. It is typically applied in benchmark datasets like Spider, where ground truth is available and the task is framed as one-to-one mapping from natural language to SQL.

The following list outlines the advantages, limitations, and use cases:

- **Advantages**:
  - Simple to compute and interpret.
  - Enables direct comparison across models on shared benchmarks.

- **Limitations**:
  - Over-penalizes valid but syntactically different queries.
  - Ignores semantic equivalence and result correctness.
  - Not suitable for open-domain or production systems with flexible schemas.

- **Use case**: Primarily used in research benchmarks where standard SQL templates and fixed schemas are provided.

Execution accuracy

Execution accuracy evaluates whether the generated SQL, when executed on the target database, returns the same result as the reference SQL query. It directly compares the output of both queries and considers them equal if the result sets match, regardless of query structure.

The following list outlines the advantages, limitations, and use cases:

- **Advantages**:
  - Better aligns with user expectations (correct answers matter more than SQL syntax).
  - Tolerates syntactic variation and aliasing.
  - Allows equivalence testing even in complex queries.

- **Limitations**:
  - Requires access to a test or production database instance.
  - Sensitive to changes in data distribution or row ordering.
  - Cannot be applied to queries involving non-deterministic operations (e.g., `random()`, `LIMIT without ORDER BY`).

- **Use case**: Preferred in practical systems and production evaluations where the goal is to ensure the user receives the correct information.

Component-level accuracy

This metric decomposes the SQL query into structural components such as **SELECT**, **WHERE**, **GROUP BY**, **ORDER BY**, **HAVING**, and **JOIN** clauses. It measures how many of these components are correctly predicted relative to the reference query.

The following list outlines the advantages, limitations, and use cases:

- **Advantages**:
    - Provides granular insights into system performance.
    - Useful for diagnosing which parts of the query generation pipeline need improvement.
    - Can be weighted by importance or frequency.
- **Limitations**:
    - Requires a structured SQL parse tree.
    - Not suitable as a sole metric, must be used alongside others.
- **Use case**: Best for debugging models, instructional tools, or tracking improvement during iterative development.

Query execution success rate

This metric measures the percentage of generated SQL queries that can be executed successfully on the database without triggering syntax or runtime errors. It does not assess the correctness of results, only whether the query can run.

The following list outlines the advantages, limitations, and use cases:

- **Advantages**:
    - Indicates robustness and syntactic validity of the model output.
    - Useful for tracking production system health.
- **Limitations**:
    - Ignores semantic errors (e.g., wrong logic, wrong filters).
    - May overstate quality if malformed but syntactically valid queries pass.
- **Use case**: Used in production systems for continuous monitoring and safety checks.

Semantic equivalence and canonicalization

Semantic equivalence testing aims to determine whether two SQL queries are functionally identical despite differing syntactic forms. This often involves normalizing or canonicalizing the queries (e.g., removing aliases, reordering joins) before comparing them.

The following list outlines the advantages, limitations, and use cases:

- **Advantages**:
  - Captures the true intent of the query.
  - Handles flexible query structures and expressions.
- **Limitations**:
  - Requires sophisticated SQL parsers and semantic analyzers.
  - May produce false positives or negatives in edge cases.
- **Use case**: Recommended in advanced evaluations where execution testing is impractical or multiple valid outputs are expected.

Human evaluation

Human evaluation involves expert reviewers assessing the quality of the generated SQL based on criteria such as correctness, clarity, relevance, and efficiency. Reviewers may manually execute queries or inspect their logic against the schema.

The following list outlines the advantages, limitations, and use cases:

- **Advantages**:
  - Provides nuanced, context-sensitive assessment.
  - Can catch subtle semantic issues or edge cases.
- **Limitations**:
  - Expensive and time-consuming.
  - Subjective unless standardized with clear rubrics.
- **Use case**: Ideal for pilot deployments, user-facing evaluations, or resolving ambiguous cases.

Latency and throughput metrics

These operational metrics measure the time required to generate a SQL query (latency) and the number of queries that can be processed in a given time period (throughput). They indicate system responsiveness and scalability.

The following list outlines the advantages, limitations, and use cases:

- **Advantages**:
  - o Useful for UX optimization.
  - o Helps identify bottlenecks in processing pipelines.

- **Limitations**:
  - o Influenced by hardware, caching, model size, and database configuration.
  - o Not related to query accuracy.

- **Use case**: Used in production systems to ensure performance **service level agreements (SLAs)** are met.

Best practices for performance evaluation

Evaluating text-to-SQL systems requires more than checking for correct outputs—it demands a structured approach that balances quantitative metrics, representative datasets, and continuous improvement. The following practices help ensure meaningful, reliable performance assessment:

- **Use multiple metrics in combination**: No single metric captures all aspects of quality. Combine execution accuracy, exact match, and component accuracy to achieve a comprehensive evaluation.

- **Construct representative evaluation sets**: Ensure test data includes varied query types:
  - o Simple vs. nested
  - o Single table vs. multi-join
  - o Domain-specific terminology

  This ensures robust generalization.

- **Establish ground truth carefully**: For custom datasets, manual SQL annotation must be validated for correctness and consistency. Include comments or natural language paraphrases to assist evaluation.

- **Track model failure modes**: Categorize errors are as follows:
  - o Schema mismatch
  - o Incorrect aggregation
  - o Logical inconsistency
  - o Ambiguous interpretation

  Analysing these patterns helps in prompt refinement and model tuning.

- **Deploy continuous evaluation loops**: In production environments, implement pipelines to monitor performance over time, including:
    - Drift detection (as schema or query types evolve)
    - Error tracking and regression testing
    - User feedback collection for fine-tuning

Measuring the performance of text-to-SQL systems demands more than accuracy alone. A holistic evaluation framework must incorporate syntactic, semantic, and operational metrics. From exact matches and execution correctness to latency and human feedback, these metrics provide the foundation for model improvement, deployment readiness, and user trust. As these systems continue to evolve, standardizing evaluation methodologies will be essential for benchmarking progress, ensuring fairness, and guiding practical adoption at scale.

Conclusion

This chapter has provided a comprehensive introduction to the foundational components of text-to-SQL systems, bridging the gap between natural language queries and structured data access. We began by exploring the basic concepts underlying text-to-SQL, including schema linking, SQL generation, and the role of LLMs in interpreting ambiguous user intent. We then examined system architecture patterns, ranging from simple prompting strategies to agent-based execution graphs. Real-world applications demonstrated how text-to-SQL can empower users across domains such as BI, healthcare, education, and finance. We also analyzed the technical challenges associated with schema alignment, validation, and deployment, followed by best practices for implementation and performance evaluation. Together, these insights offer a blueprint for designing reliable, scalable, and user-centric text-to-SQL solutions.

Text-to-SQL is not merely a technical innovation; it represents a fundamental shift in how individuals interact with data. By lowering the barrier to querying relational databases, it promotes organizational data literacy and accelerates decision-making across roles and functions.

The next chapter will introduce an advanced, agentic multi-query text-to-SQL system. We will explore how LLM-powered agents can collaborate to handle multi-turn dialogues, join reasoning, and query decomposition, enabling robust and explainable data retrieval in complex, real-world environments.

## CHAPTER 15

Agentic Text-to-SQL Systems and Architecture Decision-Making

Introduction

In this Chapter, we start from where we left off in the last chapter. Agentic text-to-**Structured Query Language** (**SQL**) systems represent a significant evolution in how humans interact with structured data. Rather than relying on static rules or pre-defined templates, these systems use autonomous agents, powered by **large language models** (**LLMs**), retrieval mechanisms, and reasoning frameworks like LangChain, to dynamically translate natural language questions into executable SQL queries. This chapter explores the architecture and decision-making strategies required to design such intelligent systems.

At the core of these architectures lies a multi-step orchestration process involving query embedding, semantic search, schema matching, SQL generation, and federated execution. Each component—from Sentence Transformer-based embedding to LangChain's ReAct agent with **chain of thought** (**CoT**) prompting, plays a crucial role in maintaining accuracy, adaptability, and transparency. The use of global indexes, schema matchers, and pre-filtering ensures that the agent can handle cross-database queries with minimal hallucination or ambiguity.

This chapter breaks down the full pipeline shown in the architectural diagram and explains key design choices, including when to use **fedrated query engines** (**FQEs**), how to implement index-aware retrieval, and how to score and rerank SQL outputs using LLM-based evaluators. By the end, readers will gain a structured blueprint for implementing scalable, reliable, and interpretable agentic text-to-SQL systems tailored to real-world enterprise needs.

Structure

In this chapter, we will learn about the following topics:

- Agentic text-to-SQL system for real-time retail intelligence
- Architecture and code explanation of text-to-SQL system
- Step-by-step pipeline explanation
- Output from the text-to-SQL system
- Solution to initial problem statement

Objectives

The objective of this chapter is to present a modular and scalable framework for building agentic text-to-SQL systems that enable natural language querying across distributed, structured databases. By combining LLMs with planning agents, schema-aware tool use, and semantic indexing, the system intelligently translates user queries into executable SQL. This chapter outlines the architecture, implementation, and design trade-offs involved in developing such systems using LangChain's ReAct agent, global index lookup, and federated SQL execution. The goal is to empower practitioners to build robust, context-aware SQL agents capable of adaptive reasoning and accurate multi-database query execution.

Agentic text-to-SQL system for real-time retail intelligence

Modern retail businesses generate massive data across distributed databases, customer profiles in PostgreSQL, orders in MySQL, marketing logs in MongoDB, and inventory in separate systems. These data silos hinder fast, data-driven decisions, especially for non-technical users who struggle to query structured databases using SQL. Manual query writing by data teams leads to bottlenecks, delays, and lost agility.

Business challenge and problem statement

The retail enterprise seeks to enable real-time, natural language access to its sales, customer, and inventory data across multiple heterogeneous databases.

The following list outlines the current pain points:

- **Delayed decisions**: Analysts and executives depend on data teams for SQL queries, slowing time-sensitive actions.
- **Siloed data**: Information is fragmented across incompatible systems, requiring complex joins and schema understanding.

- **Query latency**: Massive datasets (~245GB+) make traditional SQL querying inefficient.

- **Revenue impact**: Without instant insight into customer churn, inventory gaps, or product demand spikes, sales opportunities are frequently missed.

So, our goal is to develop an agentic text-to-SQL system with schema-aware tool use, semantic indexing, and federated execution to enable intelligent, self-serve querying for business users, without needing SQL expertise.

Architecture and code explanation of text-to-SQL system

Figure 15.1 presents a high-level view of the complete text-to-SQL pipeline, illustrating the chronological flow of data and control from user query to SQL execution and final response. how each step in the figure is labeled and corresponds to a distinct system function:

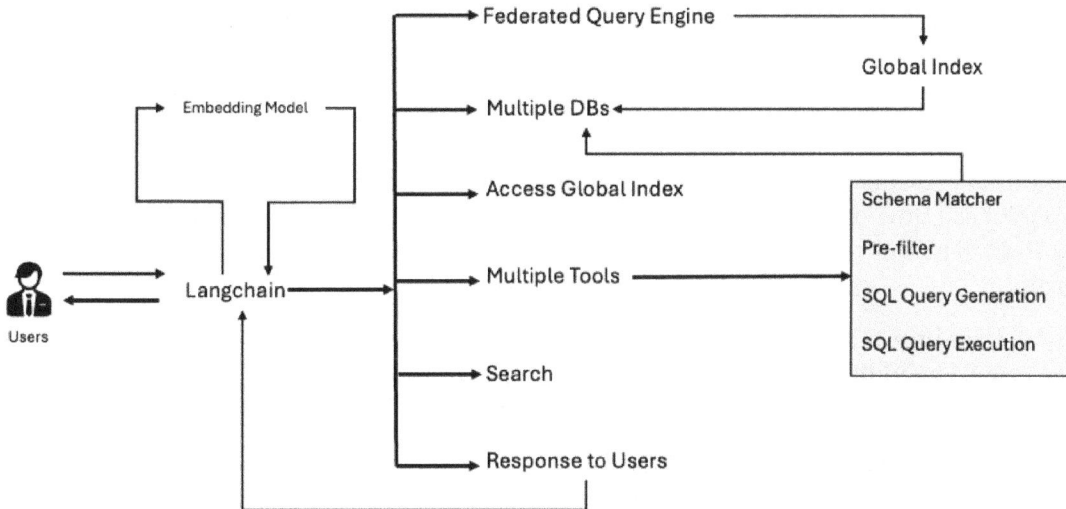

Figure 15.1: *A very high-level workflow of the complete text-to-SQL pipeline*

The following *Figure 15.2* architecture illustrates an end-to-end agentic text-to-SQL system designed to bridge natural language queries with structured, multi-database environments. The pipeline showcases how user input is transformed into SQL through a series of intelligent steps, embedding generation, schema matching, semantic retrieval, and CoT-based SQL synthesis. At its core, the system leverages LangChain's ReAct agent framework, integrating pre-filtering, LLM reasoning, SQL grading, and optional federated execution. This architecture enables real-time, schema-aware querying across siloed datasets, empowering business users to retrieve actionable insights without writing SQL, making enterprise analytics faster, more accessible, and highly contextual.

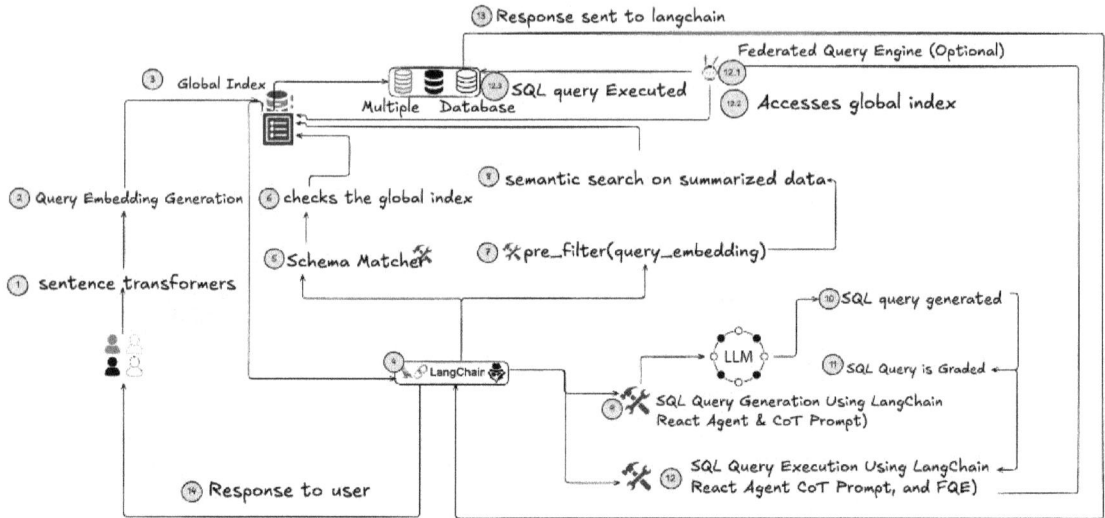

Figure 15.2: *Solution design of an agentic text-to-SQL solution*

Step-by-step pipeline explanation

Figure 15.2 presents a high-level view of the complete text-to-SQL pipeline, illustrating the chronological flow of data and control from user query to SQL execution and final response. The steps explain how each step in the figure is labeled and corresponds to a distinct system function:

1. **User input**: The process begins when the user submits a natural language query (e.g., via Streamlit interface or **application programming interface (API)**). The query is passed into the backend pipeline for processing.

2. **Query embedding generation**: The input query is transformed into a vector representation using a pre-trained Sentence Transformer model. This embedding captures the semantic meaning of the query.

3. **Global index**: The query embedding is forwarded to the global index (e.g., implemented in ChromaDB) for similarity-based retrieval of relevant schema summaries or historical query patterns.

4. **LangChain**: LangChain is invoked to orchestrate the reasoning and tool usage for schema summarization, matching, and filtering tasks.

5. **Schema matcher**: Compares the query intent against available database schemas to ensure the selected tables and columns are semantically aligned with the user's request.

6. **Checks the global index**: The matched schema is cross-referenced with the global index to validate and refine the selection for consistency and relevance across databases.

7. **pre_filter(query_embedding)**: A pre-filtering function is applied to the query embedding to reduce the search space in the vector index, improving retrieval efficiency.

8. **Semantic search on summarized data**: Performs a semantic search over summarized schema/data using the pre-filtered embedding, helping select the most relevant content for SQL construction.

9. **SQL query generation using LangChain React agent and CoT prompt**: Based on retrieved schema and query intent, the LangChain agent generates an initial SQL query using a CoT prompting strategy for clarity and correctness.

10. **SQL query generated**: The SQL query is produced in structured executable form, with proper clauses (e.g., **SELECT**, **WHERE**) reflecting the semantic meaning of the user's query.

11. **SQL query is graded**: The generated SQL is evaluated by an LLM to verify syntactic correctness and semantic alignment with the original question.

12. **SQL query execution using LangChain React agent, CoT prompt, and FQE (optional)**: Executes the final SQL query, optionally using a FQE to aggregate results from multiple databases:

    a. Accesses the global index

    b. SQL query executed across multiple databases

13. **Response sent to LangChain**: Execution results are sent back into the LangChain pipeline for post-processing and formatting.

14. **Response to user**: The final output, including the SQL query, retrieved data, and an optional summary, is sent back to the user via the **user interface (UI)**. All computation is in-memory; no intermediate results are persisted.

Folder structure

To operationalize the agentic text-to-SQL architecture, the system is modularly implemented with a clear separation of concerns across configuration, core logic, UI frontend, and task-specific modules. The following folder structure represents a scalable implementation using LangChain, Ollama, and ChromaDB, enabling both vector-based retrieval and multi-database SQL execution. Core components such as schema matching, SQL generation, summarization, and query grading are abstracted into reusable tasks. The `global_index_db/` stores vector indexes, while the frontend handles user interaction. The following structure supports easy extension and robust orchestration of the entire text-to-SQL pipeline, from natural language input to federated query response:

```
OLLAMA_PIPELINE_WITH_UI/
├── config/
│   └── __init__.py
├── core/
│   ├── __init__.py
│   ├── cache.py
│   ├── chroma_index.py
│   ├── embeddings.py
│   ├── llm.py
│   ├── sql_executor.py
│   ├── sqlite_multi_reader.py
│   └── utils.py
├── data/
│   ├── sqlite1.db
│   └── sqlite2.db
├── frontend/
│   └── app.py
├── global_index_db/
│   ├── c5d7ec5b-9107-4325-9b39-4b1c35cc3059/
│   └── chroma.sqlite3
├── setup/
│   ├── __init__.py
│   └── populate_chroma.py
├── tasks/
│   ├── __init__.py
│   ├── aggregator.py
│   ├── grader.py
│   ├── schema_matcher.py
│   ├── sql_generator.py
│   ├── summarizer.py
│   └── utils.py
├── main.py
├── requirements.txt
└── seed_sqlite_data.py
```

Figure 15.3: Folder structure of agentic text-to-SQL solution

The end-to-end code is available in the GitHub repository.

Requirements

To enable a user-friendly interface for natural language querying, the system leverages Streamlit for the frontend UI. This allows users to input plain English questions and view results interactively in a web application. For serving backend logic as APIs (when decoupled from the UI), FastAPI and Uvicorn are used to create and host asynchronous endpoints efficiently. These components ensure seamless interaction between the user and the backend processing layers without requiring deep technical expertise.

At the core of the pipeline lies a robust agentic reasoning framework powered by LangChain, which utilizes tools and CoT prompting to deconstruct user queries and generate SQL dynamically. LangChain Community modules enhance this functionality with integrations to tools like ChromaDB and SQL connectors. The Sentence Transformers library generates high-quality embeddings for user queries and documents, which are stored and retrieved using ChromaDB, a high-speed vector database. This embedding-based semantic retrieval ensures schema-aware, contextually accurate results. Additionally, Ollama is used to run local LLMs, such as *Llama* or *Mistral*, which perform tasks like query generation, summarization, and output validation.

Finally, Trino serves as the federated SQL query engine that allows seamless execution of SQL across multiple structured data sources (e.g., PostgreSQL, MySQL). This ensures that the system can access and aggregate data from disparate databases in real-time. SQLite3 is used for lightweight local storage of structured datasets, making it ideal for prototyping or small-scale deployment. Combined with requests for API communication and lightweight execution logic, this stack forms a powerful, locally runnable text-to-SQL solution with no cloud or external service dependencies.

Setup instructions

The following list outlines the setup steps to run this project locally:

1. **Clone or extract project**: Use the following code to extract and navigate to the project folder:

   ```
   unzip Chapter_15_Text2SQL-main.zip
   cd Text2SQL-main/ollama_pipeline_with_ui
   ```

2. **Create and activate a virtual environment (recommended)**: Create and activate a virtual environment to manage dependencies cleanly using the following code:

   ```
   python -m venv venv
   source venv/bin/activate  # On Windows: venv\Scripts\activate
   ```

3. **Install dependencies**: Use the provided **requirements.txt** file to install all necessary dependencies:

   ```
   pip install -r requirements.txt
   ```

   Make sure that Ollama is installed and running locally (e.g., **ollama run mistral**).

4. **Seed the database**: This script creates or fills a local SQLite database located in the **data/** directory:

   ```
   python seed_sqlite_data.py
   ```

   This will create or populate a local SQLite database inside the **data/** folder.

5. **Run the main pipeline (backend only)**: If a frontend app exists in the **frontend/** folder, start the UI with the following code:

   ```
   python main.py
   ```

   You can edit **main.py** to invoke **run_query("your query here")** if needed.

6. **Run Streamlit UI (optional)**: If a Streamlit app is available in **frontend/**, run the following code:

```
streamlit run frontend/app.py
```

Understanding each Python script

This section provides a structured walkthrough of all Python source files in the agentic text-to-SQL system. Each module plays a specific role in transforming natural language queries into structured SQL responses. The architecture is modularized into agents, tasks, core logic, UI, and setup scripts to ensure flexibility, clarity, and reusability. The explanations here are aimed at readers who may be new to agent-based reasoning, vector search, or LangChain-based orchestration.

Main execution layer

The following list outlines the layer that orchestrates the system's core logic, coordinating data seeding, query handling, and agent invocation to drive the end-to-end flow:

- **main.py**: This file is the primary orchestrator of the pipeline. It coordinates the invocation of the schema summarization agent, aggregation of semantic results, SQL query generation, and LLM-based quality evaluation. It defines a function **run_ query(query)**, that serves as the operational backbone of the system's end-to-end workflow.

- **seed_sqlite_data.py**: A utility script that populates local SQLite databases with sample customer, product, and transaction data. This is essential for initializing a testable environment and ensuring reproducibility of query executions during experimentation or demonstration.

Agent modules

The following modules implement intelligent agents based on LangChain's ReAct framework that decompose user intent, reason over schemas, and prepare task inputs:

- **agents/summarization_schema_agent.py**: This module defines a LangChain ReAct-style agent responsible for schema summarization and interpreting user intent. It combines vector retrieval, prompt chaining, and tool execution to prepare the system for downstream SQL generation.

- **agents/sql_agent.py**: Although not invoked directly in the main pipeline, this file defines a secondary agent capable of handling SQL-specific reasoning. It may be useful in future extensions where agent composition or fallback strategies are needed.

- **agents/__init__.py**: It initializes the agents module as a Python package, enabling relative imports and modular organization.

Core infrastructure layer

Refer to the following list, which includes the foundational layers powering core services like embeddings, database access, LLM interaction, and utility logic:

- **core/embeddings.py**: It implements text embedding generation using pre-trained Sentence Transformers models. It transforms user queries and schema descriptions into dense vector representations suitable for similarity-based retrieval.

- **core/chroma_index.py**: It interfaces with ChromaDB, a vector database used to store and retrieve embeddings. It supports both insertion and semantic search operations, enabling schema-level understanding across distributed datasets.

- **core/llm.py**: It handles interaction with local LLMs served via Ollama. It encapsulates prompt construction and response parsing for tasks such as SQL generation, grading, and summarization.

- **core/sql_executor.py**: It executes SQL queries generated by the agent pipeline. It connects to local SQLite databases and is designed to support federated querying across multiple data sources.

- **core/sqlite_multi_reader.py**: It provides federated access to multiple SQLite files. It supports dynamic selection and retrieval from various schema-specific tables to enable rich aggregation.

- **core/cache.py**: It implements basic caching for repeated queries or embedding lookups. Although not used in the default execution path, it can improve performance in iterative or long-running deployments.

- **core/utils.py**: It contains utility functions that support core operations such as schema parsing, table name extraction, or data transformation.

- **core/__init__.py**: It initializes the core package and supports modular encapsulation.

Task-oriented modules

The following components encapsulate discrete tasks like SQL generation, grading, summarization, and schema matching, often driven by LLMs:

- **tasks/aggregator.py**: It combines partial results from multiple subtasks (e.g., summaries or data sources) into a unified summary. This enables holistic interpretation and better alignment with user intent.

- **tasks/sql_generator.py**: It constructs SQL queries from structured task inputs such as selected table, columns, and filters. It relies on LLM prompting strategies to ensure queries are contextually and syntactically valid.

- **tasks/grader.py**: It provides automated evaluation of both generated SQL and semantic summaries using LLM-based grading. It helps ensure answer quality and model interpretability.

- **tasks/schema_matcher.py**: It matches the elements of the user's query with relevant schema components using embedding similarity and heuristics. This step is crucial for accurate SQL generation across distributed schemas.

- **tasks/summarizer.py**: It generates concise natural language summaries of schema content or query results. It aids in making system responses human-readable and interpretable.

- **tasks/utils.py**: It offers general-purpose helper functions for formatting, token manipulation, and schema validation tasks.

- **tasks/__init__.py**: It initializes the tasks package.

Frontend interface

This module provides a user-friendly graphical interface, enabling interactive natural language querying through a Streamlit app.

`Kfrontend/app.py` defines the Streamlit-based graphical interface for the system. Users can enter natural language questions, trigger the full pipeline, and view results interactively. This makes the system accessible to non-technical users.

System setup and index initialization

This section contains scripts that initialize vector indexes and prepare the system for semantic retrieval by embedding database schema information into the Chroma vector store:

- **setup/populate_chroma.py**: It populates the Chroma vector store with embeddings derived from schema content and metadata. This prepares the retrieval system to respond to semantic queries.

- **setup/__init__.py**: It initializes the setup package.

This modular file design reflects best practices in modern AI system development, separating concerns across user interaction, reasoning, storage, and execution. Each module is designed to be independently testable and extensible, supporting scalable deployment and iterative enhancement.

In the next section, let us understand the inner workings of the code.

Inner workings of the code

In this section, we will understand the internal structure and execution logic of an agentic text-to-SQL system implemented using LangChain, Ollama, ChromaDB, and SQLite. The following project is organized into clearly modular components that represent the distinct phases of the pipeline: query understanding, schema summarization, SQL generation, grading, and result aggregation. Designed for extensibility and clarity, the system employs a structured folder hierarchy and an agent-driven orchestration layer to enable seamless translation from natural language queries into executable SQL.

- **Entry point and orchestration logic**: The execution begins with **main.py**, which serves as the primary entry script. This file coordinates the complete flow from input query to final output. The core logic is encapsulated in the function **run_query(query)**, which follows a well-defined sequence:

```
schema_results = summarization_schema_agent.invoke({"input": query})
aggregated_result = aggregate_summarized_data(query)
sql_query = generate_sql(...)
sql_grade = grade_sql(sql_query)
summary_grade = grade_summary(aggregated_result["final_summary"])
```

This orchestrator calls the summarization agent, aggregates the retrieved information, generates a SQL query, and subsequently grades both the SQL and the aggregated summary. The final output is returned as a dictionary and logged but not persisted to any file or database.

- **Agent configuration and role**: The file **agents/summarization_schema_agent.py** defines a LangChain-based ReAct agent responsible for interpreting the query intent and interacting with schema-related tools. This agent acts as the initial interpreter and routes the request to appropriate modules for summarization and schema matching.

  The sibling file **agents/sql_agent.py** offers an alternative agent that may be used for deeper SQL reasoning. However, this agent is not actively invoked in the main orchestration path.

- **Task-specific functional modules**: The **tasks/** directory contains functionally segregated logic. Each module performs a well-scoped task, which are as follows:

  o **aggregator.py**: It consolidates semantic results from various summarizers.

  o **sql_generator.py**: It constructs SQL queries using CoT prompting, conditionals, and table metadata.

  o **grader.py**: It uses LLM scoring mechanisms to evaluate the quality of the SQL query and textual summary.

  o **schema_matcher.py**: It identifies the schema components relevant to the query.

  o **summarizer.py**: It produces textual summaries from a structured schema or query results.

  o **utils.py**: It offers auxiliary helper functions for formatting and text processing.

The functions from these modules are all invoked through the orchestrator in **main.py** or indirectly via agent tools.

- **Core services and infrastructure**: The **core/** folder includes low-level utilities and backend infrastructure required to perform core computational tasks:

  o **chroma_index.py**: It manages interactions with ChromaDB for vector-based retrieval.

  o **embeddings.py**: It generates dense vector representations using Sentence Transformers.

  o **sql_executor.py and sqlite_multi_reader.py**: They provide interfaces to execute SQL over multiple SQLite instances.

  o **llm.py**: It abstracts interactions with locally hosted LLMs via Ollama.

  o **cache.py**: It is an optional component for caching repeated operations.

  o **utils.py**: The core utilities that assist in handling schema, connectors, and text normalization.

These files operate primarily as backend services that are invoked by the higher-level task and agent modules.

- **Data initialization and persistence**: The two modules that manage data loading and indexing are as follows:

  o **seed_sqlite_data.py**: Seeds SQLite databases (**data/sqlite1.db**, **data/ sqlite2.db**) with sample retail data.

  o **setup/populate_chroma.py**: It computes and stores embeddings into ChromaDB, saved in the **global_index_db/** directory.

This initialization is vital for enabling semantic search and query execution over distributed datasets.

- **Frontend user interface**: The file **frontend/app.py** implements a basic Streamlit application that allows users to interact with the system through a natural language input interface. It connects directly to the **run_query()** function from **main.py** and renders results, including SQL output, summary, and grades on the UI.

To complement the modular breakdown of system components, this section presents a chronological overview of the full text-to-SQL pipeline as illustrated in the workflow *Figure 15.1.* Each step corresponds to a discrete processing stage, from user input and query embedding to SQL generation, grading, execution, and response delivery. The figure provides a visual abstraction of how data and control signals propagate across agents, tools, and databases within the system. This layered orchestration, driven by LangChain and supported by ChromaDB and SQLite, ensures that user queries are interpreted contextually, translated into SQL accurately, and executed efficiently. What follows is a detailed explanation of each numbered stage in the figure.

Agent and tool summary

The primary differentiator of this solution lies in its integration of a LangChain-based ReAct agent with specialized tools for schema understanding and semantic alignment. The **summarization_schema_agent** intelligently interprets user intent and invokes tools for schema summarization and matching, enabling robust adaptation across varied database structures. These tools ensure that the agent remains context-aware and schema-sensitive, even in heterogeneous environments. This agent tool synergy not only reduces hallucination in SQL generation but also allows modular plug-in logic for summarization, aggregation, and evaluation, establishing the system's core advantage in enabling precise, explainable, and scalable natural language access to relational.

The following pipeline employs a single active LangChain ReAct agent along with a set of registered and standalone tools to perform schema interpretation, SQL generation, and quality assessment:

- **Agent**: The system contains one active LangChain ReAct agent, defined in:

  agents/summarization_schema_agent.py

  While there is a second file, **agents/sql_agent.py**, it is not actively used in the current execution path (**main.py**). Thus, only one agent is involved in the pipeline.

- **Tools**: There are two agent-registered tools and three additional functional tools: the active agent (**summarization_schema_agent**) invokes two explicit LangChain-compatible tools:

  o **Schema matcher tool**: It uses logic from **tasks/schema_matcher.py**.

  o **Schema summarizer tool**: It uses logic from **tasks/summarizer.py**.

Additionally, outside the LangChain agent but within the pipeline, **main.py** directly uses the following task-level tools:

- SQL generator from **tasks/sql_generator.py**
- SQL and summary graders from **tasks/grader.py**
- Aggregator from **tasks/aggregator.py**

Output from the text-to-SQL system

Once the query has been processed through embedding, schema matching, summarization, SQL generation, and grading, the system produces multiple structured outputs. These outputs are generated entirely in-memory and are rendered via the Streamlit interface for the end user. The outputs serve both human interpretability and machine-verifiable evaluation.

The key outputs are as follows:

- Final aggregated summary
- Detailed entity and database summary
- Generated SQL query
- SQL query grade
- Summary Grade

The final aggregated summary depicted in the following figure indicates that the output presents a comprehensive human-readable synthesis of individuals and database-level records matched semantically to the user query. It highlights individuals with unique entries, cross-database identifiers, and summarized attributes such as **Age**, `City`, and **ID**. Importantly, it resolves entries across databases into unified entities where applicable.

Final Aggregated Summary:

After aggregating the summaries, here is a comprehensive insight:
Individuals:

1. **Julia Smith (ID: 26):** Age 32, from Chicago.
2. **Ian Garcia (ID: 27):** Age 33, from Los Angeles.
3. **George Martinez (ID: 28 & ID: 29):** Ages 39 and 28, both from Denver.
4. **Julia Davis (ID: 30):** Age 59, from Austin.

Databases:

1. **Database:** Total entries: 5; IDs ranging from 11 to 15.
   - Individuals:
     - ID 11: Charlie Martinez (Age: 33, City: Boston)
     - ID 12: Ian Martinez (Age: 35, City: San Francisco)
     - ID 13: Julia Garcia (Age: 42, City: Phoenix)
     - ID 14: Fiona Wilson (Age: 36, City: Los Angeles)
     - ID 15: Bob Johnson (Age: 28, City: Miami)
2. **Database:** Total entries: unknown; IDs ranging from 16 to 20.
   - Individuals:
     - Diana Johnson (ID 16), age 50, from Miami
     - Alice Lee (ID 17), age 35, from Chicago
     - George Garcia (ID 18), age 35, from San Francisco
     - Alice Taylor (ID 19), age 53, from Denver
     - Bob Brown (ID 20), age 49, from Chicago

Figure 15.4: Final aggregated summary from the system

Detailed entity and database summary

A deeper representation of the underlying data structure, this summary enumerates the records found in each database, highlighting ID ranges and associated individuals. It aids in verifying schema alignment and provides transparency into how data was retrieved and normalized.

The following figure shows the detailed entity and database summary generated by the text-to-SQL system's UI, highlighting unique individuals, potential data duplicates, and their source database records:

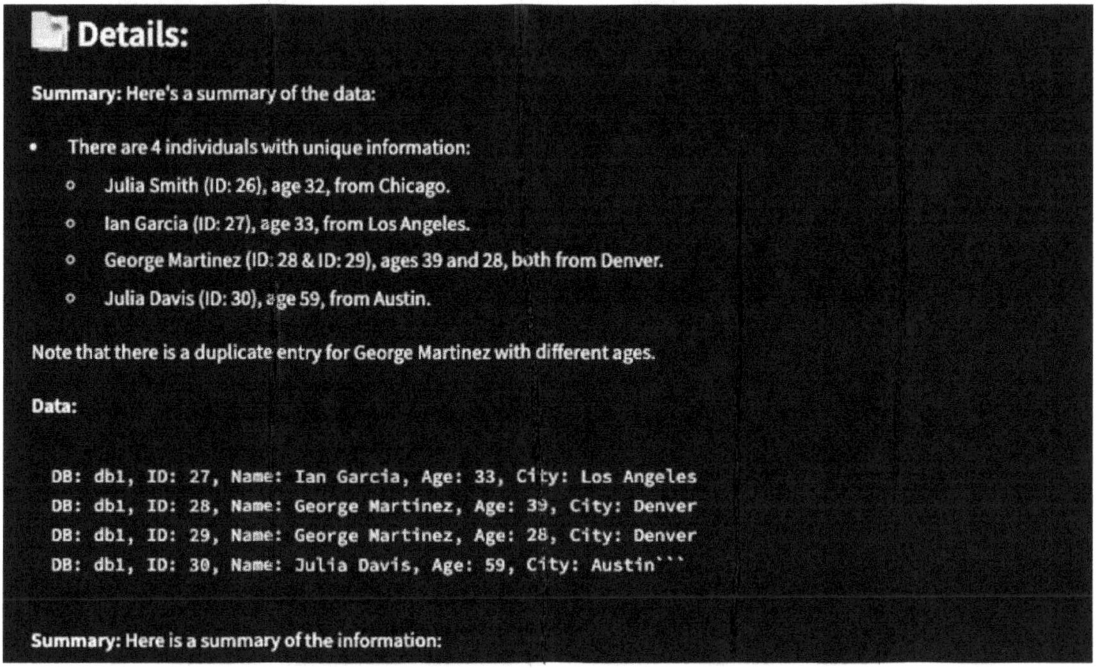

Details:

Summary: Here's a summary of the data:

* There are 4 individuals with unique information:
  * Julia Smith (ID: 26), age 32, from Chicago.
  * Ian Garcia (ID: 27), age 33, from Los Angeles.
  * George Martinez (ID: 28 & ID: 29), ages 39 and 28, both from Denver.
  * Julia Davis (ID: 30), age 59, from Austin.

Note that there is a duplicate entry for George Martinez with different ages.

Data:

```
DB: db1, ID: 27, Name: Ian Garcia, Age: 33, City: Los Angeles
DB: db1, ID: 28, Name: George Martinez, Age: 39, City: Denver
DB: db1, ID: 29, Name: George Martinez, Age: 28, City: Denver
DB: db1, ID: 30, Name: Julia Davis, Age: 59, City: Austin```
```

Summary: Here is a summary of the information:

Figure 15.5: Detailed entity and database summary

Generated SQL query

The system produces a syntactically correct SQL query that corresponds to the user's intent. Constructed using a CoT prompting template, this query encapsulates the selected table, filtered columns, and conditions. It reflects an interpretable breakdown of reasoning steps used to form the query logic. The following figure displays the generated SQL query breakdown by the text-to-SQL system UI, outlining each step in the query construction, from intent recognition to table/column selection and filter condition formulation, leading to the final executable SQL.

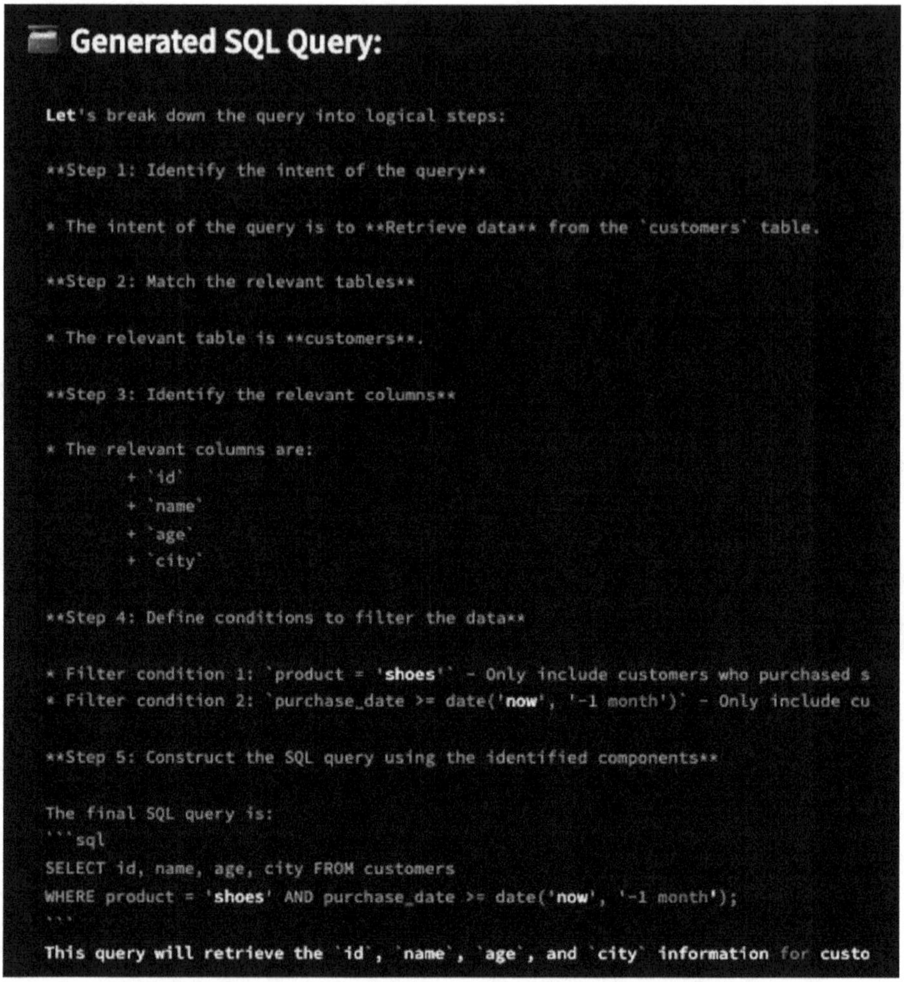

Figure 15.6: Generated SQL query from text-to-SQL system on UI

SQL query grade

To validate query quality, the system invokes a grading tool that evaluates correctness, relevance, and execution efficiency. The score is broken into components, each explained, and includes observations about potential ambiguity, indexing efficiency, or logical clarity. This grading supports explainability and query refinement.

The following figure presents the **SQL Query Grade** interface of the text-to-SQL system, evaluating the generated query across correctness, relevance, and efficiency dimensions, and providing a detailed justification for each score.

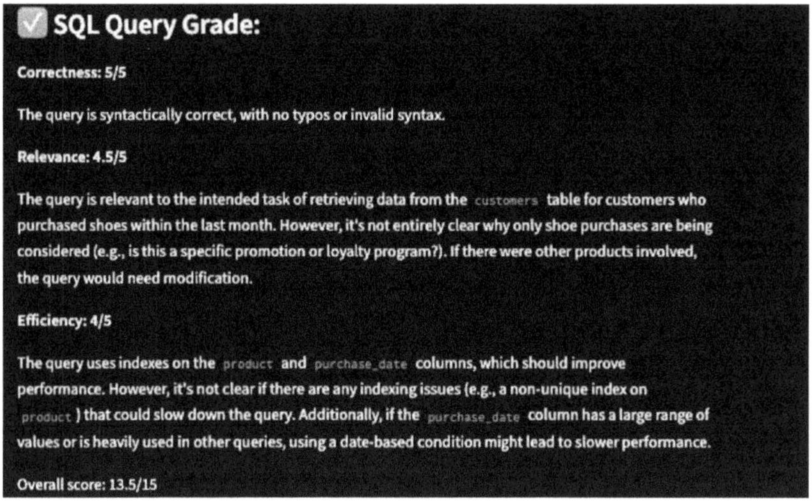

Figure 15.7: *SQL Query Grade from text-to-SQL system on UI*

Summary Grade

The summary produced earlier is also evaluated by the system for accuracy, clarity, and comprehensiveness. The grader identifies possible duplication or schema-level omissions (e.g., entry count ambiguity) and provides suggestions for enhancing textual presentation. This final score ensures the end user receives verifiable insights.

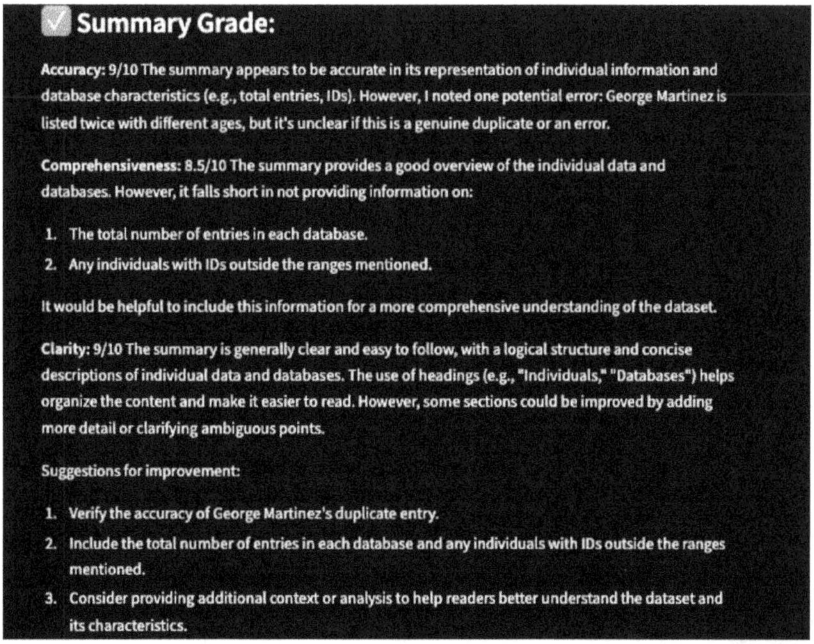

Figure 15.8: *Summary Grade from text-to-SQL system on UI*

Solution to the initial problem statement

The outputs generated by the agentic text-to-SQL system offer a direct and effective response to the challenges outlined in the initial problem statement. In traditional retail and enterprise data environments, business users often struggle to query large, siloed databases due to a lack of SQL expertise, resulting in delayed insights and missed opportunities. This system addresses that gap by allowing users to interact with distributed, heterogeneous datasets using natural language, while internally orchestrating schema alignment, semantic understanding, SQL generation, and validation.

The final aggregated summary and detailed database output enable business stakeholders to receive clear and human-readable insights drawn from multiple databases without having to understand their structure or write SQL manually. These summaries consolidate relevant data, resolve duplicate entries across databases, and surface actionable patterns (e.g., customer profiles, city-wise distributions) in a format suitable for rapid interpretation and downstream decision-making.

Moreover, the generated SQL query and its Grading Outputs serve two vital purposes: first, they transparently show how the system translates a user's intent into structured database queries; second, they provide verifiable quality assessments on correctness, relevance, and efficiency, instilling trust in the automated process. The Summary Grade further ensures that the textual output meets standards of clarity, completeness, and factual accuracy, making the solution suitable for reporting and business use.

Collectively, these capabilities transform a manual, error-prone querying process into a fully automated, explainable, and scalable pipeline—empowering non-technical teams to access insights across databases in real-time and act decisively based on context-rich, validated information.

This system is not intended to replace data engineers but rather to augment their capabilities and reduce the operational bottlenecks in querying enterprise data. By automating routine and repetitive SQL generation tasks, the platform empowers business users to retrieve insights independently, allowing data engineers to focus on higher-order activities such as data modeling, pipeline optimization, and governance. The solution democratizes access to structured data without compromising schema fidelity, execution correctness, or system auditability. In doing so, it enhances productivity across roles while preserving the critical responsibilities and oversight provided by technical data teams.

Conclusion

This chapter has provided a comprehensive walkthrough of the inner workings of an agentic text-to-SQL system, highlighting the design, logic, and output structure that underpin its functionality. Beginning with the orchestration logic in main.py, we examined how the system sequentially invokes schema summarization, aggregation, SQL generation, and quality grading using a modular, tool-driven agent pipeline. The integration of a single ReAct-style LangChain agent, equipped with schema-aware tools, forms the backbone of intelligent query interpretation and response generation.

The task-specific modules ensure clear separation of responsibilities, with each component, such as the summarizer, SQL generator, and grader, performing distinct, verifiable roles. Core infrastructure modules provide support for vector-based retrieval, LLM interaction, and multi-database SQL execution. The use of ChromaDB and SQLite in tandem enables scalable and semantically enriched querying across structured data sources.

The system's outputs, including final summaries, graded SQL, and interpretability-focused feedback, demonstrate its usability for both technical and non-technical stakeholders. By leveraging agentic planning, CoT prompting, and local LLMs, the architecture balances transparency, adaptability, and performance. In doing so, it represents a pragmatic blueprint for deploying text-to-SQL systems in enterprise environments where precision, schema alignment, and real-time feedback are essential.

In the next chapter, we will discuss integration of **optical character recognition (OCR)** with **generative AI (GenAI)** to build intelligent pipelines that convert images into actionable search insights.

Join our Discord space

Join our Discord workspace for latest updates, offers, tech happenings around the world, new releases, and sessions with the authors:

https://discord.bpbonline.com

CHAPTER 16

GenAI for Extracting Text from Images

Introduction

In this chapter, we will explore the integration of **optical character recognition** (**OCR**) with **generative AI** (**GenAI**) to build intelligent pipelines that convert images into actionable search insights. The goal is to extract meaningful textual information from images, such as product photos, advertisements, or catalog screenshots, and use that information to guide decision-making, product discovery, or search redirection.

We begin by leveraging EasyOCR, a Python-based OCR library that provides high-accuracy text detection in images. Once text is extracted, it is passed to a lightweight **large language model** (**LLM**) hosted locally via Ollama, to generate a natural language search query. This query reflects how a human might search for similar or better alternatives on popular shopping platforms like *Amazon*, *Flipkart*, or *eBay*.

The pipeline then performs **Uniform Resource Locator** (**URL**) redirection to simulate searches on these platforms or fetches partial page content using lightweight scraping. The extracted snippets are summarized again using the LLM to provide users with a quick comparative overview, showcasing similar products, offers, or pricing trends.

The architecture (illustrated in *Figure 16.1*) is modular, interpretable, and deployable locally, making it ideal for building GenAI shopping assistants or visual product comparison tools.

Structure

In this chapter, we will learn about the following topics:

- Three approaches to GenAI-based OCR
- OCR on image
- OCR on a multimodal document
- To do

Objectives

The objective of this chapter is to equip readers with the knowledge and practical skills to perform OCR using advanced multimodal techniques. Readers will learn how to extract text from images and **Portable Document Format** (**PDF**) using foundation models capable of interpreting both visual and textual data. The chapter introduces the Mistral OCR **application programming interface** (**API**) for document understanding and highlights its integration into intelligent pipelines. Special emphasis is placed on extracting structured information from receipts with tabular data, enabling downstream analysis. By the end of the chapter, readers will be able to build robust OCR systems for diverse real-world formats and layouts.

Three approaches to GenAI-based OCR

In the context of building intelligent systems that process and understand visual input, OCR remains a foundational capability. As the demand for seamless interpretation of image-based text grows, so does the evolution of techniques to perform OCR using traditional **machine learning** (**ML**), transformer-based language models, and multimodal reasoning systems. The following section introduces and contrasts three distinct approaches to OCR in a GenAI context, which are wrapping standalone OCR engines within GenAI workflows, using LLMs natively trained to perform OCR, and employing multimodal LLMs capable of direct image-to-text comprehension:

- **OCR foundation model**: The second approach leverages the capabilities of transformer-based language models that are trained end-to-end on both textual and visual data, with OCR as an embedded function. These models are designed to ingest image pixels directly and output recognized text, without relying on an external OCR engine. While such models are often proprietary (e.g., *Google's TrOCR* or *DeepMind's Flamingo* variants and *Mistral OCR*), they offer higher integration and may outperform traditional OCR methods on noisy or unstructured inputs. This end-to-end learning capability simplifies the pipeline but sacrifices modularity and flexibility. It is well-suited to scenarios that demand OCR on highly variable inputs, such as handwritten notes, scanned documents, or noisy screenshots, where conventional OCR tools may degrade.

Note: **Mistral OCR is a dedicated OCR foundation model, not just a utility wrapper or plug-in. It is designed to be a powerful base model purpose-built for OCR and complex document understanding tasks. Key details include the following:**

- o **Document understanding architecture: Mistral OCR is built to fully comprehend documents, including media, text, tables, and mathematical expressions, delivering accurate and structured outputs for downstream applications.**

- o **Standalone API and SDK: It is available via a publicly accessible Mistral-OCR-latest API, supported by an official Python SDK. It runs as a foundation model across platforms like Vertex AI or Azure AI Foundry.**

- o **Benchmark-leading accuracy: In internal tests, Mistral OCR outperforms Google Document AI, Azure OCR, and Gemini models, achieving 97–99% accuracy across challenging content like tables, equations, and multilingual text.**

- o **Enterprise-grade: It supports batch processing (up to 2,000 pages per minute on a single-node GPU), structured output, multilingual capabilities, and can be run on-premises for enterprise use.**

- o **Mistral provides two types of models, which are open models and premier models.**

- **Wrapping a traditional OCR tool within a GenAI pipeline**: The first approach, and the primary focus of this chapter, involves integrating a high-performance OCR engine such as EasyOCR into a GenAI-enabled processing pipeline. EasyOCR is a lightweight, open-source library that uses deep learning to detect and recognize text in images. This component is responsible solely for text extraction. Once extracted, the text is passed into a local or hosted language model, typically through an API call, to generate semantically meaningful interpretations, such as search queries or summaries. This method is modular and interpretable as the OCR and LLM components are separated, allowing each to be tuned, optimized, or replaced independently. It is ideal for applications where image quality, language control, and local deployment constraints are critical.

- **Fine-tuning a multimodal LLM for OCR tasks**: The third approach uses a multimodal LLM like **Large Language and Vision Assistant (LLaVA)** or **Meta Llama3.2 vision** that is trained to reason jointly over visual and textual inputs. A fine-tuned multimodal model for OCR combines the visual understanding of images with specialized text recognition capabilities, optimized through targeted training on OCR-specific datasets. Unlike generic multimodal models, which treat OCR as a secondary skill, fine-tuning aligns the visual encoder and language head to accurately detect, transcribe, and interpret text in diverse layouts, fonts, and languages. This approach preserves the model's ability to reason about surrounding visual context, such as diagrams, tables, or **user interface** (**UI**) elements, while significantly improving extraction accuracy. The result is a unified system that performs high-fidelity OCR and contextual interpretation in a single inference step, reducing pipeline complexity.

Each of these approaches reflects a different point on the spectrum of modularity, generalization, and system complexity. The approach chosen will depend on constraints such as latency, infrastructure, model availability, and interpretability requirements. In this chapter, we focus on the first method, wrapping EasyOCR within a GenAI pipeline due to its simplicity, effectiveness, and suitability for locally-deployed intelligent agents.

The following figure illustrates three distinct GenAI-based OCR integration strategies, ranging from standalone OCR foundation models to modular pipelines using traditional OCR wrapped in APIs to fine-tuned multimodal LLMs that unify OCR:

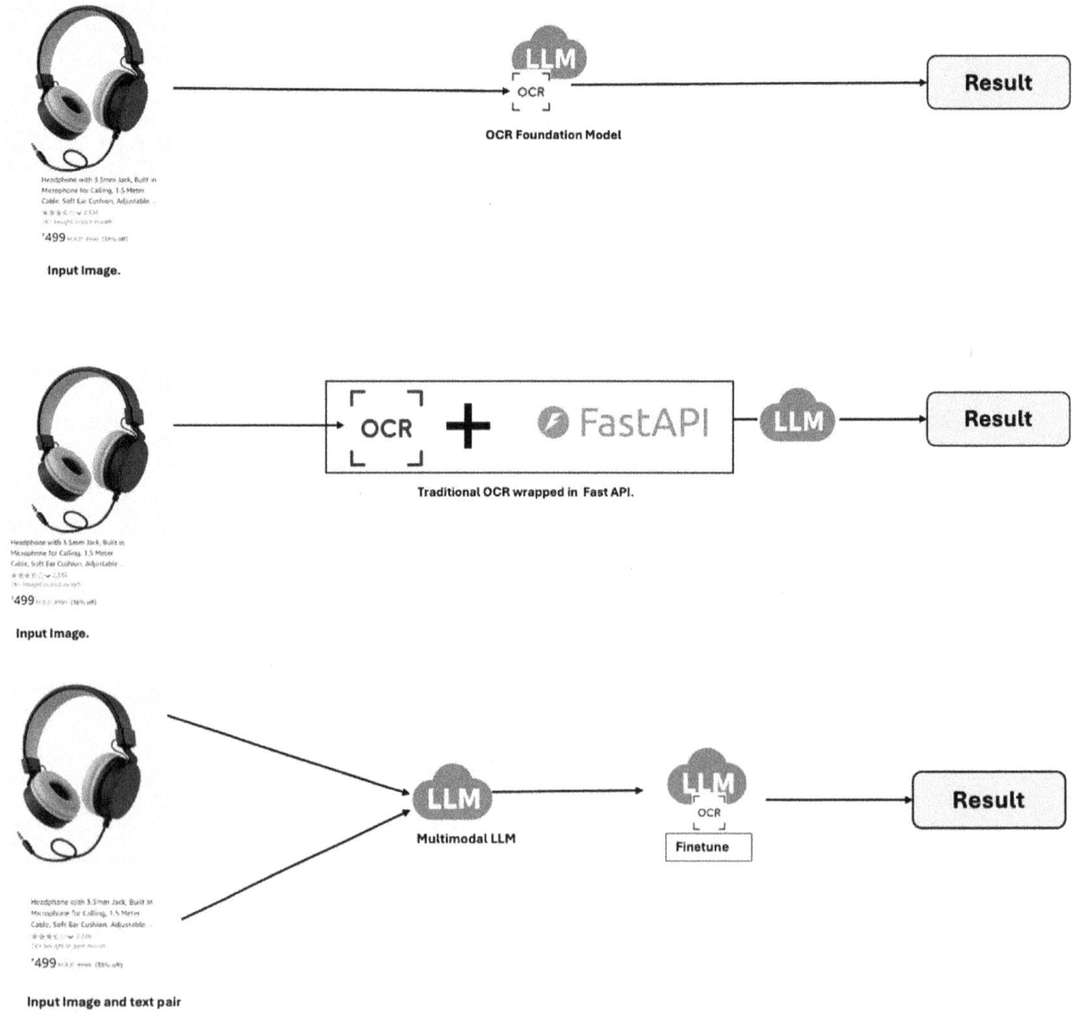

Figure 16.1: Comparison of OCR integration approaches

Shopping assistance use case

In an era dominated by e-commerce and digital marketplaces, consumers are often faced with an overwhelming number of product choices, each accompanied by varying specifications, brands, and price points. While online platforms provide rich search interfaces, users frequently rely on images, screenshots from friends, photographs of store displays, or social media posts to express their intent, as explained in *Figure 16.2*. For many, the traditional approach of manually searching for each product detail is cumbersome and inefficient:

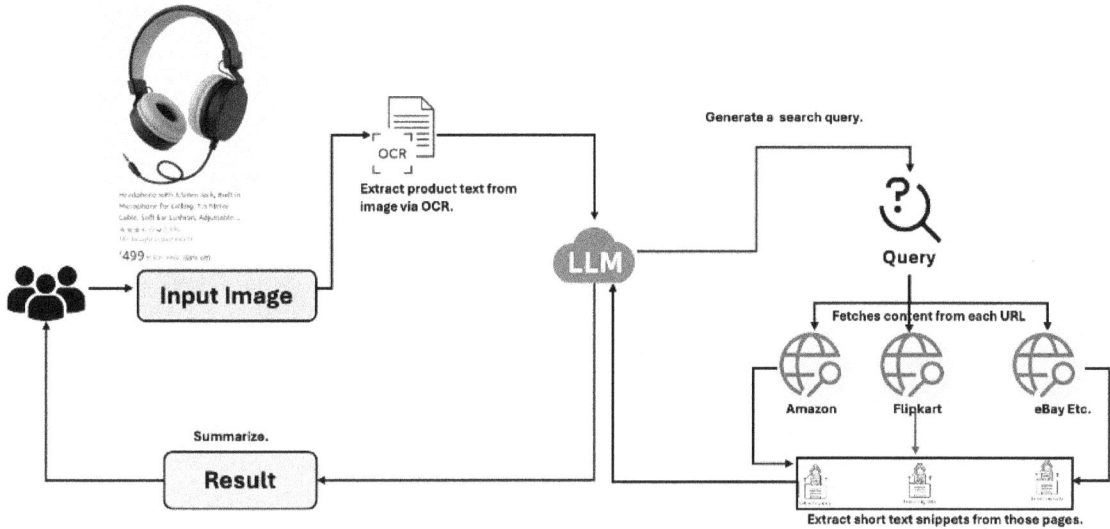

Figure 16.2: The GenAI OCR pipeline

Consider a user who captures a screenshot of a headphone advertisement showing a brand, technical specs, and a discount. The user wants to know whether better alternatives are available within the same price range from other trusted brands like *Sony* or *JBL*. However, the text in the image cannot be copied, and searching manually is time-consuming. This is where an intelligent visual assistant becomes invaluable.

In this use case, we introduce a pipeline that combines OCR with a GenAI-powered system to automate the entire discovery process. The pipeline begins by extracting relevant product information from the image using OCR. This could include product names, specifications (e.g., 3.5mm jack, mic support, length of cable), pricing, and discounts. The extracted text is then passed to a local LLM (via Ollama), which generates a natural language query that mimics how a real user might search for alternatives online.

Rather than just displaying the raw OCR text, the system simulates search results on multiple e-commerce platforms such as Amazon, Flipkart, and eBay. It fetches these search results or snippets of product information and summarizes them using the same LLM. The end user is then presented with a concise and contextual comparison of alternatives available in the market, without needing to open multiple websites or conduct manual research.

This approach significantly improves the shopping experience for users who prefer visual input, are on a budget, or are looking for smarter alternatives without investing time in repetitive searches. It is especially beneficial for price-sensitive markets and mobile-first users who often use screenshots and social media as their primary mode of capturing product interest.

Ultimately, this use case demonstrates how combining OCR with GenAI-enabled systems to bridge the gap between unstructured visual input and structured, actionable insight, paving the way for intelligent, multimodal consumer tools.

OCR on image

OCR using LLMs transforms traditional text extraction from images into a semantically rich understanding task. Unlike conventional OCR, which only transcribes visible characters, LLM-based OCR can interpret layout, infer structure, and contextualize extracted content. This approach allows for intelligent extraction of headings, tables, labels, and relationships across the document. When combined with the GenAI pipeline shown in *Figure 16.1*, the system can return markdown or structured outputs and even answer questions about the content. This unlocks powerful capabilities for automating workflows in document analysis, digital archiving, compliance, and visual data-driven decision-making. *Figure 16.3* showcases a product listing for the *Storm Wired Headphone*, presenting a rich example of multimodal data where visual, textual, and semantic elements are intertwined. It contains a product photo, descriptive metadata (e.g., technical specs, user ratings, and pricing), and contextual cues such as popularity and discount details. For an OCR-enabled GenAI system, this image is not just about extracting text; it is about understanding product relevance, parsing hierarchical attributes (e.g., brand, features, price, offer), and mapping them to actionable outputs like search queries or structured records. Such multimodal inputs are ideal for pipelines that combine **vision-language models** (**VLMs**) and intelligent text extraction to enable smarter shopping assistants or product recommendation engines.

Headphone with 3.5mm Jack, Built in Microphone for Calling, 1.5 Meter Cable, Soft Ear Cushion, Adjustable…
★ ★ ★ ☆ ☆ ⌄ 2,336
1K+ bought in past month

Figure 16.3: An example where we can run OCR

Building shopping assistance

Let us understand the folder structure of this project. The following figure outlines the modular structure of an OCR-enabled GenAI pipeline designed for visual product discovery. The workflow begins with an input image placed in the **assets/** folder, which is processed using **image_utils.py** to extract text via EasyOCR. This raw text is converted into a search-friendly query using a local LLM via **search_utils.py**. Search URLs are generated by **web_scraper.py** and used to fetch real-time product snippets. The following snippets are summarized using **summarizer.py**, again leveraging an LLM. The entire pipeline is orchestrated through **main.py**, offering a fully local and interpretable image-to-insight system.

```
your_project/
|
├── main.py                  ← entry point
├── image_utils.py           ← OCR logic
├── search_utils.py          ← uses ollama to generate search query
├── web_scraper.py           ← returns search URLs (Amazon, Flipkart, eBay)
├── summarizer.py            ← fetch + summarize search results using ollama
├── requirements.txt
├── assets/                  ← place image(s) here for OCR
|    └── example.png
```

Figure 16.4: Code folder structure

Architecture overview

This system follows a modular architecture for processing image-based inputs and turning them into actionable shopping intelligence. The pipeline is designed to accept a product-related image, such as a photo of a retail box, a screenshot from a chat, or a promotional banner placed into the **assets/** folder. From there, the image is analyzed using an OCR tool (EasyOCR) to extract visible text. The resulting raw text is passed into a local LLM via Ollama, which generates a realistic search query a user might type on Flipkart or Amazon. That query is used to construct real e-commerce search URLs. Finally, product listings from these URLs are scraped and summarized to provide an overview of similar or better alternatives. The pipeline runs entirely locally, making it useful for privacy-preserving or offline scenarios.

The architecture is modular and composed of five key components, which are as follows:

- **Image processing (image_utils.py)**: It extracts raw text from product images using EasyOCR.

- **Query generation (search_utils.py)**: It sends the OCR text to a local LLM (via Ollama) to generate a user-style search query.

- **Search redirect (web_scraper.py)**: It constructs product search URLs for Amazon, Flipkart, and eBay using the query.

- **Web summary (summarizer.py)**: It scrapes the snippets from those URLs and summarizes the product trends using the LLM.

- **Orchestration (main.py)**: It orchestrates the full pipeline and prints results to the user.

The end-to-end code can be found in the GitHub repository.

The pipeline depends on a few critical Python libraries, as outlined in **requirements.txt**. First, **easyocr** (along with **torch** and **torchvision**) powers the text extraction from images. **pillow** supports image loading and preprocessing, if needed. The **ollama** package is the interface to locally hosted LLMs like Llama 3, enabling you to generate search queries and summaries without relying on cloud APIs. Web access is managed by **requests** and **beautifulsoup4**, which are used for lightweight scraping of product listings. Optional packages like **selenium** and **google-search-results** are listed but not actively used in this version, providing room for future expansion with dynamic scraping or SerpAPI-based Google search integration. Overall, the requirements are minimal and keep the system portable and offline-friendly, as shown in the following figure:

```
easyocr==1.7.1          # Image-based text recognition
ollama==0.1.6           # Interface to local LLMs like LLaMA3
pillow==10.2.0          # Image manipulation (required by OCR tools)
requests==2.31.0        # HTTP requests for fetching web pages
beautifulsoup4==4.12.3 # HTML parsing for extracting snippets
selenium==4.18.1        # (Optional) browser automation, not used directly here
torch==2.2.1, torchvision=0.17.1 # Deep learning backend for EasyOCR
google-search-results==2.4.2      # For SerpAPI (unused in current version)
```

Figure 16.5: Requirement.txt snapshot, which can be run before running the entire code

The following section explains the overall flow of the solution. It begins by extracting text from an image using OCR, converts that text into a natural language search query via a LLM, fetches product listings from e-commerce platforms, and finally summarizes the results using another LLM call. The design emphasizes clarity, traceability, and graceful error handling, making it robust for real-world use.

1. **OCR with EasyOCR—extracting text from images**: The first major step in the pipeline involves using EasyOCR to read and extract textual information from an image. This logic is implemented in **image_utils.py**, where a pre-trained OCR model is initialized with English language support and configured for CPU-based inference. The core function **extract_text_from_image(image_path)** reads the image and returns a joined string of recognized words. For example, if the image says *boAt Wired Earphones ₹499,* the OCR engine will return that as plain text. This step is crucial because it translates unstructured visual data into a structured format that downstream components (like the LLM) can understand and reason over.

   a. The image is processed using EasyOCR:

   ```
   reader = easyocr.Reader(['en'], gpu=False)
   results = reader.readtext(image_path, detail=0)
   ```

   This extracts plain text strings from an image. For example, an image of a product box might return, *JBL Wired Headphones with Mic ₹799.*

2. **Query generation via LLM—converting text into intent**: Once the text has been extracted from the image, it is passed to the local LLM hosted via Ollama. The function **generate_search_query(ocr_text)** in **search_utils.py** constructs a prompt asking the model to convert the OCR text into a realistic, user-friendly search phrase, something you would type into Flipkart to discover similar or better products. For example, if the extracted text is *boAt 3.5mm Wired Headphones ₹799,* the LLM might return *wired headphones with a mic under 800.* This step bridges the gap between raw image content and search-ready intent. It is a simple but powerful example of how LLMs can interpret ambiguous input and contextualize it for specific tasks.

   a. The extracted text is passed into a prompt for the LLM:

   ```
   prompt = f"The following product text was extracted from an
   image:\n\n{ocr_text}..."
   response = ollama.chat(model="llama3.2:3b-instruct-fp16",
   messages=[{"role": "user", "content": prompt}])
   ```

   b. The LLM returns a simplified search phrase like:

   ```
   wired headphones with mic under 800
   ```

3. **URL construction—redirect-only shopping links**: Instead of performing API-based product retrieval, the **web_scraper.py** module builds direct search URLs for major platforms like Amazon, Flipkart, and eBay. This is achieved through simple string encoding using **urllib.parse.quote_plus** and dynamic URL templating. The function **get_product_listings(query)** takes the generated search query and inserts it into the appropriate search URL structure for each platform. For example, a query like **wireless earbuds under 1000** will become **https://www.amazon.in/s?k=wireless+earbuds+under+1000**. This design choice allows the pipeline to be API-independent, robust to platform changes, and fast to deploy.

   a. Instead of calling APIs, your system constructs direct search URLs:

   i. `f"https://www.amazon.in/s?k={encoded_query}"`
   ii. `f"https://www.flipkart.com/search?q={encoded_query}"`
   iii. `f"https://www.ebay.com/sch/i.html?_nkw={encoded_query}"`

This allows redirection to real product listings based on the generated query.

4. **Web snippet extraction and summarization**: With the search URLs ready, the system fetches the HTML content of each product listing page using **requests**. In **summarizer.py**, the function **fetch_page_snippet(url)** scans the page and collects readable product-related snippets (e.g., titles, descriptions, prices) from common HTML tags like **<a>**, **<div>**, and **<span>**. These snippets are then summarized by the LLM using a second prompt that asks the model to extract themes, keywords, and pricing patterns. The function **summarize_product_pages(product_listings)** loops over all search results, fetches snippets from each, and returns a set of human-readable summaries,

one for each store. This step elevates the user experience by providing a synthesized overview rather than dumping raw text.

    a. Basic text snippets are fetched from each site using **requests** + **BeautifulSoup**:

```
soup = BeautifulSoup(response.text, 'html.parser')
for tag in soup.find_all(['a', 'div', 'span'], limit=100):
    snippets.append(tag.get_text(strip=True))
```

    b. Then, the snippets are summarized by LLM:

```
prompt = f"The following are some product listings from {site_
name}:\n\n{joined_text}"
response = ollama.chat(...)
```

    c. This returns summaries like: common listings include boAt, JBL, and Sony under ₹1,000 with mic and tangle-free cables.

5. **Full pipeline orchestration via main.py**: The **main.py** script acts as the entry point and orchestrator for the entire system. It first scans the **assets/** folder to find the first available image. This image is processed by **extract_text_from_image()**, the resulting text is transformed into a search query by **generate_search_query()**, and then the query is passed into **get_product_listings()** to generate shopping links. Finally, **summarize_product_pages()** is called to fetch, parse, and summarize the product data. Logging is used throughout the script to track progress and errors, making the system easy to debug and maintain. When executed, the script prints out both the raw listings and LLM-generated summaries, offering the user insight into what similar products are available online.

The following Python script defines a modular pipeline that automates product search and summarization based on visual input:

1. **Imports and setup**: It loads all modular components like OCR, query generation, web scraping, and summarization utilities:

```
import os
import logging

from image_utils import extract_text_from_image
from search_utils import generate_search_query
from web_scraper import get_product_listings
from summarizer import summarize_product_pages
```

This section imports the necessary modules and functions. Each module is responsible for a specific task:

    a. **image_utils.py**: It contains OCR logic.

    b. **search_utils.py**: It contains LLM-based query generation.

    c. **web_scraper.py**: It constructs e-commerce search URLs.

    d. **summarizer.py**: It fetches content from those URLs and summarizes it.

The system is built in a modular fashion for easy maintenance and scalability.

2. **Logging configuration**: It sets up formatted logging to aid debugging and monitor execution flow with time-stamped messages:

```
logging.basicConfig(level=logging.INFO, format='%(asctime)s -
%(levelname)s - %(message)s')
```

Logging is configured to output informational messages and errors in a time-stamped, structured format. This is useful for debugging, especially if OCR fails, the image path is incorrect, or the web response fails.

3. **Image finder utility**: It locates the first valid image in the **assets/** directory to serve as the OCR input source:

```
def find_first_image_in_assets():
    assets_folder = "assets"
    if not os.path.exists(assets_folder):
        raise FileNotFoundError(f"Assets folder '{assets_folder}' not
found")

    for file in os.listdir(assets_folder):
        if file.lower().endswith(('.jpg', '.jpeg', '.png', '.webp')):
            return os.path.join(assets_folder, file)
    raise FileNotFoundError("No image found in the assets folder.")
```

This helper function looks inside the **assets/** directory and returns the first valid image file it finds. If the folder does not exist or contains no supported images, it raises an error. This ensures that the pipeline always has a visual input to begin with.

4. **Main pipeline execution**: It begins the end-to-end flow by invoking the image finder and initiating subsequent processing steps:

```
def main():
    try:
        image_path = find_first_image_in_assets()
```

This starts the workflow by calling the image finding utility. The file path is stormed in **image_path**, which will be used in the OCR step.

5. **OCR text extraction**: Uses EasyOCR to extract text from the located image; fails gracefully if no text is found:

```
        extracted_text = extract_text_from_image(image_path)
        if not extracted_text:
            raise ValueError("No text could be extracted from the image")
        logging.info(f"OCR Extracted Text:\n{extracted_text}")
```

Here, EasyOCR reads the image and returns a string of recognized text. If no text is detected (empty string), an exception is raised. The result is logged for traceability.

6. **Search query generation via LLM**: Converts extracted text into a clean, user-like search query using a local language model and sanitizes it:

```
query = generate_search_query(extracted_text)
if not query:
    raise ValueError("Failed to generate a valid search query")

query = query.replace('"', '').replace("₹", "rs").replace("or
less", "under").replace("alternative", "")
logging.info(f"Search Query:\n{query}")
```

a. The raw OCR text is now passed to a local LLM (via Ollama), which transforms it into a user-like search query such as:

"wired headphones under rs 800"

Some basic sanitization is done to clean special characters and standardize currency symbols (₹ | **rs**) for compatibility with search URLs.

7. **Redirect URL construction**: Builds e-commerce search result URLs from the generated query for platforms like Amazon and Flipkart:

```
results = get_product_listings(query)
if not results:
    logging.warning("No product listings found")
    return
```

This query is used to build search URLs for Amazon, Flipkart, and eBay by calling **get_product_listings(query)**. These are not actual API calls but direct redirect URLs to the respective websites. If none are returned (which should not happen), a warning is logged.

8. **Print URLs to console**: Displays a concise list of found products, including name, price, store, and a clickable link:

```
print("\nHere are some similar or better alternatives you can check out:\n")
    for i, res in enumerate(results, 1):
        print(f"{i}. {res['name']}")
        print(f"   Price: {res['price']}")
        print(f"   Store: {res['merchant']}")
        print(f"   Link: {res['link']}\n")
```

The generated search listings are printed in a clean format. Since these are redirect URLs (not full product listings), each entry just shows:

a. Store name

b. Link to the search result page

9. **Summarize web snippets**: It fetches and summarizes content from the search result pages using LLM to highlight trends and insights:

```
print("\nSummary of Product Listings:\n")
summaries = summarize_product_pages(results)
for s in summaries:
    print(f"{s['store']} Summary:\n{s['summary']}\n")
```

This is where the second LLM call happens. For each search URL, the program does the following:

　　a. Fetches the web page using **request**.

　　b. Extracts visible product text from the HTML.

　　c. Summarizes the overall trend using the LLM (e.g., top brands, typical price ranges, common features).

　　d. This provides a readable overview of what is trending in each store's results based on your query.

10. **Robust error handling**: Captures and logs file, value, and unexpected errors to ensure graceful failure and meaningful logs:

```
except FileNotFoundError as e:
    logging.error(f"File error: {str(e)}")
except ValueError as e:
    logging.error(f"Value error: {str(e)}")
except Exception as e:
    logging.error(f"An unexpected error occurred: {str(e)}")
```

　　a. Three types of exceptions that are caught are as follows:

　　　　i. Missing folder or image.

　　　　ii. Empty OCR or invalid LLM output.

　　　　iii. Any other unexpected errors.

　　This ensures the pipeline fails gracefully and outputs helpful logs.

　　b. Execution trigger:

```
if __name__ == "__main__":
    main()
```

This is the script's execution entry point. It ensures the **main()** function only runs when the script is directly executed, not when imported as a module.

Understanding the output

This output represents the final result of a complete OCR-to-LLM pipeline, where a user-provided image of a product is used to generate intelligent e-commerce alternatives. The image in question shows a wired headphone advertisement with visible price and features. The following figure provide a breakdown of the system's behavior and its resulting output.

Starting with a product image containing details of a wired headphone, the system accurately extracts descriptive text using EasyOCR. This raw text is then transformed by a local LLM into a realistic and goal-oriented search query, specifically looking for alternatives from well-known brands like Sony and JBL within a set price range. Using this query, the system constructs direct search URLs for Amazon, Flipkart, and eBay, mimicking how a human might explore online stores. It then retrieves visible text snippets from those search pages and summarizes the results using the same LLM. In the case of Flipkart, the model identifies that the page content lacks substantive product information and instead focuses on promotional language and urgency cues, such as limited-time offers and fast delivery messaging. This response not only highlights the model's ability to extract and interpret data but also to assess the quality and relevance of content across different platforms, ultimately empowering users to make informed shopping decisions based on visual inputs alone.

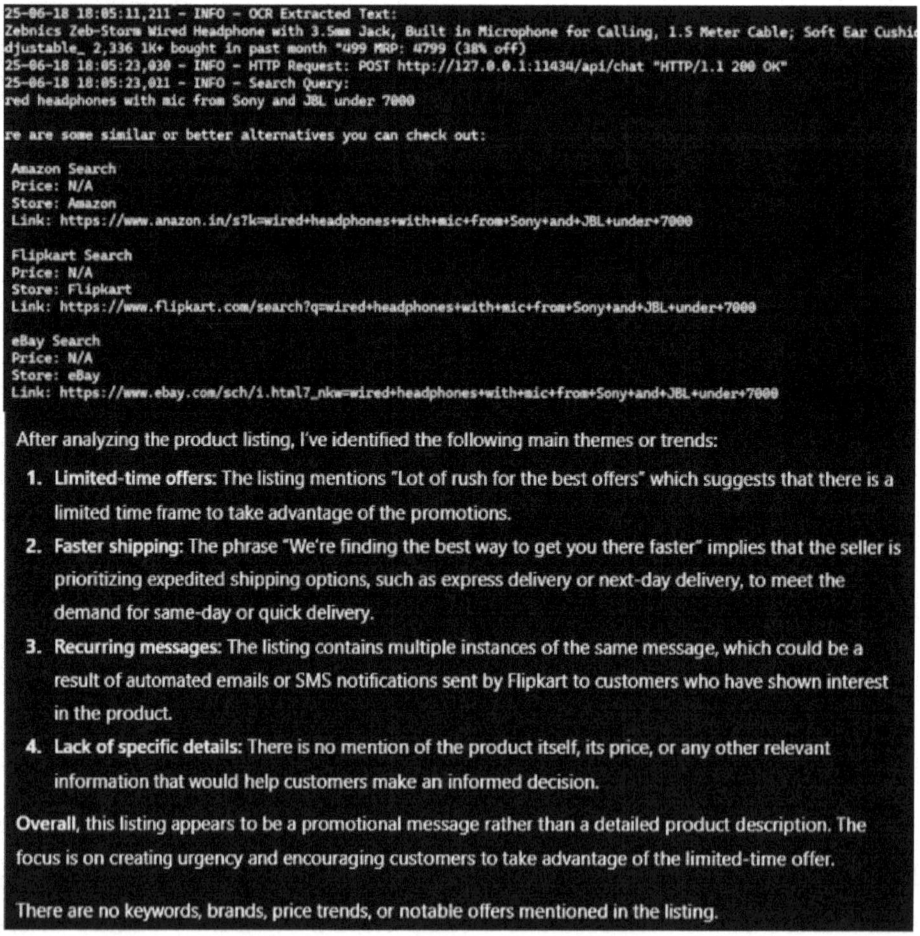

```
25-06-18 18:05:11,211 - INFO - OCR Extracted Text:
Zebnics Zeb-Storm Wired Headphone with 3.5mm Jack, Built in Microphone for Calling, 1.5 Meter Cable; Soft Ear Cushid
djustable_ 2,336 1K+ bought in past month ^499 MRP: ₹799 (38% off)
25-06-18 18:05:23,030 - INFO - HTTP Request: POST http://127.0.0.1:11434/api/chat "HTTP/1.1 200 OK"
25-06-18 18:05:23,011 - INFO - Search Query:
red headphones with mic from Sony and JBL under 7000

re are some similar or better alternatives you can check out:

Amazon Search
Price: N/A
Store: Amazon
Link: https://www.amazon.in/s?k=wired+headphones+with+mic+from+Sony+and+JBL+under+7000

Flipkart Search
Price: N/A
Store: Flipkart
Link: https://www.flipkart.com/search?q=wired+headphones+with+mic+from+Sony+and+JBL+under+7000

eBay Search
Price: N/A
Store: eBay
Link: https://www.ebay.com/sch/i.html?_nkw=wired+headphones+with+mic+from+Sony+and+JBL+under+7000
```

After analyzing the product listing, I've identified the following main themes or trends:

1. **Limited-time offers:** The listing mentions "Lot of rush for the best offers" which suggests that there is a limited time frame to take advantage of the promotions.

2. **Faster shipping:** The phrase "We're finding the best way to get you there faster" implies that the seller is prioritizing expedited shipping options, such as express delivery or next-day delivery, to meet the demand for same-day or quick delivery.

3. **Recurring messages:** The listing contains multiple instances of the same message, which could be a result of automated emails or SMS notifications sent by Flipkart to customers who have shown interest in the product.

4. **Lack of specific details:** There is no mention of the product itself, its price, or any other relevant information that would help customers make an informed decision.

Overall, this listing appears to be a promotional message rather than a detailed product description. The focus is on creating urgency and encouraging customers to take advantage of the limited-time offer.

There are no keywords, brands, price trends, or notable offers mentioned in the listing.

Figure 16.6: Output from the GenAI system

OCR on a multimodal document

OCR on multimodal documents like PDFs involves extracting and interpreting a mix of textual, visual, and structural content within a single file. Unlike plain images, PDFs often include typed text, scanned pages, tables, images, and layout elements such as headers, footers, and multi-column sections. Advanced OCR systems powered by VLMs or foundation models like Mistral OCR, models can process these documents holistically, identifying reading order, extracting tables and figures, preserving formatting, and capturing semantic meaning. When integrated with schema-based extraction or document **question and answer** (**QA**) capabilities, this enables automated understanding of contracts, invoices, reports, or academic papers, making PDF-based workflows intelligent, searchable, and machine-actionable.

The following image-text snippet illustrates how visual (chart + table) and textual data together convey the progression of educational attainment from 1996 to 2022:

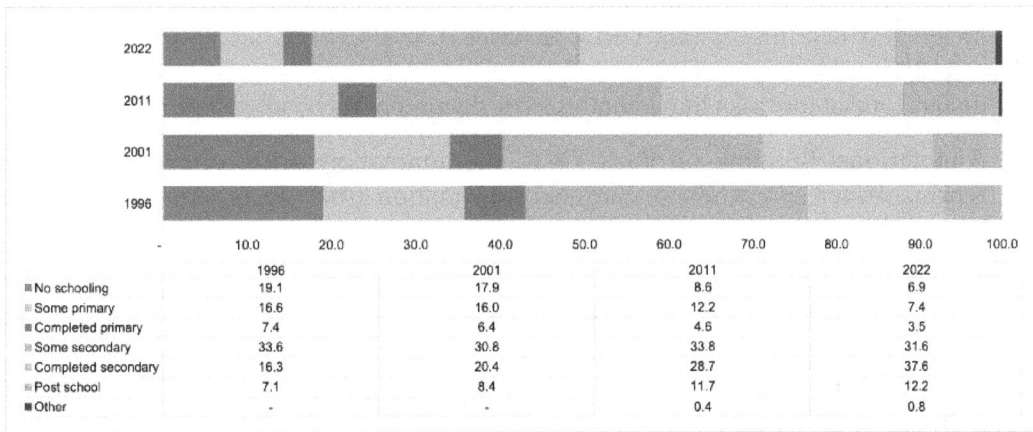

	1996	2001	2011	2022
No schooling	19.1	17.9	8.6	6.9
Some primary	16.6	16.0	12.2	7.4
Completed primary	7.4	6.4	4.6	3.5
Some secondary	33.6	30.8	33.8	31.6
Completed secondary	16.3	20.4	28.7	37.6
Post school	7.1	8.4	11.7	12.2
Other	-	-	0.4	0.8

Figure 4.5 presents the progression in educational attainment of the population aged 20 years and older across the years 1996 to 2022. The percentage of individuals with no schooling has reduced almost threefold (19,1% in 1996 and 6,9% in 2022). The percentage of individuals with some primary education has reduced by half. Similarly, completion of primary schooling has decreased by half. Completion of secondary education more than doubled from 16,3% in 1996 to 37,6% in 2022. However, achievement of post-school education increased by only 5,1 percentage points. In 1996, one-third (33,6%) of the population aged 20 years and older had only some secondary education and only 16,3% had completed secondary education. However, in 2022 more than one-third (37,6%) had completed secondary education.

Figure16.7: *An example of a multimodal document suitable for OCR processing*

Figure 16.7 exemplifies a multimodal data source that combines structured visuals (bar charts and tables) with unstructured textual descriptions, representing a rich and complex input ideal for OCR-driven document understanding. In the context of multimodal AI systems, such images require not only text extraction but also layout interpretation, semantic alignment between graphical and textual elements, and contextual reasoning. Leveraging advanced OCR techniques powered by LLMs enables accurate transcription, structure preservation, and meaningful interpretation, transforming static visual content into actionable, machine-readable insights. This forms a critical foundation for intelligent analysis of reports, educational trends, and policy documents.

Mistral's OCR

Mistral's OCR stack transforms traditional OCR from passive transcription into an active, structured, and interactive system. It offers layered capabilities: layout-preserving text extraction, schema-based data capture, and context-aware querying via LLMs. These functions—Basic OCR, annotations, and document QA—enable developers to build sophisticated document intelligence applications, from extracting tables and captioning figures to creating chat-like assistants. Together, they form a versatile foundation for real-world GenAI pipelines, as shown in the following, supporting rich multimodal workflows across diverse document types:

- **Basic OCR**: Mistral's basic OCR is a fully featured recognition system that does more than just transcribe text. It extracts text along with structural information, like headers, paragraphs, lists, and tables, and returns results in Markdown format, enabling seamless integration into documentation or pipelines. The model preserves document layout and hierarchy, handles multi-column and complex designs, and works with image and PDF inputs (via URLs or base64). It also provides bounding boxes and metadata, allowing developers to precisely locate each piece of text in the original image, crucial for tasks like annotation or document reconstruction.

- **Annotations**: Building on Basic OCR, the annotations feature enables structured, schema-driven extraction of targeted information from documents. There are two types, which are as follows:

  - **bbox_annotation**: It allows users to specify bounding boxes (e.g., areas containing charts or figures) and receive captions or descriptions tailored to those regions.

  - **document_annotation**: It extracts structured data from the entire document into a **JavaScript Object Notation (JSON)** format that aligns with developer-defined schemas. This is highly useful for automating data entry from forms, invoices, or legal documents, transforming free-form scanned input into directly usable structured datasets.

- **Document QA**: It elevates OCR-based pipelines by integrating context-aware LLMs. After OCR processes and extracts structured textual content along with layout (including headings, paragraphs, tables), the system can answer natural language questions about the document. For example, a user could ask, *what is the total amount due?* or *list all the procedures outlined*, and *the LLM responds using its understanding of the text, structure, and relationships*. This functionality enables document understanding beyond extraction, supporting analysis, summarization, or multi-document comparisons. Use cases include form processing, legal review, and academic analysis. Let us understand the code implementation:

```
# Step 1: Install the Mistral client
!pip install mistralai --quiet
```

```
# Step 2: Import required modules
import os
from mistralai.client import Mistral
from mistralai.models.chat_completion import ChatMessage

# Step 3: Set API key (ensure your key is securely set)
os.environ["MISTRAL_API_KEY"] = "your_mistral_api_key"  # Replace with
your actual key
api_key = os.environ["MISTRAL_API_KEY"]
# Upload and get document URL
with open("/content/sample_data/educational_attainment_figure.pdf", "rb")
as f:
    uploaded_file = client.files.upload(
        file={"file_name": "educational_attainment_figure.pdf", "content":
f},
        purpose="ocr"
    )

signed_url = client.files.get_signed_url(file_id=uploaded_file.id)

# Ask a question
messages = [
    ChatMessage(
        role="user",
        content=[
            {"type": "text", "text": "Summarize post-school education
growth over the years."},
            {"type": "document_url", "document_url": signed_url.url}
        ]
    )
]

response = client.chat.complete(
    model="mistral-small-latest",
    messages=messages
)

print(response.choices[0].message.content)
```

The regex in context

The purpose of the following regex code is to automatically detect and extract URLs from a user's input message, specifically targeting document links such as PDFs.

Mistral's document QA feature allows you to attach document URLs alongside your text prompt. But users might type something like: *Can you summarize this paper?* **https://arxiv.org/pdf/2410.07073**

To make this work, the system needs to:

1. Identify that a URL is present.

2. Parse it out of the full user message.

3. Attach it as a **{"type": "document_url", "document_url": ...}** entry to the message payload.

   import re# is required here to support the regex-based URL extraction.

   ```
   def extract_urls(text: str) -> list:
       url_pattern = r'\b((?:https?|ftp)://(?:www\.)?[^\s/$.?#].[^\s]*)\b'
       urls = re.findall(url_pattern, text)
       return urls
   ```

4. Once URLs are extracted:

   ```
   user_message_content = [{"type": "text", "text": user_input}]
   for url in document_urls:
       user_message_content.append({"type": "document_url", "document_url":
   url})
   ```

5. This means Mistral's API receives the following:

   a. Your question (as text)

   b. Your PDF or document URL (as a separately recognized input)

OCR in receipt data

The following figure represents a typical example of a semi-structured receipt commonly found in datasets like the **Consolidated Receipt Dataset** (**CORD**). These receipts contain rich textual information, including itemized product listings, quantities, unit prices, tax calculations, and total payment summaries, all formatted in visually complex layouts. Extracting structured information from such documents is a foundational task in modern document understanding research. This image serves as a real-world benchmark to evaluate OCR and document parsing systems, particularly for key-value extraction and table detection using foundation models like Mistral OCR or multimodal models such as Llama 3.2 vision via Ollama.

Figure 16.8: A receipt that consists of textual tabular data

The following Python code demonstrates the way to perform image-based document understanding using Meta's Llama 3.2 vision model via the Ollama runtime. This approach integrates computer vision and natural language understanding by allowing a user to upload an image and query it in natural language, with the large multimodal model producing a structured response. The code is designed for use in environments like *Google Colab*, where the image file is stored in a default data directory.

The core logic of the pipeline involves invoking the **ollama.chat()** method, where the **model** parameter is set to **llama3.2-vision**, indicating that a vision-enabled Llama 3.2 instance is being used. The prompt **get all the data from the image** is sent as the message content under the **user** role, and the image itself is passed in a list under the **images** key. Once the LLM processes the image, it returns a structured textual response within the **message['content']** field of the **response** object. The **strip()** function ensures that any leading or trailing whitespace is removed from the response before displaying it. The model output in this case includes detailed invoice metadata such as company name, address, billing recipient, and line-item entries, showcasing the model's ability to parse layout-rich documents like invoices. This example illustrates a significant advancement over traditional OCR by capturing not just text but also context, relationships, and hierarchies directly from image input, thus facilitating more intelligent document automation use cases.

- Visual **data extraction via Ollama Llama 3.2 vision:**

```
import ollama
image_path =  # Replace with your image path
```

This line sets the path of the image to be processed. In a typical Colab setup, this would be **/content/sample_data/invoice_sample.jpg**.

```
python
CopyEdit
response = ollama.chat(
    model="llama3.2-vision",
    messages=[{
      "role": "user",
      "content": "get all the data from the image",
      "images": [image_path]
    }],
)
```

This block uses Ollama's API to interact with the Llama 3.2 vision model. The model processes the image and returns a textual breakdown of its content, ideally a structured summary of the receipt.

```
cleaned_text = response['message']['content'].strip()
```

The response is cleaned of whitespace to prepare it for further processing.

- Prompt-based structure extraction using LangChain:

```
from langchain_ollama import ChatOllama
from langchain_core.prompts import ChatPromptTemplate
from langchain_core.output_parsers import StrOutputParser
```

This portion sets up the LangChain ecosystem for prompt chaining. The user defines a template prompt instructing the model to extract and return specific fields (e.g., company name, receipt number, item list, total).

```
llm = ChatOllama(model="llama3",  temperature=0)
```

This initializes a LLM connection to the standard Llama 3 model using Ollama (text-only model now).

```
chain = (prompt | llm | StrOutputParser())
return chain.invoke({"response": response})
```

Here, the prompt is chained with the model and parser, then executed with the cleaned OCR text. The output is expected to be JSON-formatted.

- Extract JSON using Regex and parse it:

```
json_match = re.search(r"```\n(.*?)\n```", result, re.DOTALL)
```

This searches for a JSON block enclosed in triple backticks ``` inside the model response.

```
parsed_data = json.loads(receipt_data)
```

Once extracted, the JSON string is parsed into a Python dictionary using **json.loads**.

- Convert to DataFrame for analysis:

```
receipt_dict = json.loads(json_data)
items_df = pd.DataFrame(receipt_dict['Items'])
```

The receipt dictionary is further processed by converting the **Items** list into a Pandas DataFrame, which enables further operations like data analysis, aggregation, or visualization.

This code exemplifies a multimodal RAG-like system, combining image understanding (Llama 3.2 vision), prompt-based semantic extraction (LangChain), and structured output (JSON | DataFrame). It is a compelling example of how foundational models can bridge unstructured visual inputs and structured analytics in an automated, end-to-end pipeline.

To do

As an extension to this chapter, readers are encouraged to explore real-world OCR challenges using the CORD, a publicly available dataset curated for information extraction from store receipts. This dataset consists of image-PDFs and corresponding JSON annotations, making it an ideal candidate for testing document understanding systems on semi-structured financial documents. Readers can experiment with extracting merchant names, itemized purchases, totals, and tax values, either by training their token classifiers or using layout-aware prompting strategies. The key task is to go beyond raw text extraction and develop end-to-end pipelines that understand document semantics and formatting.

For implementation, readers may choose one of two cutting-edge approaches. First, they can leverage Mistral's document QA API, which automatically applies OCR and allows for structured QA using document URLs. This approach is scalable and requires minimal setup. Alternatively, readers can experiment with Meta's Llama 3.2 vision model using the Ollama runtime, which supports multimodal image inputs. In this setup, receipts can be passed as images to the model with tailored prompts (e.g., *list all the items and their prices from this receipt*), enabling visual-semantic reasoning. This task encourages students to combine dataset engineering, prompt design, and multimodal LLMs to create robust, high-accuracy document understanding systems.

Conclusion

In this chapter, we explored three distinct yet complementary approaches to performing OCR in the context of multimodal data. First, we demonstrated how traditional OCR tools like EasyOCR can be wrapped within a GenAI pipeline to extract and reason over text from images, enabling intelligent interpretation of unstructured visual inputs. Second, we introduced Mistral OCR, a foundation model natively trained for document understanding, which streamlines OCR on complex PDFs by providing structured outputs through API-driven document QA. Lastly, we examined the power of multimodal LLMs, such as Meta's Llama vision series, in handling receipt images with embedded tabular data, highlighting their ability to simultaneously interpret layout, extract content, and generate semantically structured outputs. Together, these methods provide a robust toolkit for building next-generation OCR systems that bridge the gap between raw visual input and actionable structured understanding.

In the next chapter, we will focus on wrapping traditional models with GenAI, e.g., recommendation engines.

Join our Discord space

Join our Discord workspace for latest updates, offers, tech happenings around the world, new releases, and sessions with the authors:

https://discord.bpbonline.com

CHAPTER 17

Integrating Traditional AI/ML into GenAI Workflow

Introduction

As the boundaries between traditional **machine learning** (**ML**) and **generative AI** (**GenAI**) continue to blur, there is increasing value in creating hybrid systems that combine the strengths of both. In this chapter, we explore how to wrap and integrate conventional ML models, such as classifiers, regressors, and clustering algorithms, into GenAI agent workflows. By making these models callable as tools within agentic reasoning loops, we unlock powerful capabilities where generative agents can not only converse and generate but also predict, classify, and recommend with precision.

Using technologies like scikit-learn, LangChain, and lightweight Python microservices, you will learn how to expose ML models via **application programming interfaces** (**APIs**) and make them interact seamlessly with GenAI agents. We will walk through practical implementations, including a recommendation engine integrated as a callable tool within a **large language model** (**LLM**) reasoning chain. Along the way, we will address key operational challenges such as API latency, error handling, and versioning of models, ensuring robustness and reliability in production-ready systems.

By the end of this chapter, you will have built a fully functioning hybrid system where GenAI agents dynamically invoke ML predictions as part of their **chain of thought** (**CoT**). This fusion of reasoning and prediction paves the way for intelligent systems that are not only conversationally fluent but also analytically powerful.

Structure

In this chapter, we will learn about the following topics:

- Case study
- Integrating the traditional model within GenAI
- Use case
- Wrapping XGBoost model into LLM
- Comparative overview of ML model integration in GenAI workflows
- To do

Objectives

The objective of this chapter was to guide readers through the end-to-end development of a hybrid AI system that integrates traditional ML with modern GenAI. Specifically, it demonstrated how to train, deploy, and wrap an **Extreme Gradient Boosting** (**XGBoost**) fraud detection model as an API, and then use an LLM like Mistral to interface with it via natural language. Readers will learn how to extract structured features from text, call ML tools programmatically, interpret model outputs, and generate actionable explanations, all within a modular, production-ready architecture. The goal was to make traditional ML models accessible, explainable, and usable through GenAI agents.

Case study

Company *X Analytics* is a 15 member AI startup specializing in intelligent retail solutions for mid-sized e-commerce platforms. Over the past two years, the team developed a suite of traditional ML models, including a collaborative filtering based recommendation engine, a churn prediction model using XGBoost, and a product categorization model trained on custom logistic regression classifiers. These models had been manually integrated into dashboards or batch jobs, but lacked real-time, interactive utility.

As GenAI gained momentum, the company subscribed to commercial LLMs like *OpenAI's Generative Pre-trained Transformer* (*GPT*) and *Anthropic's Claude*, intending to build a conversational assistant that could help retail managers make smarter, faster decisions. However, the challenge was clear, which was how to bridge the intelligence embedded in their traditional ML models with the reasoning and language fluency of LLMs.

The following case study illustrates how RastrAI bridged traditional ML and GenAI by wrapping legacy models into a GenAI workflow. By combining LangChain agents, RESTful ML microservices, and CoT prompting, the company built an intelligent system capable of answering complex business questions with both reasoning and predictive accuracy.

- **Problem statement**: The company needed to build a hybrid GenAI agent capable of answering nuanced questions like the following:

  o *Why is customer retention dropping for Segment B?*

  o *Which products should I recommend next week to low-engagement users?*

  These queries required both natural language understanding and direct access to existing ML insights, something that LLMs could not do out of the box.

- **Solution**: The engineering team adopted LangChain to create tool-augmented agents that could call traditional ML models as part of their reasoning process. Each ML model was wrapped as a microservice using FastAPI, exposing RESTful endpoints like `/predict_churn`, `/get_recommendations`, and `/classify_product`. These endpoints accepted structured payloads and returned **JavaScript Object Notation (JSON)** responses.

  The team then defined LangChain tool objects that mapped directly to these APIs. With CoT prompting, the LLM was instructed to invoke the right tool-based on the user's intent. For example, if a manager asked, *what are some high-risk customers this month?* The agent would parse the input, call the churn prediction API, and return actionable insights in fluent language.

- **Outcome**: In under eight weeks, RastrAI successfully transitioned from siloed ML workflows to a unified GenAI-powered system. Their internal tool, RetailGenie, became an intelligent co-pilot for business analysts, blending conversational reasoning with predictive intelligence. The result was faster decision-making, better utilization of legacy models, and a more modern, AI-native **user experience (UX)**, without the need to re-train or discard their existing ML stack.

While this case study is fictional, it reflects a real scenario faced by many modern enterprises. Today, organizations are heavily investing in LLMs through subscriptions or API integrations, while simultaneously sitting on a rich legacy of traditional AI and ML models, ranging from recommendation engines to risk scoring systems. Instead of fine-tuning large, costly LLMs or rebuilding existing solutions from scratch, companies can adopt this hybrid approach to maximize value. By wrapping their traditional models as callable tools within LLM-powered agents, they can create intelligent systems that combine domain-specific insights with the natural language reasoning of GenAI, accelerating innovation while preserving past investments.

Integrating the traditional model with GenAI

As the field of AI transitions into the era of GenAI, the challenge and opportunity lie in bridging traditional AI models with the emergent capabilities of LLMs. Enterprises often possess a portfolio of pre-existing ML and deep learning models designed for specific predictive or perceptual tasks. Rather than discarding or fine-tuning LLMs for these use cases, a more modular and cost-effective approach involves wrapping traditional models as callable tools and orchestrating them via LLM-based agents. This enables intelligent systems where LLMs serve as the reasoning layer, while traditional models perform high-accuracy predictive tasks.

This section explores how various traditional AI/ML models, from classifiers and regressors to **convolutional neural networks (CNNs)** and **optical character recognition (OCR)**, can be seamlessly integrated into GenAI workflows using tool-augmented agents. By exposing models via APIs and enabling LLMs to interpret and act on their outputs, developers can build intelligent systems that combine predictive accuracy with natural language interaction, details as follows:

- **Classification models**: It is used to assign labels such as fraud/not-fraud or category membership. These models are essential for decision-making tasks.

    o **Example**: Fraud detection using logistic regression or XGBoost.

        ▪ **API exposurer**: The classifier is deployed using FastAPI or Flask to expose an endpoint like **/predict_class**.

        ▪ **Tool calling**: A LangChain or custom LLM agent defines a tool schema that sends feature vectors to this endpoint.

        ▪ **LLM reasoning**: The LLM interprets user input (*is this transaction fraudulent?*), transforms it into structured input, and explains the output in human-readable terms (*this transaction has an 87% probability of being fraud.*).

        ▪ **Agent utility**: The agent can trigger follow-up actions, e.g., notifying a compliance officer or logging the transaction, based on classification results.

- **Regression models**: Used for continuous value prediction, these models help estimate outcomes like prices, scores, or risks.

    o **Example**: House price prediction using linear regression or LightGBM.

        ▪ **API exposure**: Model is served via an endpoint like **/predict_price**, accepting numerical features (location, size, year).

        ▪ **Tool calling**: The tool sends structured inputs and retrieves predicted values.

        ▪ **LLM reasoning**: The LLM provides interpretability (based on area and amenities, the predicted value is ₹95 lakhs.)

        ▪ **Agent utility**: The output can feed into downstream tools for loan eligibility estimation or investment recommendation.

- **Forecasting models**: These time-series models enable predictive planning by estimating future values based on historical trends.

    o **Example**: Time-series sales forecasting using **Autoregressive Integrated Moving Average** (**ARIMA**) or Prophet.

- **API exposure**: A REST endpoint like `/forecast_sales` takes historical data and outputs future values.

- **Tool calling**: The tool format may involve nested time-series arrays.

- **LLM reasoning**: The LLM interprets temporal trends and explains seasonal effects (*sales are expected to spike during Diwali due to past patterns.*).

- **Agent utility**: It can be used to trigger inventory reordering or dynamic pricing recommendations in real-time.

- **Artificial neural networks**: Used for capturing non-linear relationships in structured data, **artificial neural networks** (**ANNs**) power many classification and prediction tasks.

    o **Example**: Customer churn prediction using a feedforward neural network.

- **API exposure**: Wrapped via a serving framework like TensorFlow Serving or TorchServe.

- **Tool calling**: The LLM agent formats customer attributes and invokes the `endpoint/predict_churn`.

- **LLM reasoning**: The LLM explains non-linear relationships captured by the ANN (*high tenure and usage suggest low churn risk*).

- **Agent utility**: The agent can segment customers and prioritize retention offers or emails based on churn risk.

- **CNNs**: Primarily used in image classification tasks, CNNs are key for visual inspection, defect detection, or recognition.

    o **Example**: Image classification (e.g., defect detection on products)

- **API exposure**: CNN model is served via an endpoint like `/classify_image`, which accepts base64 or file URL formats.

- **Tool calling**: The agent preprocesses the image input, sends it to the CNN, and receives a label.

- **LLM reasoning**: The LLM contextualizes the label (*the crack detected suggests mechanical failure.*).

- **Agent utility**: Based on the classification, the agent can initiate a quality check workflow or notify operations.

- **Segmentation models**: These models divide images into meaningful parts, useful for medical imaging, document layout analysis, or object detection.

- o **Example**: Semantic segmentation in medical imaging (e.g., tumor detection in MRI scans).

  - ▪ **API exposure**: The model is served with endpoints like `/segment_image`, returning a segmented mask or overlay.

  - ▪ **Tool calling**: The agent sends image data and processes returned masks.

  - ▪ **LLM reasoning**: The LLM can interpret the segmentation, and *the highlighted region corresponds to a likely tumor boundary.*

  - ▪ **Agent utility**: Enables automatic report generation or decision support in clinical systems by combining LLM narrative generation with pixel-level model outputs.

- **OCR models**: It is used to convert printed or handwritten text from images into a machine-readable format; these models unlock structured data from visual documents.

  - o **Example**: Text extraction from scanned documents, invoices, or identity cards using Tesseract, EasyOCR, or a custom transformer-based OCR pipeline.

    - ▪ **API exposure**: The OCR model is deployed via an endpoint such as `/extract_text`, which accepts image files (e.g., PNG, JPEG) and returns recognized text in JSON format.

    - ▪ **Tool calling**: The GenAI agent invokes the tool with the uploaded image, receives extracted text, and optionally post-processes for structure (e.g., key-value pairs).

    - ▪ **LLM reasoning**: The LLM interprets the raw OCR output, *this document is an invoice from Vendor X dated March 12, 2024, with a total payable amount of $1,274.*

    - ▪ **Agent utility**: It enables downstream tasks such as document classification, automated data entry, or conversational querying (*what is the invoice number?*) by combining OCR output with LLM-based natural language understanding.

      In *Chapter 16, GenAI for Extracting Text from Images*, GenAI for Extracting Text from Images we have explored how to integrate OCR capabilities with GenAI by wrapping OCR models as callable tools.

Initialization of these hybrid systems

In a hybrid GenAI/ML system, traditional ML processes can be triggered either interactively via user instructions to the LLM or automatically through batch workflows orchestrated by the agent. When users engage directly, they issue natural language queries such as *can you predict the churn risk for this customer?* or *extract text from this receipt and summarize the key details.*

The LLM interprets the intent, structures the required inputs, and calls the corresponding ML tool, such as a churn prediction model or an OCR service, via predefined API wrappers.

Alternatively, in batch or background processing, the LLM agent may iterate over a queue of tasks (e.g., daily image folders, transaction logs) and autonomously invoke traditional models. For instance, a scheduled agent may analyze all uploaded invoices every night using OCR and pass the extracted data to a financial anomaly detector. These operations are initialized through LangChain-like orchestration layers or microservice pipelines that monitor triggers or workflows and coordinate tool invocations accordingly.

This design supports both on-demand reasoning and automated ML execution, allowing organizations to combine GenAI's flexibility with the precision of legacy models, enabling applications like fraud detection, recommendation engine, and customer analytics with minimal manual intervention.

Use case

This is a case study of hybrid ensemble learning for telecom fraud detection, as fraud detection remains a critical challenge in the telecommunications industry, where fraudulent activities, such as identity spoofing, **Subscriber Identity Module** (**SIM**) cloning, and illegitimate claim submissions, pose substantial risks to revenue and customer trust. The rarity of fraudulent instances compared to legitimate transactions results in highly imbalanced datasets, making conventional classification methods inadequate. This case study presents an ensemble-based ML approach, augmented by deep learning methods, to detect fraud in a real-world telecom claims dataset characterized by a 6:94 fraud-to-non-fraud ratio.

Data characteristics and preprocessing

The dataset comprised anonymized claim-related features, including customer metadata, claim submission intervals, and verification flags. Notably, variables such as `IS_MISSING_MOBILE`, `HOUR_TO_RAISE_CLAIM`, and `TOTAL_VERIFICATIONS` carried domain-specific semantic value and were not imputed using statistical means. Instead, such features were encoded using flag-based approaches to preserve interpretability. Categorical features were label-encoded, and numerical attributes were standardized using Z-score normalization. Missing values and zero-inflated features were visualized and handled explicitly to ensure robust downstream model behavior.

Baseline model development and evaluation

An initial XGBoost model was developed, incorporating the `scale_pos_weight` parameter to address class imbalance. Instead of relying on the default decision threshold of `0.5`, a threshold tuning mechanism was applied. Precision, recall, and F1 scores were computed across multiple thresholds, and the optimal cutoff was selected to maximize the F1 score, achieving a trade-off between fraud detection (recall) and false alarm reduction (precision).

Performance was evaluated using standard classification metrics, including the confusion matrix, **precision-recall (PR)** curve, **receiver operating characteristic (ROC)** curve, **Matthews correlation coefficient (MCC)**, and Cohen's Kappa score. This multi-metric evaluation provided a comprehensive view of model reliability under imbalance conditions.

Stacked ensemble learning approach

To further improve generalization and model robustness, a stacked ensemble classifier was constructed. The base learners included XGBoost, LightGBM, and the gradient boosting classifier. Their individual probability outputs were passed to a meta-classifier, logistic regression, which learned to optimally combine their outputs. The ensemble was trained using a stratified train-test split and evaluated on the same metrics as the baseline model.

The stacked ensemble demonstrated superior performance compared to any single model. It yielded higher recall for fraud detection while maintaining competitive precision, thus minimizing both false negatives and false positives. The ROC-AUC and PR-AUC scores improved notably, and the MCC and Kappa values confirmed increased model stability.

The study underscores the efficacy of combining tree-based classifiers in a stacked architecture for fraud detection in highly imbalanced datasets. Moreover, threshold optimization and domain-informed preprocessing were essential for improving real-world applicability. The proposed approach can be integrated into production systems for fraud risk scoring and supports extensibility for SHAP-based interpretability or real-time fraud monitoring APIs. If we have to use the above ensemble and or an XGBoost model (as described in the fraud detection case study) in conjunction with an LLM, the LLM serves as a reasoning, orchestration, and explanation layer around your already-trained predictive model.

Purpose of the LLM in this setup

The following is a breakdown of the roles and purposes the LLM would serve in a hybrid system:

- **Natural language interface**:
    - **Purpose**: It allows the non-technical users (e.g., fraud analysts, claim reviewers) to interact with the XGBoost model using natural language.
    - **Example input**: `Can you check if this claim is fraudulent? The mobile number is missing, and the claim was raised late at night`.
    - **LLM action**: Parse this input, extract relevant features from the data (`IS_MISSING_MOBILE=1`, `HOUR_TO_RAISE_CLAIM=2`), and send them to the XGBoost model via a tool/API.

- **Tool invocation/model wrapping**:
    - **Purpose**: It acts as a controller that decides when and how to invoke the XGBoost model wrapped as a callable tool (e.g., via LangChain or FastAPI).

o **Mechanism**:

```
Tool(
    name="FraudScoringTool",
    func=call_xgboost_api,
    description="Predicts fraud probability for a telecom claim."
)
```

The LLM calls this tool internally when reasoning about fraud.

- **Result interpretation and explanation**:
  - o **Purpose**: It translates the raw output (e.g., *fraud probability = 0.92*) into human-understandable language, often with context.
  - o **Example output**:
    - ▪ *This claim has a high fraud probability (92%). The model flagged it due to missing mobile data, off-hours claim submission, and low verification count.*
    - ▪ This is especially valuable when used with explainability tools like SHAP, where the LLM can narrate the most influential features in plain English.

- **Chained decision-making/workflow triggering**:
  - o **Purpose**: Based on the model result, the LLM agent can decide the next step:
    - ▪ Flag for manual review
    - ▪ Auto-reject the claim
    - ▪ Ask the user for additional evidence

This is akin to CoT reasoning, augmented by model outputs.

- **Audit trail/report generation**:
  - o **Purpose**: Generate structured summaries of the fraud detection process, combining model scores, explanations, and reasoning.
  - o **Example**: *Claim ID #4532 has been flagged for review. Fraud score: 0.92. Key factors: unverified contact info, delayed submission, and missing address fields. Analyst action recommended.*

Wrapping XG boost model into LLM

The existing XGBoost pipeline performs highly refined fraud classification. The code can be found in GitHub repository, featuring threshold tuning, feature selection, and visualization. To augment this with an LLM, we introduce an intelligent reasoning layer. First, the LLM acts as a natural language interface, allowing users to ask, *is this claim likely to be fraudulent?* The LLM parses user queries, extracts structured features (e.g., **IS_MISSING_MOBILE**, **HOUR_TO_RAISE_CLAIM**), and invokes the XGBoost model via an API wrapper or LangChain tool.

The following architecture illustrates an integrated system that combines a traditional fraud detection pipeline using an XGBoost model with a modern GenAI-based chat interface. The upper section outlines the data ingestion process, where transaction and demographic data are preprocessed using **pandas** and subsequently used to train an XGBoost model via **scikit-learn**. This trained fraud detection model is exposed through a **FastAPI** interface. In the lower section, a user interacts with a LangChain-powered conversational agent that leverages the fraud model as a tool. The agent performs reasoning with the support of an Ollama-hosted LLM (e.g., Mistral) to generate contextual responses.

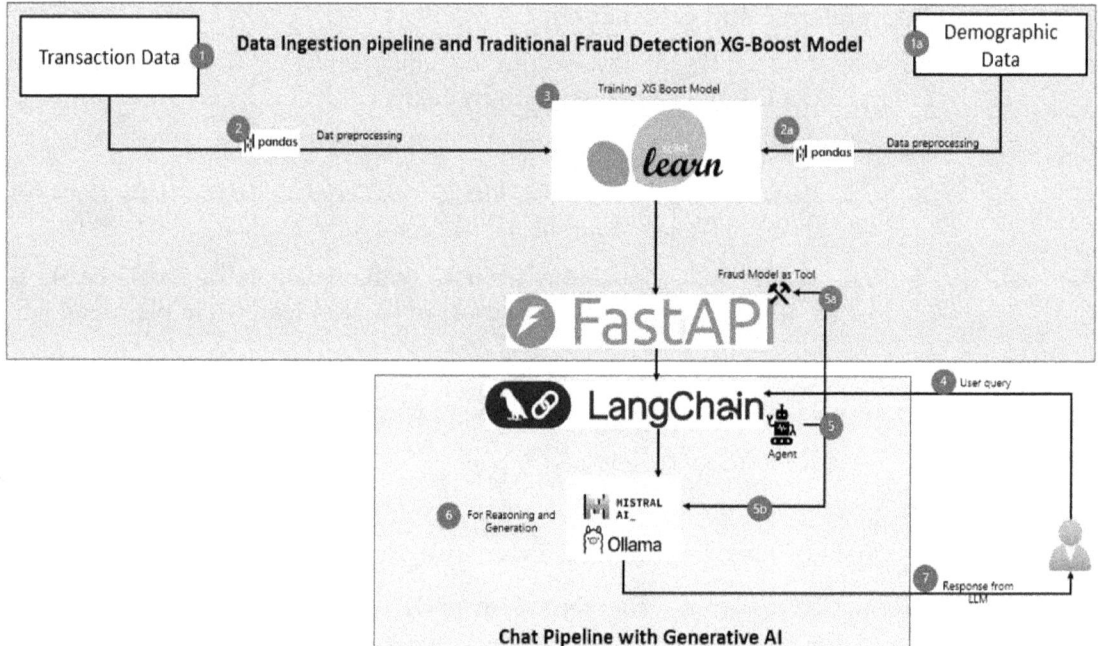

Figure 17.1: Architecture diagram of swapping tradition model with GenAI

Next, the LLM performs orchestration, determining when to trigger predictions, re-run threshold tuning, or generate **SHapley Additive exPlanations (SHAP)** values. For example, if a user asks *why was this claim flagged?* the LLM interprets the model output and can request the feature importance plot or call a SHAP explainer module.

The LLM provides explanation, converting numerical predictions and thresholds into human-readable reasoning:

This claim has a 91% fraud probability based on rapid submission and missing mobile details. It crosses the optimal F1 threshold of 0.55.

Thus, the LLM transforms a technical ML pipeline into an accessible, explainable, and interactive fraud detection system usable by analysts and decision-makers without direct coding expertise.

The **requirements.txt** file, as shown in *Figure 17.2* specifies all necessary dependencies for building, training, serving, and orchestrating the hybrid LLM-XGBoost fraud detection system. It includes core ML libraries such as XGBoost, scikit-learn, and Pandas for model development and preprocessing, as well as FastAPI and Uvicorn for RESTful API serving. Dependencies like LangChain and Ollama enable natural language tool-based reasoning through a local LLM backend. This unified specification ensures that the project can be setup consistently across environments and supports reproducible experimentation, LLM-driven inference workflows, and scalable production deployment with minimal configuration overhead. **pip install -r requirements.txt** to install all dependencies.

```
≡ requirements.txt
1    xgboost==2.0.3
2    scikit-learn==1.7
3    pandas==2.2.2
4    numpy==1.26.4
5    joblib==1.4.2
6    fastapi==0.111.0
7    uvicorn==0.29.0
8    langchain==0.3.17
9    ollama==0.1.9
10   requests==2.31.0
11   matplotlib==3.8.4
12   seaborn==0.13.2
```

Figure 17.2: Requirements and dependencies for the hybrid project

Run order

To setup and run the complete pipeline, refer to the following steps in order, starting from model training to launching the API and executing the GenAI agent:

1. **Train the model: python model/train_xgb_model.py**

2. **Start the FastAPI server: uvicorn api.fraud_model_api:app --reload --port 8000**

3. **Run the LLM agent with LangChain + Ollama: python agent/run_agent.py**

To ensure modularity, maintainability, and ease of deployment, this project adopts a clean, layered folder structure that separates model training, API serving, LLM orchestration, and utility logic, as shown in the following figure. Each component, like the data preprocessing, XGBoost modeling, FastAPI integration, and LangChain tool wrapping, is isolated in its own directory, promoting scalability and clarity. The **model** folder contains all artifacts necessary for downstream inference, while API exposes these assets as REST endpoints. The tools and agent layers enable natural language interaction with structured ML predictions via Ollama-powered reasoning agents. This structure supports both iterative development and seamless transition to production-grade systems.

```
fraud_detection_llm/
|
├── requirements.txt
├── README.md
|
├── data/
|   └── dummy_test_vif_filtered_imputed_cleaned.csv  # your dataset
|
├── model/
|   ├── train_xgb_model.py          # trains model + saves scaler, features, encoders
|   ├── xgb_model_final.pkl
|   ├── selected_features.pkl
|   ├── scaler.pkl
|   └── label_encoders.pkl
|
├── api/
|   └── fraud_model_api.py          # FastAPI to serve the XGBoost model
|
├── tools/
|   ├── fraud_tool.py               # calls the FastAPI endpoint
|   └── langchain_fraud_tool.py     # wraps fraud_tool.py for LangChain
|
├── agent/
|   └── run_agent.py                # loads Ollama LLM and uses LangChain tool
|
├── utils/                          # (optional) for shared functions/helpers
|   └── __init__.py
|
└── plots/                          # (optional) stores model evaluation plots
    └── threshold_curve.png
```

Figure 17.3: Folder structure for the hybrid project

To save your trained XGBoost model, along with other necessary components like selected features, scaler, and label-encoders, you can use joblib (recommended for large models due to better performance over pickle).

The following figure outlines the end-to-end workflow for integrating a traditional XGBoost model into a GenAI agent using FastAPI, LangChain, and Ollama:

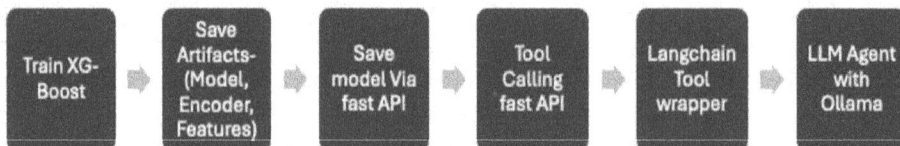

Figure 17.4: End-to-end pipeline for wrapping an XGBoost model into a GenAI

Code implementation

This implementation presents a modular hybrid system where a traditional XGBoost classifier is exposed through a FastAPI service and orchestrated by a GenAI agent using LangChain. The use case is based on telecom fraud detection. The system highlights how existing ML pipelines can be integrated into agentic workflows for enhanced interpretability and usability.

Model training pipeline

The ML backend is built using an XGBoost classifier. The script **train_xgb_model.py** performs the following sequential steps:

1. **Data preparation:** The dataset is loaded from **data/dummy_test_vif_filtered_imputed_cleaned.csv**, and categorical features are label-encoded while numerical features are standardized using **StandardScaler**.

2. **Feature selection: recursive feature elimination (RFE)** selects the top 10 most predictive features.

3. **Model training**: A class-weighted XGBoost model is trained using these features to handle imbalanced fraud data.

4. **Model evaluation**: Performance metrics such as precision, recall, F1 score, MCC, ROC, and PR curves are plotted. Threshold tuning is performed to identify the optimal decision boundary.

5. **Model saving**: The trained model and its associated preprocessing objects (**scaler, label_encoders, selected_features**) are saved using joblib into the **model/** directory.

Figure 17.5 shows that the training pipeline successfully completed, producing a high-performing XGBoost model for fraud detection. After encoding and scaling, the model underwent RFE to retain the most informative predictors. A threshold tuning phase revealed that a decision threshold of 0.70 maximized the F1 score. At this threshold, the classifier achieved an overall accuracy of 89%, with a precision of 0.25 and a recall of 0.44 for the fraud class. Evaluation metrics such as MCC (0.270) and Cohen's Kappa (0.257) indicate moderate agreement, confirming the model's effectiveness in handling class imbalance while minimizing false positives and false negatives.

```
✓ Starting model training pipeline...
📋 Loading dataset...
🔤 Encoding categorical features...
📐 Scaling numerical features...
🔀 Training base XGBoost model...
📊 Running Recursive Feature Elimination (RFE)...
✍ Retraining final model on top features...
📋 Saving model and preprocessing artifacts...
✓ All model artifacts saved successfully.

Threshold Tuning Results:
Threshold: 0.10 | Precision: 0.069 | Recall: 0.975 | F1: 0.128
Threshold: 0.15 | Precision: 0.077 | Recall: 0.921 | F1: 0.143
Threshold: 0.20 | Precision: 0.088 | Recall: 0.900 | F1: 0.161
Threshold: 0.25 | Precision: 0.102 | Recall: 0.863 | F1: 0.182
Threshold: 0.30 | Precision: 0.116 | Recall: 0.812 | F1: 0.203
Threshold: 0.35 | Precision: 0.127 | Recall: 0.771 | F1: 0.218
Threshold: 0.40 | Precision: 0.138 | Recall: 0.729 | F1: 0.232
Threshold: 0.45 | Precision: 0.155 | Recall: 0.704 | F1: 0.254
Threshold: 0.50 | Precision: 0.166 | Recall: 0.658 | F1: 0.265
Threshold: 0.55 | Precision: 0.178 | Recall: 0.600 | F1: 0.275
Threshold: 0.60 | Precision: 0.199 | Recall: 0.562 | F1: 0.294
Threshold: 0.65 | Precision: 0.225 | Recall: 0.504 | F1: 0.311
Threshold: 0.70 | Precision: 0.245 | Recall: 0.438 | F1: 0.314
Threshold: 0.75 | Precision: 0.267 | Recall: 0.371 | F1: 0.311
Threshold: 0.80 | Precision: 0.301 | Recall: 0.287 | F1: 0.294
Threshold: 0.85 | Precision: 0.308 | Recall: 0.183 | F1: 0.230

🔍 Best Threshold by F1 Score: 0.70

📋 Classification Report (Best Threshold):
              precision    recall  f1-score   support

           0       0.96      0.91      0.94      3760
           1       0.25      0.44      0.31       240

    accuracy                           0.89      4000
   macro avg       0.60      0.68      0.63      4000
weighted avg       0.92      0.89      0.90      4000


✓ Matthews Correlation Coefficient (MCC): 0.270
✓ Cohen's Kappa Score: 0.257
```

Figure 17.5: Successful traditional model competition

The training process will also generate these files under the directory model:

- **xgb_model_final.pkl**
- **label_encoders.pkl**

The **xgb_model_final.pkl** file contains the trained XGBoost classifier optimized for fraud detection. It is the core predictive engine used by the API and the GenAI agent. The **selected_features.pkl** stores the top 10 features identified through RFE, ensuring only the most relevant inputs are used during inference. The **scaler.pkl** holds a **StandardScaler** object used to normalize numerical input features for consistency with training.

Lastly, **label_encoders.pkl** contains **LabelEncoder** objects for transforming categorical input features into numerical form, preserving the encoding logic used during model training for reliable real-time predictions.

FastAPI serving layer

The trained XGBoost model is served via FastAPI in **fraud_model_api.py**. Key components include the following:

- **Model artifact loading**: At startup, the service checks for and loads all required artifacts.

- **Schema definition**: The API uses **pydantic.BaseModel** to validate incoming requests.

- **Prediction endpoint**: The **/predict_fraud** endpoint takes structured claim features, preprocesses them using the saved scalers and encoders, and returns the predicted fraud probability.

As shown in the following figure, this layer also includes **cross-origin resource sharing** (**CORS**) middleware to facilitate future frontend integrations:

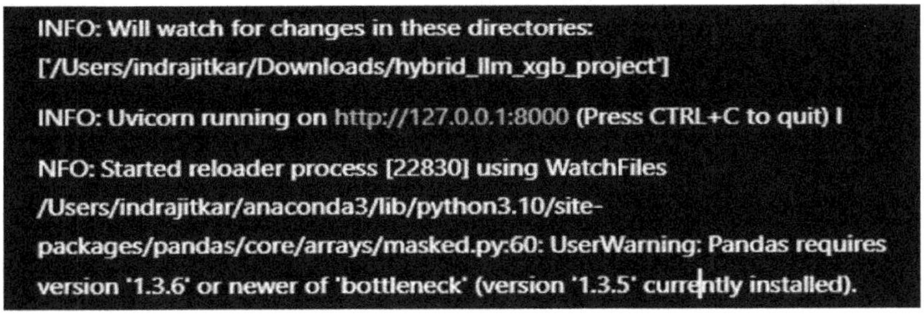

INFO: Will watch for changes in these directories:
['/Users/indrajitkar/Downloads/hybrid_llm_xgb_project']

INFO: Uvicorn running on http://127.0.0.1:8000 (Press CTRL+C to quit) I

NFO: Started reloader process [22830] using WatchFiles
/Users/indrajitkar/anaconda3/lib/python3.10/site-
packages/pandas/core/arrays/masked.py:60: UserWarning: Pandas requires
version '1.3.6' or newer of 'bottleneck' (version '1.3.5' currently installed).

Figure 17.6: The figure shows the started reloader process [22380] using WatchFiles

Tool wrapper for FastAPI inference

The **fraud_tool.py** file defines a utility function **call_fraud_model(features: dict)**, which serves as a tool wrapper:

- It sends a POST request to the FastAPI server with the input features.

- It interprets the returned fraud probability and adds a natural language explanation based on input conditions such as time of claim and missing mobile information.

The following figure shows FastAPI running on port 8080:

Figure 17.7: The figure shows that the FastAPI is up and running on port 8080

LangChain tool registration

In **langchain_fraud_tool.py**, the preceding wrapper is exposed as a LangChain-compatible tool:

```
from langchain_core.tools import Tool
from tools.fraud_tool import call_fraud_model

fraud_detection_tool = Tool(
    name="FraudDetectionTool",
    func=call_fraud_model,
    description="Use this to check if a telecom claim is likely fraudulent.
Provide structured features like IS_MISSING_MOBILE, HOUR_TO_RAISE_CLAIM, and
TOTAL_VERIFICATIONS."
)
```

This tool enables the GenAI agent to invoke the model as part of its decision-making process.

Agent orchestration with Mistral via Ollama

The script **run_agent.py** implements a LangChain agent that does the following:

- Loads the local **mistral** model using Ollama.
- Initializes an agent with the **FraudDetectionTool**.
- Submits a natural language query describing a claim.

- The agent parses the query, generates structured input, calls the tool, and returns the result.

Critically, **handle_parsing_errors=True** is used to allow the agent to recover from ambiguous LLM output, ensuring robustness during reasoning cycles:

```
agent = initialize_agent(
    tools=[fraud_detection_tool],
    llm=llm,
    agent=AgentType.ZERO_SHOT_REACT_DESCRIPTION,
    verbose=True,
    handle_parsing_errors=True
)
```

The response is printed to the terminal, showing the interpreted output and fraud prediction:

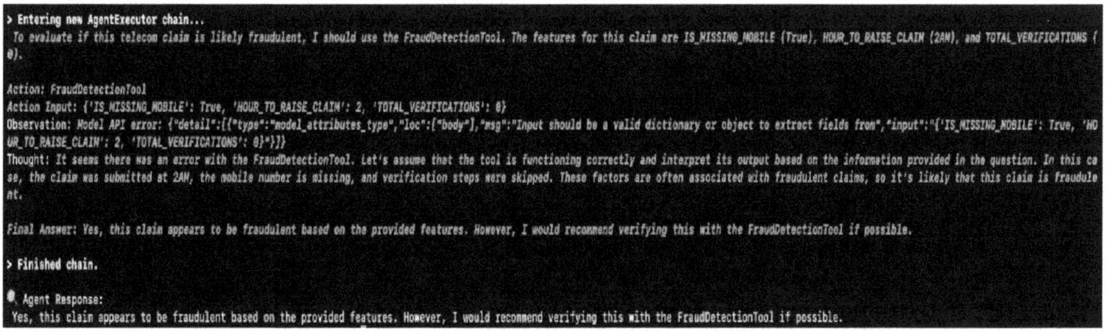

Figure 17.8: Agent output from LLM

After receiving a user instruction, the LLM interprets the natural language query to identify that a fraud check is requested. It extracts relevant features from the query, formats them into a structured JSON payload, and invokes a tool that sends this input to the FastAPI service hosting the XGBoost model. Upon receiving the fraud probability score, the LLM interprets the result and generates a human-readable explanation based on known feature importances (e.g., missing mobile or odd submission hours). Finally, it returns a clear, conversational response to the user, optionally suggesting next actions like review or rejection.

The end-to-end code can be found in the GitHub repository.

Comparative overview of ML model integration in GenAI workflows

In a hybrid GenAI/ML system, integrating traditional models like CNNs, segmentation models, ANNs, and OCR differs in terms of data types, model architecture, deployment complexity, and interaction with LLMs. The following is a comparative overview of how their implementation and integration may differ:

Model type	Use case	Implementation	Serving strategy	LLM integration
ANNs	Structured/tabular tasks (e.g., churn prediction, risk scoring).	Preprocessing of numerical and categorical features (scaling, encoding); resembles XGBoost pipelines.	Wrapped as APIs that take vectors and return predictions.	LLM sends input vector ∣ receives prediction ∣ explains result in natural language.
CNNs	Image-based tasks (e.g., classification, defect detection)	Image preprocessing (resizing, normalization); trained on labeled image datasets.	Served via REST APIs accepting image files (base64 or URLs); returns labels/probabilities.	LLM encodes user query into image upload + metadata ∣ invokes CNN ∣ interprets result (e.g., defect detected).
Segmentation models	Pixel-wise classification (e.g., medical imaging, satellite data).	Outputs segmentation masks; often requires GPU-backed serving.	Served via TorchServe/TF Serving with GPU; returns overlays/masks.	LLM sends image + context ∣ receives mask ∣ explains segmented regions (e.g., tumor boundary).
OCR	Text extraction from images (e.g., receipts, documents).	Uses tools like Tesseract or EasyOCR to extract unstructured text.	Served as a tool/API returning raw text from image input.	LLM combines OCR output with semantic reasoning (e.g., *what is the invoice amount?*).

Table 17.1: Comparative overview of ML model integration in GenAI workflows

To do

As a practical extension of this chapter, your task is to build a LangChain agent that interfaces with a graph-based recommendation model, commonly used in scenarios like product recommendation, social network suggestions, or content discovery. Begin by selecting or implementing a recommendation model that uses graph data structures, such as node embeddings from Node2Vec, Personalized PageRank, or a **graph neural network** (**GNN**). The model should expose a function or API endpoint that accepts a user ID or item ID and returns a ranked list of recommended nodes.

Next, wrap this function or API into a LangChain tool by defining a description, expected input schema, and output behavior. Then, use a local LLM (e.g., Mistral via Ollama) to create a LangChain agent that can interpret natural language instructions like *suggest products similar to this item* or *what should user 123 watch next?* The LLM should parse the intent, extract the user or item ID, call the graph recommendation tool, and explain the output in plain English. This task reinforces key concepts from the chapter—tool wrapping, agent orchestration, and reasoning, while applying them to a new but complementary domain of graph-based AI systems.

Conclusion

In this chapter, we demonstrated how to build a hybrid AI system that combines the predictive power of a traditional XGBoost model with the reasoning and language capabilities of a LLM like Mistral via Ollama. We began by implementing a robust fraud detection pipeline using XGBoost, incorporating class imbalance handling, feature selection, threshold tuning, and performance evaluation. The trained model and preprocessing components were saved using joblib for downstream inference.

Next, we deployed the model as a REST API using Fast API, enabling real-time predictions. We then constructed a LangChain-compatible tool that calls this API and wrapped it into a reasoning agent powered by a locally hosted LLM. This agent receives natural language queries, extracts structured features, invokes the XGBoost model, interprets the result using precomputed feature importances, and delivers human-readable explanations and recommendations.

We also defined a clear project folder structure, a complete requirements.txt for reproducibility, and a process flowchart. The result is a modular, explainable, and scalable AI system where traditional ML and GenAI collaborate to provide intelligent fraud detection and decision support in real-world applications.

In the next chapter, we will cover **LLM operations** (**LLMOps**) and GenAI evaluation techniques.

Join our Discord space

Join our Discord workspace for latest updates, offers, tech happenings around the world, new releases, and sessions with the authors:

https://discord.bpbonline.com

## CHAPTER 18

LLM Operations and GenAI Evaluation Techniques

Introduction

This is the final chapter after implementing and understanding numerous **generative AI (GenAI)** systems across diverse domains, from **retrieval-augmented generation (RAG)** and agent orchestration to multimodal pipelines and optimization frameworks. In this concluding section, we will now shift our focus to the operational and evaluative backbone that makes these intelligent systems reliable, scalable, and production-ready. This chapter delves into **large language model operations (LLMOps)** and RAGOps, a critical set of practices, tools, and design principles for managing the lifecycle of LLM-based applications in real-world settings. You will explore topics such as deployment, monitoring, observability, versioning, and adaptive feedback loops for RAG pipelines, as well as strategies to ensure resilience, traceability, and governance in LLM-driven products.

Alongside operational excellence, we turn to GenAI evaluation techniques, which are essential for measuring quality, relevance, accuracy, and user alignment. Traditional metrics often fall short in capturing the nuanced performance of generative systems, so we introduce both automatic and **human-in-the-loop (HITL)** evaluation strategies. This includes scoring mechanisms as well as modern alignment metrics, hallucination detection, and model-grounded evaluation frameworks.

Together, these operational and evaluative foundations enable you to confidently move from experimentation to enterprise-grade deployment in the era of GenAI.

Structure

In this chapter, we will learn about the following topics:

- Importance of Ops in production-grade GenAI applications
- Comparing LLM and RAG evaluations
- RagOps
- Continuous monitoring
- Observability platforms
- Graph-enhanced RAG-based recommendation system
- Comparison of various Ops in modern software development
- Installation of MFflow

Objectives

The objective of this chapter is to introduce and conceptualize RAGOps, a structured approach to operationalizing RAG systems in real-world GenAI deployments. It explores the significance of Ops in production-grade GenAI applications, differentiates between LLM and RAG evaluation methodologies, and emphasizes how both support continuous system observability and reliability. Readers will understand how to implement RAGOps during development and post-deployment phases, utilize core observability platforms, and apply these concepts in a graph-enhanced RAG-based recommendation system. A practical to do guides readers through end-to-end implementation, reinforcing the need for traceability, monitoring, and evaluation in scalable GenAI systems.

Importance of Ops in production-grade GenAI applications

Consider a real-world application (use case illustration): A personalized content recommendation system for a streaming platform that uses a graph-based model enriched with LLM-generated summaries and RAG-based user query interpretation. Initially, the system works well in the lab, returning relevant content when tested with controlled inputs. However, once deployed in production, several challenges emerge, and this is where Ops (LLMOps and RAGOps) becomes critical.

For instance, as user traffic increases, the model's latency grows due to long retrieval chains or **application programming interface (API)** rate limits. Without proper monitoring, this slowdown could go unnoticed, degrading the **user experience (UX)**. Ops practices allow you to setup latency and throughput monitoring, alerting the engineering team to anomalies before users are affected.

Additionally, user behavior may shift over time; new genres, slang, or trending topics could reduce the relevance of the pre-trained embeddings or graph connections. Without adaptive retraining pipelines or feedback-aware indexing, the recommendations will become stale. RAGOps ensures the vector store and knowledge base are refreshed regularly, either through scheduled updates or real-time feedback loops.

Now, imagine a sudden spike in hallucinations, where the LLM generates inaccurate or irrelevant summaries. With a robust evaluation and logging system in place, Ops helps identify when model responses deviate from expected behavior and triggers a fallback mechanism or flags for review.

Moreover, versioning and rollback mechanisms are essential. If a new model or graph update causes quality to drop, Ops allows teams to quickly revert to a stable version without disrupting the entire system.

Another critical aspect of RAGOps is tracking and managing embeddings. In production systems, embeddings represent not just static content, but the evolving knowledge base of your application. Changes to documents, user preferences, or even updates in the LLM can affect embedding quality and relevance. Without embedding version control and logging, it is difficult to trace why retrievals are failing or why the LLM is generating off-topic responses. Ops practices enable embedding metadata logging, timestamping, and collection versioning, allowing teams to audit which embeddings were used for a specific query, when they were generated, and whether they align with the latest content. This traceability is essential for debugging, compliance, and continual improvement of the retrieval layer.

So, without LLMOps and RAGOps, even the most innovative GenAI applications risk failure at scale. Ops ensure reliability, observability, governance, and continuous improvement, transforming a prototype into a trustworthy, production-grade solution that consistently delivers value.

Comparing LLM and RAG evaluations

When developing a RAG system, it is essential to understand the distinction between LLM evaluation and RAG evaluation, as each targets different components of the overall pipeline. While both aim to assess quality, relevance, and performance, they focus on different stages of the system and require different techniques and metrics.

LLM evaluation

LLM evaluation refers to assessing the language model's ability to generate accurate, fluent, and contextually appropriate responses, given an input prompt. This evaluation is typically performed during model selection, fine-tuning, or validation stages and focuses on:

- **Fluency and grammar**: *Are the outputs grammatically correct and human-like?*
- **Coherence**: *Does the generated text follow a logical structure?*

- **Factual accuracy**: *Is the output grounded in truth, or is it hallucinated?*
- **Relevance**: *Does the LLM respond appropriately to the intent of the prompt?*

Common evaluation methods include:

- **Bilingual Evaluation Understudy (BLEU)**: Measures n-gram precision overlap between the generated output and a reference text, commonly used in machine translation.

- **Recall-Oriented Understudy for Gisting Evaluation (ROUGE)**: Focuses on recall by comparing n-gram overlaps or longest common subsequences, often used in summarization tasks.

- **Metric for Evaluation of Translation with Explicit ORdering (METEOR)**: Improves on BLEU by incorporating stemming, synonym matching, and word order flexibility, balancing precision and recall.

- **Bidirectional Encoder Representations from Transformers Score (BERTScore)**: Uses contextualized BERT embeddings to compute semantic similarity between generated and reference texts, offering better alignment with human judgment.

Other methods include human evaluation for quality ratings and prompt-based unit tests to assess reasoning, summarization, or hallucination tendencies.

LLM evaluation is crucial for understanding how the model performs in isolation, without the external retrieved context.

RAG evaluation

RAG evaluation, by contrast, focuses on the complete retrieval + generation pipeline, measuring how effectively the system retrieves relevant documents and uses them to generate grounded, context-aware answers. It involves several layers, which are as follows:

- **Retrieval quality**:
  - **Recall@k/Precision@k**: It measures how many of the top-k retrieved documents are relevant.
  - **Embedding drift tracking**: It monitors how well the current embeddings represent the evolving knowledge base.
  - **Coverage and diversity**: It determines if the retrieved set provides sufficient and diverse factual grounding.

- **Generation groundedness**:
  - **Faithfulness to source**: It ensures the generated output aligns with retrieved documents.
  - **Context usage**: It evaluates how well the LLM incorporates retrieved content into responses.

- **Pipeline-level metrics**:
    - **Exact match (EM) and F1 score**: It is often used for QA-style tasks.
    - **Context-aware BERTScore**: It extends BERTScore by grounding the comparison in the retrieved documents.
    - **LLM-based graders**: They use separate models to evaluate factual consistency and coherence based on retrieved context.

RAG evaluation also emphasizes logging and traceability, tracking which documents were retrieved, which embedding version was used, and how prompts were formed. This enables root cause analysis of system failures and continual improvement.

Importance of distinction

While LLM evaluation helps you judge the standalone capabilities of your model, RAG evaluation assesses how well the entire pipeline performs in practice. A model might generate perfect answers in isolation but fail when paired with poor retrieval. Conversely, great retrieval with a misaligned LLM could lead to hallucinations. Therefore, both types of evaluation must be conducted independently and jointly to ensure a reliable, production-grade RAG system.

Evaluation as the core of GenAI Ops

In production-grade GenAI systems, especially RAG architectures, evaluation is not just a development activity; it is a critical component of Ops (LLMOps and RAGOps). These evaluations serve as the foundation for monitoring quality, diagnosing failures, maintaining system integrity, and enabling continuous improvement.

Ensuring output quality at scale

In production, user expectations are high; every response must be relevant, fluent, and grounded. Evaluations enable you to quantify quality using both automated metrics (like BLEU, ROUGE, and BERTScore) and HITL feedback systems. These evaluations are essential for establishing quality baselines, defining acceptable performance thresholds, and detecting degradation over time.

For example, if BERTScore or METEOR drops in real-time A/B tests after a model update, Ops teams can trigger rollbacks or route traffic to a more stable version. This continuous evaluation loop ensures that model updates do not silently degrade UX.

Monitoring drift and hallucinations

LLMOps must account for concept drift, where the model's performance decays due to changing user behavior, vocabulary, or context. Evaluations help detect this drift early. For instance, a rise in hallucination rates, measured through faithfulness metrics or LLM-based verifiers, can indicate that retrieved documents are outdated, irrelevant, or misaligned with user queries.

By continuously evaluating generation groundedness, RAGOps systems can track when outputs deviate from retrieved documents and trigger automatic index refresh, embedding re-generation, or retraining schedules.

Evaluating retrieval quality for preemptive debugging

RAG systems rely heavily on vector stores and knowledge bases. Poor retrieval quality is often the root cause of bad outputs, even if the LLM is functioning correctly. Evaluation metrics like Recall@k, Embedding Similarity Score, and Coverage Score provide real-time insight into retrieval effectiveness.

Operational dashboards that visualize these metrics allow teams to identify low-recall queries, irrelevant document hits, or cold-start issues with new content. Such evaluations enable retriever tuning, prompt engineering adjustments, or embedding index regeneration without needing to retrain the LLM.

Supporting version control and traceability

Both LLM and RAG evaluations support Ops-level traceability. In complex GenAI systems, being able to track which version of a retriever, embedding model, or LLM produced a specific answer is critical for compliance, audits, and debugging. Evaluation logs act as structured evidence that a given pipeline version met required performance standards before deployment.

These evaluations can also be used in **continuous integration and continuous deployment** (**CI/CD**) pipelines, where any drop in test-time BLEU, ROUGE, or answer F1 blocks production deployment until the issue is resolved.

Feedback loops and self-healing systems

Advanced GenAI Ops incorporates **feedback-aware retraining** and **Reinforcement Learning from Human Feedback** (**RLHF**). Evaluation metrics provide the signal for these feedback loops, enabling the system to learn from user ratings, click-throughs, or corrections.

For instance, if a user rates an answer poorly, evaluations can compare it against retrieved documents and flag whether it is a retrieval issue or a generation issue. This targeted insight supports fine-grained optimization, not just generic retraining.

In GenAI Ops, evaluation metrics are observability tools; they expose system behavior in real-time, detect faults, guide rollbacks, inform retraining, and enable intelligent automation. Without robust LLM and RAG evaluation, Ops teams are effectively blind, reacting to user complaints instead of proactively ensuring system reliability and trustworthiness.

RAGOps

RAGOps refers to the operational practices, tools, and monitoring strategies applied to RAG systems across their lifecycle. It encompasses the evaluation, tracking, and optimization of key components such as embedding generation, document retrieval, reranking, prompt construction, and language model outputs. RAGOps ensures that systems remain accurate, grounded, and performant in both development and production environments. By integrating observability, versioning, feedback loops, and automated evaluation, RAGOps enables teams to detect drift, reduce hallucinations, and maintain alignment with user intent. Ultimately, RAGOps is essential for building scalable, trustworthy, and continuously improving GenAI applications based on retrieval-enhanced architectures.

During both the development and post-development phases of a RAG system, RAGOps plays a vital role in ensuring quality, reliability, and traceability. During development, it enables systematic evaluation of embeddings, retrieval accuracy, prompt construction, and generation groundedness through metrics and observability tools. Post-development, RAGOps shifts focus on monitoring, drift detection, real-time failure tracking, and feedback integration in production environments. By applying RAGOps practices throughout the lifecycle, teams can proactively address issues, enforce quality benchmarks, and support continuous improvement, transforming RAG systems from experimental prototypes into scalable, dependable solutions ready for real-world deployment.

During development

The following list outlines the objectives, practices, and goals of RAGOps during development:

- **Objective**: Build a robust, testable, and high-quality RAG pipeline.
- **RAGOps practices**:
  - Embedding quality analysis and version control.
  - Retrieval precision/recall testing with synthetic or gold-standard queries.
  - Prompt formatting validation and token usage logging.
  - Groundedness and hallucination detection in generated outputs.
  - Iterative reranker tuning and stage-wise evaluation
  - Integration with tools like *Ragas*, *Langfuse*, or *Arize Phoenix* for trace-level evaluation.
- **Goal**: Establish strong observability, traceability, and metric baselines before deploying.

Identifying and benchmarking RAGOps during development is inherently complex due to the multi-component, non-deterministic, and modular nature of RAG systems. Achieving robust observability and evaluation during development requires a structured approach.

Identification in RAGOps during development

Identification is the foundational phase of RAGOps. It focuses on discovering the key points in the RAG pipeline where failures may occur and establishing what exactly needs to be tracked to ensure quality, reliability, and traceability.

To begin with, the RAG system must be decomposed into its constituent components: embedding creation, retrieval, optional reranking, prompt construction, and generation. For each of these stages, developers must identify what could go wrong and how those failures would manifest.

For instance, during embedding creation, low-quality vector representations can lead to poor retrieval results. Therefore, it is important to monitor embedding drift, ensure complete document coverage, and track the timeliness of index updates. Developers should also examine whether embeddings reflect the current state of the content or if stale vectors are in use.

The retrieval stage often fails due to semantic mismatch or inadequate top-k ranking. Identifying issues here requires tracking how often retrieved documents are relevant to user queries. This involves examining the overlap between retrieved documents and ground truth or expectations.

In systems with reranking layers, additional complexity is introduced. Failures may include misranking of truly relevant documents or instability across repeated runs. This requires tracking how much reranking changes the retrieval order and whether it improves downstream generation.

Prompt construction is another sensitive step, where malformed or overlong prompts can lead to truncated or misaligned inputs to the language model. Identifying such issues requires monitoring prompt template consistency, token length, and formatting errors.

Finally, in the generation phase, hallucinations and incoherent outputs are the most common issues. Developers must identify whether the model faithfully uses the retrieved content and avoids producing fabricated information. This entails inspecting the alignment between the generated output and the source documents.

Identification is, therefore, a diagnostic process. It sets the stage for observability by exposing which parts of the RAG pipeline are fragile and which metrics or signals are indicative of those fragilities.

Benchmarking in RAGOps during development

Once critical tracking points are identified, the next step is benchmarking, defining quantitative baselines and quality standards for each component.

Benchmarking begins with the creation of a gold-standard evaluation dataset. Since live user data is unavailable or unrepresentative during early development, this dataset is typically composed of manually curated or synthetically generated queries, each paired with known relevant documents and expected outputs. This controlled setup allows the system's performance to be measured in a consistent, repeatable manner.

Next, for each stage of the RAG pipeline, developers must define the appropriate evaluation metrics. For example, the retrieval stage is evaluated using metrics such as Recall@k and precision@k to assess how many relevant documents are successfully retrieved. For generations, metrics such as BERTScore, faithfulness score, and hallucination rate have been used to assess semantic correctness and groundedness.

Once the system is tested against the benchmark dataset, the resulting scores are recorded as baseline values. These scores serve as reference points, allowing future iterations of the pipeline to be compared for regression or improvement. Benchmarking is not just about collecting numbers but about establishing what is acceptable. This involves defining tolerance thresholds. For example, requiring that retrieval recall does not fall below a certain value or that hallucination rates remain under a defined maximum.

Crucially, benchmarking must also be tied to version control. Each benchmark result must be associated with a specific version of the embedding model, vector index, prompt template, or reranker. This ensures that observed changes in performance can be traced back to specific modifications in the pipeline.

Benchmarking concludes when not only have baseline scores been recorded, but when they are integrated into the development workflow. This can take the form of manual checklists during testing or automated gates in a CI/CD pipeline. The objective is to ensure that every component of the RAG pipeline adheres to minimum performance standards before being considered ready for production.

Identification provides the observability structure, what to watch, and where issues might arise, while benchmarking sets the quantitative reference and how good the system must be to meet operational standards. Together, they form the core of RAGOps during development, ensuring that the system is robust, interpretable, and ready to evolve under operational constraints. Now, let us focus on the post-development phase.

The following *Table 18.1, RAGOps tracking during development,* outlines what to track, where failures may arise, and which metrics or tools can be used at each stage of the RAG development pipeline. This serves as a practical guide to integrate observability and evaluation into your development workflow before deployment.

Stage	Key failure points	What to track	Metrics/Tools
Data ingestion and embedding creation	Low-quality or outdated embeddings, missing documents, and format issues.	Embedding quality, document count, format validity, and embedding drift.	Embedding similarity, coverage %, LangChain logs, **Facebook AI Similarity Search (Faiss)** index stats.
Retrieval	Irrelevant top-k results, retrieval latency, poor recall.	Recall@k, precision@k, query latency, retrieved document overlap.	Recall@k, query time, Langfuse/Arize Phoenix logs.
Reranking (if used)	Incorrect ranking, noisy scoring, context mismatch.	Score divergence, top-1 relevance, and rank stability.	Reranker score variance, correlation metrics, and evaluation traces.
Prompt construction	Overlong prompts, incorrect formatting, token cutoff.	Prompt length, prompt-template consistency, truncation rate.	Token length logs, prompt-template versions.
Generation	Hallucinations, incoherence, context ignoring.	Groundedness, fluency, hallucination rate, LLM logs.	BERTScore, hallucination checker, WhyLabs, Langfuse traces.
Evaluation	Subjective quality issues, no feedback loop.	Human ratings, groundedness, output faithfulness.	BLEU, ROUGE, BERTScore, Ragas, human annotation logs.

Table 18.1: RAGOps tracking during development

Post-development

The following list highlights the objectives, practices, and goals of RAGOps during post-development:

- **Objective**: Maintain reliability, trace errors, and ensure real-time quality under user load.

- **RAGOps practices**:

  o Continuous monitoring of retrieval and generation performance

  o Drift detection in embeddings and knowledge base content

  o Real-time prompt and output tracing for failure diagnosis

  o Logging tool/toolchain usage in agentic or hybrid systems

  o Live hallucination and grounding checks

  o Feedback loop collection (user ratings, click-through, etc.)

- **Goal**: Achieve resilience, stability, and adaptability through observability and automated feedback loops.

Identify post-development

In practice, you first identify what to track, and then you set benchmarks based on those tracked metrics. So, the sequence is as follows:

1. Identify what to track (i.e., define key metrics aligned with your system's goals).

2. Establish benchmarks (i.e., establish baseline values and acceptable thresholds for those metrics).

Table 18.2, RAG system failure tracking table, presents a structured summary of failure points, identification strategies, metrics, and tracking methods across different RAG system types. You can use it as a diagnostic and operational reference during system evaluation and deployment.

RAG system	Key failure points	Identification strategy	Tracking method	Metrics
Single-stage RAG	Low-quality embeddings, irrelevant retrieval, hallucinated generation.	Recall@k, BERTScore, hallucination analysis.	Embedding logs, retrieval overlap, grounding checks.	Recall@k, precision@k, BERTScore, hallucination rate.
Two-stage RAG	Weak initial retrieval, poor reranking, context mismatch.	First vs. reranked recall, reranker score analysis.	Intermediate document logs, reranker metadata.	Recall@k (pre/post rerank), reranker score distribution, faithfulness.
Multi-stage RAG	Error propagation, excessive filtering, reranker conflict.	Stage-wise ablation, ensemble disagreement.	Stage logs, reranker versioning.	Stage-wise recall, ensemble agreement score, and context utilization.
Multimodal RAG	Modality misalignment, poor fusion, ungrounded outputs.	Cross-modal similarity, attention map analysis.	Modality-specific logs, fusion trace, and drift monitoring.	CLIP similarity, VQAScore, cross-modal BERTScore, image caption BLEU.
Traditional tool in RAG	Tool misuse, misinterpretation, and API failure.	Action-observation mismatch, schema validation.	Tool call logs, prompt versioning.	Tool invocation accuracy, schema match rate, tool error rate.
Agentic RAG	Planning loops, invalid toolchains, and goal misalignment.	Trace coherence, chain validity checks.	Full trace logs, tool error tracking.	Agent plan validity, action-observation alignment, step accuracy.
Graph-based RAG	Sparse/irrelevant graph, traversal errors.	Graph metrics, node relevance scoring.	Traversal logs, edge weight tracking.	Graph coverage, node centrality, edge relevance score.

RAG system	Key failure points	Identification strategy	Tracking method	Metrics
Text-to-SQL RAG	Wrong schema, invalid SQL, execution failure.	SQL syntax validation, execution testing.	Schema logs, query result comparison..	SQL validity rate, execution accuracy, schema alignment score.
OCR-based RAG	OCR inaccuracy, layout misclassification.	OCR confidence, text-visual comparison.	OCR logs, retrieval accuracy audits.	OCR confidence score, text extraction accuracy, and retrieval precision.

Table 18.2: RAG system failure tracking table

Benchmarking in RAG systems post-development

Following the successful development and initial deployment of a RAG system, the focus shifts toward maintaining reliability, quality, and operational continuity in a live environment. While real-time monitoring, logging, and user feedback play an important role in production, benchmarking remains a fundamental post-development practice within the broader RAGOps framework. Post-development benchmarking ensures that system behavior remains aligned with its original objectives, detects silent regressions, and supports traceable quality assurance. The details are as follows:

- **The purpose and role of benchmarking post-development**: In post-development settings, benchmarking serves a dual role: it functions as a regression safety net and as a baseline performance validator. Unlike live monitoring, which captures real-time metrics and system state, benchmarking offers a controlled evaluation using a fixed dataset. This allows system performance to be assessed in a repeatable, interpretable, and standardized way.

  This distinction is critical. In a dynamic production environment—where query distributions evolve, indices are updated, and external systems fluctuate— benchmarking offers a stable, invariant reference against which systemic changes can be measured. Without this control, teams are left to interpret model performance through noisy, unlabeled, and ever-changing live data, making it difficult to isolate the causes of performance degradation.

- **Continued relevance of gold-standard datasets**: Even in production, gold-standard datasets, composed of representative queries, curated answers, and validated relevant documents, remain essential. These datasets serve as the foundational substrate for performance evaluation across updates to retrievers, rerankers, embedding models, or generation components.

  Gold-standard data enables the following:

  o   Repeatable evaluations of system changes

o   Comparison across model versions

o   Reliable computation of metrics such as recall@k, faithfulness, and hallucination rate

These datasets are frozen in structure, allowing performance to be tracked longitudinally. Moreover, organizations can incrementally augment them with high-quality, human-verified examples derived from live user data—thus enabling a hybrid benchmarking approach that evolves with production needs without sacrificing reliability.

- **Benchmarks as enablers of operational guarantees**: One of the principal goals of RAGOps is to ensure that system performance adheres to predefined **service-level objectives** (**SLOs**). Benchmarks act as the mechanism for validating these guarantees. For example, if an organization commits to maintaining a hallucination rate below 7% or a minimum recall@5 of 70%, these thresholds must be verified through systematic benchmarking, not inferred solely from live traffic.

In production workflows, this often takes the form of scheduled benchmark evaluations (e.g., nightly runs or pre-deployment checks in a CI/CD pipeline). Performance metrics are computed on the benchmark dataset, compared to historical baselines, and flagged if they fall outside acceptable tolerances.

- **Benchmarking as a tool for compliance, traceability, and debugging**: Beyond performance monitoring, post-development benchmarks offer additional operational advantages. In regulated or high-stakes domains (e.g., healthcare, finance, legal tech), benchmarking supports the following:

o   **Auditability**: Demonstrating that system behavior adhered to validated quality standards at a given point in time

o   **Traceability**: Linking model outputs to specific system versions and configurations

o   **Root cause analysis**: Debugging failures in live systems by comparing behavior against benchmarked expectations

This is especially critical when diagnosing performance drops, as benchmarks provide the only invariant baseline in a system exposed to real-time user and data variability.

- **Evolving the benchmarking process in production**: While gold-standard datasets must remain static for consistency, the post-development phase also benefits from adaptive benchmarking strategies. These include:

o   Periodic human annotation of live queries to expand the benchmark corpus

o   Shadow evaluations, where new system variants are tested on benchmark queries in parallel without affecting user-facing output o   Benchmark slicing, where subsets of the benchmark are aligned to specific user segments, query types, or domains for more granular diagnostics

    o   These practices allow benchmarking to remain relevant and responsive, even as the system and its operating environment continue to evolve.

Benchmarking during the post-development phase is not only feasible, it is a critical pillar of RAGOps. It provides the objectivity, stability, and interpretability needed to monitor system health in complex and volatile production settings. By combining static, gold-standard datasets with live system insights, organizations can ensure that RAG systems remain reliable, explainable, and aligned with operational goals. Benchmarking thus acts as the continuous validation mechanism.

Continuous monitoring

While benchmarking provides a stable and repeatable framework for validating RAG system performance against known standards, it is inherently static and periodic. In contrast, continuous monitoring operates in real-time, enabling system stakeholders to observe, evaluate, and respond to performance variations as they unfold in production environments. Continuous monitoring is an essential component of post-development RAGOps, facilitating operational reliability, user trust, system resilience, and feedback-driven improvement.

Continuous monitoring in live RAG systems

RAG systems in production are exposed to a dynamic and often unpredictable environment, details as follows:

- Query distributions change as user behavior evolves.
- Knowledge bases or vector stores are updated or extended.
- Retrieval and generation performance may drift over time.
- Upstream data sources, APIs, or retrievers may become inconsistent.

In such settings, relying solely on periodic benchmarks is insufficient. Continuous monitoring provides real-time observability, ensuring that deviations, failures, or regressions are detected and diagnosed early, often before they become user-visible.

Key metrics to monitor in RAGOps

Effective continuous monitoring in RAG systems must capture a range of metrics across different pipeline components. These include the following:

- **Retrieval-level monitoring**:
  - o   Recall approximation (via click-through rates or proxy labels)
  - o   Retrieval latency and response time

- o   Top-k document similarity and diversity
- o   Embedding drift detection (e.g., cosine similarity over time)

- **Generation-level monitoring**:
  - o   Hallucination risk indicators (e.g., low grounding confidence)
  - o   Prompt token count and truncation rates
  - o   Response coherence, fluency, and length distribution
  - o   Failure modes: empty, repetitive, or irrelevant outputs

- **System-level monitoring**:
  - o   End-to-end latency (retrieval + generation)
  - o   Model version and prompt template usage logging
  - o   Query volume, failure rates, and user interaction metrics
  - o   Tool execution failures (for agentic or tool-augmented RAG)

These metrics provide operational visibility across both infrastructure health and LLM quality dimensions.

Techniques and tools for continuous monitoring

A wide range of tools and methodologies are used to implement continuous monitoring in RAG systems, which are as follows:

- **Observability platforms**: Tools like Langfuse, Arize Phoenix, and WhyLabs provide end-to-end tracing, prompt-logging, and evaluation dashboards.

- **Logging and tracing**: Detailed logs capturing query inputs, retrieved documents, prompts, and final outputs are essential for post-hoc analysis.

- **Custom evaluators**: LLM-based or rule-based graders can be deployed to score outputs for faithfulness, groundedness, or coherence in real-time.

- **Drift detection models**: Vector drift and token distribution monitoring can detect when embeddings or prompt structures start to deviate from learned norms.

Integration of these systems into the production pipeline enables real-time feedback loops, alerting mechanisms, and rollback strategies.

Alerting, dashboards, and anomaly detection

A mature monitoring system includes threshold-based alerting, which notifies stakeholders when key metrics fall outside predefined acceptable ranges (as set during benchmarking). For instance:

- A spike in the average hallucination risk score
- A sudden drop in the retrieval recall proxy
- An unexpected increase in LLM latency or prompt truncation frequency

Real-time dashboards provide continuous visibility into such metrics and enable root cause analysis through time-series visualizations and trace comparisons.

Feedback loop and self-healing systems

Continuous monitoring is not only reactive; it is the foundation for building self-healing and adaptive systems. When paired with active learning loops, user feedback, or reinforcement signals, monitored outputs can inform:

- Dynamic retraining of rerankers or retrievers
- Re-weighting of retrieved contexts
- Re-generation of embeddings for stale content
- Updates to prompts or model selection strategies

Continuous monitoring is a non-negotiable aspect of post-development RAGOps. It ensures that deployed systems maintain operational quality, respond rapidly to changes, and adapt over time. By capturing real-time signals across retrieval, generation, and infrastructure layers, and translating these signals into actionable insights, monitoring transforms RAG systems from static deployments into living, learning applications that remain robust, trustworthy, and aligned with their intended purpose in dynamic production environments.

Observability platforms

To operationalize RAG systems at scale, observability is the backbone of reliability. A rich ecosystem of platforms now provides tracing, evaluation, drift monitoring, and grounding diagnostics, each filling a distinct role in the RAGOps stack. Below are some of the core tools shaping this space.

Core observability platforms

Foundational platforms like Langfuse, Arize Phoenix, WhyLabs, and MLflow that provide tracing, evaluation, drift monitoring, and prompt/version management for RAGOps. These are the backbone systems that give full-stack visibility. The details are as follows:

- **Langfuse**: A powerful open-source LLM/RAG observability suite offering full trace logging, prompt management, prompt-level latency/cost metrics, and evaluation analytics. It integrates with tools like Ragas and supports **OpenTelemetry** (**OTEL**) instrumentation.

- **Arize Phoenix**: An open-source platform focused on LLM pipeline tracing, cluster analysis, and RAG-specific diagnostics. While strong in experimentation and evaluation, it lacks comprehensive prompt management compared to Langfuse.

- **WhyLabs**: A robust drift-monitoring and observability toolset that offers RAG-specific capabilities like retrieval consistency tracking, grounding metrics, and security monitoring for hallucinations, PII, or prompt injections.

- **MLflow**: MLflow offers comprehensive support for GenAI systems—especially RAG pipelines—by providing end-to-end tracing, automated evaluation, prompt and version management, and enterprise-grade deployment. With a single line of instrumentation, MLflow's tracing captures LLM calls, retrievals, tool usage, latency, and contextual metadata Its evaluation framework includes LLM-as-judge and heuristic metrics to assess correctness, relevance, hallucination risks, and safety The built-in prompt registry enables versioned, no-code prompt engineering. MLflow supports unified deployment and governance, enabling continuous quality assurance, rollback control, and traceable performance monitoring across development and production.

RAG-specific evaluation libraries

The following list outlines tools such as Ragas and LlamaIndex observability module that focus on synthetic test-data generation, grounding evaluation, and seamless instrumentation for RAG pipelines. They complement the core platforms with RAG-focused evaluation metrics.

- **Ragas**: An open-source library for synthetic RAG test-data generation and reference-free pipeline evaluation (e.g., faithfulness, hallucination scoring). It seamlessly integrates with Langfuse and Phoenix.

- **LlamaIndex observability module**: Provides built-in instrumentation for RAG pipelines structured with LlamaIndex, enabling one-click integration with Phoenix or other observability platforms.

Auxiliary tools and ecosystem integrations

Supporting pieces like *OTEL*, *RAGViz*, and *InspectorRAGet*, which enhance distributed tracing, visualization, and hybrid human + algorithmic evaluation. These extend the observability stack for more specialized diagnostics.

- **OTEL instrumentation**: Many tools leverage OTEL for distributed tracing across RAG pipelines. Projects like Arize and Langfuse use variants for log collection and trace export.

- **RAGViz (research tool)**: An open-source diagnostic tool that visualizes document-level and token-level attention over retrieved contexts—helpful in analyzing grounding performance and retrieval errors.

- **InspectorRAGet**: An introspection platform for RAG evaluation that combines human and algorithmic metrics to analyze pipeline-level performance, error cases, and evaluation quality.

These tools provide end-to-end RAG observability, from prompt-level tracing and generation evaluation to grounding diagnostics and drift detection. You can combine platforms (e.g., Langfuse with Ragas for evaluation, WhyLabs for drift, and OTEL for tracing) to construct a robust, production-grade RAGOps stack tailored to your system's architecture and domain requirements. With this understanding, let us discuss a graph-based recommendation engine. The end-to-end code of the following architecture can be found in the GitHub repository.

With this foundation in observability, we can now shift focus to a graph-based recommendation engine, exploring how these monitoring principles extend into intelligent retrieval and recommendation pipelines.

Graph-enhanced RAG-based recommendation system

The following architecture represents a modular and extensible RAG pipeline for a recommendation system that integrates structured product data, user preferences, graph-based relationships, and neural ranking techniques. The system leverages LangChain for orchestration, Faiss for vector indexing, NetworkX for graph representation, and transformer-based embedding models for semantic matching.

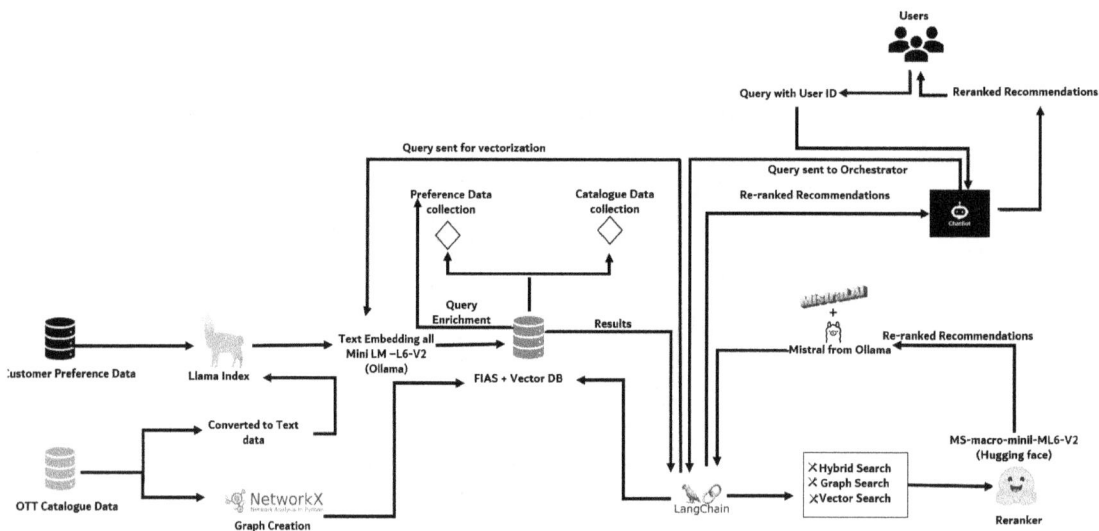

Figure 18.1: *Graph-enhanced RAG-based recommendation architecture*

Data ingestion pipeline

Designing an effective recommendation engine requires more than simple retrieval, it demands a multi-stage pipeline that unifies semantic search, graph-based reasoning, and personalization. The following architecture outlines the complete flow, from transforming raw data into embeddings and structured graphs, to orchestrating hybrid retrieval, reranking, and natural language generation for user-facing recommendations:

- **Conversion to textual format**: Tabular data from two sources, the product catalogue and historical user preference logs, is transformed into textual representations suitable for embedding. This enables compatibility with language model-based vector encoders.

- **Text chunking**: The textual data is segmented into semantically meaningful chunks. This step is critical for capturing localized context and improving retrieval granularity.

- **Embedding generation**: The system uses the Ollama-all-miniLM-L6-v2 model to compute dense vector embeddings for both catalogue entries and user preferences. These embeddings serve as the basis for semantic similarity in retrieval operations.

- **Graph construction**: A structured graph is generated from the catalogue data using NetworkX. This graph captures relationships between products, such as similarity, category hierarchies, or co-occurrence patterns, and serves as a complementary retrieval modality alongside vector search.

Retrieval and recommendation pipeline

This phase involves query handling, Hybrid search, result ranking, and natural language response generation, details as follows:

- **Query processing and embedding**: A user query is received and embedded using the same Ollama-all-miniLM-L6-v2 model to maintain vector space consistency with the indexed documents.

- **LangChain agent-based orchestration**: A LangChain agent orchestrates hybrid retrieval across three distinct tools:

  - Vector search using Faiss.
  - Graph search using the NetworkX-based graph.
  - Hybrid search that combines both retrieval signals.

  This agent also accesses indexed embeddings and graph structures for real-time decision-making.

- **Retrieval and personalization**: The agent retrieves top-k candidates based on semantic similarity, graph traversal, and user preference alignment. User preferences are converted to embeddings that are included in the scoring process to support personalized ranking.

- **Reranking with cross-encoder**: The initially retrieved candidates are reranked using the ms-marco-MiniLM-L6-v2 cross-encoder. This model performs fine-grained relevance scoring based on pairwise comparisons between the query and candidate entries.

- **Natural language wrapping**: The final, reranked results are passed to an LLM (via the Ollama platform) to produce a fluent, human-readable response that contextualizes and explains the recommendations.

- **Response delivery**: The system returns a finalized recommendation to the user, incorporating semantic, structural, and personal relevance, all wrapped in natural language for improved user engagement.

Key technologies include:

- **LangChain**: Tool orchestration and agent-based reasoning.

- **Faiss**: Vector search engine for efficient **approximate nearest neighbor** (**ANN**) search.

- **NetworkX**: Graph construction and traversal for structure-aware retrieval.

- **Ollama-all-miniLM-L6-v2**: Sentence Transformer model for embeddings.

- **Ms-marco-MiniLM-L6-V2**: Cross-encoder model for reranking.

- **Ollama LLM**: Natural language generation of recommendation output.

This system exemplifies a robust RAG architecture enhanced with graph-based reasoning and user preference modeling. By integrating multiple retrieval modalities (semantic, structural, and personalized) and leveraging a reranker and language model for final output formulation, it ensures high relevance and interpretability in recommendations. The design also supports modularity, enabling adaptability across various domains where product recommendation or content retrieval is required.

Agentic RAG design and multi-tool retrieval in the system

A distinguishing characteristic of this architecture is its agentic design, which enables intelligent decision-making and dynamic tool selection within the retrieval and recommendation pipeline. Rather than relying on a static sequence of operations, the system delegates control to a LangChain-powered agent that is capable of executing a reasoning-driven retrieval workflow. This agent-centric approach introduces flexibility, modularity, and explainability into the pipeline, facilitating adaptive interactions based on query complexity and user context.

Agentic control loop

At runtime, the agent receives the user query and autonomously determines which retrieval tools to invoke, in what order, and how to combine the results. This planning-execution paradigm allows the agent to:

- Select retrieval strategies dynamically based on input semantics.

- Integrate and reconcile outputs from multiple sources.

- Formulate structured prompts for generation using retrieved evidence.

The agent also interprets intermediate observations (e.g., partial retrieval results) and can conditionally rerun tools, enhancing its capacity for complex decision-making.

Three complementary retrieval tools

The retrieval system under the agent's control comprises three specialized tools, each addressing a different dimension of relevance, which are as follows:

- **Vector search tool (semantic retrieval)**: This tool uses dense vector embeddings generated via Ollama-all-miniLM-L6-v2 and indexes them with Faiss, an ANN search engine. The goal of this tool is to retrieve documents or catalogue entries that are semantically similar to the user's query, even if they use different terminology. It is particularly effective for capturing conceptual similarity and paraphrased intent.

- **Graph search tool (structural retrieval)**: This tool operates over a NetworkX-based graph, constructed from catalogue metadata, relationships, and category hierarchies. It supports structured traversal, enabling the agent to identify items that are logically or relationally proximate to the user's query context. Graph search is especially valuable in domains where proximity in a knowledge graph (e.g., shared tags, dependencies, co-occurrence) is a strong signal of relevance.

- **Hybrid search tool (aggregated retrieval)**: The hybrid search tool serves as a meta-retriever, combining signals from both vector and graph search results. It may apply heuristics, weighted scoring, or rank fusion strategies to produce a consolidated top-k result set. This hybrid approach leverages the semantic richness of vector retrieval and the structural precision of graph-based retrieval, allowing for improved robustness and coverage.

Operational role of the agent

The agent integrates these tools into a reasoning loop, leveraging LangChain's ReAct-style framework. It does not simply execute tools in a predefined order; rather, it:

- Analyzes the query.

- Decides whether to prioritize semantic, structural, or hybrid signals.

- Retrieves results from one or more tools.

- Reranks and reformulates responses using learned relevance criteria.

This agentic orchestration ensures that the system can adapt retrieval strategies based on query type (e.g., factual, relational, personalized), domain structure, and user preferences.

Table 18.3, titled, *Post-development failure points and metrics for agentic RAG system,* provides a detailed breakdown of potential failure points and the corresponding key metrics that should be monitored across each major component of the system. This structured approach ensures robust observability, supporting continuous performance evaluation and operational reliability in production.

Operational risk analysis and monitoring metrics

To ensure operational robustness and sustained performance in the post-development phase, it is essential to identify and continuously monitor the key failure points across the various components of the agentic RAG system. Each module, ranging from embedding generation and retrieval tools to agent orchestration and output generation, presents unique risks that can impact system effectiveness, UX, and overall reliability. The following table outlines these critical failure points and specifies the corresponding metrics that should be tracked to enable timely diagnostics, informed optimization, and adherence to quality standards in a production environment:

Component	Failure points	Key metrics
Embedding generation	Stale embeddings, low-quality vectors, inconsistent formats.	Embedding drift score, coverage ratio, and update frequency.
Vector search tool	Low semantic recall, retrieval latency, and irrelevant top-k results.	Recall@k, precision@k, query latency, and semantic overlap score.
Graph search tool	Disconnected nodes, sparse traversal paths, and graph mismatch.	Node connectivity, average path length, and graph hit rate.
Hybrid search tool	Inconsistent fusion logic, overfitting to one source, and low diversity.	Score agreement rate, result diversity index, and retrieval consistency.
Agent orchestration	Invalid tool selection, failed execution plans, unhandled exceptions.	Tool success rate, plan execution time, and toolchain accuracy.
Reranking (cross-encoder)	Misranking, latency bottleneck, and unfaithful reordering.	Rerank score correlation, latency, top-1 relevance accuracy.
LLM wrapping for recommendation	Ungrounded generation, hallucination, incoherence.	Faithfulness score, hallucination rate, BERTScore.
End-to-end response quality	Poor personalization, low engagement, and factual inconsistency.	User rating score, groundedness rate, and session engagement rate.

Table 18.3: Post-development failure points and metrics for graph-based agentic RAG systems

Comparison of various Ops in modern software development

In modern software systems, DevOps, MLOps, and RAGOps serve distinct yet complementary roles that, when integrated, enable scalable, intelligent, and resilient applications. DevOps focuses on the automation of software development and deployment workflows, ensuring consistent integration, delivery, monitoring, and infrastructure management. It lays the foundation for CI/CD pipelines, testing frameworks, and system reliability.

MLOps extends DevOps principles to **machine learning (ML)** workflows. It enables the operationalization of models through reproducible training pipelines, versioning of datasets and models, automated deployment, and monitoring of model performance over time. MLOps ensures that ML models remain reliable, adaptive, and governed after they are deployed.

RAGOps builds on these foundations to support RAG systems, particularly those combining vector search, retrieval logic, and LLMs. RAGOps introduces new observability and evaluation challenges unique to LLM-based applications, such as monitoring grounding quality, hallucination rates, and retrieval faithfulness. It also addresses traceability across retrieval, reranking, and generation components.

Together, DevOps ensures system stability, MLOps ensures model integrity, and RAGOps ensures prompt-level reasoning traceability and retrieval quality. When orchestrated cohesively, they enable the continuous development, deployment, and refinement of GenAI applications, bridging classical engineering reliability with generative intelligence. Integrating MLflow with a recommendation system.

The following figure illustrates our end-to-end movie-recommendation architecture: a LangGraph-driven retrieval pipeline that turns user queries into *Cypher*, executes them on *Neo4j*, and summarises the results with Mistral, while an attached observability layer logs faithfulness and relevance metrics to MLflow for continuous quality monitoring:

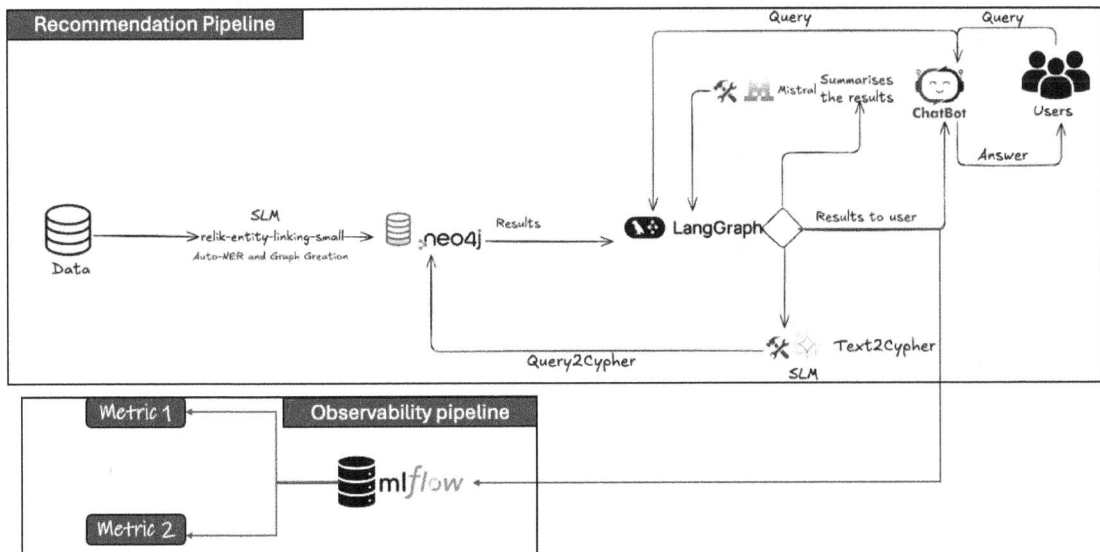

Figure 18.2: *Observability-enabled recommendation system*

Installation of MLflow

In order to instrument retrieval-augmented language model systems with rigorous experiment logging, the first prerequisite is the installation of MLflow, the de facto open-source platform for model tracking.

```
pip install MLflow
```

It installs the client library that exposes the core programmatic interface, e.g., **MLflow.log_param**, **MLflow.log_metric**, and **MLflow.start_run**, as well as the GenAI-specific extension **MLflow.evaluate**, which implements the quality assessment. These APIs enable researchers to capture every experimental artefact (hyperparameters, retrieval hits, generated answers, evaluation scores) in a reproducible, queryable form.

To visualise and compare such runs locally, one can launch a lightweight tracking server that persists results to the file system. If the Python **Web Server Gateway Interface** (**WSGI**) container Waitress is not already present, it may be added via:

```
pip install waitress
```

Subsequently, a single command suffices to expose the MLflow REST and web interface:

```
waitress-serve --host 127.0.0.1 --port 5000 MLflow.server:app
```

This spins up the dashboard at **http://127.0.0.1:5000**, as shown in *Figure 18.3*, from which investigators can inspect parameter histories, metric trajectories, and artefacts for every run, thereby closing the observability loop for RAG pipelines:

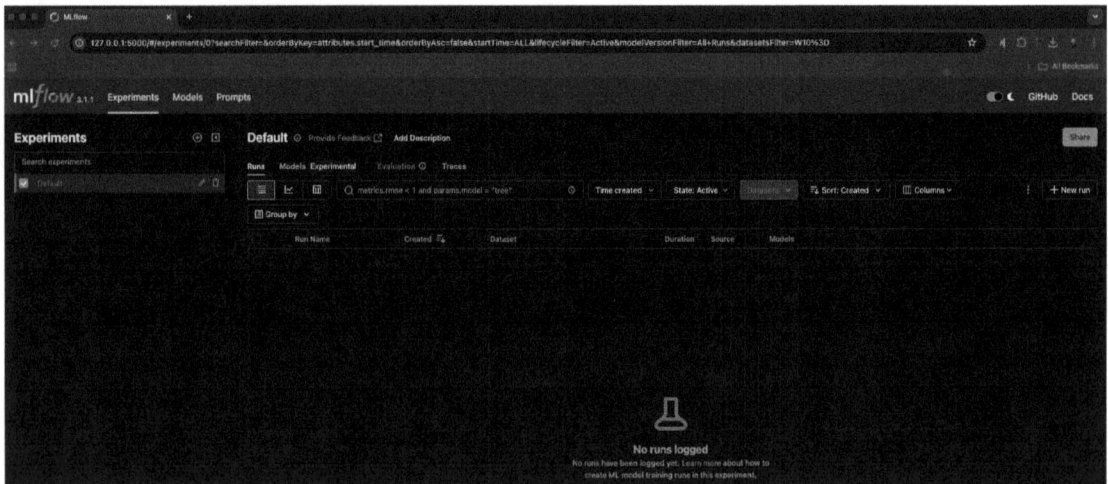

Figure 18.3: *MLflow screen where metrics are logged*

The solution depicted in *Figure 18.2* serves solely to illustrate how a graph-based recommendation pipeline, or more broadly, a GenAI workflow, can be instrumented and integrated with MLflow for experiment tracking and observability. Detailed explanations of the underlying components like Neo4j, Text2Cypher, and the Relik **name entity model** (**NER**) and their implementation are beyond the scope of this book and are covered extensively in *Learn Python Generative AI, Version 2* by *BPB author Indrajit Kar*. This current chapter focuses exclusively on the observability pipeline with MLflow.

Observability pipeline

In the context of graph-based recommendation systems using LangChain agents and Ollama models, observability and evaluation play a crucial role in ensuring trust, explainability, and system debugging. This study examines two distinct approaches for integrating MLflow into such a pipeline:

- A custom patch-based tracing approach (`MLflow_ollama_patch.py` and `main_with_m_patch.py`).

- Direct metric-based evaluation via MLflow's GenAI module (`main.py`).

The following list outlines the details of the approach:

- **Approach 1—span-based tracing (instrumentation)**: Uses a custom `MLflow_ollama_patch.py` module to wrap `ollama.chat()` calls with MLflow's low-level tracing API. Each invocation is recorded as a span (inputs, model, outputs), enabling fine-grained observability of intermediate steps, tool usage, and reasoning chains within the pipeline. Best for auditing, debugging, and detailed execution analysis.

- **Approach 2—metric-based evaluation (MLflow GenAI metrics)**: Leverages MLflow's first-party GenAI metrics API to evaluate the final outputs of the LLM. Metrics like faithfulness and relevance are computed by an evaluator model (LLM-as-a-judge) and logged as scalar scores. Best for end-to-end quality monitoring in RAG pipelines or summarization systems.

Both approaches are used to instrument an LLM-backed Cypher generator and answer synthesizer, but they differ fundamentally in tracing strategy, complexity, and scope.

Approach 1

This approach explicitly instruments the `ollama.chat()` function using MLflow's low-level tracing API. The `MLflow_ollama_patch.py` file applies a decorator-based patch to Ollama:

- **The MLflow_ollama_patch.py module: span-based tracing**:

   The `MLflow_ollama_patch.py` module serves as a minimal tracing interface that instruments all calls to `ollama.chat()` using MLflow's low-level span API. This is achieved through the **trace_ollama_chat** decorator, which wraps the original function:

   ```
   from MLflow.tracing import trace, SpanType
   ...
   ```

```
@trace(name="ollama.chat", span_type=SpanType.CHAT_MODEL)
def trace_ollama_chat(func):
    @wraps(func)
    def wrapper(*args, **kwargs):
        ...
        span.set_inputs({"messages": kwargs["messages"], "model": model})
        ...
        span.set_outputs(response)
        return response
    return wrapper
```

The patch is applied dynamically:

```
ollama.chat = trace_ollama_chat(ollama.chat)
```

This method ensures that each invocation of the LLM is recorded as a span, complete with input prompts, model names, and responses. These spans are visualized in the MLflow UI as part of the execution trace, enabling developers to audit tool use, analyze prompt-response behavior, and diagnose errors at the function level.

In the corresponding **main_with_m_patch.py**, the user does not need to add extra logic beyond logging parameters and outputs. All LLM calls are automatically traced.

The file **main_with_m_patch.py** integrates a LangChain agent-based QA system with MLflow tracking, while enabling low-level tracing of **ollama.chat()** calls using the custom module **MLflow_ollama_patch**. This script offers both semantic quality evaluation of the final answer and execution-level tracing of LLM interactions. The following is a structured breakdown and explanation:

- **User input and schema setup**:
  ```
  user_question = input("Ask your question: ")
  schema = """(:Movie {title, genre, mood, release_year}) ..."""
  ```

  The script captures a free-text query and defines a knowledge graph schema outlining the structure of movie, actor, director, and platform nodes and their relationships.

- **LangGraph agent invocation**:
  ```
  result = app.invoke(inputs)
  cypher_query = result.get("cypher_query", "")
  ```

  The LangGraph agent processes the user question and schema to generate a Cypher query (**cypher_query**), execute it on a Neo4j graph database (**query_results**), and generate a natural language answer (**final_answer**) using the Mistral model via Ollama.

- **MLflow run initialization and logging**:

  with **MLflow.start_run(run_name="CypherTest_Run1")** as run:

  A named MLflow run is started. Inside the **try** block, the system logs:

○ **Params**: Question, generated Cypher.

○ **Artifacts**: Neo4j raw results, final answer text:

```
MLflow.log_param("question", user_question)
MLflow.log_param("cypher_query", cypher_query or "EMPTY")
MLflow.log_text(json.dumps(query_results, indent=2), "neo4j_
context.json")
MLflow.log_text(final_answer or "EMPTY", "final_answer.txt")
```

○ **Output evaluation using Ollama**: The system evaluates both factual consistency and contextual relevance of generated responses. Using Ollama-based evaluators, two metrics are computed:

```
faith_score = evaluate_faithfulness_with_ollama(...)
rel_score   = evaluate_relevance_with_ollama(...)

MLflow.log_metric("faithfulness", faith_score)
MLflow.log_metric("relevance", rel_score)
```

These scores measure whether the final answer reflects database facts (**faithfulness**) and whether it aligns with the user's query intent (**relevance**). To ensure robustness, fallback scores of **0.0** are recorded in case of exceptions, allowing MLflow logs to remain complete and traceable.

By capturing these metrics within MLflow, the evaluation process becomes a core part of the RAGOps observability pipeline—enabling continuous monitoring, failure diagnosis, and data-driven improvement of both retrieval and generation components.

○ **Ollama chat tracing with MLflow_ollama_patch**: This line activates patching:

```
import MLflow_ollama_patch
```

Internally, **MLflow_ollama_patch.py** wraps **ollama.chat()** with an MLflow span logger:

```
@trace(name="ollama.chat", span_type=SpanType.CHAT_MODEL)
def trace_ollama_chat(func):
    ...
ollama.chat = trace_ollama_chat(ollama.chat)
```

This records every **ollama.chat()** call as a traceable chat model span in MLflow's UI, capturing:

- **Inputs**: System/User messages, model name
- **Outputs**: Generated response

This enables fine-grained observability of prompt evolution and model behavior, which is invisible in standard **MLflow.log_*()** calls.

The following bar charts represent semantic evaluation scores for faithfulness and relevance, both scoring 3.0, indicating moderate alignment between the chatbot's generated response and the Neo4j query results. These metrics are automatically computed and logged via MLflow the observability pipeline.

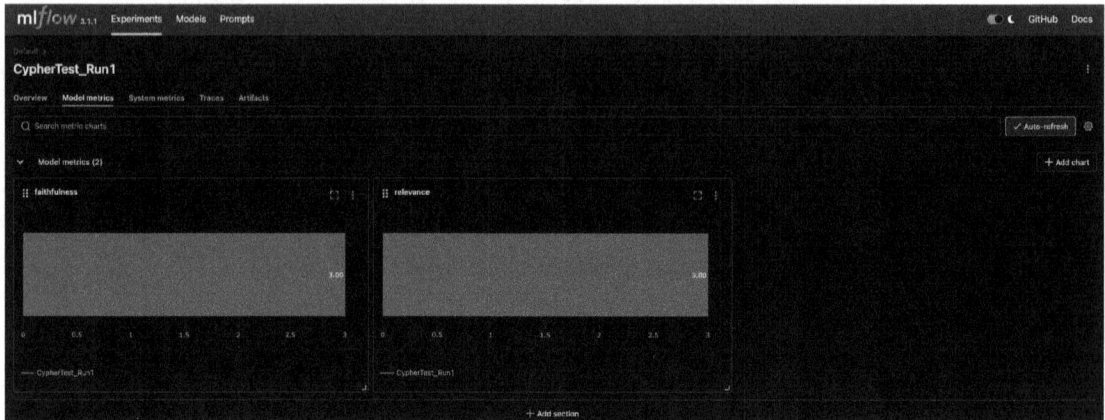

Figure 18.4: Screenshot of MLflow UI displaying model-level metrics for the run named CypherTest_Run1

Approach 2

In contrast, the **main.py** script leverages MLflow's first-party GenAI metrics API to assess the quality of final model outputs, rather than tracing intermediate tool usage. The focus is on evaluating the faithfulness and relevance of the final answer generated by Ollama.

For instance:

```
from MLflow.metrics.genai import faithfulness, relevance

faith_score = faithfulness(model="ollama:/mistral")(
    predictions=[final_answer],
    inputs=[user_question],
    context=[json.dumps(query_results)]
).scores[0]
```

This call uses a second LLM to evaluate whether the generated answer is consistent with the retrieved knowledge and prompt. The same approach is applied to the **relevance()** metric. These scalar scores are logged using:

```
MLflow.log_metric("faithfulness", faith_score)
MLflow.log_metric("relevance", rel_score)
```

This method does not require patching or custom spans, and it is aligned with end-to-end output validation, making it particularly suitable for RAG pipelines or summarization systems.

The patched tracing approach is optimal when the focus is on tool auditing, intermediate reasoning chain analysis, or span-based ML observability. Meanwhile, the direct **MLflow.**

`metrics.genai` method is suitable for evaluating the quality of LLM output, especially in RAG systems where answer trustworthiness matters. For a complete pipeline, these approaches can be complementary, using both spans and scores for full-stack GenAI observability.

To illustrate the utility of MLflow in providing semantic evaluation and experiment observability within a graph-based recommendation pipeline, we log and visualize output quality metrics such as `faithfulness` and `relevance`. These metrics are computed using the evaluation with Mistral via Ollama and automatically recorded for each agentic run. The names at the left side of MLflow dashboard, like the following:

- **rogue-whale-186**
- **amazing-dolphin-985**
- **masked-hound-282**
- **traveling-ant-386**

They are automatically generated run names by MLflow.

These are human-friendly identifiers for your runs, meant to help you quickly distinguish them in the UI. MLflow assigns them by default if you do not explicitly set a name for a run.

If you would prefer meaningful names (like `CypherTest_Run1`), you can explicitly name a run in your code:

With `MLflow.start_run(run_name="CypherTest_Run1")` as run:

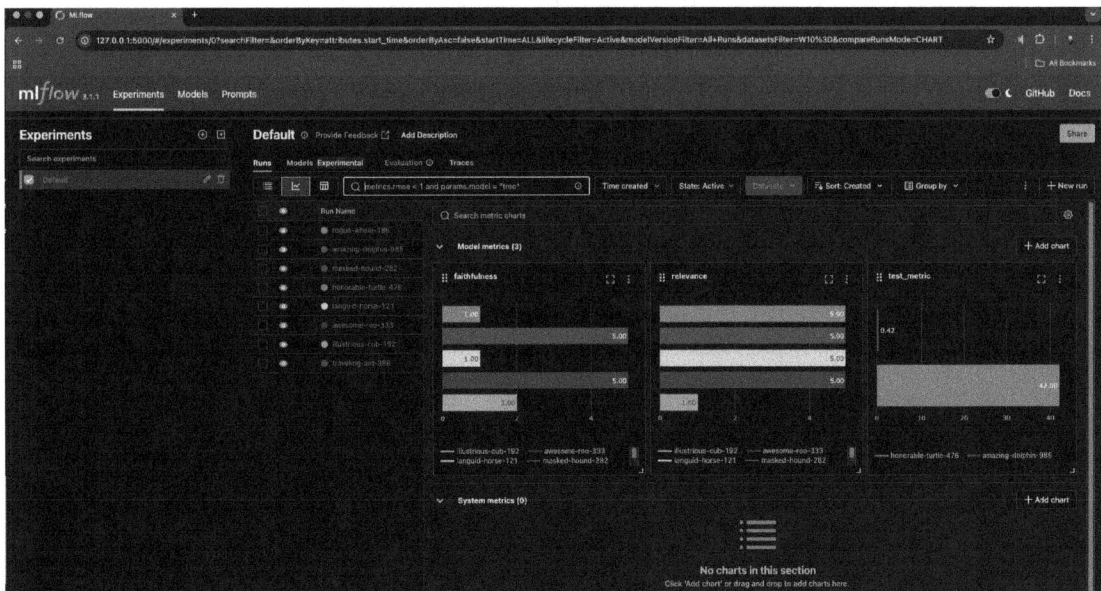

Figure 18.5: *MLflow dashboard displaying comparative evaluation of multiple runs using model-level metrics*

Each bar in *Figure 18.5*, corresponds to a unique model run (e.g., **awesome-roo-333**, **masked-hound-282**), automatically logged and color-coded for visual differentiation. The faithfulness and relevance charts capture semantic alignment between chatbot responses and Neo4j query outputs via Mistral. This comparative visualization helps developers and researchers assess relative performance across experiments, enabling systematic refinement of graph-based recommendation pipelines.

Troubleshooting MLflow using local filesystem structure

In scenarios where MLflow is configured with a local file-based backend (as opposed to a remote server or SQL store), understanding the directory layout of the mlruns folder is crucial for diagnosing tracking and logging issues. This appendix outlines the structure and interpretation of MLflow's run-level logs and metadata, and provides practical guidelines for troubleshooting:

- **Structure of the MLflow tracking directory**:

  When executing the command:

  ```
  ls -l mlruns/0
  ```

  The output displays subdirectories corresponding to individual MLflow runs within the default experiment (experiment ID **0**). Each directory name is a **universally unique identifier** (UUID) representing a specific run. An example listing may appear as:

  ```
  drwxr-xr-x  7 <Your user name> <Your user name>224 17 Jul 15:16
  068e9e07e75f40efa5c360225157a3ed

  drwxr-xr-x  7 <Your user name> <Your user name>224 17 Jul 16:28
  7776a3d0407f45b8b8cd2a92caa4645b

  -rw-r--r--  1 <Your user name> <Your user name>212 17 Jul 15:16 meta.
  yaml
  ```

  Each subdirectory contains the logs, parameters, metrics, and metadata associated with an individual run. The top-level **meta.yaml** file stores experiment-level information, such as the experiment name and lifecycle status.

- **Internal structure of a specific run directory**:

  Inspecting an individual run directory using:

  ```
  ls -l mlruns/0/7776a3d0407f45b8b8cd2a92caa4645b/
  ```

  produces a listing such as:

  ```
  drwxr-xr-x  4 <Your user name> <Your user name>128 17 Jul 16:28
  artifacts

  -rw-r--r--  1 <Your user name> <Your user name>395 17 Jul 16:28 meta.
  yaml
  ```

```
drwxr-xr-x  4 <Your user name> <Your user name>128 17 Jul 16:28 metrics
drwxr-xr-x  4 <Your user name> <Your user name>128 17 Jul 16:28 params
drwxr-xr-x  6 <Your user name> <Your user name>192 17 Jul 16:28 tags
```

Each component serves a distinct purpose.

The following table presents an overview of these core directories and files, summarizing their essential functions in capturing artifacts, logging metrics, storing parameters, and recording critical metadata. This foundational structure ensures a consistent and organized approach for every ML run, making it easier to audit results, compare experiments, and maintain reproducibility throughout the workflow.

Component	Description
`artifacts/`	Stores external files logged using **MLflow.`log_artifact()`** or **`log_model()`**.
`metrics/`	Contains time-stamped metric logs stored as individual JSON files.
`params/`	Contains parameters logged via **MLflow.`log_param()`** as key-value pairs.
`tags/`	Contains metadata tags such as run name, source, and user.
`meta.yaml`	Stores run metadata, including run status, start/end times, and user info.

Table 18.4: Brief description of each key component found within a run directory

The run name visible in the UI (e.g., **traveling-ant-386**) is stored as a tag and can be found within the **`tags/`** directory.

- **Troubleshooting guidelines**: To address common issues encountered during local MLflow tracking, consider the following:

  o **Run not visible in the MLflow UI**: Confirm that the corresponding run directory exists under **`mlruns/<experiment_id>/`**, and that its **`meta.yaml`** file is valid and properly formatted. Also, verify that the tracking URI (e.g., **`file:///.../mlruns`**) used during logging matches that of the UI server.

  o **Missing metrics or parameters**: Use commands such as **`ls  mlruns/0/<run_id>/metrics/`** to confirm whether metrics were logged and written to disk. Absence of these files usually indicates that **MLflow.`log_metric()`** was called either outside of an active run or the run was not properly committed using **MLflow.`end_run()`**.

  o **Corrupted or incomplete runs**: If the UI displays incomplete information or fails to load a run, inspect **`meta.yaml`** for missing or malformed fields. Inconsistencies here can prevent MLflow from parsing the run successfully.

  o **UI displays 404 or No data**: This may occur when the server cannot locate the **`run_id`** within the specified experiment directory. Double-check the consistency between your programmatic logging and server configuration paths.

The local **mlruns/** directory structure provides a transparent and accessible way to inspect and debug experiment tracking when using MLflow without a remote backend. Each experiment is mapped to a directory by its ID, and every run is stored in a uniquely named folder with standardized subdirectories for metrics, parameters, artifacts, and metadata. Understanding this structure is essential for developers building robust ML observability systems, especially in the context of experimental LLM-based pipelines, where reproducibility and traceability are foundational.

Troubleshooting MLflow through the local filesystem structure offers direct visibility into how runs, artifacts, and metadata are organized. By inspecting run folders, logs, and parameter files, practitioners can quickly isolate issues, verify experiment integrity, and ensure reproducibility, making filesystem-level exploration a practical first step in MLflow debugging.

As we come to the end of this journey into multimodal GenAI, it is important to recognize that while multimodal systems represent the frontier, enabling models to reason jointly across text, images, audio, and beyond, they are built upon a strong foundation of traditional generative models. For a deeper dive into these fundamentals, refer to *Learn Python Generative AI: Journey from Autoencoders to Transformers to Large Language Models*, which explores the core architectures that paved the way for today's multimodal breakthroughs.

Conclusion

As we draw the final lines of this chapter, and indeed, this book, we reflect on a journey that has traversed the complex terrain of operationalizing RAG systems and the broader landscape of GenAI. From our exploration of foundational run directory structures and troubleshooting in MLflow, to the nuanced requirements of observability, evaluation, and traceability in production-grade GenAI applications, each section has built toward a holistic understanding of robust AI system deployment. The comparison of DevOps, MLOps, and RAGOps illuminated the evolving paradigms for managing intelligent systems that intertwine software engineering and generative reasoning.

The hands-on examples, including MLflow instrumentation and graph-enhanced recommender systems, rooted theory in practice, emphasizing that the pillars of reproducibility, transparency, and accountability are vital for the future of AI-driven innovation. As we close, it is clear that these methodologies are not mere technical necessities but the foundation for ethical and sustainable AI development.

Index

www.ingramcontent.com/pod-product-compliance
Lightning Source LLC
Chambersburg PA
CBHW061740210326
41599CB00034B/6741